The Theory and Practice of Legislation

Essays in Legisprudence

Edited by

LUC J. WINTGENS
European Academy of Legal Theory,
Center of Legislation, Regulation and Legisprudence,
University of Brussels (K.U. Brussel)

Assistant Editors
PHILIPPE THION and MELANIE CARLY

Routledge
Taylor & Francis Group
LONDON AND NEW YORK

First published 2005 by Ashgate Publishing

Published 2016 by Routledge
2 Park Square, Milton Park, Abingdon, Oxon OX14 4RN
711 Third Avenue, New York, NY 10017, USA

Routledge is an imprint of the Taylor & Francis Group, an informa business

British Library Cataloguing in Publication Data
The theory and practice of legislation : essays in
legisprudence. - (Applied legal philosophy)
1. Legislation 2. Law
I. Wintgens, Luc
340.1

Library of Congress Control Number: 2005923703

Transfered to Digital Printing in 2010

ISBN 9780754624615 (hbk)

Contents

Series Preface

The objective of the Applied Legal Philosophy series is to publish work which adopts a theoretical approach to the study of particular areas or aspects of law or deals with general theories of law in a way which focuses on issues of practical moral and political concern in specific legal contexts.

In recent years there has been an encouraging tendency for legal philosophers to utilize detailed knowledge of the substance and practicalities of law and a noteworthy development in the theoretical sophistication of much legal research. The series seeks to encourage these trends and to make available studies in law which are both genuinely philosophical in approach and at the same time based on appropriate legal knowledge and directed towards issues in the criticism and reform of actual laws and legal systems.

The series will include studies of all the main areas of law, presented in a manner which relates to the concerns of specialist legal academics and practitioners. Each book makes an original contribution to an area of legal study while being comprehensible to those engaged in a wide variety of disciplines. Their legal content is principally Anglo-American, but a wide-ranging comparative approach is encouraged and authors are drawn from a variety of jurisdictions.

Tom D. Campbell
Series Editor
Centre for Applied Philosophy and Public Ethics
Charles Sturt University, Canberra

Introduction

Luc J. Wintgens

Legisprudence is a new domain in legal theory aiming at a theoretical reflection on legislation. Most of the time, legislation is considered too much from the political perspective, which puts it in the field of study of political scientists. Legisprudence for its part focuses on legislation from the perspective of legal theory.

Current legal theory emerged from the 19th century method of study of law known as general theory of law or *allgemeine Rechtslehre*. The general theory of law aimed at providing legal scholarship with a scientific status, upon the general secularisation of philosophy. The exploration of principles like *pacta sunt servanda*, concepts like property, and distinctions like private-public law were deemed common to all legal systems. Upon that characteristic, they constituted the proper domain of a scientific analysis. The search for and exploration of the basic structure, principles, and concepts of law gave rise to a discipline that intended to be value free, and therefore could allow for scientific propositions.

While the general theory of law focused on a comparison of the content of legal rules and concepts, it gradually evolved towards a search for the structure and function of legal norms and systems as its main theme. With Kelsen it was conceived as the theory of positive law. Together with this shift in focus, the general theory of law got a new label in 1926 as it appeared in the title of a new journal, *Revue internationale de théorie du droit – Internationale Zeitschrift für Theorie des Rechts*. From then on, the focal point of legal scholarship has included the relation between law and state, and between different normative systems among many others.

Another milestone in the emergence of legal theory as an autonomous branch of legal scholarship, has been the publication of the journal *Rechtstheorie* since 1970. The purpose of *Rechtstheorie* is to combine several disciplines that have law as their object of study, in view of a need to integrate these disciplines into an interdisciplinary matrix of research.

The conjunction of law with a number of non-legal disciplines that can however have law as an object of study, like sociology, economics, and logic has given rise to legal theory as it appears nowadays. Its main idea is to throw different disciplinary lights on law in order to understand better normative behaviour. From that perspective, legal theory deals with problems, and is no longer confined to structures, concepts, and principles any more.

One of the problems that emerge in our societies is legislation. While legal theory works on its interpretation and systematisation, it hardly deals with its creation. This is what legisprudence aims at.

The creation of law in the large sense is one of the problems that deserve attention. Many legal systems suffer from legislative inflation and a decreasing quality of legal rules. The nearly exclusive attention of legal theory for problems of interpretation of law at the neglect of its creation makes the latter a blind spot on the map of legal theory. It is here that legisprudence turns out to be helpful.

As a theory of rational legislation, legisprudence focuses on the creation of legislation and the theoretical articulation of these processes. This book contains the results of a long-run project to which a considerable number of scholars have contributed.

The five parts of this book reflect as many perspectives on the rationality of legislation. In the first part, some theoretical issues are dealt with. The epistemological framework of legisprudence, together with a critique of instrumentalism involve a quest of the rationality of law making. It includes a critical investigation of legalism while at the same time opening up economic exploration of the creation of legislation.

Part two examines the relation between legislation and democracy. Hercules is not only a extraordinary judge. He may be involved in democratic law making as well. From the perspective of democratic law making, the problem of judicial review and of constitutionalism are taken into consideration.

Part three focuses on the legitimacy of law making. The procedural approach is weighed against the argumentative approach, while at the same time the legislative elaboration of human rights gets the attention it deserves.

Part four further elaborates this theme from the perspective of practical reason. Legislative deliberation, argumentation in and evaluation of legislation are critically exposed as part of legisprudence.

Part five finally deals with practical issues, including the drafting of legislation in European law and the justification of legislative ruling in view of its optimisation in the field of nuclear law.

Legisprudence is an interdisciplinary theory of legislation. Rational legislation is the result of a collaboration between disciplines. It is only upon this collaboration that we can expect legal theory to contribute to better legislation.

PART I

LEGISPRUDENCE: THEORETICAL ISSUES

Chapter 1

Legisprudence as a New Theory of Legislation

Luc J. Wintgens*

The search for balance between law and politics has the advantage of drawing in two poles in legal research. In this chapter I will argue that the separation of law and politics that has been predominant in legal thinking until recently, makes that the creation of law via legislation has not been deemed a proper theme of attention for legal theory (Waldron, 1999, pp. 2 ff). Legislation belongs to the realm of politics focused upon by political scientists of different sorts.

Law for its part is recognized to root in politics, though it lives its own life being cut off from this root. Law has its own method of study, called legal dogmatics or, more broadly, legal theory of different sorts. The way law is created throughout the process of legislation does not appear on the screen of the legal theorist. The question of why this is so, and a critique of this position are the topics of this contribution.

The central thesis is that law is separated from politics for a political reason. The separation is operated on epistemological grounds, which contribute to the concealment of the political choices made. As a result, the domain of values, both moral and political, is structured on a "neutral" basis that prevents the elaboration of a rational theory of legislation.[1]

The Social Contract and the Three Axes of Modern Philosophy

The elaboration of legisprudence as a rational theory of legislation starts with a reflection on the organisation of political space since Modernity. The basic model of this organisation is the social contract. This contract is an act of will of the subjects. Upon its conclusion, a sovereign is called into being. From the moment of his emergence, the sovereign has the power to decide about matters of practical reason. He decides the what and how of human actions (Hobbes, 1966; Rousseau, 1964; Locke, 1963; Kant, 1983).

The articulation of the sovereign is premised by a reflection on freedom. This reflection articulates the three main axes of the Modern philosophical project, that is, the epistemological axe resulting in the epistemologization of philosophy, the political axe resulting in the construction of the state and the moral axe, mainly concentrating on the freedom of the individual.

The basic premise that both Hobbes and Rousseau adopt is freedom unlimited.

For Hobbes, everyone can act in freedom on the *ius naturale*. It includes a right of all to all. The laws of nature impose some duties that, however, are unworkable in the state of nature. This is because of his nominalistic epistemology. According to this epistemology, concepts have no ontological value. They depend on definition by the subjects. Because everybody is more likely to define these concepts following his own biases, the laws of nature are unworkable. In short, they do exist although they are semantically empty. Only a sovereign can define their content in a binding way. Unless this is the case, there is a war of all against all.

A similar though slightly different thesis is found in Rousseau. According to him, man is born free and everywhere he is in chains. Rousseau's is mainly an economic theory. For Rousseau like for Hobbes the conclusion of a contract is a necessary condition for warding of the dangers of this war.

From there, it follows that freedom is mainly considered a political theme. Freedom comes to its realisation in political space as a result of the will of individual subjects.

The latter's freedom as a moral issue is only a secondary matter. Individual freedom and the possibility of subjects to interact on their own insights in social space are surpassed by the political variant of freedom or freedom according to the law. The organisation of political space is superimposed on some form of self-regulating social space in which neither Hobbes nor Rousseau believes. As long as the sovereign does not regulate an issue, subjects can act as they please. The sovereign though can intervene whenever he deems it fit, in view of the finality of his position.

Apart from the political and moral components of freedom the theory of the social contract, as it seems, is mainly coloured by the third axe, that is, the epistemological perspective.

In comparison with Descartes (Descartes, 1996), both Hobbes and Rousseau face freedom as a problem. While Descartes is of the opinion that morality would unfold as a rational system, Hobbes and Rousseau consider this not possible. They are in a way more realistic than their forerunner. They do espouse however his basic insight that comes to an epistemologization of philosophy in general and of practical philosophy in particular.

Philosophical truth for Descartes comes to securing the latter's certainty. Ideas having the same clarity and distinctiveness as the *cogito* can be logically concatenated to the latter, and so to each other. Upon this, reality can be unfolded in a rational way. At the reverse, what is not capable of logical or empirical proof is therefore not rational (Perelman and Olbrechts-Tyteca, 1976, pp. 2-5).

Fruitful as this may have turned out for scientific thinking, it strongly reduces though the action radius of practical reason. Values, or goals and ends of action are not capable of logical or empirical proof; hence, they are not rational. These effects have been felt for some three centuries, and persist throughout the programme of logical positivism.

The model of the social contract as Hobbes and Rousseau conceive it purports to solve the problem of political integration as it follows from individualism. They do so by applying and enlarging the Cartesian method of transforming thinking into knowing. They deliver, that is, a specific exercise of epistemologized philosophy.

To begin with, the social contract is a true idea. In making use of his rational capacities, the subject cannot but conclude that entering into the contract is preferable to staying in the state of nature. In Razian language, the reason for entering the contract is an exclusionary reason (Raz, 1990). While Hobbes can be read to hold some utilitarian version of rationality, Rousseau's theory most obviously is of a more purified brand. It is reason itself that unfolds and induces to the adherence to the true principles of public law, as he calls the social contract.

Both variants of the contract result however in the same thing: the sovereign's rules are morally true. They are so in the Hobessian variant because the rules of the sovereign are implementations of the laws of nature. The latter being commands of God, they are the only true morality (Hobbes, 1966, p. 147). They are also true in Rousseau's version because no law, because it is a law, can be unjust (Rousseau, 1964, p. 379).

The logic of both the variants of the social contract is nearly inescapable. From the truth of the premise, that is, the social contract one can logically conclude the truth of propositions based on it, that is, laws.

Legalism

From the above diagnosis, we can proceed to an articulation of the main characteristics of the pattern of legal thinking that has been dominant from the 17th century to the middle of the last century. It is commonly labelled as "legalism". Legalism, so we can read from Judith Shklar, takes normative behaviour to be a matter of rule following (Shklar, 1964, p. 1). Zenon Bankowski has added to this that it does not matter where these rules come from (Bankowski, 1993). Law, that is, is "just there".

This addition brings also to light a characteristic of legalism shared by positivism and jusnaturalism. Both hold that law represents reality. This is obvious for jusnaturalism. The content of law is dictated by a substantial transcendent norm that is reproduced through the law of the sovereign. Representationalism is less obvious in positivism. Law as a command of a sovereign is a decision of the latter. It is however true as both Hobbes and Rousseau claim, because it is based on the social contract. The latter is true, and consequently the rules based on it must also be true. It is a consequence of their epistemologized version of philosophy.

Representationalism as the basic metaphysical premise of their theories is supplemented with four other aspects that identify legalism. First, if the construction of laws results in true normative propositions, the latter must be timeless. If they are not, they could hardly be held true since truth is eternal.

Secondly, since laws are true there can be no discussion about their content. This entails that the disputable nature of values, goals and ends is concealed. Any rule is true, which means that the value, goal or end is morally correct. In this view, laws are considered instruments for their realisation without any need to be chosen. This characteristic of legalism can be called its concealed instrumentalism.

Thirdly, upon the conclusion of the social contract any normative proposition of the sovereign *ipso facto* outweighs any other proposition that would pretend to have normative value. Personal moral insights of the subjects as to what is right or wrong is conclusively waved from the normative screen. It is the law of the state that prescribes what is right and wrong. This aspect of legalism can be qualified as etatism.

Fourthly and finally, the study of law is confined to the study of true propositions. As to its method, the study of law is held identical to that of the science of nature. Scientific method as a description and explanation of an object found "out there" equally applies to law as to nature. The study of law then is aptly labelled as the "science of law". Propositions resulting from the science of law can operate as a supplementary source of law. This conclusion is a logical result of the truth of the premises – the law – and the uniqueness of the method of science. Hence, the legal system is a closed set of logically connected propositions.

Legalism then consists of a conjugation of these five characteristics – representationalism, timelessness, concealed instrumentalism, etatism and the scientific method of study of law. I propose to call this form of legalism "strong legalism" and will qualify it later.

Strong Legalism and the Proxy Model of the Social Contract

The foregoing brief articulation of legalism sheds some light on the theory of legislation. Legalism mainly attempts to exclude any form of theorizing on legislation. Legislation is a matter of politics. Politics is a matter of choice. Choices are disputable, so that a theory that would take them to be the object of knowledge is condemned to failure from the very beginning. Legalism then solves this problem by epistemologizing it and transforming practical reason into a branch of theoretical reason. What ought to be done is confined to the knowledge of the rules that contain rights and duties. Following rules is a matter of knowledge; their enforcement is a matter of application.

As a consequence, the central position of the judge as the main actor within the legal system and the subsequent reduction of jurisprudence to the theory of the application of rules goes without saying. The legislator operates behind the scene of the legal system. His role is confined to political decision-making. The true principles of public law, as Rousseau had labelled the social contract (Rousseau, 1964, p. 470), concern the establishment of the institutions, and not the content of the decisions that result from that.

This is a consequence of sovereignty. The legislator is a sovereign actor within political space. He cannot be bound to rules, at least not in the sense a judge is. If he were, he would not be a sovereign. On this view, the constitution is a political programme that steers legislation. It is not a set of binding rules for the legislator. As a consequence, the legislator is not considered a legal actor. He is only a political actor. Legislation then is a matter of politics. In severing law from its political origin, law making is not a matter of legal theory.

In the pages to come, I will challenge this view. The argument of this paper aims at articulating the position of the legislator as a legal actor. I will do so in three steps. In the rest of this section, I will briefly explore the meaning of freedom. The next section is dedicated to the articulation of the contours of an alternative version of the social contract. In the last section, four principles of legisprudence will be identified, that allow for a rational elaboration of legislation.

This tentative sketch has not the ambition of being complete. It only contains a rudimentary outline of legisprudence as a theory of legislation, that is elaborated at more length in a forthcoming publication.

I propose to start with the concept of freedom. In the absence of any external limitation, any subject is free to act as he pleases (Hart, 1979). Both Hobbes and Rousseau take this as a starting point. As a matter of logic, the subject faces an infinite variety of possibilities to concretise the concept of freedom. The concept of freedom allows any action. Paradoxically, freedom has to be limited for action to be possible at all. If no choice is made from the infinite variety of possibilities, no action ever takes place.

This is saying that action in order to be possible is preceded by a limitation of freedom. Freedom-unlimited is only a concept; it must be supplemented by a concretisation that I propose to call a "conception". Conceptions are a necessary condition for action.

In the absence of any external limitation of freedom, subjects are to act on their own conceptions. They have to choose the limitations of freedom that I propose to call "conceptions *of* freedom". Conceptions of freedom are concretisations thereof and these concretisations are determinations of the infinite variety of possibilities. Conceptions of freedom are limitations of freedom by the subject. When the subject acts on a concretisation of freedom that is not his own, he acts on a conception *about* freedom. A conception about freedom can also be called an external limitation of freedom, since the limitation that is necessary for action is *external* to the subject. At the opposite, a conception of freedom can be considered an *internal* limitation of freedom.

What both Hobbes and Rousseau are eager to show is that social interaction cannot take place on the basis of conceptions of freedom. This is most obviously the case with Hobbes. According to him, subjects do not dispose of the true meaning of the laws of nature. This is because of their semantic emptiness. Once we would achieve the true meaning of the laws of nature, social interaction disposes of rules.

Unlike Hobbes, Rousseau holds that there exists a society before a state comes into being. His theory embraces the possibility of social interaction based on meaning. Subjects, that is, interact in the context of participation. It is within this context of participation that they recognize each other as members of a social bound. The existence of a war of all against all is a sign that there is a society. War, that is, is a form of social interaction.

Meaning, however, is different from truth. Truth is unique while meanings are multiple. Social interaction based on meanings, that is, social interaction from the perspective of a context of participation, is deemed to failure. This is so because of man's wicked nature, as can be read from Hobbes. It is due to relations of dependence resulting from the economic settings within social space, according to Rousseau.

This can be reframed in the above terminology. Subjects acting on conceptions of freedom do not dispose of its "true" meaning. Conceptions of freedom are of an infinite variety; the "true" meaning of freedom for its part must be unique.

The three axes that were pointed to above appear in the contractual setting in the following way. Conceptions of freedom as the basis of action of the subject are a practical necessity. Without concretisations of freedom in terms of conceptions there can be no action. This practical necessity includes, at the same time, a priority of the subject. If there are no external limitations of freedom, that is, conceptions about freedom, the subjects can act as they please. However, as Hobbes and Rousseau argue, the practical necessity of concretisations of freedom is reframed as a political priority. Concretisations of freedom by the sovereign, that is, conceptions about freedom, predominate over conceptions of freedom. They do so for an epistemological reason.

This reason is epistemological in that it has an exclusionary character. Hobbes and Rousseau presume that all subjects are endowed with an identical rational capacity. Upon using their rational capacity, they will all come to the conclusion that entering into the contract is preferable to remaining in the state of nature. On this presumption, truth is rationally preferred to mere meaning.

The political organisation of freedom then, for an epistemological reason, outweighs the moral priority of the subject to act on conceptions of freedom. From the "moment" of the contract on, subjects primarily act on conceptions about freedom. Their consent to the contract includes a proxy to the sovereign. On this proxy, they consent to abide by any of the sovereign's external limitations of freedom whatever their content may be.

The mechanism of the proxy model operates itself however as a conception of freedom. It is the subjects who act on a conception of freedom when they enter into the social contract. The conceptions about freedom that result from there are ascribed to them as if it were conceptions of freedom. That is what the general proxy comes to.

It relies however on a misconception of freedom. Freedom means the possibility to act on conceptions of freedom in the absence of any external limitations, that is, conceptions about freedom. Speaking more generally, freedom is the starting point of the organisation of political space. This is the meaning of freedom as a principle or *principium*. A *principium*, however, also means guiding principle as "leitmotiv". From this perspective, freedom is not only the starting point of the organisation of political space.

It has however also a moral dimension that is outweighed by the political dimension. As was argued above, this happens for an epistemological reason. The consequence of this is the following. If the political organisation of freedom outweighs its moral dimension, action on conceptions about freedom always automatically outweighs conceptions of freedom. The latter however affects the reflexive character of the concept of freedom. The reflexive character of freedom is what makes it a moral concept. As a moral concept, it articulates moral autonomy. Moral autonomy requires freedom to be exercised in freedom. This is the same as saying that acting on conceptions of freedom has priority over acting on conceptions about freedom.

This is what is denied in the theory of the social contract. The proxy outweighs freedom in the moral sense in that conceptions about freedom always have priority over conceptions of freedom.

Weak Legalism and the Trade-off Model of the Social Contract

Against the proxy model of the social contract, I propose to sketch the characteristics of a different model. If any external limitation of freedom is by its very existence *ipso facto* legitimate, this results in what we testify nowadays as the exponential growth of legal systems. Any external limitation of freedom that is formally legitimated as a saying of the sovereign is a valid rule.

Because the proxy is a general one, the legal system as a whole is supposed to have a general purpose. The proxy is given for a reason – safety of one's life in Hobbes, or equality in Rousseau – and this reason is the purpose of the legal system as a whole. It *a priori* justifies any of the future external limitations, the content of which is yet unknown at the "moment" of the contract. Therefore, both the proxy and the purpose of the legal system are general. In this characterisation, any of the external limitations is covered by the proxy and serves the purpose of the legal system. Their number is not limited on any criterion.

The quantitative aspect of the legal order is a well-known problem nowadays. However important it is, it will not be dealt with in the limits of this contribution. It will be limited to the qualitative transformation of freedom on the basis of the social contract.

The latter is a rational reconstruction of the Aristotelian paradise lost, that is, natural political society (Aristotle, 1972). Methodological individualism is hard to conjugate within a body politic without some rational conceptual glue that integrates the individual parts into some whole. Rational political society is substituted for natural political society with the help of the social contract.

As a hypothetical reconstruction, however, it jeopardizes the moral dimension of freedom. If any external limitation or conception about freedom can be legitimately substituted for any internal limitation or conception of freedom, it follows that a concretisation of freedom in the moral sense can always be replaced by a concretisation of freedom in the political sense.

The reason for concluding the social contract coincides with the finality of the state or the general purpose of the legal system. From this perspective, it can be asked whether freedom in the moral sense can be the general purpose of the legal system?

If freedom in the moral sense is considered the general purpose or the *leitmotiv* of the legal system, we get a thinner version of the social contract. In this version, *it is law that is to make morality possible.* This includes a different characterisation of the relation between law and morality, to which I just point without going deeper into it. Suffice it to say that on this characterisation of the relation between law and morality, morality has a priority over law.

It is not to be concluded from the above that this priority is absolute. It is a relative priority in that conceptions about freedom can outweigh conceptions of freedom. The challenge of the absolute priority of conceptions about freedom refers to an alternative model of the social contract, that I propose to call the *trade-off model*.

In the trade-off model, subjects do not give a general proxy to the sovereign. On the contrary, the model says that freedom is traded off with each and every external limitation. Put differently, the proxy model contains a general and *a priori* trade-off of freedom. The trade-off model on the contrary qualifies the proxy character of the social contract, in that the subjects do not trade off their capacity to act on conceptions of freedom; they only trade off a conception of freedom.

Unlike Hobbes' model this trade-off model is not based on a general assessment of human nature that makes action on conceptions of freedom unworkable. It is different from Rousseau's in that it does not take in a general appraisal of human society that affects social interaction and culminates in war.

The trade-off model fits the three axes of the Modern philosophical project and puts them in a new setting.

The epistemological axe is reframed in that the meaning of a concept is not identical to truth. Concepts, that is, can have different meanings dependent on the context of participation. The denial of the distinction between truth and meaning comes to a denial of the idea of a context of participation altogether. Truth exists independently of any context, although meaning does not. The equalisation of truth and meaning, or the idea of "true meaning" results in adopting some "view from nowhere" (Nagel, 1986) that underlies representationalism proper to the Modern philosophical project.

The political axe of the project aims at institutionalising truth thus discovered, or discoverable in principle. The result of this for the moral axe is quite clear: subjects are not supposed capable of acting on their own moral insights or conceptions of freedom, due to their nature (Hobbes) or due to their life in society (Rousseau).

The epistemological distinction between "concept" and "conceptions" for its part has the potential to strike the balance between the political and the moral axe. Concretisations of freedom by way of conceptions about freedom then do not automatically outweigh conceptions of freedom. If they did, there simply is no balance to strike.

There is however a balance to find on the trade-off model. This is precisely what trading off comes to. Any rule of the sovereign is an external limitation of freedom. On freedom as *principium*, the political and moral concretisations of the concept of freedom – that is, conceptions about and conceptions of freedom – have to be weighed and balanced.[2]

On freedom as *principium*, conceptions of freedom have a *prima facie* priority. They can be outweighed by conceptions about freedom on the condition that the latter are justified as preferable to conceptions of freedom. This justification aims at striking the balance between the political and the moral axe.

The requirement of justification for its part expresses the priority of the moral over the political concretisations of freedom. In addition, the possibility that a moral concretisation is outweighed by a political concretisation of freedom shows that the priority is only a relative one.

The Principles of Legisprudence

On freedom as *principium*, any external limitation of freedom must be justified. This comes to a justification of the substitution of a conception about freedom for a conception of freedom. The duty of justification is what legisprudence is about. Legisprudence is defined as a rational theory of legislation. It consists of an elaboration of the idea of freedom as *principium*.

The justification of legislation is marked as a process of weighing and balancing the moral and the political limitations of freedom. Upon the rational character of legislation, a principled framework is required. With the help of this framework, external limitations can be justified. Justification is part of the process of legitimation. It does not lead to an external limitation to be ultimately justified.[3] External limitations are never legitimate as such. They are submitted to an ongoing legitimation, as will be clarified in the following pages.

The framework is made up of four principles that I will briefly expose and comment upon hereafter. The four principles are: the principle of alternativity, the principle of normative density, the principle of temporality, and the principle of coherence.

The Principle of Alternativity (PA)

The PA requires that an external limitation of freedom be justified as an alternative for failing social interaction. The PA is the most obviously related to freedom as *principium* in that it expresses the priority of the subjects' action, that is, action on a conception of freedom. This priority, again, is not absolute. It is relative in that social interaction can fail. This failure however should not be presumed, as do Hobbes and Rousseau.

What must be justified is that an external limitation of the sovereign is preferable to the absence of an external limitation. The relation between the sovereign and subjects is of an asymmetric nature (Ricoeur, 1986, p. 310). This involves the existence of a gap between the sovereign's claim to legitimacy and the subjects' belief in it. If the relation were symmetrical, any of the sovereign's claims to legitimacy would be *ipso facto* filled with the subjects' belief in it. This puts the argument back on the track of the proxy model of the social contract with strong legalism in its wake.

The PA as a principle of justification is based on the subject's capacity to act on conceptions of freedom. This involves that social practices are presumed to be self-regulating. Subjects involved in interaction create meaning. Meaning that emerges from social interaction refers to rules that are embedded in a social practice. At the same time, these rules are constitutive of these practices.

Scientific research, musical performance, carpentry, education, and religion are all types of practices. Any of these practices has its own rules upon which these practices are meaningful forms of interaction. Mark Hunyadi has convincingly argued that the existence of these rules comes to the surface in the case of a conflict (Hunyadi, 1995). Conflicts reveal the existence of rules together with the practices in which they emerge. Conflicts, rules, and meaning are necessary conditions for a practice to exist. Social space can be considered an intertwinement of an innumerable variety of practices, involving conflicts within, as well as between, them.

Would any conflict be *a priori* prevented, we face a situation that is similar to Hobbes' epistemologized version of politics. The sovereign's definitions of meaning may be apt to prevent or to solve conflicts. At the same time, however, it jeopardizes the existence of social practices altogether. As a consequence, social and political space, or society and state would be identical.

The result of this is that the subject as an autonomous moral agent is brushed aside. What is left over to him are accidental domains where he can act on conceptions of freedom as long as they are not regulated by the sovereign. The latter can intervene in any of them whenever he deems fit.

On the PA, the opposite is the case. The sovereign can only intervene on the condition that it is argued that his external limitation is preferable to an internal limitation of freedom as a reason for action, due to a failure of social interaction.

The Principle of Normative Density (PN)

The PN submits an external limitation to justification as far as the density of the normative impact is concerned. Put briefly, sanctions need a special justification because they include a double restriction of freedom. First, external limitations are conceptions about freedom. They exclude action on a conception of freedom. This is a first constraint. Secondly, if they are accompanied by a sanction, the purpose, goal, or end of the rule can only be realised in the way that is prescribed. If the pattern of behaviour is not realised that way a sanction is imputed. This prevents the subject from acting on conceptions of freedom.[4]

External limitations are not by themselves exclusionary reasons for action. If they were, we are again on the track of the proxy model. In the trade-off model, however, the legal system has only a modest general purpose that is making morality possible.

If the trade off is justified on the PA, it does not automatically follow that a sanction is the most preferable manner to get the purpose, goal or end of the external limitation realised.

Hart has convincingly criticised both the Austinian and Kelsenian concepts of a legal rule. According to him, any legal system contains rules that confer powers. Rules can confer powers to officials. Such rules allocate a power on an official to create or change a rule and to apply it. At the same time, these rules make the recognition of rules possible, both for officials and citizens. Generally speaking, power-conferring rules do not prescribe sanctions (Hart, 1994, pp. 91 ff).

Yet, rules can also confer power on private persons. In virtue of such rules, private persons can create wills, get married or make contracts. Again these rules are not orders, far less are they backed by threats (Austin, 1971) or there is an "essential connection" with a sanction (Kelsen, 1967). No one has an obligation, e.g., to get married. If a person wants to get married, he or she has to realise the pattern of behaviour of what counts as a valid marriage. If he or she does not, there simply is not a marriage, although there may be another form of relationship.

While Hart achieves disconnecting the validity of an external limitation and a sanction, the PN requires one more step. If there is no essential or necessary connection between a rule and a sanction, the relation is a contingent one. In this characterisation, the relation between a rule and a sanction must be justified.

The justification of a sanction includes an argument of why the supplementary limitation freedom is necessary. A sanction in pecuniary terms or as a physical constraint of freedom is only one option among a wide variety of possibilities to realise some pattern of behaviour. The extension of these possibilities has a variable degree of normative density, with a sanction as the maximum. It includes regulative techniques like information, incentives like tax reductions, self-regulation based on codes of conduct or covenants, labelling and the like

The point is that punishing behaviour must be justified because freedom as *principium* requires that action on a conception of freedom has priority over action on a conception about freedom. On the PA, the latter must outweigh the former. As a result, the type of conception to be realised is a conception about freedom. The substitution of a conception about freedom for a conception of freedom does not, however, automatically justify that the latter be enforced with a sanction. What must be realised is an end, purpose, or goal.

The PN then requires that the means of realisation of the rule's end, purpose, or goal result from a process of weighing and balancing of the alternatives. An alternative for a rule punishing possession and use of drugs could be an information campaign in schools. Such a campaign informs about the negative consequences of drug use. It can go along with by a covenant between the government and a school aiming at keeping the establishment drug free. In addition, a label can be conferred to a school that adopts this line of conduct. This label can be complemented with an additional subvention. An award may be conferred to a school that has respected the covenant for a certain period and so forth.

For the realisation of an end, goal or purpose, a variety of possibilities turn out to be available. Sanctions are only one among others. If the essential connection between a rule and a sanction is broken, a connection between the end, goal, or purpose and the means to realise it must be established. The establishment of this connection is what the PN is about.

It is needless to add that the different means have a different normative density. Their impact on freedom is dissimilar. It goes without saying that the instrument with the lowest normative density compared to sanctions is to be preferred. Put differently, if a sanction is used, its justification involves an outweighing of the alternatives with a weaker normative impact.

The Principle of Temporality (PT)

The PT brings the time dimension into the legal system. On strong legalism, the legal system is a timeless set of rules. They represent reality and absorb the realm of meaning. On the legisprudential view of the matter, rules, or external limitations, are a matter of human creation. Rule creation is like any human activity related to historical conditions. Human activity is replete with temporality.

Theories that claim to have direct access to reality, like Hobbes' or Rousseau's, deny the temporal character of this access. Knowledge provided by these types of theories is ontologically true. As opposed to these theories *of* reality, theories *about* reality consider this access to be mediated. Access to reality, that is, is mediated by a theory. I propose to call the latter type of theory an analytical theory or "paradigm". Analytical theories rely for their part on yet another analytical theory, and so forth. Theories of reality deny the mediation by an analytical theory. Unlike theories about reality, they claim truth unqualified. Theories about reality for their part only claim objective knowledge or knowledge unqualified. Knowledge unqualified refers to a theoretical framework on which it is dependent.

Theory dependence of a theory can be apprehended as the epistemological translation of human imperfection due to the temporality of the human condition. Consciousness of the historical nature of knowledge should not turn over into scepticism. It only induces a form of relativism as to the ontological truth of knowledge.

This view on temporality corroborates the distinction between truth and meaning. Meaning is connected to a context of participation. Logically speaking, truth in the philosophical sense cannot, while truth exists independently of any context. Something is true or it is not. A proposition can be true given a certain context. This is, however, different from the claim that a proposition is ontologically true.

Moral and political action does not qualify for ontological truth. This is the basic error of the social contract theories. They claim to have direct access to reality and so they set up the unique normative framework for the organisation of political space.

What applies for explanation in the field of knowledge similarly applies to justification in the domain of action.[5] On this claim, truth comes to justified belief. For reasons of brevity, I will not enter into the justification of this. Suffice it to say that justification is a form of action. If truth can be reached, it is mediated by a theory. The analytical theory that mediates access to reality at the same time bars direct access to it. Truth is qualified as "true knowledge" that is itself premised by what I propose to call "temporal cognitivism".

The variety of possible concretisations of the concept of freedom rules out the very option of any "true meaning" of freedom. The choice for a conception about freedom is submitted to justification. In the PA, this justification focuses on the external justification as an alternative for failing social interaction. In the PN, this normative density of the external justification must be justified. The PT in its turn stresses the general historical character of any justification.

The PT constrains a normative proposition submitted to justification on the PA and the PN from the perspective of time. An external limitation can be justified on both these principles at a certain moment of time.

Two important aspects of the PT are to be noted in this respect. First, the external limitation, apart from its content that is constrained in the PA and the PN must be shown to come on the "right time". Concrete circumstances *hic et nunc* may justify the issuing of an external limitation.

At the opposite of concrete circumstances, we find ahistorical social reality. This is social reality as it is conceived through the looking glass of strong legalism. Strong legalism aims at turning off the button of time. Weak legalism or the form of legalism underlying legisprudence on the contrary takes the temporal dimension of human action seriously. The rationality of legislation as the main concern of legisprudence compels the legislator to take concrete circumstances into consideration. These circumstances are replete with temporality.

As a consequence, what once was at the right moment may, after a lapse of time, be misplaced. This is the second aspect of the PT. It shows that what once was justified may turn out to have become unjustified. The justification of external limitations then is an ongoing process of justification. This process of justification should include the consciousness that external limitations must be kept in track with changing circumstances. Obsolete legislation or external limitations that are eroded by desuetude are no longer legitimated. They are to be withdrawn, changed or qualified in view of the PA and the PN.

The Principle of Coherence (PC): the Level Theory of Coherence

The PC is a principle of justification of external limitations from the perspective of the legal system as a whole. A legal system is not a static chain of external limitations; it is, on the contrary, a complex and dynamic set of intertwined propositions concerning what ought to be done and how it ought to be done.

On a somewhat strong claim, it could be said that any change in the system affects it as a whole. Complex as it may be by its very nature, it turns out to become increasingly complicated. The complication of a legal system is mainly due to its exponential growth. Consequential upon this, the systematic character of the legal system risks being jeopardized.

From there, the idea of coherence of a legal system can be articulated. Coherence is often interconnected with consistency. Consistency means the absence of contradictions within the set of propositions that is called a theory. One contradiction makes the system inconsistent. On the idea that consistency is considered a condition for coherence, a contradiction would make the system also incoherent.

Apart from this relation between coherence and consistency, some would say that consistency is a matter of all or nothing. Coherence in its turn is a matter of degree. In this view, consistency is a logical requirement while coherence refers to "making sense as a whole".

The relation between coherence and consistency can be defined in yet a different way. If coherence means "to make sense as a whole" consistency can be taken to be a specific and strong way of making sense. It then only looks as if consistency is a matter of all or nothing, while coherence is a matter of degree.

From the perspective we are dealing with here, coherence concerns discourse or a set of propositions. These propositions can hang together in different ways. Consistency is one of them. If they cohere in a consistent way, we have a logical or consistent whole, that is, a set of contradiction-free propositions. The set of propositions can be said to make sense as a whole. On consistency as a conception of coherence, there exist other ways of making sense.

These appear when the "whole" is enlarged so as to include the context of participation. Law is not a set of propositions "turning on its own". It is to get in touch with social interaction, that it regulates. When the whole is enlarged that way, the distinction between consistency and coherence becomes all the more clear.

With this in mind, we can proceed to the articulation of the PC. The PC can be distinguished as a distinct theory that I propose to call the level theory of coherence. Generally speaking, four levels of coherence can be distinguished.

Coherence$_0$ The first level is not specific for the theory. It is a level of coherence below which nothing makes sense. It is called the level of coherence$_0$. This level concerns the elementary level of speech (say, a sentence, a judicial or legislative decision). If there appears a contradiction at this elementary level of speech, the subsequent elements of the discourse will be affected by that. Coherence$_0$ is a necessary condition for any discourse to make sense. It requires the absence of contradictions at the elementary level of speech. It has been aptly labelled "simultaneous consistency" (Kornhauser and Sager, 1986, pp. 105-106; Winch, 1990, p. 61).

Yet, the requirement of coherence$_0$ is not universal in that it is an identical requirement for each and every type of discourse. It depends on what counts as an elementary level of speech. The latter, in its turn, depends on the context. In poetic discourse is will be less constraining than in logical discourse. Every type of discourse has, so to say, an elementary level of speech. Although this level may be different depending on the type of discourse, the requirement of coherence$_0$ itself is a universal one. In this way it is unaffected by time.

The Level of Coherence$_1$ The requirement of coherence changes when the time dimension is added. When the time dimension is taken into consideration, the level of coherence$_0$ is not affected. When two judicial decisions on a similar case are compared, both should meet the requirement of coherence$_0$. Further, we want the decisions to be similar because the cases are similar. If a judge condemns a thief to a fine of €100, formal justice compels pronouncing the same fine in a subsequent and similar case. Our sense of justice may be shocked if this were not the case.

Formal justice looks most similar to consistency. There are two reasons main for this. The first reason is the rule character of law. The rule character of law is founded in the process of epistemologisation of philosophy. This process gave rise to the development of natural science. For natural science, reality is expressed in rules. The grammar of reality is expressed in mathematical rules. Scientific truths are mathematical equations. At least on some interpretation of modern science, reality is, ontologically speaking, mathematical. The mimicking of natural science by the sciences of man results in the rule character of the latter.

The second reason is related to the first. Legal rules like scientific rules are to be applied equally to equal cases. If they were not, their rule character would be affected. Unlike logical rules, however, the rule character of external limitations expresses a value judgement. The value that is expressed by the rule character of law is equality. On freedom as *principium,* freedom must be equal for all. Consequential upon that, the necessity of equal treatment of equal cases results from a normative demand. This demand dictates and corroborates the rule character of law. It is because we care for equality that law as rules is preferred to, e.g., law as a command.

The assimilation of law to natural science according to strong legalism then must lead to identical requirements as to consistency. The main reason why this is not the case is that the time dimension is left out of the view. This means that no distinction is made between coherence$_0$ and coherence$_1$. Coherence$_0$, as one remembers, requires the absence of contradictions at the elementary unit of speech of a discourse. The absence of the distinction between coherence$_0$ and coherence$_1$ for its part denies that elementary units of speech can be identified. It takes consistency to be a matter of all or nothing. As a consequence, it is the whole that must be consistent in order to make sense at all.

Once the time dimension is brought in, it affects the process of application of rules. It can be said that it is the time dimension that makes law different from natural science. If the application of rules is mainly a logical operation the introduction of the time dimension involves the temporal aspects of this operation being taken into account. These temporal aspects ensure that a justification of decisions is substituted for a mere application of rules. Justification includes that the identity of cases is tempered to their similarity. The conclusion that two cases are similar involves a value judgment that requires a justification. This conclusion is not compelling; it is at best convincing.

Since justification is submitted to temporal conditions, it could hardly be expected that the set of external limitations that result from there is logically consistent. On the contrary, it varies over time.

As far as judicial decision-making is concerned, this means that one can depart from earlier decisions. Formal justice as a rule of decision-making is not absolute, since decision-making is dependent on time. Departure from a rule or a precedent is possible on the condition that it is justified, while following precedent needs no justification.

Things are similar, although slightly different, from the perspective of the legislator. As a matter of fact the latter's freedom is much larger than the judge's. Judges are bound by the rules of the legal system. Since legislators create and can change these rules they are, logically speaking, not bound by any of them. The aspects of change and creation of external limitations call for two different sets of observations. The first relates to coherence$_1$, while the second deals with another level of coherence that will be treated in the next subsection.

A judge must not justify the fact that he follows the rule or the precedent. The only thing he has to justify is departure from them. The legislator for his part can be called to justify both the *status quo* and a departure from an existing situation on the PA, the PN, and the PC. Paradoxically, the legislator's duty of justification in view of the PC is in a sense stronger than the judge's.

This specific character of the legislator's duty is connected to the fact that external limitations of freedom are submitted to justification on the PA and the PN. As long as the situation S does not change, a change of the external limitation would entail a formal injustice. If all As are to be treated as Bs on an existing external limitation R, any change of R results in a different treatment of A from that moment on. Therefore, a justification is required.[6]

If no distinction were made between coherence_0 and coherence_1, no changes would be possible. Any change, that is, would be barred by the requirement of formal justice. The judge has not to justify adherence to the precedent though he has to justify departure from it. The legislator for his part has to justify both the status quo and the change of external limitations. This is, briefly, what the level of coherence_1 from the legisprudential perspective requires.

When we focus on the change of external limitations from the perspective of the judge, a further distinction has to be made that opens the way for a different level of coherence.

The Level of Coherence$_2$ A judge who departs from precedent violates the requirements of formal justice. This violation can be outweighed by justification. The view needs some qualification. It is premised by the idea that rules are "just there" and that they jump from the rulebook right on to the judge's desk. Reality however is more complex. Judges are to choose the rule they apply to a case. A textbook example is whether a lease is ruled by a contract regime or by a property regime. The specific set of rules has to be chosen. This choice is not compelling. The consequences of both regimes embrace serious differences as to the rights and duties of the landlord and tenant. On coherence_1, the line of decision along one of these regimes has to be followed. Departing from it is possible if it is justified. For this justification, a supplementary level of coherence is needed.

This level of coherence, that is, the level of coherence_2, provides arguments for departing from the requirements of coherence_1.[7]

It follows from the above that departure from a line of precedent is permitted if it is justified. Arguments that justify such a departure are of a different level than coherence_1. They belong to the level of coherence_2. Systematic interpretation is an exemplary case of argumentation on the level of coherence_2 from the perspective of the judge. On this level, the whole of the legal system is taken into account. Yet, similar observations can be made for other methods of interpretation.

Apart from the requirements of coherence_1, legislative activity is also submitted to the constraints of the level of coherence_2. As is the case with the judge, coherence_2 arguments from the perspective of the legislator require him to take the system as a whole into consideration. On arguments of coherence_2, the judge can rely on the systematic character of the legal system. The corresponding perspective of the legislator comes to the requirement to constitute the legal system as a whole.[8]

When the judge argues on the level of coherence$_2$ – e.g., in systematic interpretation – he assumes the unity of the legal system, in that he takes it as a whole. Coherence$_2$ argumentation from the perspective of the legislator requires the latter to constitute this unity.

Unlike in strong legalism, the rationality of the legislator is not irrefutably presumed. If it were, the proxy model would again be substituted for the trade-off model. The legislator, that is, has to justify his external limitations so that they allow the judge to make coherence$_2$ arguments at all.

Once the central position of the judge is qualified, the legislator's place becomes more apparent. Legislative activism includes an active justification of external limitations. Unlike the judge, the legislator cannot assume the systematic character of the legal system.

The more external limitations are shown, apart from their coherence$_0$ and coherence$_1$ aspects, to fit the system as a whole when seen from inside the system, that is, the better they satisfy coherence$_2$ justification. The assumption of rationality of the legislator, typically, belongs to the premises of strong legalism since, on the latter, external limitations are considered representations of reality. In strong legalism, the creation of rules or external limitations is considered a reproduction of reality; in weak legalism, the construction of rules is just a construction of rules, and not a reconstruction of reality.

In this reinterpretation of the premise of rationality of the legislator, he is not presumed to be rational. His rationality is to follow from his acts. If the latter presumption is part of the premises of strong legalism, on weak legalism, however, the rationality of the legislator is a matter of justification, not of presumption.

The Level of Coherence$_3$ On strong legalism, judges apply rules that legislators create. Rule application is a theoretical matter, as it is in mathematics. Rule creation for its part is considered a political matter that does not appear on the screen of legal theory.

On weak legalism, however, both judge and legislator create rules and follow rules. The judge follows rules in the application of rules. At the same time, he creates individual rules. The legislator for his part follows rules while creating general rules or external limitations. The differences between these positions may be considerable; they are not opposite, however.

As far as the judge's position is concerned, rules are not self-interpreting (Perelman, 1970). The process of the determination of meaning as well as the choice of the rule needs a theory in order to be rational. Rationality in decision-making however is not limited to fitting new decisions into a set of existing rules. This is only one way of putting the matter that can be labelled "internal rationality" (Wroblewski, 1984). So all of the existing rules can be said to be rational or coherent or to make sense from this perspective.

However, on the articulation of coherence as "making sense *as a whole*" one needs another perspective. You cannot see something as a whole unless an external perspective is included. While the legal system as a set of external limitations can be internally rational or coherent, its making sense as a whole requires a perspective that allows it to be seen as a whole. This is only possible by leaning over the edges of what is considered the whole. In addition, saying that the whole becomes *more* coherent by transforming some of its elements, the comparative term necessitates that the whole *qua* whole is taken into consideration. This again requires an external perspective that I propose to call "external rationality". While the levels of coherence$_1$ and coherence$_2$ refer to internal rationality, their operationalisation is conditioned by external rationality. This relation can be articulated in the following way.

The basic premise of the argument is that things do not have meaning of their own. Meaning is conveyed upon something. On this objection against the plain-meaning doctrine, it follows that the meaning of a rule is subsequent to interpretation, since rules do not speak of themselves. From this perspective, the rule-following judge and the rule-following legislator are in a similar position.

The meaning of rules does not stem from the rules itself. Meaning cannot be grasped by merely gazing at them (Perelman, 1970). Interpretation, and meaning resulting from that, is a theoretical construction that itself depends on a theory. The plain meaning doctrine as an ally of strong legalism denies this theory dependence. Strong legalism, one remembers, relies on a direct access to reality; weak legalism for its part relies only on an indirect access to it. This indirect access means that a theory is about reality and that its access to it is mediated by a theoretical framework. This theoretical framework is the analytical theory of a legal system referred to below.

In order for the legal system to make sense as a whole, the legal officials operating its buttons are to keep an eye on what makes it a whole; and that is a theoretical framework on which the legal system depends.[9] This theory dependence of the legal system is what the level of coherence$_3$ is about.

The level of coherence$_3$ is best articulated via the distinction between the internal and the external points of view that can be adopted towards a rule. While the external point of view expresses the behavioural regularities that can be connected to rule-following behaviour, the internal point of view expresses the rule's normative character. MacCormick's qualification of this original insight of H.L.A. Hart comes to saying that the legal scholar, while adopting an external perspective, at the same time includes in his description the internal point of view. On that view, legal scholarship gives full weight to rules as reasons for action.

MacCormick's qualification of Hart's moderately external point of view, that he aptly labels the "hermeneutical point of view" (MacCormick, 1981, pp. 37-40; MacCormick, 1978, pp. 290-292) refers to specific dynamics. It is a perspective that starts *from* the external point of view *towards* the internal point of view. The connection between the scholar's own method – economics, morals, history, sociology, comparative law, etc. – and the object "law" is likely to result in a different understanding of the object altogether.

Yet, in my view of the matter, the dynamics of the MacCormickian hermeneutical perspective can be reversed. Roughly speaking, a scholar revealing an alternative reading of a set of legal rules according to his own method adopts an "as if" position. His scholarly conclusions, it can be said, do not have the same authority as a judicial decision. Yet, in as far as his reading includes the internal point of view of the judge, his conclusions may come very close to the way the judge reads the statute. The latter, in taking cognisance of the scholar's work, sees a virtual image of himself.

This image is a virtual one as long as the judge did not adopt this position. The law and economics research illustrates this point. From an external point of view the law and economics scholar may reveal a new reading of the torts rule.

A textbook example is Calabresi's and Melamed's approach that eloquently reveals a different view of the cathedral of torts (Calabresi and Melamed, 1972). Apart from the meanings of the tort rule considered from within the legal system, an economic analysis informs an alternative meaning from an external perspective. When this external perspective is a moderately external one, or as MacCormick calls it a "hermeneutical" perspective, the mirror effect is obtained. A judge withholding the new meaning reverses the dynamics of the hermeneutical point of view. That is to say, that *from* an internal point of view which expresses the rule being a norm for him, he goes *towards* the external point of view.

It may look as if the level of coherence$_3$ is some supplementary level that is relevant only when the rules to be applied need some interpretation. Put differently, only if rules are unclear, are they to be interpreted. In order to determine their meaning, the judge is then to lean over the edge of the system as a set of rules. There he finds supplementary tools to interpret these rules.

This view is however wrong. The clarity of a rule does not precede interpretation, so that only unclear rules must be interpreted. If rules were held clear by themselves, meaning would exist on itself or "out there", which is clear nonsense. On the contrary, the clarity of a rule is the result of an interpretation that may be concealed.

A theory of interpretation with the help of which rules are interpreted is not itself law (Troper, 2001, p. 212). It does not belong to the legal system that consists of a set of rules; it is though necessary for a legal system to dispose of such a theory.

Summarizing, rule-following behaviour includes a cognitive and a volitional aspect. The volitional aspect of the internal point of view, however, is not a pure act of will. It is, so to say, replete with theory that is not contained within the rule. It is contained in the analytical theory of the legal system saying why rules are preferable to commands, and so why freedom and equality are preferable to arbitrariness, and why therefore it is preferable that the powers in political space are separated, and so on. From that perspective, the analytical theory of the legal system orients the choice of acceptable theories of interpretation, that is, theories to determine the meaning of rules of the legal system result in the legal system making sense as a whole. In short, the analytical theory of the legal system is what makes the legal system a legal order.

On the thesis that the legislator, like the judge, is a rule follower, a similar account can be given of his activity. Like the rules of the legal system not being self-interpreting, the rules of the constitution rarely contain a positive indication as to the substance of legal rules issued by the legislator. His rule-following behaviour is then confined to not violating the rules he is supposed to follow. Following rules however includes more than the minimalist duty not to violate them (Bankowski, 1993).

If following rules by the legislator involves, as a minimum or negatively, that they are not violated, it includes positively, however, or as a matter of aspiration, that the rights and duties it includes can be effectively exercised, that they are sufficiently protected and enforced respectively, and so on. The legislator's aspiration is more than a matter that deserves a prize when effectuated. It resembles a duty to aspire to the best possible rules rather than a simple political aspiration to do so. It is on this condition that the legal system starts making sense as a whole from the legisprudential point of view.

It would be tempting to say on this point that the "best possible rules" are a matter of politics, and that politics is a matter of disagreement. Here come in though the principles of legisprudence, the PC on top. The circumstances of politics ensure there exists disagreement among people, while at the same time there is a need to act in concert, at least in some domains (Waldron, 1999a, pp.102 ff; Waldron, 1999b, pp.156 ff). Politics does not aim at disagreement evaporating; it must make disagreement workable.

Some would say that this is achieved by respecting human rights. This is correct, and so it is also correct to say that human rights are part of the analytical theory of the legal system. The respect for human rights is achieved by not violating them. Individual freedom is protected by human rights as the requirement of respect for individual freedom.

This is, however, only one way of making sense of freedom. It is a negative stipulation that stems from the analytical theory of the legal system making it a legal order. The reflexive character of freedom however requires more than a negative protection of some essential features of freedom. From this perspective, legal rules or external limitations of freedom are submitted to justification on the principle of alternativity, the principle of celerity, and the principle of normative density. This justification comes to a positive implementation of the moral autonomy of the subject. The supplementary justification on the principle of coherence underpins the connection between the concept of freedom as part of the analytical theory of the legal system and the system's rules.

* Professor of Law and Jurisprudence at the K.U. Brussel and the European Academy for Legal Theory, Director of the Center for Legislation, Regulation and Legisprudence, Brussels.

Notes

1 In this respect, I disagree with Jeremy Waldron, who claims that: "We paint legislation up in these lurid shades [deal-making, horse-trading, log-rolling, etc.] in order to lend credibility to the idea of judicial review (…)." (Waldron, 1999, p. 2). Although this thesis may be correct for the American legal system where judicial review exists, albeit

largely criticised, it is incorrect for civil law systems where no judicial review existed until recently (e.g. in Belgium) or does not exist at all (e.g. in the Netherlands). From this perspective, the reasons for the lack of interest in or the absence of a theory of legislation must be sought elsewhere.

2 This means to be weighed and balanced against each other, as conceptions of or conceptions about. It does not only mean a weighing and balancing of two or more conceptions about freedom.

3 I thank Manuel Atienza for his comment on this point.

4 When a person is in jail, his capacity to act on conceptions of freedom is by definition limited. If he has to pay a fine, he cannot spent the money according to his own wish.

5 This does not suggest that explanation would not be of a justificatory type.

6 If a tax measure is justified on the PA and the PN in order to increase economic activity, it may well be that the effects of R are insufficient to realise the goal. Therefore, R is to be changed. This change is submitted to justification. If S changes over time, this may be a reason for changing R. It may, on the contrary, also be a reason for not doing so. In the first hypothesis, a justification is required on the PN and the PA. In the second, a reason must be given for not changing R. It may indeed turn out that the tax measure did realise its goal. If economic production has reached the level, the measure purported to realise the tax measure becomes unjustified

7 The potential of the level of coherence$_2$ can be illustrated with an example from judicial decision-making. According to a rule from 1963, a spouse staying home and taking care of her children qualified for the sc. "premium for the spouse at the fireside". In 1979, a husband claimed the premium. Over against the plain meaning of the text of the law, the judge decided for the plaintiff. His argument involved a reference to other rules of the system that proclaimed the principled equality of husband and wife. The matrimonial act of 1976, the European Convention on Human Rights (1950, ratified by Belgium in 1955), the Universal Declaration of Human Rights (1948) as well as legal doctrine supported this view. The decision was inconsistent with the preceding line of jurisdiction. Despite the violation of the requirements of coherence$_1$, this decision was held to make more sense as a whole. Hence, it was more coherent than earlier decisions. The decision relied on a systematic interpretation of the 1963 rule. A systematic interpretation comes to reading this rule in the light of other rules of the system.

8 An example will illustrate this position. On rule R_1, unemployed persons receive an unemployment benefit U according to fixed criteria of distribution. Some time later, the sovereign issues R_2. On rule R_2, companies who employ a person qualifying for the unemployment benefit under R_1 on their turn qualify for a premium encouraging the employment of the economically inactive. Both premiums are paid by the state. A person P_2 who, in doing so, qualifies for the premium on R_2 offers a person P_1 qualifying under R_1 for the unemployment benefit a job. Both P_1 and P_2 can be thought to have an interest, in that P_1 gets a job and a salary S and P_2 gets the premium. However, if P_1's S only slightly exceeds his U, he may be entitled to think that he is paid very little for his work. He may think that what he "really" earns by working comes to [S – U]. The smaller the result of [S – U], the more he will be encouraged to think that way. This problem is known as the unemployment trap. The simultaneous effects of R_1 and R_2 do not contradict. They simply annul each other's effect to a large extent. If both R_1 and R_2 are valid rules and, *ex hypothesi*, satisfy coherence$_0$ requirements and are justified on coherence$_1$, they do not necessarily satisfy the requirements of coherence$_2$. Their combination impairs the systematic character of the legal system. Their simultaneous existence causes a lot of hay, including administrative bother, eventually procedures in court, and the like, for an effect that is close to zero. R_1 and R_2, it can be said, are not

efficacious. R_2 then needs a supplementary justification in the PC in order to show that it fits with the system as a whole. Coherence$_2$ from the perspective of the legislator requires him to take the systematic character of the system as a whole into consideration. Even while avoiding violations of coherence$_0$ and coherence$_1$, he can violate coherence$_2$ in adding rules that are inefficacious, or impair the systematic character of the whole, or annul other rules' effects.

9 Together with this I should like to argue that the legal system is itself a theory. Unfortunately, this proposition is to keep its dogmatic formulation as space is lacking here.

References

Aristotle (1972), *Politics*, H. Rackham (tr.), Harvard University Press, Cambridge (Ma).

Atienza, M. (2005), 'Reasoning and Legislation' in this volume.

Austin, J. (1971), *The Province of Jurisprudence Determined and the Uses of the Study of Jurisprudence*, 4th ed., H.L.A. Hart (ed.), Weidenfeld & Nicholson, London.

Bankowski, Z. (1993), 'Don't Think About It : Legalism and Legality', in M.M. Karlsson (ed.), *Rechtstheorie*, Beihefte, 15, 45-57.

Berlin, I. (1969), *Four Essays on Liberty*, Oxford University Press, Oxford.

Blumenberg, H. (1983), *The Legitimacy of Modernity*, R.M. Wallace (tr.), MIT Press, Cambridge (Ma)/London.

Calabresi, G. and Melamed, A.D. (1972), 'Property Rules, Liability Rules and Inalienability : One View of the Cathedral', *Harvard Law Review*, Vol. 85, pp. 1089-1128.

Cassirer, E. (1932), *Die Philosophie der Aufklärung*, Mohr Siebeck, Tubingen.

Descartes, R. (1996), *Discours de la méthode pour bien conduire sa raison et chercher la vérité dans les sciences,* in C. Adam and P. Tannery (ed.), *Œuvres de Descartes*, VI, Vrin, Paris.

Fuller, L.L. (1978), *The Morality of Law*, 15th ed., Yale University Press, New Haven.

Hart, H. L. A. (1994), *The Concept of Law*, 2nd ed., J. Raz and P.A. Bulloch (eds.) Clarendon Press, Oxford.

Hart, H.L.A. (1979), 'Are There Any Natural Rights ?' in D. Lyons (ed.), *Rights*, Wadworth Publ. Comp., Belmont, 14-25.

Hobbes, T. (1966), *Leviathan: or, the Matter, Form, and Power of a Commonwealth, Ecclesiastical and Civil*, 2nd ed., in W. Moleworth, (ed.), *The English Works of Thomas Hobbes of Malmesbury*, III, Scientia Verlag, Aalen.

Hunyadi, M. (1995), *La vertu du conflit. Pour une morale de la médiation*, Cerf, Paris.

Kant, I. (1983), *Metaphysik der Sitten. Metapysische Anfangsgründe der Rechtslehre*, 5th ed., in *Kant Werke*, IV, Wissenschaftliche Buchgesellschaft, Darmstadt.

Kelsen, H. (1967), *Reine Rechtslehre*, 2nd ed., Deuticke, Vienna.

Kornhauser, L.A. and Sager, L.G. (1986), 'Unpacking the Court', *Yale Law Journal*, Vol. 96, pp. 82-117.

Locke, J. (1963), *Two Treatises of Government* in *The Works of John Locke*, V Scientia Verlag, Aalen.

MacCormick, N. (1981), *H L A Hart*, in W Twining (ed.), *Profiles in Legal Theory*, Arnold, London.

MacCormick, N. (1978), *Legal Reasoning and Legal Theory*, Clarendon Press, Oxford.

Nagel, N. (1986), *The View from Nowhere*, Oxford University Press, Oxford.

Noll, P. (1973), *Gesetzgebungslehre*, Rowohlt, Reinbek.

Perelman, C. (1970), 'Avoir un sens et donner un sens', in *Le champ de l'argumentation*, Presses Univ. Bruxelles, Brussels.

Perelman, C., and Olbrechts-Tyteca, L., (1976), *Traité de l'argumentation. La Nouvelle Rhétorique*, 3rd ed., Ed. University Bruxelles, Brussels.

Raz, J. (1990), *Practical Reason and Norms*, Princeton University Press, Princeton, NJ.

Ricoeur, P. (1986), 'Science et idéologie' in *Du texte à l'action*, Seuil, Paris.

Rousseau, J.-J. (1964), *Du contrat social* in *Œuvres complètes*, III, (Bibliothèque de la Pléiade), Gallimard, Paris.

Shklar, J.N. (1964), *Legalism. Law, Morals and Political Trials*, Harvard University Press, Cambridge (Ma).

Taylor, C. (1995), *Philosophical Arguments*, Harvard University Press, Cambridge (Ma).

Taylor, C. (1983), *Social Theory as Practice*, Oxford University Press, Delhi.

Toulmin, S. (1990), *Cosmopolis. The Hidden Agenda of Modernity*, Free Press, New York.

Troper, M. (2001), *La théorie du droit, le droit, l'Etat*, in *Leviathan*, P.U.F., Paris.

Ullman, W. (1979), *Medieval Political Thought*, Penguin, London.

Waldron, J. (1999a), *The Dignity of Legislation*, Cambridge University Press, Cambridge.

Waldron, J. (1999b), *Law and Disagreement*, Oxford University Press, Oxford.

Weber, M. (1964), *The Theory of Social and Economic Organisation*, A.M. Henderson (tr.), T. Parsons (ed.), Free Press, New York.

Winch, P. (1990), *The Idea of Social Science and its Relation to Philosophy*, 2nd ed., Routledge, London.

Wroblewski, J. (1984), *Einführung in die Gesetzgebungstheorie*, Manz, Vienna.

Chapter 2

The Quest for Legisprudence: Constitutionalism *v.* Legalism

Imer B. Flores*

Introduction: Why Legisprudence?

Reintegrating legislation to the nucleus of law implies not only reviewing the conditions of why it has been on leave or in the periphery of the legal processes, but also revising the possibilities – and even the necessity – of "legisprudence" as the theory of legislation; its characteristics as a theory of legislators and legislatures, on one side, and of lawmaking, on the other; its relationships to other legal process within the "legal" or "juridical" science, namely "jurisprudence", and to "legal rationality" in the search for an appropriate "rationality of legislation". In addition, as the main aim of this contribution is to seek out for the proper place for legisprudence in legal or juridical analysis, it is imperative to contrast it to both "constitutionalism" and "legalism".

Accordingly, the paper has two major parts: 1) depicted by the comparison amid the absence and presence of a theory of legislation; and 2) described by the contrast between constitutionalism and legalism to house legisprudence. In my opinion, legisprudence is incompatible with a strong version of legalism and compatible with a weak one. But my hunch is that, albeit it is by the same token congruent with a weak version of constitutionalism, it will be much more consonant with a stronger one.

Legislation and Legisprudence: From Absence to Presence

Legislation, legislators and legislatures have a "bad name" in legal and political philosophy (Waldron, 1999b, p. 1) and are considered the "poor cousins" of legal education to the extent that statutory drafting and implementation are to be learned by osmosis, if at all (Froomkin, 1988, p. 1071). A partial explanation can be traced at least to the publication of the essay *Of the Vocation of Our Age for Legislation and Jurisprudence* of Friedrich Karl von Savigny, which developed the view that legal institutions are an indigenous expression of the national culture and history of a people as expressed in their spirit: law is the product of the collective conscience. As such, the institutions cannot be externally imposed without representing an arbitrary interference with the *Volkgeist*. This conception strengthens the prejudice against codification and what's more is contrary to the idea that it is possible to amend law – and reality – merely by legislative decrees (of the sovereign or popularly elected legislatures).

Besides, the absence of a theory of legislation, together with the non-appearance of legislators and non-attendance of legislatures creates the presumption that judges and courts are what law is all about. It also explains the obsession with law-application: adjudication. Paradoxically, the least dangerous branch of government is the more – and arguably better – examined, meanwhile the most dangerous one is the less – and presumably worse – studied.[1] Roscoe Pound's statement is revealing (1921, pp. 46-47):

> Hence the orthodox tradition of our law schools wholly ignores the enactment element in law. In its teaching the older element, represented by the traditional course of decision, stands for the real law and furnishes principles and analogies, while the newer element, represented by legislation, is regarded as something alien, intruding in the body of the law, and may furnish only detailed rules for the cases expressly covered.

In that sense, legal theory tends to focus exclusively on adjudication – as law-application or lawfinding – and judiciary – judges and courts – whereas legislation – as law-creation or lawmaking – and legislative – legislators and legislature – are almost neglected as they are considered rather a matter of politics, and as such the object of study not for jurists but for political scientists. Although this may explain why legal science appears to be limited to a science of the application of rules and legal theorists obsessed with the person of the judge and the role of the courts, it does not justify that the creation of rules by the legislator is set aside (Hart, 1994, p. 1). Especially since judges and legislators are and must be closely allied in the endeavor of law constructing as they employ more or less the same rationality and fix similar things. Neither courts nor legislative assemblies – or even executive agencies – alone can be completely accountable of the edifice of law. Instead, judges and legislators – and other officials – are co-responsible and must collaborate in this joint venture together with the citizenship. Lon L. Fuller's quote seems appropriate: "[T]here is a kind of reciprocity between government and the citizen with respect the observance of rules" (Fuller, 1969, p. 39).

The search for a theory of legislation is not a completely new enterprise, since legislation has been a primary concern for philosophers from Aristotle to Bentham, including Hobbes, Locke, Montesquieu, Rousseau and Kant, and to legal scholars, pre-eminently Henry Sumner Maine. The latter even highlighted that the last stage in the evolution of law was precisely that of *legislation.*[2] Nevertheless, as Fuller (1968, p. 87) revealed, Maine's account is doubly mistaken by presuming that all societies have followed exactly the same course set by his six stages and presupposing that each one is entirely closed out before the next begins. On the contrary, he argued extensively in favor of the distinctiveness of each society and the coexistence of several legal processes such as adjudication, contract, customary law, legislation, managerial direction, mediation, and so on, all of which spill over both backward and forward in time (Fuller, 1981).

In recent times, the configuration of an alternative legal theory and the reappearance of a theory of legislation are amongst the main consequences of the criticism directed against the dominant legal theory and its obsessional focus upon adjudication, particularly to the question: How should judges decide cases? (Kennedy, 1996, and Unger, 1986 and 1996). Jeremy Waldron, in a book review of Roberto Unger's *What Should Legal Analysis Become?*, encourages: "[T]o start the construction of a jurisprudence appropriate to the aspiration of a free people to govern themselves under laws that they themselves have made" (Waldron, 1998, p. 522). That's why he has embarked the task of presenting legislation as a dignified mode of governance and a respectable source of law, and placing legislators and legislatures at the center of our philosophical thinking about law (Waldron, 1999a and 1999b).

What is distinctively in the configuration of a new-fangled theory of legislation is the call for a shift from adjudication to legislation: from a judge-centered approach to a legislator-oriented attitude in law and legal analysis, as advanced and advocated prominently among others by Luc J. Wintgens in a crusade in the quest for the holy grail of legisprudence (2002). Jurists have paid too much attention to the judicative side of law and the legislative trait has not been taken care of appropriately. The obvious answer to redress this evil is to concentrate now in this long neglected field and reallocate it in the focal point of legal inquiry. Appealing as this idea might be, we must be careful in the hunt for a Panacea of opening a Pandora's box instead. In this sense, a moderate version as the one attributed to Julius Cohen is preferable: legisprudence should be a coordinate branch of jurisprudence, parallel to what he called "judicativeprudence" (Cohen, 1983).

As legal – or juridical – science has been obsessed with adjudication-application, and not so much with legislation-creation, it seems that "jurisprudence" is reduced to the judicative part (*application* of law by the *judge*) leaving no space left for the legislative realm (*creation* of law by the *legislator*) – and as a result neglecting that the judge does legislate.[3] Nonetheless, since the Romans defined *iurisprudentia* ("jurisprudence") as *divinarum atque humanarum rerum notitia; iusti atque iniusti scientia* and *ius* ("law") as *ars boni et æqui*, they established that the noun *ius* and the adjective *iuris* ought to prevail over the similar expressions *lex* and *legis*. Such priority is grounded in the fact that the former terms are far more general to the extent that they are comprehensive of the latter ones: *ius* and *iuris* refer to "the law" and to "legal" and "juridical", correspondingly; *lex* and *legis* relate to "a law", i.e. "legislation", as a distinctive legal or juridical source, and to "legislative", respectively. In this order of ideas, the same rationale applies to "adjudication", as another distinct source, and to "judicative".

In sum, even if legisprudence as a theory of legislation is a part of jurisprudence as a legal – or juridical – science, it is imperative that our traditional jurisprudential approach to law, which is biased and almost one-sided in favor of the judicative area to the detriment of the legislative one, be completed with an alternate legisprudential attitude and with as many alternative prudential analyses to other legal sources – processes and products – as necessary.

Legisprudence as a Theory of Legislation

Etymologically, "legisprudence" derives from *legis*/*lex* ("a law" or "legislation") and *prudentia* (practical knowledge, reason and wisdom) and alludes to the "study and theory of legislation", to the "science, theory and technique of legislation" or to the "rational theory of legislation". In any event, legisprudence is defined mainly as a "theory of legislation" and is characterized both as "a new theory" – or "a new theoretical approach" – and as "an object of study of legal theory" (Wintgens, 2002).

As stated above, it is not a completely new-fangled endeavor, but a call for a novel theory or theoretical approach to law. Clearly, law and legal analysis require a major shift in the mentality of jurists and legal theorists towards a complementary legisprudential method to jurisprudence – to include the perspective of the legislator – and to other methodologies. The shift implies the reallocation of the study or theory of legislation inside the legal or juridical science and the revision of some of the "great dichotomies", such as the distinctions between adjudication-legislation, law-application – or lawfinding – and law-creation – or law making – judges-legislators, courts-legislatures, and so on, which reinforce the apparent separation between law and politics.[4]

At this point I would like to bring to mind that the word "legislation" is ambiguous as it implies activity-process, on one side, and product-result, on the other. In clarifying the concept, let me suggest that in the, until now, dominant view, legislation as a process has been depicted as political not legal, and legislation as a product (of the "political process") has been described chiefly as political, but to some extent as pre-legal: it is not-yet-law until a legal authority or official says it is law.

This gap opened at least the back door for a minimalist analysis from the legal point of view of statutes as a specific result of legislation, leaving the activity that originated them largely unexplored. For instance the Supreme Court of the State of Wyoming in the United States of America has defined legisprudence as the "jurisprudence of legislation" and elucidated that it "is helpful in determining what the legislature intended" to resolve an ambiguity of a statute.[5] Evidently, legisprudence is reduced to a "theory of the creation and application of statutes" (Eskridge and Frickey, 1988). Moreover, legisprudence aspires as a legitimate heir to the main entrance and to a maximum assay not only of legislation – and statutes – both as activity-process and product-result, but also of legislators and legislatures themselves.

Consequently, a new theory or theoretical approach of legislation from the legal standpoint must focus: 1) on lawmaking – legislation itself and statutes – covering everything from the final product to the whole process from the conception and gestation of a statute – through its drafting and implementation – to its death – either by fleeting derogation or lingering desuetude; and 2) on legislators and legislatures, beginning with the regulation of elections through which legislators as representatives are voted into the Congress or Parliament, continuing with the organization of the legislature at large and/or through committees and even subcommittees, and finishing with the supervision of what they – and others – might do and not do "lawfully" in the way of lawmaking.

Let me also suggest that legislation is itself in crisis and that both legislators and legislatures are immersed in it. On one side, there is a crisis of the qualitative and quantitative merits of legislation, which by the by amplify each other: defective or flawed legislation (decreased quality) is one of the causes of *legislative inflation* (increased quantity); and, excessive or flecked legislation (increased quantity) is one of the causes of *legislative deflation* (decreased quality). On the other, there is a crisis of representation, which affects the democratic nature of legislators as elected representatives and legislatures as the forum for deliberation. Let me start first with the latter and then return to the former.

Legisprudence as the study of legislators and legislatures Legisprudence must incorporate into its object of study not merely the functional purpose of legislators and legislatures, but their structural election and organization. According to the mainstream theory of representation (Pitkin, 1967): 1) legislators should mirror their constituencies and the legislature should look like the electorate in miniature: they are "standing for" them; 2) legislators as their agents – or delegates – should do what the constituents want them to do regardless of their own preferences: they are "acting for" them; and 3) legislators as their trustees should act professionally and independently of the mandate of the represented and even depart from their freewill: they are "acting on behalf of" them.

The problem is that the representation has remained mostly as "virtual": legislators and legislatures neither reflect the standing point of their constituencies nor are acting for them or on their behalf, reinforcing that minorities are being left out the political process and oppressed by the "tyranny of the majority" (Flores, 1999, pp. 204-206). On this regard, to enable a "real" representation that mirrors the citizenry, at the time that acts for and on behalf of them, it is imperative first to take a look to the electoral systems through which the election and organization of our representatives takes place. If a legislature is a mirror of the citizenry, our electoral system – whether it is oriented towards majority, plurality or proportionality – must be open and remain so in order to be legitimate by representing the interests of both majorities and minorities at the same time that a governing coalition is guaranteed to rule (Flores, 2002).

Along similar lines, Waldron has argued: if a legislature is a mirror of the constituency, our legislative body – namely Assembly, Congress or Parliament – the larger the better (Waldron, 1999a, 1999b, and 2002). For him, size matters and has a positive effect in the proportionality of legislators-citizens and in the debate itself: large gatherings of representatives air their disagreements and make better laws as a direct effect of such deliberation and voting.

It is well known that legislative assemblies can operate at large or through committees – and even subcommittees. As Woodrow Wilson (1981, p. 69) expressed: "Congress in session is Congress on display. Congress in committee is Congress at work." But the inquiry goes far beyond the question of whether the courts when construing ambiguous statutes should examine only floor debates or rely on committee discussion. If they consider it necessary, the query into the reliability of such committees comes into play, which brings their selection and composition into scrutiny. Presumably the bigger the committee the more likely they are to mirror the interest of the community and the more reliable they are. At the end of the day the committees are nothing but little legislatures.

In addition, much of the work in any Congress is done not by representatives themselves but by groups of experts and professionals either hired temporarily or working permanently as congressional staff. In fact, Parliaments rely not just on information from the inside but from the outside as well – either by outsourcing an initiative, ordering a congressional hearing or requiring some specific information to be evaluated in-house.

Furthermore, if legislators are agents – or delegates – of the people, they should do what the constituents want them to do regardless of their own preferences. Elections must be made with certain periodicity and close to each other: arguably the more frequent they are the greater the fidelity of legislators to the will of the people must be. In parliamentary democracies the call for anticipated elections follows a parallel rationale: ask the people what is truly its opinion through ballots at polls. Likewise, legislators are trustees that should act independently of those represented because they are professionals that know as connoisseurs themselves what to do or at least to whom look after for a piece of advice.

The issues range from provisions created to regulate districting and apportionment, especially malapportionment and gerrymandering; nomination and election; age and other requirements to vote and being voted in; terms and sessions; reelection and term-limits; to regulations produced to control the money spent on political campaigns, bribery and other improper attempts to influence the legislative process, lobbying and other proper means, a regimen of incompatibilities and so on. The guiding principle is that democracy is not only formal or adjective, but also real and substantive. Hence, the discussion of what is "lawful" in the way of lawmaking cannot be reduced merely to "who" is entitled and "how" to make the decisions but to "what" can actually be decided (Ferrajoli, 1999).

Legisprudence as a study of lawmaking Legisprudence must include as its object of study the whole activity-process of lawmaking and its final product-result, in order to improve both. Following Schäffer (1988), it is necessary to eliminate the deficits of rationalization and to integrate the most rational and convenient configuration possible: any legal system is not – and cannot – be perfect, but, perfectible. Besides, legisprudence must pay attention to all the legal mandated phases of the legislative *iter*, counting those preceding or following it. As a matter of fact, the problems of lawmaking are not exclusively legal-technical but political-axiological. The latter varies from the categorization of ends, goals and purposes, interests, principles and values in a society to the decision to legislate in order to solve a social conflict proactively or leave it to the executive or judicative to resolve them retroactively (Bulygin, 1990).

The outcomes of legislation are not completely predictable, but by the same token a previous examination of its probable effects and a subsequent investigation of its tangible upshots is desirable. And so legisprudence has to include a survey of the impact of legal norms *ex ante* and *ex post* not only to avoid, as far as possible, undesired and undesirable effects, but also to rectify those negative consequences not expected nor intended. Additionally, it must improve legislation by attacking the multiple causes of what we label as "legislative inflation" and "legislative deflation".

Let me clarify that the former – legislative inflation – corresponds to an increase in the quantity of legislation, considering "quantity" as equivalent to "amount" or "number" and "extent", not "size". So, "more legislation" means an increase in its quantity: in the amount or number of pieces of legislation and extent of topics covered by it, not in the size of a specific statute, which is a different matter related more to its quality, to which it is subordinated.[6] The latter – legislative deflation – relates to a decrease in the quality of legislation, considering "quality" as parallel to "virtue" and "worth". Along these lines, "bad legislation" levels a decrease in its quality: in the virtue and worth of legislation itself.

On the one hand, legislative hypertrophy and overproduction of legal norms – and endless reforms – are related to the suspicious legalist belief that law represents reality: law alters or captures reality, either by introducing a piece of legislation, rectifying an old one or merely replacing it, when it obviously does not amend or grasp it, preserving the same deficiencies or putting similar deficits instead. Even as such, increased quantity of law is not recommendable: it has become a normal condition of democracy. In peculiar, as democracy becomes normality, society expects and requires more from the government, but its capacity to deliver effective solutions is reduced. In other words, demand increases in quantity causing legislative inflation, supply decreases in its quality producing legislative deflation (Flores, 1996).

If truth be told, there is a direct link between quantity and quality contributing to both more laws and bad laws. For instance, excessive or flecked legislation leads to different qualitative problems, such as the inconsistency derived from the presence of antinomies, contradictions and redundancies; along with a inconstancy of law through time in order to be more or less certain and stable instead of ever-changing; and even incongruity between rules in paper and in action, all of which impede both governed and government to observe rules: to be governed by rules under a government of laws.

What is more, it is said that "the supreme lawgiver cannot himself be out of step since it is he who calls the tune." As Fuller revealed in the following passage (Fuller, 1968, p. 40-41):

> In reality, some of the most grievous offenses against the integrity of the law come not form the lower levels of the hierarchy of offices, but from the legislator himself. The catalog of his sins is a long one. It includes vague and contradictory laws, laws changed capriciously and in response to passing political pressures, esoteric legal compulsions hidden in obscure corners of the code book, and a hundred and one other ways of writing confusion into what is supposed to be the prime source of social order.

Among the most serious offenses, Fuller lists "passing (or retaining on the statute books) laws that are not intended to be enforced at all" and "passing laws that are intended to be enforced only in selected cases" (Fuller, 1968, pp. 41-42). Openly, the problem of legislative inflation is more political than legal or technical, as it depends on political will and can be controlled even by self-regulation. However, legisprudence has a great share in a law's quality and in the adherence to legal principles such as consistency, constancy and congruity. In order to curb irresponsibility in law-making and to keep law simple, it is necessary to control the excesses and flecks of legislation that impoverish the quality of law, by including prohibitions that limit the sovereign power of the legislature, e.g. forbidding changes to a piece of legislation before a certain period or allowing them only if they have been previously justified or requiring some extra-qualification. Similarly it is necessary to curb the passing or retaining of symbolic law, i.e. law not intended to be enforced, without a concrete legal function, or merely as political manifestos through legislation (*legge manifiesto*); and, to restrict not addressing complicated questions directly in the text of the statute but answering them indirectly via pre-legislative materials such as the *travaux préparatoires*, and even leaving them to be solved in judicial practice.

On the other hand, legislative lowliness and poor standards have become the general rule and direct product of both legislative inflation and deflation. Plainly, the problem is not exclusively political but legal and technical. The defects and flaws of legislation, following Eng (2002, pp. 68-78), can be: 1) substantial; 2) technical; or 3) instrumental. The first brand contends from moral and/or political concerns that legislation is unfair, unjust, or the like. The second class contests since linguistic, logical-systematic and logical-dynamic considerations that legislation is incoherent or inconsistent.[7] Finally, the third category questions under means-ends correlations that legislation is inefficacious, ineffective or even inefficient.

As defective or flawed legislation causes legislative inflation the answer is not more legislation but better legislation. In enriching the quality of law the first step seems to be the incorporation of checklists (*checklisten*) and questionnaires (*fragenkataloge*) to verify that some minimal benchmarks are met. The convenience or necessity of legislation and the importance or indispensability of its intended purpose, including an analysis of its systematic adequacy and hierarchic sufficiency, of its intensity for being effectual and successful, on the one hand, its acceptability and predictability for the public, on the other hand, both require an *ex ante* and *ex post* critical examination of its causes and effects.

In this regard, Lars D. Eriksson (2002, p. 47) has suggested "[T]he lawgiver has to base his or her legislative decisions on detailed analyses of what the consequences will be of the legislative decisions made. The lawgiver has to be able to foresee the effects of his or her decisions". Moreover, as the principles of "good" legislation imply a constant criticism of both the activity-process and the product-result, we shall briefly enunciate some aspects that must improve the quality of a bill throughout the whole legislative *iter*.

In the pre-legislative: drafting the initiative itself and preparing a brief with information in advance on the problem and the solution proposed, together with the analysis of its merits compared with the other options and their costs (*vorblatt*). The preliminary draft and its final version must be: clear and precise, avoiding ambiguous and vague concepts, definitions and term;[8] coherent and consistent, eluding antinomies, contradictions and redundancies, on one side, and escaping gaps or normative conflicts of rules and collision of principles, on the other; and congruent, evading the mismatch between means-ends.

In the strictly-legislative: holding hearings; creating *ad hoc* committees – or subcommittees – if necessary; including some sort of preliminary discussion within them, recommending through committee reports passage or not and even – as a result of a rules committee – determining length of debate to elude "filibusters" and ability to amend it in the floor by declaring it as a "close-rule" instead of an "open-rule" to evade "riders"; and, finally; debating and passing after thoughtful and truthful deliberation.[9]

In the post-legislative: incorporating some sort of sanction or ratification immediately after its approval and before its enactment into law by an executive agent, who must either sign it or exercise its veto, and even via judicative tribunals, which would examine its coherency and consistency, as well as its constitutionality (or legality), and so on. In addition, even though publicity does not enhance the quality of a law by itself it would improve its understanding and compliance. The *vacatio legis* is an adequate means to get both citizen and authority or official to know the law and adapt to it. "Legisvacancy" or prospective legislation must be the general rule and immediate or retroactive legislation the exception. Anyway, regarding the use of derogatory clauses and transitory directives, it is necessary to restrain them to avoid the abuses of a general derogatory clause or of a transitory directive that is, in effect, permanent and as such must be in the main text.

Let me advance that legisprudence implies and requires an information-evaluation-oriented approach, and an interdisciplinary one, that must borrow from economics, ethics, informatics, logics, politics and so on, to assure the rationality of legislation regarding the correct use of scientific methodology and the degree to which it is influential in the legal process and its final product.

On the one side, Heinrich Winter in his call for a forum model of the legislative process and systematic evaluation of legislation argues: "[T]he quality of the laws produced by the legislative process increases when more and better verifiable information is available on the circumstances under which the law has to function… Evaluation adds value to the legislative process because it tests the assumptions on which a law is based. It supplies the legislator with information on the functioning of a law and on the circumstances that influence the law's performance. This information enlightens the legislative process and contributes to the quality of the debate on legislation [and legislation itself]" (Winter, 2002, pp. 146 and 148).

On the other side, for instance, Wim Voermans claims that "legimatics", as the use of informatics in the legislative process, in general, and in the drafting of legislation, in particular, will enhance the rationality of legislation, not merely by supplying the information needed in the legislative process but what's more by adopting the artificial intelligence approach to solve problems based on the information supplied and related to legislative drafting for which he has developed the Legislative Design and Advisory system (LEDA), using a checklist based on the governmental guidelines for legislative drafting in The Netherlands (2002).

Rationality of Legislation: Formal versus Substantial

Although the idea of a rational creation and application of law, i.e. founded in reason (*ratio*), and its corresponding rationalization – or formalization – are not novel, they can be traced back to the era of the great codifications and the common saying: "the code was the purest exercise of reason"; which reaches its climax with legal formalism in general and in particular with Weber's celebrated typologies of domination[10] and of categories of legal thought (Weber, 1968, pp. 212 and 656-657):

> Both lawmaking and lawfinding may be either rational or irrational. They are *formally* irrational when one applies in lawmaking or lawfinding means which cannot be controlled by the intellect, for instance when recourse is had to oracles or substitutes therefor. Lawmaking and lawfinding are *substantively* irrational... to the extent that decision is influenced by concrete factors of the particular case as evaluated upon an ethical, emotional, or political basis rather than by general norms. "Rational" lawmaking and lawfinding may be rational in a formal or substantive way. All formal law is, formally at least, relatively rational. Law, however, is "formal" to the extent that, in both substantive and procedural matters, only unambiguous general characteristics of the facts of the case are taken into account. This formalism can, again, be of two different kinds. It is possible that the legally relevant characteristics are of a tangible nature, i.e., that they are perceptible as sense data. This adherence to external characteristics of the facts, for instance, the utterance of certain words, the execution of a signature, or the performance of a certain symbolic act with a fixed meaning, represents the most rigorous type of legal formalism. The other type of formalistic law is found where the legally relevant characteristics of the facts are disclosed through the logical analysis of meaning and where, accordingly, definitely fixed legal concepts in the form of highly abstract rules are formulated and applied. This process of "logical rationality" diminishes the significance of extrinsic elements and thus softens the rigidity of concrete formalism. But the contrast to "substantive rationality" is sharpened, because the latter means that the decision of legal problems is influenced by norms different from those obtained through logical generalization of abstract interpretations of meaning. The norms to which substantive rationality accords predominance include ethical imperatives, utilitarian and other expediential rules, and political maxims, all of which diverge from the formalism of the "external characteristics" variety as well as from that which uses logical abstraction. However, the peculiarly professional, legalistic, and abstract approach to law in the modern sense is possible only in the measure that the law is formal in character. In so far as the absolute formalism of classification according to "sense-data characteristics" prevails, it exhausts itself in casuistry. Only that abstract method which employs the logical interpretation of meaning allows the execution of the specifically systematic task, i.e., the collection and rationalization by logical means of all several rules recognized as legally valid into an internally consistent complex of abstract legal propositions.

In sum, if lawmaking and lawfinding are irrational or rational and formal or substantive, it follows that law can be either: 1) formally irrational; 2) substantively irrational; 3) formally rational; and 4) substantively rational. In addition, formally rational law can be "formal" either in an "extrinsic" or in a "logical" sense, which can be re-characterized as "intrinsic". Weber favors rationality over irrationality, formality over substantively, and logical – or intrinsic – over extrinsic, and thus logical-formal rationality trumps everything. What remains unclear is: Why he dismisses or rules out the case for a substantive-rationality? The only basis to exclude it seems to be quite simple: it is not the logical-formal rationality, as it "is influenced by norms different from those obtained through logical generalization of abstract interpretations of meaning" and because "the peculiarly professional, legalistic, and abstract approach to law in the modern sense is possible only in the measure that the law is formal in character".

Our main concern is to explore the possibilities of a substantive rationality and find which sort, if any, can be properly reintegrated into law. But, first of all, we must complete our criticism of the logical-formal rationality. In the way, this cut-rate and low-price version of legal rationality reinforces the lack of a theory of legislation. Once law-creation is excluded the only thing left as legal rationality is law-application: adjudication. For that purpose let me quote Weber again (Weber, 1968, pp. 657-658):

> Present-day legal science, at least in those forms which have achieved the highest measure of methodological and logical rationality, i.e., those which have been produced through the legal science of the Pandectists' Civil Law, proceeds from the following five postulates: viz., first, that every concrete legal decision be the "application" of an abstract legal proposition to a concrete "fact situation"; second, that it must be possible in every concrete case to derive the decision from abstract legal propositions by means of legal logic; third, that the law must actually or virtually constitute a "gapless" system of legal propositions, or must, at least, be treated as if it were such a gapless system; fourth, that whatever cannot be "construed" rationally in legal terms is also legally irrelevant; and fifth, that every social action of human beings must always be visualized as either an "application" or "execution" of legal propositions, or as an "infringement" thereof, since the "gaplessness" of the legal system must result in a gapless "legal ordering" of all social conduct.

In this statement Weber characterizes "legal rationality" in the form of "logical-formal rationality": 1) to application of an abstract legal proposition to a concrete situation; 2) to derivation – deduction – in every case from such abstract legal propositions; 3) to a gapless system of legal propositions; 4) to construal interpretation; and 5) to a gapless legal ordering of all social conduct. All of which contribute to a compacted legal rationality, namely a logical-formal rationality, and even worse to a condensed variety of it, focused exclusively in adjudication through construal interpretation, derivation – or deduction – and application of abstract legal propositions to concrete situations in an actual – or virtual – gapless legal system that constitutes a gapless legal ordering of all social conduct.

With the reappearance of legal theories of argumentation, the approach to legal rationality is not merely logical but rhetorical and dialogical (Feteris, 1999, pp. 15-19). Law requires "internal" – formal – and "external" – substantial – justifications.[11] Correspondingly, Manuel Atienza has criticized the "standard" theory of legal argumentation on the basis that it tends to focus only on adjudication as a law-application process, when in reality legal argumentation also plays a key role in legislation as a law-creation process (Atienza, 1990, pp. 39-40).

According to Henry M. Hart and Albert M. Sacks (1958, p. 166): "[L]aw is a doing of something, a purposive activity, a continuous striving to solve the basic problems of social living". Under their view of the "legal process", statutes as a purposive act designed to achieve an ascertainable objective in a society are as much a source of law as are judicial decisions, and require to be justified too. Hence, legal rationality is as important in adjudication as in legislation. The justification of judicial decisions is as necessary as the justification of legislative decisions: the rule itself; its correlative sanction, negative or positive, increased or decreased; ends, goals and purposes, as well as interests, principles and values.

By ascertaining that legal rationality is quintessential to legislation, we do not mean to suggest that the rationality of legislation is different from the rationality of adjudication, like other authors do. For instance, Tuori declares that "the rationality of legislation should be assessed with different yardsticks than the rationality of adjudication and legal science" (Tuori, 2002, p. 105). Quite the contrary, legislation to be rational from a significant legal point of view requires to meet not different, but the very same standards as other legal processes, such as adjudication.

We agree with Atienza (1989a, 1989b and 1997a), who argues that there are at least five different models of rationality in legal argumentation that can be applied to legislation: *linguistic rationality* (R1); *legal-formal rationality* (R2); *pragmatic rationality* (R3), *teleological rationality* (R4), and *ethical rationality* (R5). None of these models exclude nor imply each other and can be integrated in an *integral legal rationality* of adjudication or legislation, and of all legal processes.

Moreover, several distinctions are useful: First, whereas R1-R4 are alike, as they share the notion of *instrumental* rationality – in a broad sense – as adequacy of means-ends, R5 is not, as it requires a *principled* rationality to justify ethically both means and ends. Second, although R1-R4 are instrumental rationalities – *lato sensu* – R1-R2 necessitate an *internal* or *technical* rationality, which aim to maintain its intrinsic coherence and consistency logically, both linguistic and legal-formal as a *deontological* rationality, and R3-R4 need an *external* or *instrumental* rationality – in a strict sense – which aspire to retain some sort of extrinsic efficacy, effectiveness and efficiency as a *consequential* rationality. Third, even though R3-R4 are external or instrumental rationalities – *strictu sensu* – that require sustaining some sort of correspondence means-ends, R3 entails application and observance to be pragmatically efficacious and R4 expects realization of its objective to be teleologically effective and even fulfillment with the minimal cost to be efficient. Fourth, R1-R2 are emblematic of a *traditional-dogmatic* and *formal* rationality and R3-R5 are symbolic of a *non-traditional-dogmatic* and *substantial* rationality. Fifth, last but certainly not least, R3-R5 embody substantial rationality, R3-R4 are illustrative of an *extrinsic substantial* rationality of norms and its consequences and R5 is representative of an *intrinsic substantial* rationality of the content of rules and its principles.

In other words, legal rationality calls not merely for an *intrinsic formal rationality* (R1-R2) but for an *extrinsic substantial rationality* (R3-R4) and an *intrinsic substantial rationality* (R5).[12] Therefore, the formal rationality, which is mainly intrinsic and technical (R1-R2), is to be compatible and must be complemented by a substantial rationality, which can be either extrinsic or instrumental (R3-R4) and intrinsic or ethical (R5). In short, the *substantive rationality* that can be properly reintegrated into law is, on one side, *extrinsic* or *instrumental* to the substantive realization of means-ends, and, in the other, *intrinsic* or *ethical* to the substantive justification of means and ends.

Legisprudence: Constitutionalism *vis-à-vis* Legalism

In this part, our ambition is to find the proper place for legisprudence in legal or juridical analysis by contrasting it to both "constitutionalism" and "legalism", but in doing so it is necessary to recall first of all why legislation has been neglected and why it need not to be so; and, later, to criticize the, until recently, dominant legal theory, and to develop an alternative one, while at the same time challenging some traditional distinctions such as adjudication-legislation, law-application – or lawfinding – and law-creation – or lawmaking – judges-legislators, courts-legislatures, and so on, which reinforce the apparent separation between law and politics.

The lack of a theory of legislation – or legisprudence – can be explained, following Wintgens, in a very straightforward way. For the dominant legal theory and its formal rationality, there is no place for any theory of legislation: "The absence of a theory of legislation, and the limitation of legal science to a science of judicial decisions can further be explained by the reduction of law to a (complete) system of legal rules based on pseudo-cognitive pattern of legalistic thought" (Wintgens, 2002, p. 14).

A theory of legislation is simply unnecessary either for modern natural law theories, where positive law is legitimated if deduced correctly from natural law, and for legal positivism, where positive law is legitimized by sole reference to the sovereign. Law is based on *knowledge* of natural law, on one side, and on a *decision* of the legislator, on the other. In the former, for epistemological reasons, there is no need for a theory of legislation, distinct from a theory of natural law. In the latter, there is no room for a scientific theory of legislation, as legislation appears to be a matter of political choice, and as such considered subjective and irrational, ruling out the possibility for an objective and rational theory, at least from the legal perspective.

In a nutshell, the absence of a theory of legislation is a result of a limited understanding of the interrelation science – or theory – and law, in general, and between scientific and legal positivism, in particular (Fuller, 1968, pp. 177-178):

> At this juncture it will be helpful to offer some comparisons between legal positivism and its counterpart in science. Scientific positivism condemns any inquiry projecting itself beyond observable phenomena; it abjures metaphysics, it renounces in advance any explanation in terms of ultimate causes. Its program of research is to chart the regularities discernible in the phenomena of nature at the point where they become open to human observation, without asking - as it were - how they got there. In the setting of limits to inquiry there is an obvious parallel between scientific and legal positivism. The legal positivist concentrates his attention on law at the point where it emerges from the

> institutional processes that brought it into being. It is the finally made law itself that furnishes the subject of his inquiries. How it was made and what directions of human effort went into its creation are for him irrelevancies.

This belief has been reinforced by the separation of powers doctrine, which is premised in the distinction between law and politics. This distinction, which has been predominant in legal – and political – thinking until recently, suggests that lawmaking as law-creation through legislation belongs to the realm of politics and lawfinding as law-application via adjudication goes to the legal realm. This clear distinction between "law" or "already-law" and "non-law" or "not-yet-law", excludes any form of legal or scientific theorizing on legislation. In this fashion, legislation as the creation of law is considered a political and sovereign activity, whereas adjudication as the application of law is not. The "application attitude", which was originally the attitude of the legislator with respect to natural law, is now emblematic of the judge regarding positive law (Wintgens, 2002b, p. 12).

Moreover, the separation of powers doctrine comprises the idea of setting limits to the abusive exercise of power and contains the notion of government under law. Supposedly, the rule of law entails the primacy of law and of legality. Yet, under the traditional conception such primacy has been identified not with legal but political principles, such as the "omnipotence of majorities (over minorities)" and the "supremacy of legislative (over judiciary)". Paradoxically the primacy of law is subordinated to the ascendancy of politics and sovereignty reduced to omnipotent and supreme legislative majorities.

In the traditional *legalist* archetype, separation of powers overemphasizes dominance of legislative over judiciary and predominance of politics over law. In order to re-balance the interactions judiciary-legislative and law-politics, we must re-assemble an alternate comprehension where both relations are symmetrical. Separation of powers does not necessitate domination or preponderance. On the contrary, a sense of equilibrium and a weighing scale, namely a *constitutionalist* prototype with checks and balances, is required (Flores, 2003b).

Legalism

Judith N. Shklar has indicated that both natural law theories and legal positivism "allow judges to believe that there always is a rule somewhere for them to follow" (Shklar, 1986, p. 12). Despite all their differences, *iusnaturalism* and *iuspositivism* have one thing in common, a strong tendency towards legalism, which is defined as "the ethical attitude that holds moral conduct to be a matter of rule following, and moral relationships to consists of duties and rights determined by rules" (Shklar, 1986, p. 1).

Legalism is not only "an ideology internal to the legal profession as a social whole" or "the operative ideology of lawyers" and of those who have a "rule-oriented thinking" (Shklar, 1986, pp. vii-viii and 5), but also a background theory of law (Unger, 1986 and 1996), which implies a rule-based way of looking at things and a tendency to treat law as just "there" (Shklar, 1986, pp. ix-x and 35) and separated of non-law (Shklar, 1986, pp. 2-3):

> Law is endowed with its own discrete, integral history, its own "science," and its own values, which are all treated as a single "block" sealed off from general social history, from general social theory, from politics, and from morality. The habits of mind appropriate, within narrow limits, to the procedures of law courts in the most stable legal systems have been expanded to provide legal theory and ideology with an entire system of thought and values. This procedure has served its own ends very well: it aims at preserving law from irrelevant considerations, but it has ended by fencing legal thinking off from all contact with the rest of historical thought and experience.

The "thereness" of law entails that "Within a legalistic form of thinking, there is no need for a *theory about* rules, since the only thing that is to be taken into account *are* rules" (Wintgens, 2002b, p. 12). Conversely, law is not just "there", it must be rather regarded as part of a social continuum (Shklar, 1986, p. 3):

> At one end of the scale of legalistic values and institutions stands its most highly articulate and refined expressions, the courts of law and the rules they follow; at the other end is the personal morality of all those men and women who think of goodness as obedience to the rules that properly define their duties and rights. Within this scale there is a vast area of social beliefs and institutions, both more and less rigid and explicit, which in varying degrees depend upon the legalistic ethos. This would provide an approach suitable to law as an historical phenomenon, and would replace the sterile game of defining law, morals, and politics in order to separate them as concepts both "pure" and empty, divorced from each other and from their common historical past and contemporary setting.

The absence of a theory of legislation, and the reduction of legal science to the study of adjudication can be explained by the reduction of law within legalism to rules regardless their origin. Legality, as the formal aspect of legal rules, is the necessary and sufficient condition for the legal character of rules. This unmistakably leads to legislative inflation – increased quantity – and deflation – decreased quality – since there are no other requirements than formal ones for a rule to exist and to be valid. In as far as a legal system provides a method of constitutional or judicial review of legislation, there exists a possibility of control, but legalism presupposes the constitutionality and rationality of the legislator's ruling.

Strong and Weak Legalism Given that legalism is the dominant background theory of law and thinking in terms of rules the dominant pattern, any critical attitude to legal thinking is necessarily external to the legal system, because a critique from an internal position is impossible. In this manner, any criticism of legislation is external. Seemingly, if the theory of legislation is neglected within legal theory, a new theory will have to be external to law and as such not legal.

In this form of legalism, which Wintgens calls *strong legalism*: "legality is a necessary and sufficient condition for the *existence* and the *meaning* of law." And *a contrario*, in the one that he labels *weak legalism*: "legality or formal validity of a rule is only a necessary and not a sufficient condition for its existence" and the idea that rules themselves do have a meaning of their own, must be rejected

(Wintgens, 2002b, p. 19). Rules and meaning are not something just out there, less neutral.[13]

Besides "representationalism", the characteristic of legalism shared by both natural law theories and legal positivism, which holds that "law represents reality", "strong legalism" consists of a conjugation of four other dispositions: ["eternalism" or] "timelessness"; "concealed instrumentalism"; "etatism"; and ["logicism" or "positivism" as the proper] "scientific method of study of law" (Wintgens, 2003).

In contraposition, "weak legalism" challenges that there is not a representational theory *of* reality but theories *about* reality and also that the rationality of legislation compels the legislator to take the temporal dimension of human action seriously: "temporalism"; to justify the rule, its correlative sanction, its ends, goals and purposes, as well as interests, principles and values: "revealed instrumentalism"; to weigh and balance the options and the concrete possibilities for a society: "societism"; and a different method of study of law: "non-logicism" or "non-positivism".

From the comparison between the two it follows: firstly, on "strong legalism" the creation – and the application – of rules is considered a "direct" reproduction of reality, on "weak legalism" it is just a construction of rules and never a direct reconstruction of reality, but an "indirect" one; secondly, on the latter, the rationality of the legislator is a matter of justification, not of presumption as in the former; thirdly, on "strong legalism" judges apply rules that legislators create, on "weak legalism" both judge and legislator apply and create rules; and, fourthly, on the latter, judge and legislator follow rules, not as in the former where supposedly the judge is the only one that follows rules because the legislator as a sovereign actor cannot be bound to rules. If the legislator were bound to rules, he would not be a sovereign.

Constitutionalism

As Shklar (1986, p. 3) suggests it is "not only important to understand legalism, but also to suggest other ways of thinking about law". The distinction between strong and weak legalisms is helpful to understand legalism, but a different set of distinctions is needed to suggest another way of thinking about law. The double-distinction involves: first, legalism and constitutionalism; and, then, weak and strong versions of the latter.

As the constitution is nothing but a rule, constitutionalism *prima facie* as rule following can be a form of legalism and as such it can be companionable to both versions of legalism. If we take "constitutionalism" as a simple rule following of existing and so valid rules it is subordinated to "strong legalism", but if we take it as a complex rule following of existing rules that are valid if they derive from and are compatible with the constitution it is incorporated to "weak legalism". Undoubtedly the first version of constitutionalism is meaningless as it is secondary to "strong legalism", while the second is meaningful as it is primary to "weak legalism".

Strong and Weak Constitutionalism In view of the fact that constitutionalism, as a form of legalism, is a matter of rule following it also contributes to the implementation of the rule of law: "It brings about predictability and security in the relations of individuals to the government by defining in advance the powers and limits of that government" (Alexander, 1998, p. 4). In the process of demarcating such powers there are two general possibilities: either we delimit the sovereign or we do not. The version that set limits to sovereign power can be labeled as a "strong constitutionalism" and the one that does not can be marked as a "weak constitutionalism".

On the one hand, in "weak constitutionalism" there are no limits to the sovereign. The Latin adage *Quod principi placuit vigorem legis habet* ("Whatever pleases the prince has the force of law") has become the family motto. It conveys a very sovereign - and sovereignty-oriented notion of law, with the prince, emperor or king conceived as an inherent law-maker, and law understood as its command or, literally, as the prince's pleasure (Waldron, 2002, p. 10).

The legislator is a sovereign actor that cannot be bound to rules, if that were the case it would not be considered as such: "On this view, the constitution is" – as Wintgens draws attention to – "a political programme that steers legislation. It is not a set of binding rules for the legislator. As a consequence, the legislator is not considered a legal performer but a political player: legislation then is a matter of politics. In severing law from its political origin, law making is not a matter of legal theory" (Wintgens, 2002).

On the other hand, in "strong constitutionalism" there are – and must be – limits to the sovereign. The omnipotent and supreme legislative majorities abide by law and above all must act fitting the constitution: within its rules and underlying principles (Dworkin, 1977, 1985, 1986 and 1996), including those identified as the internal morality of law: "generality", "publicity", "irretroactivity" or "prospectivity", "clarity", "non-contradictoriness", "possibility", "constancy" and "congruity" (Fuller, 1969, p. 39), which even legislators and other elected officials cannot override or overrule.

The rules of the constitution are more than negative limits to the legislator's power: it contains rules and principles regarding the guarantee of rights and the separation of powers. If truth be told, article 16 of the Declaration on Rights of Men and Citizen is self-evident: *Toute société dans la quelle la garantie des droits n'est pas assurée, ni la séparation des pouvoirs déterminée, n'a point de constitution.* In the hunt for such rules and principles we can go back to Cicero himself and to Coke, and even return to twentieth century classics, for example Pound and Fuller, and to contemporaries, for instance Alexy, Dworkin and Ferrajoli.

Legisprudence and Strong Constitutionalism

The legislator, like the judge, is a rule follower. Despite being sovereign, the rule following behavior entails not violating secondary rules and respecting the principles of good legislation. As the constitution is mainly intended to protect rights and separation of powers, both judge and legislator are subordinated not to existing law, whichever its content, but to valid law that derives from and is compatible with the constitution, especially principles of political morality and rights (Flores, 2003b). Openly legisprudence sides with "weak legalism" over "strong legalism" and will be much better off with "strong constitutionalism" than with "weak constitutionalism".

In "strong legalism" the rationality of the judge and of legal decisions was very limited; reduced to a "mechanic" and deductive application of the rule, where the rationality of the legislator and of legal rules is presumed. In weak legalism and in the two versions of "constitutionalism" the rationality of judge and legislator cannot be taken for granted, as they are both bound by the constitution they must act fittingly, and so some sort of judicial – or constitutional – review is quintessential. The complete absence or a limited role are proofs of the strong legalistic attitude that strengthens legalism. In the strong legalism: "the legislator is *irrefutably presumed* to have followed the rules of the constitution even if it is patently clear that this was not the case… even an unconstitutional rule – that as a matter of fact, is not a rule – is a rule to be applied by the judiciary" (Wintgens, 2002b, p. 25). In weak legalism the legislator is presumed to have followed the constitution, but this time the presumption is held refutable.

According to the rule of law doctrine, the legislator is bound by higher norms, just as the judiciary is bound by the rules of the legislator. It appears that a sovereign legislator is by definition independent of any external forces and the supreme source of law within the legal system. If the sovereign legislator respects the rule of law and is bound by "rules" – and "principles" – it seems to be no longer a sovereign legislator. Is it possible to reconcile both? Can the sovereign legislator respect or be bounded by rules and still be a sovereign legislator? In my opinion both answers are positive: a legislator can be bounded by rules and still be sovereign. To prove the point let's take the case of James I of England – or VI of Scotland – who inherited the throne from Elizabeth I and characterized his reign for his exaltation of the royal authority and the divine right of kings, and for his exhilaration in the persecution of Catholics and extreme Protestants dissidents.

To cut a long story short, Sir Edward Coke, Chief Justice of the Court of Common Pleas, first, and of the King's Bench, later, objected the absolute sovereignty of the monarch and in opposition stated the supremacy of the "common law". Coke argued that "Reason is the life of the law, nay the common law itself is nothing else but reason" and concluded that "law is an artificial reason": "an artificial perfection of reason, gotten by long study, observation, and experience, and not of everyone's natural reason; for *nemo nascitur artifex*."

In addition he rejected the idea of the sovereign as an unlimited discretionary power, on the contrary the royal prerogative is – and must be – a checked power limited by law. For instance, Coke ruled, in the *Case of Prohibitions* (1607), that by the law of England the king in person could not adjudge any cause: all cases, civil and criminal, were to be determined in some court of justice by judges according to the law and custom of the realm: "*judex est lex loquens*"; and, in the *Case of Proclamations* (1611), that the king himself cannot reform the law, in general, and establish new crimes, in particular, with retroactive effect: "*Nova constitutio futuris formam imponere debet, non praeteritis*".

But the main chapter of the contest with the Stuarts took place on the Sunday morning of November 10th, 1612, when the judges of England were summoned before King James I upon complaint of the Archbishop of Canterbury, regarding a writ of prohibition issued by the Court of Common Pleas against the High Commission, an administrative tribunal established for the regulation of the church and that had begun to take cognizance of temporal matters and to deal with lay offenders, according to no fixed rules and subject to no appeal.

To meet the judicial insistence upon the supremacy of law, it was suggested that the king might take away from the judges any cause he pleased and decide it himself: "the judges were but the delegates of the king, wherefore the king might do himself, when it seemed best to him, what he left usually to these delegates." The Archbishop added that "this was clear, if not in the law yet beyond question in divinity, for it could be shown from the word of God in the Scripture". To this Coke answered on behalf of the judges: the king in person could not judge, he could only through a court of justice and according to law.

"But" – said James I – "I thought law was founded upon reason, and I and others have reason as well as the judges." "True it was" – Coke responded – "that God had endowed his Majesty with excellent science and great endowments of nature, but his majesty was not learned in the laws of his realm of England, and causes which concern the life or inheritance of goods or fortunes of his subjects are not to be decided by natural reason, but by the artificial reason and judgment of the law which law is an art which requires long study and experience before that a man can attain cognizance of it." At this the king was much offended, saying that in such a case he should be under the law, which it was treason to affirm. Coke answered that the king ought "not to be under any man but under God and the law": *non sub homine sed sub Deo et lege* (Pound, 1921, pp. 60-61).

Concisely *mutatis mutando* the legislator can be at the same time both sovereign and bounded to rules: above all men and under the law. Indeed, such decisions established a general doctrine explicitly of the competence of the courts and implicitly of the confines of the sovereign, since the former administered the law and law was reason, to compel not merely all private individuals, and all agents of government, but the very sovereign itself to keep within the bounds of reason, by refusing to recognize or give legal effect to acts or ordinances of the sovereign which went beyond such bounds. Coke said boldly "When an act of Parliament is against common right and reason... the common law will control it and adjudge such act to be void." "Accordingly" – as Pound noted – "it became usual to speak of limitations involved in the very idea of free government which go back of and are only declared by constitutions and bill of rights. It became usual to think, not of the text of the bills of rights, but of these supposed fundamental principles of which they were but declaratory" (Pound, 1921, pp. 74-76).

The followers of James I counterattacked and Coke, who would give no pledge to do otherwise than administer the law as a judge should, was promoted first in 1613 to Chief Justice of the King's Bench and at the end removed from his post in 1617. Among the defenders of the sovereign, Sir Francis Bacon argued that kings existed long before law and parliaments did: it is the king that makes the law and not the law that makes the king. From there – according to him – it follows that the judges' function is *jus dicere* and not *jus dare*: to apply the existing law, not to create it. It also results that the judge has several duties regarding not just the litigants and their lawyers, notaries, attorneys, clerks, and other court officials but to the prince and the government they represent. In fact, their main duty is towards the protection of the sovereign by limiting themselves to apply the law (Bacon, 1936).

Notwithstanding it was Hobbes – as main advocate for the monarchy – who strongly persuaded, on the one hand, that the "sovereign is the legislator" (Hobbes, 1991, p. 184):

> The Legislator in all Common-wealths, is only the soveraign, be he one Man, as in a Monarchy, or one Assembly of men, as in a Democracy, or Aristocracy. For the Legislator, is he that maketh the Law. And the Common-wealth only, praescribes, and commandeth the observation of those rules, which we call Law: Therefore the Common-wealth is the legislator. But the Common-wealth is no Person, nor has capacity to doe any thing, but by the Representative, (that is, the Soveraign;) and therefore the Soveraign is the sole Legislator. For the same reason, none can abrogate a Law made, but the Soveraign; because a Law is not abrogated, but by another Law, that forbiddeth it to be put into execution.

And, on the other hand, that the "sovereign is not subject to laws" (Hobbes, 1991, p. 184):

> The Soveraign of a Common-wealth, be it an Assembly, or one Nan, is not Subject to the Civill Lawes. For having power to make, and repeale lawes, he may when he pleaseth, free himselfe from that subjection, by repealing those Lawes that trouble him, and making of new; and consequently he was free before. For he is free, that can be free when he will: Nor is it possible for any person to be bound to himselfe; because he that can bind, can release; and therefore he that is bound to himselfe onely, is not bound.

What's more Hobbes directly addressed Coke, agreeing that "law is Reason" and differing on "whose Reason it is, that shall be received for law". He argues (Hobbes, 1991, p. 186-187):

> It is not meant of any private Reason... nor yet...an *Artificiall perfection of Reason, gotten by long study, observation, and experience...* and therefore it is not that *Juris prudentia*, or wisedome of subordinate Judges; but the Reason of this our Artificiall Man the Common-wealth, and his Command, that maketh Law... In all Courts of Justice, the Soveraign (which is the Person of the Common-wealth,) is he that Judgeth: The subordinate Judge, ought to have regard to the reason, which moved his Soveraign to make such Law, that his Sentence may be according thereunto; which then is his Soveraigns Sentence; otherwise it is his own, and an unjust one.

Succinctly, Hobbes' account is: the sovereign is the only legislator, and as such the only one that does make law (T1); laws do not bound the sovereign (T2); and law is reason: not the reason of the judge, but the reason of the legislator as sovereign himself (T3). Therefore, we must challenge these three theses with its matching antitheses: the sovereign is not the only legislator and as such is not the only one that does make law (A1); laws do bound the sovereign (A2); and, law is reason, of the judge and of the legislator as sovereigns themselves (A3). And, finally, replace them with our own syntheses: firstly, as the legislator is not the only one that does make law, it is not a sole sovereign but a joint sovereign: legislator and judge (S1); secondly, as laws do bound the sovereign, both legislator and judge are bounded by law (S2); and, thirdly, as law is reason, it is the reason of both legislator and judge as sovereigns themselves (S3).

In order to contrast our account it is necessary to revise, following Duncan Kennedy, some of the "great dichotomies" of both legal and political theory, such as the distinctions adjudication-legislation, law-application – or lawfinding – and law-creation – or lawmaking – judges-legislators, courts-legislatures, and so on, which reinforce the apparent separation between law and politics (Kennedy, 1996, pp. 23-38).

It is affirmed that adjudication as law-applying – or lawfinding – by judges in courts belongs to the jurisdiction of law and legislation as law-creating – or lawmaking – by legislators in legislatures corresponds to the domination of politics. Curiously, in adjudication the political – or ideological – element is denied and underestimated, while in legislation the political – or ideological – element is taken for granted and overestimated. Equally, adjudication appears to be totally objective and the political element absolutely minimized, whilst legislation seems to be wholly subjective and the political element completely maximized.

Furthermore, it is alleged that "adjudication is what courts do and legislation is what legislatures do", "But it is perfectly possible for a legislature to adjudicate and for a court to legislate" (Kennedy, 1996, p. 26). As Fuller highlighted: "the distinction between legislative and judicial functions, today taken for granted, is a comparatively modern development" (Fuller, 1968, p. 32): "The English Parliament in its origin was primarily an adjudicative or "law-finding" body, and it only gradually began openly to assert legislative powers" (Fuller, 1968, pp. 89-90). Fuller brings to light (1968, p. 135):

> This is a point on which legal scholarship has diverged sharply. The old view, still not entirely abandoned, maintained that the courts do not make law at all, but merely discover or discern it. The opposing view is that the courts just as truly make law as do legislatures; the only difference is that the legislature lays down in advance a general rule, whereas the courts develop general rules gradually in the course of a case-by-case decision of controversies as they are presented for decision.

It is also announced that "what legislatures do when they legislate is [create or] make law, and what courts do when they adjudicate is apply [or find] law" (Kennedy, 1996, p. 26). The law-making process insists on value judgments, which are subjective and political. Then, legislators as elected officials should do it and judges abstain from legislating simply because they are not elected. The law-finding process involves questions that are independent of value judgments, questions of meaning and of fact, which are objective and legal – or non-political. Thus, legal professionals – or non-elected officials – should do it and legislators refrain from adjudicating because they are not legal professionals. In spite of all, as Kennedy spotlights (Kennedy, 1996, p. 28):

> When identified with the contrast between law making and law application, the legislation/adjudication dichotomy seems to admit of no middle term. But as soon as we shift to this broader notion of legal interpretation, it follows that adjudication involves both making and applying. But it does not follow, and is controverted, that judicial law making must be or is in fact "judicial legislation" and therefore abhorrent...

According to him, there are at least four different strategies for dealing with the problem: 1) deny or at least ignore the possibility of a middle term, what is not law-application is law-creation, in the form of "judicial legislation" (Hart, 1994); 2) collapse the distinction between law-creating and law-applying, by demonstrating that any legal process entails both creation and application (Kelsen, 1992) and/or by illustrating that application cannot be insulated form the ideological, political or subjective element (Unger, 1975 and 1976); 3) curtail the distinction to the extent that the court interstitially applies law, as a general rule, and creates law, as an exception (Holmes, 1996); 4) propose a genuine middle term between law-application and law-creation: the method of "coherence" or "fit", which concedes the ideological and political character of adjudication without giving up the exigency of objectivity and maintaining that there is some sort of distinction between judging and legislating (Fuller, 1981, and Dworkin, 1985 and 1986).

Jurisprudence as "legal" or "juridical" science requires a certain uniformity and universality of its principles: the principles applied to "judicativeprudence" are – and must be - equally attached to "legisprudence" – or "legislativeprudence": from "coherence" and "consistency", "predictability" and "acceptability", and so on, to "rationality" and "objectivity".

Although Kennedy is sympathetic to the fourth strategy, he believes that adjudication is ideological, political and as subjective as legislation, ruling out the claim for objectivity. My guess is that once legisprudence is put in its place next to judicativeprudence, as in the strong version of constitutionalism, adjudication and legislation are ideological and political but still objective. They both imply law-creation and law-application at the same time that they involve a certain degree of freedom and constraint within a kelsenian "frame".

Conclusion: Whither Legisprudence?

In the coming years, legisprudence must consolidate itself by proving that it is possible to guarantee such objectivity. The main theme is to prove that the premonition is possible: to rule out subjectivity in legislation – and in adjudication – by establishing objective principles that can guide a substantial legal rationality. To conclude, let me quote Pound (1921, pp. 80-81):

> In each case the social interest in general security requires that it be guided and regulated by reason; that it conform to principles and standards formulated dispassionately in advance of controversy upon weighing of all the interests to be affected. In insisting on the supremacy of law… law is not bound of necessity to stand always against the popular will in the interest of the abstract individual. Rather its true position is one of standing for ultimate and more important social interests as against the more immediately pressing but less weighty interests of the moment by which mere will unrestrained by reason is too likely to be swayed.

* Professor-Researcher, Instituto de Investigaciones Jurídicas, Universidad Nacional Autónoma de México (UNAM). The author is grateful to Julius Cohen and Juan Vega for their comments on an earlier draft of the manuscript and to Ariadna Valdés for helpful research assistance.

Notes

1 Bear in mind Hamilton's dictum: "[T]he judiciary… will always be the least dangerous to the political rights of the Constitution"; and Madison's maxim: "In republican government, the legislative authority necessarily predominates" (Hamilton *et al.*, 1961, pp. 465 and 322).

2 According to Maine, in the first stage law is rather a *habit*; in the second reaches the footing of a *custom*; in the third is identified with *codes* (not as a legislative enactment but as a compilation of rules already established by custom through judicial decisions); in the fourth introduces *legal reform* under the cover of "legal fictions" (via judicial and legislative interpretations); in the fifth appeals to a *transcendent model* of implicit law; in the sixth and final stage to *legislation* as a explicit declaration of intention incorporated in a legislative enactment (Maine, 1912).

3 For instance, in Mexico - and I believe that in all the Spanish-speaking world and most of the civil law countries - the word "jurisprudence" is used more to refer to the "judicial function" than to the "juridical science" (Flores, 1998, p. 1005).

4 We will return to this matter, *infra*, in the last major part of this contribution: "Legisprudence: Constitutionalism *vis-à-vis* Legalism".

5 *Board of County Commissioners for Sublette County, Wyoming v. Exxon Mobil Corporation*, 151 WY 2002.

6 Although "size" is something quantifiable, whether a piece of legislation is long or short and big or small is a matter related more to quality than to quantity itself: quality overcomes size to the extent that as a general rule size does not matter. Good legislation prevails independently of size; it is in the case of equally good - or bad - where size, as an exception, does matter. Imagine as in Svein Eng's example (2002, pp. 66-67) that there are two different statutes: the first is long, but includes detailed legal definitions; and, the second is short, but framed in vague and value-laden terms. We would probably prefer the longer to the shorter: but that depends not in size itself but in the verity that the lengthy is good and the brief is bad. In the same way, suppose that we are able to draft two different initiatives on the very same subject both equally good in their merits, but one longer and bigger than the other that is shorter and smaller. We would rather prefer the second to the first: good and brief over good but lengthy.

7 The typology includes among others: A) linguistic: ambiguous and vague concepts, definitions or terms; B) logical-systematic: antinomies, contradictions and redundancies, as well as gaps; and C) logical-dynamic: normative conflicts of rules and collision of principles (Flores, 1995).

8 The homologation or standardization of legal definitions in a statute and in the legal system as a whole or at least in a part of it seems appropriate and even desirable.

9 On this regard, as the main course of the legislative *iter* is first the debate and then the subsequent approval, the deliberation practice is and must be central to legislation to the degree that the following question is quite appealing: Should apparent/virtual presence or absence of deliberation affect a court's determination of the constitutionality (or legality) of a statute? (Eskridge and Frickey, 1988, p. 336).

10 The three distinct types are: "traditional", "charismatic" and "legal". The latter is based on rational grounds, resting on a belief in the legality of enacted rules and the right of those elevated to authority under such rules to issue commands.

11 Albert Calsamiglia has distinguished between "parametric" and "strategic" rationalities. In the former, as norms themselves are the sole variable that is enough; and, in the latter, as norms and its consequences are interacting, they constantly shape and reshape each other. He also has reasoned that rationality in law and in legislation is not merely parametric but mostly strategic (Calsamiglia, 1989, pp. 124-125, and 142). As Eriksson has pointed out: "The coherence and consistency of law is not the primary problem of the lawgiver. The lawgiver's primary task is to produce laws the consequences of which correspond to the aims he or she aspires to" (Eriksson, 2002, p. 47).

12 Let me suggest that this typology, despite terminological differences, is compatible with and comprehensive of Eng's (2002, 68-78) characterization of legislative flaws: *substantive* or *material flaws* (R5), *technical flaws* (R1-R2) and *means-ends flaws* (R3-R4), and even Touri's (2002, 104-107) classification of legislative rationality: *object rationality* (R3-R4), *internal rationality* (R1-R2) and *normative rationality* (R5).
Although the statement that rationality of legislation is different from that of adjudication and legal science will be addressed in the following part, it is convenient to state briefly Tuori's account: legislation, in comparison to other legal practices, is characterized by one dimension of rationality, the one he calls "objective rationality" – corresponding to our "extrinsic substantial rationality" (R3-R4) - that lacks its counterpart in adjudication and legal science. He is also persuaded not only that the other two rationalities, those he labels "internal" and "normative" - matching our "intrinsic formal rationality" (R1-R2) and "intrinsic substantial rationality" (R5) - are highly relevant in the assessment of adjudication and legal science but also that "object rationality... is not directly relevant in the context of these practices". Finally, he reasons that as argumentation in adjudication and in legal science, usually adopts the perspective of the judge, it escapes the purposive rational pattern typical of legislation; and, concludes that "The significance of the dimension of object rationality reflects the dominance of political aspect in legislative practices: legislation is used by political decision-makers as a means to political goals and, from that perspective, its success or failure is measured in the dimension of object rationality" (Tuori, 2002, pp. 106-107).

13 Rules do not have a meaning *per se*, it is through interpretation that they acquire one: meaning is convey upon something and is subsequent to interpretation. Thus, it is false that they are clear beforehand to the extent that they need not to be interpreted as *clara non sunt interpretanda* aphorism suggests. On the contrary, the clarity or not of a rule is the result of an interpretation: it is the interpreter who says that the rule is clear and

so "p" or that it is not clear and then "q" (Flores, 2003a, Wintgens, 2003, and Cohen, 1986).

References

Alexander, L. (1998), 'Introduction' in L. Alexander (ed.), *Constitutionalism. Philosophical Foundations*, Cambridge University Press, Cambridge.

Alexy, R. (1993), *Derecho y razón práctica*, Fontamara, México.

Aristotle (1988), *The Politics*, Cambridge University Press, New York.

Atienza, M. (1989a), 'Sociología jurídica y ciencia de la legislación' in R. Bergalli (ed.), *El derecho y sus realidades. Investigación y enseñanza de la sociología jurídica*, PPU, Barcelona.

Atienza, M. (1989b), 'Contribución a la teoría de la legislación', *Doxa*, Vol. 6, pp. 385-403.

Atienza, M. (1990), 'Para una teoría de la argumentación jurídica', *Doxa*, Vol. 8, pp. 39-61.

Atienza, M. (1991), 'Razón práctica y legislación', *Revista Mexicana de Estudios Parlamentarios*, Vol. 3, pp. 9-31.

Atienza, M. (1997a), *Contribución a la teoría de la legislación*, Tecnos, Madrid.

Atienza, M. (1997b), *Las razones del derecho. Teorías de la argumentación jurídica*, Centro de Estudios Constitucionales, Madrid.

Bacon, F. (1936), *The Essays of Francis Bacon*, Riverside Press, Cambridge (Ma).

Bentham, J. (1948), *The Principles of Morals and Legislation*, Hafner Press, New York (first published in 1789).

Bentham, J. (1974), *The Theory of Legislation*, Oceana, New York (first published in 1802).

Bulygin, E. (1990), 'Teoría y técnica de la legislación', *Arbor*, Vol. 136, pp. 9-30.

Calsamiglia, A. (1989), 'Justicia, eficiencia y optimización de la legislación', *Documentación Administrativa*, pp. 113-151.

Cohen, J. (1983), 'Legisprudence: Problems and Agenda', *Hofstra Law Review*, Vol. 11, pp. 1163-1183.

Cohen, J. (1986), 'The Myth of Neutrality in Positive Legal Theory: Hart Revisited', *The American Journal of Jurisprudence. An International Forum for Legal Philosophy*, Vol. 31, pp. 97-120.

Dahlman, C. (2002), 'Predictable Rules and Flexible Principles. The Problem of Ideological Pluralism and Legitimacy' in L. J. Wintgens (ed.), *Legisprudence: A New Theoretical Approach to Legislation*, Hart Publishing, Oxford.

Dworkin, R. (1977), *Taking Rights Seriously*, Harvard University Press, Cambridge (Ma).

Dworkin, R. (1985), *A Matter of Principle*, Harvard University Press, Cambridge (Ma).

Dworkin, R. (1986), *Law's Empire*, Harvard University Press, Cambridge (Ma).

Dworkin, R. (1996), *Freedom's Law. The Moral Reading of the American Constitution*, Harvard University Press, Cambridge (Ma).

Eng, S. (2002), 'Legislative Inflation and the Quality of Law' in L.J. Wintgens (ed.), *Legisprudence: A New Theoretical Approach to Legislation*, Hart Publishing, Oxford.

Eriksson, Lars D. (2002), 'Making Society through Legislation', in L.J. Wintgens (ed.), *Legisprudence: A New Theoretical Approach to Legislation*, Hart Publishing, Oxford.

Eskridge, W.N. and Frickey, P.P. (1988), *Cases and Materials on Legislation: Statutes and the Creation of Public Policy*, West Publishing, St. Paul (Min).

Ferrajoli, L. (1999), 'Jueces y política', *Derechos y libertades. Revista del Instituto Bartolomé de las Casas*, Vol. IV, pp. 63-79.

Feteris, E.T. (1999), *Fundamentals of Legal Argumentation. A Survey of Theories on the Justification of Judicial Decisions*, Kluwer Academic Publishers, Dordrecht.

Flores, I.B. (1995), 'La técnica jurídica en la aplicación del derecho', *Revista de la Facultad de Derecho de México*, Vol. XLV, pp. 17-55.

Flores, I.B. (1996), 'Crisis, fortalecimiento y valores de la democracia' in J.A. Aguilar Rivera et al., *Los valores de la democracia*, Instituto Federal Electoral, México.

Flores, I.B. (1998), 'El porvenir de la ciencia jurídica. Reflexión sobre la ciencia y el derecho' in J.L. Soberanes Fernández (ed.), *La ciencia del derecho durante el siglo XX*, Instituto de Investigaciones Jurídicas, UNAM, México.

Flores, I.B. (1999), 'Democracia y participación: consideraciones sobre la representación política' in J. Jesús Orozco Henríquez (ed.), *Democracia y representación en el umbral del siglo XXI*, Instituto de Investigaciones Jurídicas, UNAM, México.

Flores, I.B. (2002), 'Gobernabilidad y representatividad hacia un sistema democrático electoral mayoritario y proporcional' in H.A. Concha Cantú (ed.), *Sistema representativo y democracia semidirecta*, Instituto de Investigaciones Jurídicas, UNAM, México.

Flores, I.B. (2003a), '¿Ensueño, pesadilla o realidad? Objetividad, (in)determinación e interpretación del derecho'. (Paper presented at Contemporary Problems of Legal Philosophy and Theory Congress in México, D.F., México).

Flores, I.B. (2003b), 'Assessing Democracy and Rule of Law: Access to Justice' (Paper presented at IVR Congress in Lund, Sweden).

Froomkin, A.M. (1988), 'Climbing the Most Dangerous Branch of Government: Legisprudence and the New Legal Process', *Texas Law Review*, Vol. 5, pp. 1071-1098.

Fuller, L.L. (1968), *The Anatomy of Law*, Mentor, New York.

Fuller, L.L. (1969), *The Morality of Law*, Yale University Press, New Haven (Revised edition of the originally published in 1964).

Fuller, Lon L. (1981), *The Principles of Social Order. Selected Essays of Lon L. Fuller*, K. Winston (ed.), Duke University Press, Durham (NC).

Hamilton, A., Madison, J. and Jay, J. (1961), *The Federalist Papers*, Mentor, New York (originally published in 1787-1788).

Hart, H.L.A. (1994), *The Concept of Law*, Oxford University Press, Oxford (second edition with a Postcript of the originally published in 1961).

Hart, H.M. and Sacks, A.M. (1958), *The Legal Process: Basic Problems in the Making and Application of Law*. (Unpublished manuscript tent. ed. 1958.)

Hobbes, T. (1991), *Leviathan*, Cambridge University Press, Cambridge (first published in 1651).

Holmes, O.W. (1897), 'The Path of Law', *Harvard Law Review*, Vol. 10, pp. 457-478.

Kant, I. (1991), *Political Writings*, Cambridge University Press, New York.

Kay, R.S. (1998), 'American Constitutionalism' in L. Alexander (ed.), *Constitutionalism. Philosophical Foundations*, Cambridge University Press, Cambridge.

Kelsen, H. (1992), *Introduction to the Problems of Legal Theory*, Clarendon Press, Oxford.

Kennedy, D. (1986), 'Freedom and Constraint in Adjudication: A Critical Phenomenology', *Journal of Legal Education*, Vol. 36, pp. 518-562.

Kennedy, D. (1996), *A Critique of Adjudication (fin de siècle)*, Harvard University Press, Cambridge (Ma).

Locke, J. (1988), *Two Treatises of Government*, Cambridge University Press, New York.

Maine, H.S. (1912), *Ancient Law: Its Connection with the Early History of Society and Its Relation to Modern Ideas*, John Murray Ltd, London (first published in 1861).

Montesquieu, C.L. (1949), *The Spirit of the Laws*, Hafner Press, New York (first published in 1748).

Pietilä, K. (2002), 'Rationality of Legislation in a Sociological View' in L.J. Wintgens (ed.), *Legisprudence: A New Theoretical Approach to Legislation*, Hart Publishing, Oxford.

Pitkin, H.F. (1967), *The Concept of Representation*, University of California Press, Berkeley.

Pound, R. (1921), *The Spirit of the Common Law*, Beacon Press, Boston.

Savigny, F.K. von (1831), *Of the Vocation of Our Age for Legislation and Jurisprudence*, Littlewood & Co. Old Bailey, London.

Schäffer, H. (1988), 'Rationalisierung der Rechtssetzung' in H. Schäffer (ed.), *Theorie der Rechtssetzung*, Manz Verlag, Vienna.

Shklar, J.N. (1986), *Legalism. Law, Morals and Political Trials*, Harvard University Press, Cambridge (Ma) (first published in 1964).

Tolonen, H. (2002) 'Concept and Institution of the State in the European Legal Tradition' in L.J. Wintgens (ed.), *Legisprudence: A New Theoretical Approach to Legislation*, Hart Publishing Oxford.

Tuori, K. (2002), 'Legislation Between Politics and Law' in L.J. Wintgens (ed.), *Legisprudence: A New Theoretical Approach to Legislation*, Hart Publishing, Oxford.

Unger, R.M. (1975), *Knowledge and Politics*, Free Press, New York.

Unger, R.M. (1976), *Law in Modern Society. Toward a Criticism of Social Theory*, Free Press, New York.

Unger, R.M. (1986), *The Critical Legal Studies Movement*, Harvard University Press, Cambridge (Ma).

Unger, R.M. (1996), *What Should Legal Analysis Become?*, Verso, London/New York.

Verhoeven, A. (2002), 'Legisprudence and European Law: in Search of Principles of European Legislation' in L.J. Wintgens (ed.), *Legisprudence: A New Theoretical Approach to Legislation*, Hart Publishing, Oxford.

Voermans, W. (2002) 'Rationality in Legislation by Employing Informatics' in L.J. Wintgens (ed.), *Legisprudence: A New Theoretical Approach to Legislation*, Hart Publishing, Oxford.

Waldron, J. (1998), 'Dirty Little Secret', *Columbia Law Review*, Vol. 98, pp. 510-529.

Waldron, J. (1999a), *Law and Disagreement*, Oxford University Press, Oxford.

Waldron, J. (1999b), *The Dignity of Legislation*, Cambridge University Press, Cambridge.

Waldron, J. (2002), 'Large Legislatures' in E. Villanueva (ed.), *Legal and Political Philosophy*, Rodopi, Amsterdam/New York.

Weber, M. (1968), *Economy and Society. An Outline of Interpretative Sociology*, Bedminister Press, New York (first published in 1922).

Winter, H. (2002), 'The Forum Model in Evaluation of Legislation' in L.J. Wintgens (ed.), *Legisprudence: A New Theoretical Approach to Legislation*, Hart Publishing, Oxford.

Wintgens, L.J. (2002), 'Rationality in Legislation. Legal Theory as Legisprudence: An Introduction' and 'Legislation as an Object of Study of Legal Theory: Legisprudence' in L.J. Wintgens (ed.), *Legisprudence: A New Theoretical Approach to Legislation*, Hart Publishing, Oxford.

Wintgens, L.J. (2005), 'Legisprudence as a New Theory of Legislation', in this volume.

Wilson, W. (1981), *Congressional Government*, John Hopkins University Press, Baltimore (first published in 1885).

Chapter 3

The Evolution of Economic Thinking about Legislation and its Interpretation by Courts

Richard A. Posner*

The evolution of economic thinking about legislation and the legislative process has undergone several phases. In the first phase, which was dominant until the 1970s, the prevailing economic theory of legislation was the public-interest theory. Legislation was assumed to be enacted by legislators acting in the public interest to correct market failures, redress distributional inequities, and implement the moral values of the society. This approach implied that the role of the courts in the interpretation of legislation was to identify a public interest rationale for the legislation and to interpret the legislation in such a way that would implement that rationale.

This economic theory and its application were strongly challenged, beginning in the early 1970s. The dominant figure in this reexamination was George Stigler, who formulated the interest group theory of regulation (Stigler, 1975; Magee *et al.* 1989; Posner, 1974, p. 335). Now in fact there was an earlier interest group theory, which had been formulated by the well-known political scientists Arthur Bentley and David Truman, (see Bentley, 1908; Truman, 1951) but it did not operate as a challenge to the public interest theory but rather as a complement to it, because negotiations among interest groups were assumed to result in efficient and equitable legislation. Stigler's theory, in contrast, assumed that interest groups work against the public interest. Specifically, he modeled the legislative process on cartelization. In a cartel, competing firms agree not to compete with each other, and by doing this they transform consumer into producer surplus, that is, they redistribute wealth from consumers to themselves. In so doing they reduce the efficiency with which society's scarce resources are allocated across different goods and services. To be effective, however, cartels have to overcome the free-rider problem – the temptation of each member of the cartel to undercut the cartel price slightly, thereby garnering a greater share of the cartel profits. Of course, if many members yield to the temptation, the cartel will collapse, and that is why the prevention of free riding is a central challenge to cartels even when cartelization is not illegal.[1]

Similarly, as Stigler explained, for an interest group to obtain legislation in its favor it must overcome the free-rider temptation of its members, since a member who contributes nothing to the effort to obtain the legislation will nevertheless benefit from it to the same extent as the members who bore their fair share of the burden in lobbying and other activities. A further analogy comes from the fact that cartels are able to redistribute wealth from consumers to themselves because consumers typically are unorganized. Similarly, voters tend to be unorganized unless they happen to belong to interest groups. The goal of an interest group seeking to obtain wealth through the political process is to distribute the burden of the legislation so widely – perhaps across all taxpayers – that there is no organized opposition; not only do the costs of organization rise with the number of persons who must be organized, but the incentive to organize is diminished when the benefits of organization are widely diffused, as they are if the cost of the interest-group legislation is distributed over a very large number of people. The ideal law from the standpoint of an interest group is therefore one that transfers small amounts of wealth from a large number of taxpayers to a small number of individuals or other entities constituting the interest group. The larger the burdened group, the less the incentive of each member to oppose the legislation or even to acquire the information necessary to know whether to oppose it and the greater the free-rider problem, while the smaller the interest group the larger the stake of each member and hence the less incentive to defect, and the lower the cost of organizing the group.

The interest-group approach to legislation, as articulated by Stigler, had definite implications for how courts should interpret legislation, implications first pointed out I believe by myself (see Posner, 1982, p. 263; 1983, p. 800). If much legislation is intended not to advance the public interest but rather to redistribute wealth from the public at large to an interest group able to organize effectively to plunder the public fisc in this fashion, it would be perilous for courts to impute a public interest rationale to the legislation – to assume, that is, that the legislation was in the public interest – and to seek to enforce the rationale to its hilt. Such an approach would not only tend to magnify the redistributive or cartelesque effects of the legislation; it would also disregard the extent to which legislation is a product of compromise, assuming some resistance to the pressure of the interest group that obtained, but perhaps only in truncated form, legislation redistributing wealth to it.

The interest group approach has had signal successes in explaining a broad range of legislation, including legislation conferring farm subsidies and other subsidies, imposing tariffs on imported goods, and limiting entry into various occupations and markets. However, much legislation is not explained by the interest group approach, including the many statutes, enacted as part of the deregulation movement, that dismantled a host of interest group laws; and many general laws, such as the criminal laws, that seem to serve the public interest, as well as a number of laws regulating safety, health, and the environment. Indeed, the greatest success of the interest group theory had been in explaining the pattern of regulation that existed *before* deregulation took hold. The theory taught, and empirical studies confirmed, that the principal effect of such regulation had been to bring about or shore up producers' cartels. The theory identified the demand and supply factors that explained the success of some producers and failure of others in obtaining such regulation, and those factors turned out to be much the same, as I have suggested, as those that facilitate purely private cartels. The more concentrated the cartelists' market and the more diffuse the buyer side of the market, the easier it is for the cartelists to overcome the free-rider problems that bedevil cartels – and if sellers can overcome those problems in the private marketplace, they may be able to overcome parallel problems in the political marketplace, where legislation is "bought" and taxpayers, who pay for it, correspond to consumers in an economic market. This explanation of regulation is supported by the characteristic provisions of regulatory statutes, which include limitations on price and service competition, new entry, and other such threats to the elimination of competition.

But if interest group legislation is a form of cartelization, why aren't interest groups content with cartelizing? Why do they need or want legislation? There are two answers. The first is that cartels are illegal, which, obviously, increases the difficulty of forming and maintaining them. The second is that a group may be too large to cartelize effectively, yet be able to overcome the free-rider obstacles to procuring legislative protection, especially since, the less feasible the cartel alternative, the more valuable such protection is. Agricultural quotas, acreage limitations, and subsidies illustrate this point, since farmers are too numerous to cartelize effectively even when cartelization is permitted.

Concerning the deregulation movement, however, about the best the Stiglerian approach can do is to draw attention to the fact that, in the 1970s, when the movement began, many regulated firms were becoming restive under regulation. One reason was the high rate of inflation in that decade, which interacted with regulatory control over rates, and particularly regulatory lag in granting rate increases, to impede needed pricing flexibility. A more fundamental reason, however, is the tendency of cartelization, including cartelization by regulation, over time to transform cartel profits into costs. A cartelized market is not in equilibrium. Because price exceeds marginal cost, there are unexploited profit opportunities. If price competition is prevented by agreement or regulation, the members of the cartel will vie for additional sales by increasing the quality of their product until at the margin the cost of the product equals the price. At this point, regulation becomes all costs and no benefits, at least to the most efficient firms, whose expansion is inhibited by the protectionist philosophy of the regulators. Service competition in the airline industry before deregulation illustrates this point. Airline service was luxurious and load factors (the percentage of seats on a plane that were actually occupied) were very low because restrictions on entry enabled airlines to charge supracompetitive prices, which eventually they competed away by providing more and better service, notably in the provision of frequent flights.

A new economic approach to legislation, which helps to fill the gaps in the interest group approach and, more broadly, to suggest a reconciliation or fusion of the public interest and interest group theories, builds on Joseph Schumpeter's theory of democracy. It is neither a public interest theory nor an interest group theory, but it explains why legislation is sometimes in the public interest and sometimes a product purely of interest group politics. It is my focus in the remainder of this paper.

Since Schumpeter was a great economist and announced his theory in a book published in 1942 (see Schumpeter, 1942, pp. 269-273), it may seem odd for me to call it a *new* theory. However, apart from the fact that his presentation of the theory was very sketchy and has been increasingly ignored in the more than half century that has elapsed since its publication, he did not present it as an economic theory, though it is readily translated into economic terms, as I shall show.

Schumpeter modeled the democratic process as a competitive power struggle among members of a political elite (not to be confused with a moral or intellectual elite) for the electoral support of the masses. Thus, his theory is centrally about *representative* democracy, which presupposes a division between voters and politicians, or between citizens and rulers. (In contrast, the structure of government plays little role in either the public interest or the interest group theory of legislation.) In his theory, neither citizens on the one hand nor the governing class of elected officials on the other are regarded as actuated to any great degree by motives other than self-interest in a fairly narrow sense, and the masses are regarded as poorly informed about, and except in times of crisis little interested in, political matters. And there is no presumption that what emerges from the political process is legislation that is in the public interest. At the same time, politicians place a central role in the theory, whereas in the interest group theory politicians are incidental and it is the interest groups themselves that are seen as the fashioners of public policy.

Schumpeter was, as I said, a great economist; and though his theory of democracy is not formally economic, it bears the stamp of his profession.[2] It is natural for an economist to regard political competition in a democracy (or in any other polity, but it is democracy that highlights the non-violent competitive element in politics, suggesting an analogy to economic competition) as a power struggle. The economist comes to the study of politics from the study of markets, where profit-seeking sellers compete for the favor of buyers (Schumpeter, 1942, pp. 258–260). To 'analogize' political competition to economic competition involves votes taking the place of sales and power of profits, and the observation that the two sides of the political market, like the two sides of economic markets, are sharply differentiated – the sellers (candidates) representing the active side, the buyers (voters) the passive. In economic as in political markets the buyer does not design the product; he chooses from a menu presented to him by the sellers.

Schooled in the economic advantages of the division of labor, the economist turned political scientist is alert to the advantages likely to flow from constituting a corps of specialists in governing, the representatives and other officials, thus freeing the rest of the citizenry to specialize in other pursuits. This salutary division of labor entails a separation in outlook and knowledge between governors and governed, but that is no different from the separation between sellers and buyers in economic markets.

The economist turned political scientist notices, however, that the electoral market is deficient in the conditions that would enable the "buyers", that is, the citizens, to make sound choices. The buyers in economic markets have strong financial or otherwise self-interested incentives to choose carefully between competing sellers, and usually they have enough knowledge to be able to determine which seller is offering the better value. The citizen, in contrast, the buyer in the political market, seems to have no incentive to vote at all, let alone to invest in learning which candidate offers the greatest value, since a single vote will not swing the election. And he is asked to buy a "product" – the candidate and the candidate's likely policies – the value of which is almost impossible to determine even if the voter irrationally invests a great deal of time and effort in studying the candidates and the issues.

Another way to state the difference between the economic marketplace and the political marketplace is that the "goods" in the latter are not priced. As Schumpeter's fellow Austrian Friedrich Hayek emphasized, price is a cheap and accurate signal. It compacts enormous information. High-income consumers can use price as an index of quality; low-income consumers can use price to guide them to the cheapest goods consistent with minimum quality. There is no comparably economical and informative signal to guide the voter, though we'll see that there are some substitutes.

Then too there are greater economies of scale in political than in most economic markets and therefore stronger monopolistic tendencies. The reason is the unusually serious information problems that beset political markets. "The scale of political activity is large...because many [political] offices tie together numerous activities...An electorate with a limited amount of political information finds it easier to place one person in charge of many activities than to choose one person for each activity." (Becker, 1958, pp. 105, 108).[3] As a result, the only important US political parties are national, and there are only two of them, making political competition duopolistic. Duopolists often collude, rather than competing vigorously with each other.

The economist who turns his eye to politics thus beholds an unedifying prospect from his professional standpoint. And yet his perspective offers reassurance as well. Many economic markets are oligopolistic rather than atomistic in their structure, yet still effectively competitive; this is true even of many duopolies, especially if there is at least a potential threat of new entry. Or consider voter apathy. If one looks at the buying side of a well-functioning consumer market, one sees there a good deal of, well, apathy. Another name for it is contentment. Buyers do not need to be alert, assiduous shoppers when they rightly believe that the market in which they are buying is competitive. They have reasonable assurance that the products offered them by the market will be of satisfactory price and quality.

Sellers in a competitive market, moreover, however vigorously they compete with one another, offer products similar in price and quality. Otherwise it would be not a competitive, but a monopolized, market. We can expect the same thing in the political marketplace. We should not take the Tweedledum-Tweedledee character of major-party competition in a two-party political system as a sign that competition is not working. If the parties were highly dissimilar, one of them would probably be the permanent minority party.

And while what I am calling apathy and equating to contentment could signify alienation, studies of non-voters suggest otherwise. They find that non-voters tend to have similar political views to voters (see Teixeira, 1992, pp. 94-101; Hadley, 1978, p. 149 (tab. 1)) and that non-voting is concentrated among the young and among people who move around a lot (see Hadley, 1978, pp. 150-151 (tab. 2)).[4] The young are less knowledgeable about political "commodities" and therefore "buy" fewer of them, while voting is more costly for people who change their state of residence and so must reregister. Turnout in close elections is higher not because voters irrationally believe that their vote may swing the election (the probability of an election's being swung by one vote is infinitesimal), but because the contestants spend more on political advertising and other promotional activities in a close election, thus stirring greater interest on the part of the electorate (Aldrich, 1993, pp. 246, 266-268).

Furthermore, in political as in economic markets, relatively uninformed "consumers," that is, the voters, can and do use information shortcuts to make up for their information deficits, such as by inferring a candidate's suitability from the identity of his supporters and opponents (see, for example, Wittman, 1995, chs.2-3, 5; Popkin, 1991; Lupia, 1994, p. 63; Kuklinski *et al.* 1982, p. 615. Cf. Milgrom and Roberts, 1986, p. 18).[5] Political parties reduce voters' information costs; a voter who knows a candidate's political affiliation (easy information to come by) knows something, and maybe a lot, about the policies the candidate is likely to support if elected. Party affiliation corresponds to a trademark in an ordinary market. A trademark is a low-cost signal of the quality of a product, and investment in a trademark is a commitment to maintain existing quality, since the investment will be lost if consumers defect because the producer has failed to maintain the promised quality. The broader point is that a consumer may make the same decision on the basis of incomplete information as he would on the basis of complete information; there is empirical evidence that this is the case for most voters (Lau and Redlawsk, 1997, p. 585).

There is even a respect in which information deficiencies are less serious in the electoral market than in ordinary markets. In an ordinary market, if 50 percent of the consumers are well informed and the other 50 percent are not, the latter group will make a lot of mistakes,[6] and thus incur a loss of utility. But in a political market, if only (say) 10 percent of the voters are well informed and the others vote randomly, the outcome will be the same within a small margin of error as if all 100 percent were well informed. The reason is that consumers get what they buy, but voters get what the majority "buys."

Although economists don't much stress the point, the apathy or, better, the rational inertia of consumers, besides economizing on precious time, serves to stabilize markets in important ways. The fact that most consumers are not actively shopping for most products at any given time (not that they're not buying, but that they're not considering changing their existing consumption pattern) minimizes the frequency and amplitude of fluctuations in demand and supply, averting the sudden gluts and shortages that would ensue if the entire consuming public flocked all at once to a new product. In the latter event, prices would change until equilibrium was restored, but changing prices is not costless and meanwhile there would be uncertainty, queuing, bankruptcies, and disemployment. The interest in stability is even greater in the political sphere because of the potentially disastrous consequences of sudden sharp changes in political governance. Imagine if all citizens were avid students of political theory and became mesmerized by the radically disinterested political theory of a charismatic political enterpreneur and as a result they elected officials who wanted to change the course of the nation 180 degrees. That is a terrifying prospect, held at bay by many things but among them the fact that most citizens are interested not in what is best in some sense for the nation or the world but rather in what is best from the standpoint of their self-interest. Except in circumstances of desperation, a concern with self creates resistance to radical social change.

Just the fact that sellers and consumers are assumed to be motivated wholly or at least very largely by self-interest rather than by concepts of the public good is reassuring. It shows that a market can serve the public good even if none of the participants is trying to serve it. The invisible hand of the economic market can be found at work in the political market as well. It doesn't operate as efficiently in the political market, because it lacks that valuable tool, price. But this is not a criticism of democratic government. To government falls those tasks that the price system cannot perform well. It is not an accident, or some foolish socialist project, that national defense, judicial enforcement of contract, property, and other rights, crime control, regulation of pollution and other externalities, poor relief, and internal security are not provided by private enterprise.

The role of the politician in the Schumpeterian model is central and becomes clearer when the model is inflected by economics. Critics of American democracy deride politicians as panderers to the uninformed preferences of the ordinary citizen. For the critics, the correct economic analogy is to sellers' simply giving the consumer what he wants. The analogy is incomplete. There are sellers and there are sellers. The most interesting are those who seek to create (in order, of course, to then be able to satisfy – at a price) new desires of consumers. The consuming public did not know that it wanted automobiles, radios, frozen food, compact disks, e-mail, or laptop computers before these things were invented. The voting public did not know that it wanted social security, conscription, public education, an independent central bank, an interstate highway system, a Presidency open to a divorced or Catholic person, the North Atlantic Treaty Organization, or the auctioning of rights to the use of the electromagnetic spectrum before these things were proposed by political entrepreneurs, as distinct from run-of-the-mill politicians. Schumpeterian democracy may not be edifying, but it need not be mediocre. This point is related to democracy's advantage as the system that diverts the energies of dangerously ambitious men into socially harmless, even beneficial, channels. Some of those men are practical-minded idealists (as opposed to mere dreamers) – which doesn't necessarily make them less dangerous.

The interesting sellers and the uninteresting sellers have something important in common: the profit motive. Without that, there would be no assurance that consumers were being well served. The interesting and the uninteresting politicians also have something similar, and similarly important, in common: ambition to obtain and retain public office. Without that, the voters would have no control over their representatives. "No more irresponsible government is imaginable than one of high-minded men unconcerned for their political futures" (Schlesinger, 1966, p. 2). Such government would be irresponsible in the literal sense of not being responsible to the people.

The competitive process that is the heart of Schumpeterian democracy does not operate only at election time. In between elections, and quite apart from the possibility of recalling or impeaching an elected official before his term expires, elected officials from the different parties, and their adherents, compete vigorously, for example by pointing out the errors, oversights, and iniquities of the opposition. Campaigning, actual or latent, is continuous. Compare that to a system in which the only check on officials between elections is an ombudsman (the heir of the Roman tribune) or the judiciary. Or a system, modeled on the representation of the workers in a collective bargaining unit that has voted to make the union the exclusive representative of the unit in bargaining with the employer over terms and conditions of employment, in which representatives would have a fiduciary obligation to represent all their constituents fairly, including those who had voted for the losing candidate (which is the duty of an exclusive bargaining representative). Such a duty that would inhibit representatives from courting popular support between elections.

Competition provides stronger incentives for monitoring and criticism than bureaucratic, including judicial, control mechanisms do. Schumpeter overlooked the importance of between-elections competition because his model democracy was Great Britain, which had (and still has) a highly centralized government. There were no traces of a federal system. The Cabinet had virtually unlimited power, since it controlled Parliament; thus the legislative and executive branches were fused. The judges, though independent, had no power of constitutional review. The United States, with its separation of powers, is in a constant competitive boil. The competition between Thomas Jefferson and John Marshall in the early 1800s did more to maintain a competitive political system, by preserving Federalist institutions in a period of anti-Federalist electoral dominance, than the one-sided electoral competition of that period did.

Schumpeter's implicit economic model of the democratic process was shortly made explicit by the economists Anthony Downs (1957) and Gary Becker (1958), and in succeeding decades, as we know from the earlier discussion in this paper, a substantial economic literature on politics developed. But its focus was on the manifold ways in which a public-interest model of government fails to explain policy. Missing from the analysis were the politicians and the voters – the sellers and the buyers in the political market and the focus of Schumpeter's theory. Politicians and voters were implicitly modeled as lackeys and dupes of interest groups, respectively. This is an oversimplification of the political process to the point of caricature, as even conservative economists now recognize (see, for example, Peltzman, 1998). And it disregards the refinements and criticisms of interest group theory by political scientists, notably the criticism that the theory, at least in its original economic form, is unduly pessimistic (see Ginsburg).[7]

Schumpeterians acknowledge that interest group pressures deform public policy. But as there is no evidence that non-democratic regimes are any less susceptible to those pressures, the frictions that interest groups create should be considered the ineliminable transaction costs of government, akin to transportation costs in ordinary markets. We accept the need for transportation and therefore the costs incident to it, and we should do likewise with respect to government.

Another point at which the Schumpeterian concept diverges from interest group theory concerns the need for channeling the energies of the ambitious. In Stigler's theory, officials are agents (of interest groups), not principals; they are neither a distinct nor even an important stratum of the community, let alone a dangerous elite whose domestication is a major project and achievement of democracy. The passivity of officials assumed in most interest group models is the reason economic theorists of democracy have tended to lack interest in the actual structure of a democratic system. If interest groups rule and officials merely broker the interest groups' deals, the structure of government is incidental.

The emphasis that Schumpeter's theory of democracy places on the existence of distinct tiers or classes of participants in the political process (voters and politicians, mass and elite) suggests a parallel to the long-running debate over "corporate democracy." Beginning in the 1930s with the work of Adolf Berle and Gardner Means, concern arose about the "separation of ownership and control" in the modern corporation (see Berle and Means, 1932).[8] The shareholders of a large publicly traded corporation are its nominal owners, corresponding to the electorate in the political system. They elect the board of directors, which in turn appoints the management. But like the politicians in Schumpeter's theory of political democracy, the directors and managers are the real "rulers" and have their own interests, which often diverge from those of the shareholders. The Securities and Exchange Commission has attempted to encourage greater shareholder participation in corporate management by requiring management to include shareholder proposals in the proxy materials distributed to the shareholders in advance of the corporation's annual meeting.[9] In effect, it has attempted to bring about Concept 1 corporate democracy.[10] It has failed (see, for example, Easterbrook and Fischel, 1991, p. 85). Like voters, most shareholders of publicly traded corporations have only a small stake in the corporations whose shares they own – too small to give these shareholders an incentive to invest significant time and effort in monitoring the performance of corporate management. It is easier for them either to sell their shares if the corporation is doing badly, or, by holding a diversified portfolio, to offset unusually good performance by some of their stocks against unusually bad performance by others. Still, they do have the power to oust management, and the existence of this power both is a spur to management to perform well (or at least not too badly) and enables management to be replaced when it flounders disastrously. In practice, corporate democracy is Schumpeterian democracy (see Posner, 2003, § 14.7).

The analogy is imperfect because corporate "citizens" have more options than political citizens. Expatriation is too costly an exit option to be equated to selling one's shares; and it is impossible to hold a diversified portfolio of citizenships. On the other hand, there is more vigorous competition for political office than there generally is for corporate directorships; rarely in fact are shareholders asked to choose between rival slates. And while shareholders' legal rights against management appear to be important to the welfare of investors, (Shleifer and Vishny, 1997) citizens likewise have important rights against their "rulers" under the free-speech, just-compensation, equal-protection, and other clauses of the Constitution.

Still another economic perspective on Schumpeterian democracy is provided by the economics of rent-seeking. The term refers to the dissipation of resources in efforts to obtain pure profit (what economists call "rent"). Resources devoted solely to shifting wealth from one person's pocket to another's are wasted from a social standpoint. The expenditure of such resources moves wealth around without increasing it; and since real costs are being incurred, the social pie shrinks in the process of being redivided. Universal suffrage is a method of reducing political rent-seeking, since unrepresented people are a natural prey for rent seekers who have their hands on the levers of governmental power. In addition, the larger the electorate, the more difficult it is for the would-be rent seekers to forge electoral coalitions for the exploitation of electoral minorities, because the costs of organizing rise with the number of people who must be brought into the coalition for it to be effective. It used to be feared that democracy would encourage the plundering of the rich, simply because they are a minority; and presumably they are a smaller minority the larger the electorate, since the electorate is expanded by granting the vote to the members of previously marginalized groups. But it turns out that the costs to the majority of thus killing the geese that lay the golden eggs discourage this form of exploitation. The more heavily the rich are taxed, the less taxable income they will generate, so that at sufficiently high rates of taxation the net transfer to the rest of the population will be negative (see Mulligan, 2002). And in fact we observe only moderate levels of wealth redistribution by government in modern democracies – especially the United States (see Posner, 2001b, pp. 103–104; Shapiro, 2002, p. 118).

The causality is complex; and reliance on the non-wealthy to recognize the full costs to them of soaking the rich would be a risky strategy. Reflection on rent seeking helps to explain and justify the limitations on democracy that are created by constitutional and other supermajority requirements for legislative action. Without such limitations (whose existence, by the way, complicates any effort to ascribe the failure of democratic governments to undertake ambitious schemes of wealth redistribution purely to the rational self-interest of the electorate), winning majority control of the legislature would be much more valuable to the winner, and so factions would expend greater resources on the struggle for that control (Hirshleifer, 2001, pp. 43, 63). The additional resources would be largely wasted from a social standpoint, especially if the goals of the contestants were to achieve maximum power by extinguishing democracy.

Schumpeter's theory of democracy is indebted to psychology as well as to economics. He bolstered his vision of democracy by reference to a then-influential literature on "crowd psychology" by Le Bon, Pareto, and others, who 'analogized' the voting masses to mobs. A number of present-day psychologists and economists, joined by some law professors, have questioned the accuracy of the conventional economic model of rationally self-interested behavior by invoking a variety of cognitive defects that deflect people from rational behavior (see, for example, Thaler, 1991; Jolls *et al.* 2000). These behavioralists are in the line of descent from the crowd psychologists, but their critique is more encompassing and to the extent that it undermines faith in markets it undermines faith in the democratic electorate even more. Both the ability and the incentive to overcome one's cognitive deficiencies are weaker in political markets than in economic ones because the voter has a smaller stake and less information in choosing between candidates than the consumer has in choosing between sellers of the ordinary goods and services.

In Cass Sunstein's extensive writings on the regulation of health, safety, television, and the Internet (Sunstein, 2002; 2001; 1997), for example, the cognitive defects become a basis for arguing for a shift of regulatory authority from Congress to expert administrators—precisely in order to dilute irrational democratic influence. Neither the electorate nor even its representatives can be trusted. Schumpeter might not have disagreed. If the people are incapable of any political activity other than choosing between candidates, any intelligence in government will have to be the intelligence of an elite from which the candidates (and appointed officials, including judges and experts) are drawn. Schumpeter did not deny that there *is* such intelligence. He was counting on it to hold back the tide of democratic socialism. He himself had been minister of finance in Austria's first post-World War I government.

Although Sunstein considers himself a deliberative democrat rather than a Schumpeterian, his concept of democracy, if fully fleshed out and pushed to its logical limits, might end up resembling Schumpeter's. The key to this convergence is the distinction between deliberation over means and deliberation over ends. The former is far more likely to yield productive agreement. But it is also more amenable to expert treatment. Nothing is more natural or more common than to assign the design, formulation, and implementation of specific policies to experts. This makes it possible to envisage a two-step process of government reform, the end result of which would be to limit democratic choice. First, efforts are made to instrumentalize political reasoning to the extent possible so that intractable issues of ends are transformed into issues of means. Second, the responsibility for the extensive instrumental reasoning now required of government is handed over to technical experts – instrumental reasoning is what technical expertise is good for.

Experts, however, constitute a distinct class in society, with values and perspectives that differ systematically from those of "ordinary" people. Without supposing that the "man in the street" has any penetrating insights denied the expert, or is immune from demagoguery, we may nevertheless think it reassuring that political power is shared between experts and non-experts rather than being a monopoly of the former. One reason that democracies tend to be more stable than authoritarian governments is that the latter are more susceptible to "vanguardism," the tendency to reckless social experimentation that rule by experts fosters.

This analysis casts "crowd psychology", "herd behavior", and related phenomena of imitative action in a different light from that of mere cognitive defects or limitations. The fact that voters tend to take their cues from others who are better informed, yet without blindly following either demagogues or experts, may increase rather than reduce the rationality of political action, as well as imparting to the political process a salutary inertia, impeding precipitate change. Indeed, what may appear to be cognitive quirks may actually be efficient mechanisms for coping rationally with uncertainty, including uncertainty about political candidates and issues.

* Judge, U.S. Court of Appeals for the Seventh Circuit; Senior Lecturer, University of Chicago Law School.

Notes

1 On the economics of cartels, see further Posner (2001a).
2 He did, however, though very briefly, compare political with economic competition. See Schumpeter (1942, p. 271).
3 Becker later moved away from Schumpeter's theory, substituting "a definition of democracy as free competition among pressure groups for political favors in place of Schumpeter's definition of democracy as free competition for political leadership," (Becker, 1985, pp. 120, 141).
4 Very few of the non-voters in Hadley's exhaustive study seem seriously disaffected.
5 Still, public ignorance about political matters is staggering; for a recent summary of the literature, see DeCanio (2000, pp. 215, 219-221).
6 Fewer than one might think, though, because the uninformed are protected to a certain extent by the informed, since sellers cannot easily discriminate between the two groups.
7 The optimistic and pessimistic versions are debated at length in Symposium (2002)
8 In the modern literature, this is described as a problem in "agency costs," that is, a problem arising from the fact that agents (such as corporate managers) have divergent objectives from their principals (the shareholders). See, for example, Shleifer and Vishny (1997, pp. 737, 740–748).
9 See SEC Rule 14a–8; Cox *et al.* (2001, pp. 1010–1012).
10 But this should be distinguished from the form of industrial democracy (see Introduction), also moribund, that seeks to alter the governance of the corporation to make it responsive to interests other than those of the shareholders. See, for example, Jones and Goldberg (1982, p. 603). The psychological literature is comprehensively reviewed in Shafir and LeBoeuf (2002, p. 491).

References

Aldrich, J.H. (1993), 'Rational Choice and Turnout', *American Journal of Political Science*, Vol. 37, pp. 246-278.

Becker, G.S. (1958), 'Competition and Democracy', *Journal of Law and Economics*, Vol. 1, pp. 105-109.

Becker, G.S. (1985), 'Pressure Groups and Political Behavior' in R.D. Coe and C.K. Wilber (eds.), *Capitalism and Democracy: Schumpeter Revisited*, University of Notre Dame Press, Notre Dame .

Bentley, A.F. (1908), *The Process of Government*, University of Chicago Press, Chicago.

Berle, A.A. and Means, G.C. (1932), *The Modern Corporation and Private Property*, Commerce Clearing House, New York.

Cox, J.D., Hillman, R.W. and Langevoort, D.P. (2001), *Securities Regulation: Cases and Materials,* 3rd ed., Aspen Law & Business, Gaithersburg .

DeCanio, S. (2000), 'Beyond Marxist State Theory: Autonomy in Democratic Societies', *Critical Review,* Vol. 14, pp. 215-236.

Downs, A. (1957), *An Economic Theory of Democracy*, Harper, New York.

Easterbrook, F.H. and Fischel, D.R. (1991), *The Economic Structure of Corporate Law*, Harvard University Press, Cambridge.

Ginsburg, T. (2002), 'Ways of Criticizing Public Choice: The Uses of Empiricism and Theory in Legal Scholarship', *University of Illinois Law Review*, Vol. 2002, pp. 1139-1166.

Hadley, A.T. (1978), *The Empty Polling Booth*, Prentice-Hall, Englewood Cliffs.

Hirshleifer, J. (2001), 'The Paradox of Power' in J. Hirshleifer (ed.), *The Dark Side of the Force: Economic Foundations of Conflict Theory,* Cambridge University Press, Cambridge.

Jolls, C., Sunstein, C.R. and Thaler, R.H. (2000), 'A Behavioral Approach to Law and Economics' in Cass R. Sunstein (ed.), *Behavioral Law and Economics*, Cambridge University Press, New York.

Jones, T.M. and Goldberg, L.D. (1982), 'Governing the Large Corporation: More Arguments for Public Directors', *Academy of Management Review,* Vol. 7, pp. 603-611.

Kuklinski, J.H., Metlay, D.S. and Kay, W.D. (1982), 'Citizen Knowledge and Choices on the Complex Issue of Nuclear Energy', *American Journal of Political Science*, Vol. 26, pp. 615-642.

Lau, R.R. and Redlawsk, D.P. (1997), 'Voting Correctly', *American Political Science Review*, Vol. 91, pp. 585-598.

Lupia, A. (1994), 'Shortcuts versus Encyclopedias: Information and Voting Behavior in California Insurance Reform Elections', *American Political Science Review*, Vol. 88, pp. 63-76.

Magee, S.P., Brock, W.A., and Young L. (1989), *Black Hole Tariffs and Endogenous Political Theory: Political Economy in General Equilibrium*, Cambridge University Press, Cambridge.

Milgrom, P. and Roberts, J. (1986) 'Relying on the Information of Interested Parties', *Rand Journal of Economics*, Vol. 17, pp. 18-32.

Mulligan, C.B. (2002), 'Economic Limits on "Rational" Democratic Redistribution' (University of Chicago, George J. Stigler Center for the Study of the Economy and the State, Working Paper No. 171, March 2002).

Peltzman, S. (1998), *Political Participation and Government Regulation*, University of Chicago Press, Chicago.

Popkin, S.L. (1991), *The Reasoning Voter: Communication and Persuasion in Presidential Campaigns*, University of Chicago Press, Chicago.

Posner, R.A. (1974), 'Theories of Economic Regulation', *Bell Journal of Economics and Management Science*, Vol. 5, pp. 335-358.

Posner, R.A. (1982), 'Economics, Politics, and the Reading of Statutes and the Constitution', *University of Chicago Law Review,* Vol. 49, pp. 263-291.

Posner, R.A. (1983), 'Statutory Construction—In the Classroom and in the Courtroom', *University of Chicago Law Review*, Vol. 50, pp. 800- 822.

Posner, R.A. (2001a), *Antitrust Law*, 2nd ed., University of Chicago Press, Chicago.

Posner, R.A. (2001b), *Frontiers of Legal Theory*, Harvard University Press, Cambridge.

Posner, Richard A. (2003), *Economic Analysis of Law,* 6th ed., Aspen Publishers, New York.

Schlesinger, J.A. (1966), *Ambition and Politics: Political Careers in the United States*, Rand McNally, Chicago.

Schumpeter, J. (1942), *Capitalism, Socialism, and Democracy*, Harper & Brothers, New York.

Shafir, E. and LeBoeuf, R.A. (2002), 'Rationality', *Annual Review of Psychology*, Vol. 53, pp. 491-517.

Shapiro, I. (2002), 'Why the Poor Don't Soak the Rich', *Daedalus*, Vol. 131, pp. 118-28.

Shleifer, A. and Vishny, R.W. (1997), 'A Survey of Corporate Governance', *Journal of Finance*, Vol. 52, pp. 737-783.

Stigler, G.J. (1975), *The Citizen and the State: Essays on Regulation*, University of Chicago Press, Chicago.

Sunstein, C.R. (1997), *Free Markets and Social Justice*, Oxford University Press, New York.

Sunstein, C.R. (2001), *Republic.com*, Princeton University Press, Princeton.

Sunstein, C.R. (2002), *Risk and Reason: Safety, Law, and the Environment*, Cambridge University Press, Cambridge.

Symposium (2002), 'Getting Beyond Criticism: New Theories of the Regulatory State', *Cornell Law Review*, Vol. 87, issue 2.

Teixeira, R.A. (1992), *The Disappearing American Voter*, Brookings Institution, Washington.

Thaler, R.H. (1991), *Quasi Rational Economics*, Russell Sage Foundation, New York.

Truman, D.B. (1951), *The Governmental Process: Political Interests and Public Opinion*, Alfred A. Knopf, New York.

Wittman, D.A. (1995), *The Myth of Democratic Failure: Why Political Institutions Are Efficient*, University of Chicago Press, Chicago.

Chapter 4

Legal Instrumentalism Revisited

Koen Van Aeken*

Introduction

This contribution focuses on legal instrumentalism, reconsidering its alleged deficiencies and revisiting the instrumentalist project by making use of new developments from a wide area of disciplines, including sociology, philosophy, legal studies, management sciences, communication sciences, political sciences and architecture. I feel that this multidisciplinary approach is badly needed in the complex world we live in. The old division of sciences may not be adequate anymore to tackle the problems contemporary science and society faces.

However, this multifaceted approach demands special caution. It is important to define clearly the vocabulary employed, in order to standardize the meaning of words for the different disciplines. As such, we start with defining some recurrent terms, drawing on generic definitions.

Defining the Vocabulary

To start with the most difficult one: What is law? Not so long ago, I summarized my research topics to a freshly graduated Harvard Law School student. A bit puzzled, he asked me: "What stands "law" for in your perspective?". From his experiences in Boston, law studies could be as varied as the field of social science, and law as varied as society. He differentiated between Japanese law, business law, intellectual property law, indigenous law, philosophy of law, comparative law and so on: all separated islets of legal practice and research with very specific points of interests. This is in stark contrast with the generic definition of law that I use. For me, law is the intervention from a governmental body in society through the promulgation of rules with the intention to steer the conduct of the relevant constituting parts.[1] These bodies can be situated at different levels, be it a small rural community or a federal state. Its constituting parts can be individuals, families, an industry, the educational or the judicial system, or a nation as a whole. This broad definition enables us to use a plenitude of synonyms for law, such as legal regulation, rules, legal norms, legal messages, legal norms and so on.

Defining law in relation to governmental intervention is opening up law to policy making. Indeed, in the framework of this discussion, law is related to policy, in the sense that it is one instrument in the hands of the policy-maker. Policy-making is thus, in our perspective, related to lawmaking. Put differently, the lawmaker operates as a special kind of policy-maker, with a smaller toolbox, but one that contains tools with a remarkable potential. Opening up the discussion to a revisiting of law in the world of policy-makers, synonyms such as lawgiver, lawmaker or norm constructor will be supplemented by terms such as the policy constructor, always bearing in mind that policy embraces law. Law is not the one love of the policy-maker, or should not be; but when law is deployed, it should be so from a well considered view, enhancing the policy with some of the intrinsic values of law. As the first lay rector of a Jesuit University once replied to the former and last Jesuit rector on the latter's question why he did not go to church daily: "Mass is too important for me to join the celebration on a daily basis". The recognition of the surplus value of law thus demands a scanty use of law. We will consider this statement *infra*.

By stating that law is an instrument, I arrive at legal instrumentalism. Instrumentalism considers a legislated rule as a tool in the hands of a policy-maker who is bent on realizing some sort of social change (Griffiths, 2003). More general, instrumentalism assumes that law is created with a particular result or goal in mind (Fortson, 1999), a goal that lies outside the realm of law (Summers, 1980). Although these definitions may sound very neutral, just the mere referring to the term instrumentalism causes blood pressure to rise amongst many socio-legal scholars. Before examining in-depth some of the problems associated with the instrumental project and in turn the problems associated with the defining of these problems, we first have to clear some linguistic barriers. From instrumentalism,[2] three adjectives can be derived: instrumental, instrumentalist and instrumentalistic. Since the starting point of this contribution is a neutral stance to instrumentalism, I restrict myself to the use of the less coloured adjective of the three, i.e. "instrumental", in addition to the noun "instrumentalism". Both words have strong ties with "instrument", a focal property of law in a policy context.

The positioning of law as a policy instrument implies the imposing of a strict demarcation. Put differently, I embark this vessel of thought from the policy pier. Nevertheless, I will move away from the embarkation point in the direction of legisprudence, the theoretical approach to legislation and regulation that unites the contributions in this book under one flag (see Wintgens, 2002). In the next paragraph I will outline how I will do so.

Outline

In a first stage, I track the roots of the instrumental conception of law, followed by a summary of its main critiques. These critiques fall in three categories: humanitarian, theoretical and practical. The second part of the journey reconsiders these critiques, trying to strip instrumentalism from its negative connotations. As such, the term instrumentalism should have been rendered more neutral than it appears now in the bulk of socio-legal writings. That opens the door for a third part in which I launch tentatively the term *evolutionary instrumentalism*: instrumentalism adapts itself to the socio-political context in which it operates, breaking away from its naive forms. Such an instrumentalism offers a theory of practice that not only may be useful in the field of policy, but also might contribute to the development of a theory of legisprudence. To allow instrumentalism for the necessary adapting, especially with regard to the growing complexity and fluidity of our changing life world, the revisited instrumental project has to fulfil certain conditions. The most acute of these conditions are (1) the introduction of the notion of *probability* in instrumental thinking, (2) the systematic *evaluation* of laws and (3) the opening up to *alternatives* in, to and for legal regulation.

Instrumentalism: Genesis and Critique

A term that has definitively acquired a "bad name" in the socio-legal scholarly community is instrumentalism. The critics became widespread throughout the legal-scientific space, their objections got well known, and the audience adapted their ideas with hardly any hesitation.

Without engaging in a profound discussion on the nature of instrumentalism,[3] I offer a short overview of its alleged deficiencies. These deficiencies play at three levels. On a first level, I consider the humanitarian arguments against a project of social engineering as the bare essential of legal instrumentalism. On a second level, I give a rough sketch of the critiques on the level of the presumed theoretical presuppositions of instrumentalism. On a third level, I describe in broad outline which arguments are formulated against instrumentalism in action. But before doing so, I go back to the conceptual roots of legal instrumentalism.

The Genesis of the Goal-oriented Approach in Legislative Action

To understand the very nature of the instrumental heritage, the image of the engineer at the crossroads of the 19th and 20th century is a quite useful point of referral. In early 20th century Russia, Lenin proclaimed the engineer as the ultimate hero (Johnson, 1983). At first glance, this is not surprising: Russian and later Soviet politics strived towards the expansion of industrial power, be it to emancipate the farming population or to strengthen their geopolitical power.

The idolizing of the engineer, however, reveals more than just the pragmatic orientation of the state towards industrial development. The engineering idea was, *an sich*, closely related to the concept of constructing an utopia, involving a radical change of the existing social structure. Engineering thus quickly acquired the epithet "social", and social engineering was born.

The reference to Lenin with regard to the instrumental conception of legislative policy offers a typical example of the discrediting of instrumentalism.[4] The historical "abuse" of law as an instrument in the hands of dictatorial regimes still affects contemporary thinking about the field of instrumental lawmaking,[5] in the way that it is a permanent *no-go zone*.

This used to be different. Instrumentalism has been quite a promising concept in the democratic, western world in the first half of the 20th century, as laid down in the early writings of Roscoe Pound:

> So there is, as one might say, a great task of social engineering. There is a task of making the goods of existence, the means of satisfying the demands and desires of men living together in a politically organized society, if they cannot satisfy all the claims that men make upon them, at least go round as far as possible. This is what we say that the end of law is justice. (Pound, 1968, p. 64)

First published in 1942 – historically understandable reprinted in 1968 – Pound's ideas of justice and the task of the political corpus differed significantly from Lenin's dictatorial views, although their main underlying thought, the use of law as a means to transform society, shared the same motivation.[6] Pound rejected the economic-political concept of *laissez faire*, which had been a long-standing feature of legal formalism.[7] Instead of believing in individualism as a moral and economic ideal in the courts, he promoted a sociological jurisprudence. Over time, his ideas "left" the courts. He advanced the "theory of social interests" in law, asserting that law must recognize the needs of humanity, and take contemporary social conditions into account.

Roscoe Pound's views capture very well the general evolution in attitudes regarding legal instrumentalism. As discussed above, he may be regarded as a pioneer in introducing the concept of social engineering into the domain of the law. However, when he grew older, he gradually took more distance from his original progressive views. His Obituary in the *Times* clearly expresses this shift in attitude.[8] The attempts made to foster social progress under the New Deal strategy, according to some partly a product of Pound's inspiration, were fiercely contested by the scholar towards the end of his life, since he saw the welfare state evolving towards a service state modeled to a Marxist blueprint.

Lenin's stance towards instrumentalist lawmaking behavior is probably a politically correct way to discredit instrumentalism. Pound's gradual distancing from instrumentalism may reinforce this idea. Yet the view that law could serve policy as an instrument appealed to a great number and variety of scholars and policy-makers in the democratic world in symbiosis with the development of the welfare state (see, e.g., Summers, 1980; Schuyt, 1985; Schwitters, 2000). The idea that the social environment could be manipulated towards specific politically defined goals became omnipresent in policy thinking. This is not surprising if one takes the dominant world view of that era into account. Legal realism, closely connected to the idea of instrumentalism, drew heavily on the change in scientific paradigm from a deductive to an inductive method. [9] Apart from the paradigm shift, the applied natural sciences produced one after the other cutting edge invention. The euphoric ode by Le Corbusier to the packet boat, the automobile, the airplane and numerous other innovations offers a striking illustration of the then common trust in new technology and man's ability to "mould" society (Le Corbusier, 1923).

In "Pragmatisme et Sociologie", Durkheim analyzed the writings of pragmatist philosophers James and Dewey, stating that:

> particularly in James, there is liking for risk, a need for adventure.[10] That is certainly the ideal of the strong man who wishes to expand the field of his activity. (Durkheim, 1914, 13th lecture)

The world is preferred as uncertain and "malleable" over fixed and immobile. The "transformative" vision is quite clear here. In sum, inspired by the flow of technical and industrial, managerial, commercial and architectural innovations, to name a few, the policy-maker and lawyers thus gradually started to think as (social) engineers, using legal instruments as tools.

Critique

The dark side of social engineering: humanitarian arguments against instrumentalism While the short description of the genesis of the ideas of social engineering was relatively unbiased in value judgment, most comments on social engineering (and, intrinsically connected, instrumentalism) focus on the "dark side of social engineering". Historian Paul Johnson refers cynically to the 20th century as "the age of social engineering", focusing on the megalomaniac experiments of the likes of Lenin, Stalin and Hitler (Johnson, 1983). Philosopher Popper warns against utopian, totalitarian or holistic engineering, aimed at remodeling the whole of society according to a tight scheme or blueprint. This form of social engineering tries to capture the key institutions of society, leveling off society to the state (Popper, 1964). The Polish sociologist of law Podgórecki talks about sociotechnics as a hallmark for totalitarian regimes (Podgórecki, 1996).

In short, social engineering is negatively coloured by its connection to totalitarism. For some, this historical connotation alone suffices to discredit instrumentalism.

Critique of the theoretical presuppositions of instrumentalism The idea of the instrumental use of law quickly attracted the attention of the scholarly community. The early years of academic critique are well described in *Patterns of American Jurisprudence* by Neil Duxbury, be it that the relevant parts of this publication focus more on the broader concept of Legal Realism. A more thorough analysis of instrumentalism as such is presented by Robert Summers (1982) in *Instrumentalism in American Legal Theory*.

I will restrict myself to a summary of the main objections that were prevalent in the 1990s. They can easily be structured following the early *sender-message-receptor* scheme that has dominated communication sciences for a long time.[11] This scheme captures very well the stereotypical way in which the instrumental lawgiver allegedly thinks. The legislator is portrayed as a sole sender on the top, projecting legal messages onto individuals that are on the bottom and not able to influence the sender. These individuals respond obediently to the transmitted messages. These top-down and command-and-control features are omnipresent in the traditional critique on legal instrumentalism (Griffiths, 1978).

Building on the communication metaphor, the theoretical presuppositions as identified by several authors (see, e.g., Griffiths, 1996; Griffiths, 2003; Rottleuthner, 1987) can be ordered as follows:

(1) the legislator is regarded as an autonomous, normative-monistic instance that generates unambiguous norms with clear objectives;
(2) while the transmitting process of norms is thought of as taking place in a vacuum free of noise and disturbance by other norms;
(3) and society is seen as a composition of rational, atomistic individuals.

In reality, of course, these theoretical assumptions do not hold (see, e.g., Griffiths, 2003; van Klink, 2002; Moore, 1978). Indeed,

(1) the legislator is not autonomous, since he is rooted in society, and its capacity to produce unambiguous norms with clearly defined targets may certainly not be taken for granted. In addition, the legislator is not the only creator of regulations since many competing regulators appear on the scene;
(2) legal norms do not reach their "audience" through a vacuum, but are interpreted by various enforcement actors and the addressees themselves;
(3) it is generally accepted that numerous smaller organised social fields exist between the state and the individual, which accommodate these individuals and function by their own rules. Sally Moore used the term "semi-autonomous social fields" to describe these groupings of people with the capacity to create and enforce (non-governmental) regulations

Critique of instrumentalism in action The initial euphoria that accompanied the belief in social progress through the instrumental use of law faded when the crisis of the welfare state set in. The criticism reached a high peak in the 1980s and was often influenced by neo-liberal ideas.[12] The increasing use of law as an instrument in the hands of the government has been described at some length in terms of overregulation and juridification. Teubner (1987) summarizes the main critiques in four points, merging Habermasian and Luhmannian notions (Deflem, 1992).

First, legal instrumentalism encounters effectiveness problems. Counterintuitive behavior of complex systems is the main cause of this dysfunction. Second, instrumentalism leads to the colonization of the social environment. Third, the legal system suffers from overstrain within the gigantic machinery that is the welfare state. Finally, system conflicts carry the risk of tearing the welfare state apart due to different evolutions and goals proper to distinct subsystems.

Critique Revisited

The multifaceted critique on instrumentalism has gradually taken over most of the socio-legal thinking about law. It became almost "academically incorrect" not to discredit instrumentalism. But towards the end of the 1980s, a gradual shift in attitude towards the instrumental project took placc, continuing into present day thinking. I will argue that instrumentalism rarely exists in its naive form, but is capable of adapting to the societal and political context. In the following argumentation, I stick to the threefold order of critiques from the paragraph above.

Social Engineering can be a Humanitarian Enterprise

The backtracking of the conceptual roots of instrumentalism clearly showed how the original project was motivated by a belief in social progress and transformative visions. Of course, these beliefs and visions are not value free. Hence, the application of instrumentalism could serve a fascist or communist purpose. Podgórecki and Popper both warned against the malafide use of social engineering, but also presented a righteous way to make use of the potential of social engineering and instrumentalism. Podgórecki opposes "dark social engineering" to "sociotechnics proper", the latter providing:

> the potential practitioner with a method to seek effective (adequate to expected goals) ways and means to achieve aims, provided there is a given accepted system of values as well as a usable set of verified propositions describing and explaining human behavior [...] Dark social engineering [...] is consciously used to produce harm. It is not the techniques but rather the goals that make it deplorable. (Podgórecki, 1996, p. 26)

In an analogical way, Popper distinguishes between utopian or holistic engineering, and piecemeal engineering. The first kind is characterized by a dictatorial approach, leaving no room for the historical contingencies that shape society, but suffocating that very society by imposing an invariable blueprint of reforms. The utopian engineer departs from the superiority of his plans and neglects unforeseen consequences of his actions, since he expects society to be completely manipulable. Piecemeal engineering, on the other hand, is inspired by respect for society, societal institutions and processes and their history. Piecemeal instrumental reasoning thus takes the delicate properties of the social habitat into account, a consideration that forces the policy-makers to act stepwise. This incremental approach to societal steering thus shows respect for the historically contingent characteristics of society by refraining from all-embracing, utopian projects. At the same time, it is wary of relying on *a priori* truths and predicted outcomes of the engineering (Popper, 1964).

Social engineering, intimately connected to legal instrumentalism, can thus be applied in different forms and for different reasons. The common connecting of social engineering to dictatorial regimes disregards the fact that an instrumentalist project may also consist of "sociotechnics proper" or "piecemeal engineering". As expressed by Podgórecki, it is not the techniques but rather the goals that determine if social engineering is improper. Fortunately, contemporary social theory has re-opened the discussion of utopia, the "good place" that may be reached by transformative action. Works by Ulrich Beck and Anthony Giddens reinstate important questions such as "How shall we live?" and "What is to be done?", moving away from a discourse in which utopianism was something associated with modernity and rationality, but also with totalitarianism, fascism, Stalinism and communism (Levitas, 2000).

On the Theoretical Assumptions

Regarding the theoretical presuppositions, my main objection is that they function on a conceptualizing level thriving on too radical a reduction of the complexity of the social context. I therefore put the following question forward: is it not too naive to state that the lawgiver actually thinks that a law will fulfill its expectations in a real context? I will elaborate this argument, starting with anecdotical evidence, followed by a more theoretical perspective, drawing on communication sciences and political sciences.

A fine example of politicians worried about effectiveness problems was mentioned by Dutch sociologist of law Rob Schwitters in his doctoral dissertation (1991). The author analyzed the development of the first law trying to protect the labour force in Holland, i.e. the Law on Child Labour (1874). The report of the Commission of the Senate clearly states some of the factors that could produce unintended, unwanted consequences and threats to the effectiveness of the new law – notwithstanding the fact that they were partly ideologically coloured. If children were banned from the factories, (a) the children would aimlessly roam the streets, with the potential hazards of stealing and breaking the law in different respects, (b) children would be employed in a domestic manual labour setting with even harsher working conditions and (c) since the total family income would decrease, more women would be employed to make up for the loss in income. This evidence from the 19th century, long before legal instrumentalism was studied by academics, shows that not every lawgiver reasoned according to the reductionist viewpoint that became projected onto instrumentalism.

Theorizing this argument, I stick to the representation of instrumentalism as the simple S-M-R communication model from above, which captures fine the naivety that is attributed to instrumental legal reasoning. Before engaging in revisiting the critique from the opponents of instrumentalism on the sender-, message- and receptor-levels, I would like to present a preliminary note on the communication model as a whole.

From top-down communication to transaction The reductionist view on instrumentalism depicts the instrumental lawgiver as a sender who transmits a legal message to a number of atomistic individuals. This communication is unidirectional: the audience is passive. Aristotle presented communication originally as the simple process of a sender with a message targeted at an audience.

To the early Greeks, things were either atoms (simple) or molecules (complex). Audiences were perceived as atomic. This assumed that the message reached the audience, neglecting a possibly active role of that audience (Nehiley, 1997).

However, the simple S-M-R model has already been amended by Aristotle himself through the inserting of "influential others" between the message and reception (Aristotle, 1973). Influencing the audience was important in ancient Greece, where citizens would meet and argue law and politics. Those citizens that argued in the most persuasive way made the laws and exercised political control. In the 1940s, the concept of the audience as an atom in the unidirectional transmitting process gave way to the notion that audiences have their own abilities, relationships and priorities. To put it in ancient Greek terms: audiences are complex. Not all messages are perceived, since people learn in different ways and no one system of information or instruction will work with all. In addition, the audience is not passive, but consists of groups with individual agendas, able to influence the transmitter. A good example is offered by commercial advertising: transmitters "tailor" their messages to increase their effectiveness (Nehiley, 1997). The audience thus plays an active role, rendering the feature of unidirectional communication obsolete in favour of bidirectional communication. This two way-communication generates a transaction process.

In short, contemporary communication theory no longer regards the transmission of information as a static concept, but has changed it into one of transaction. The sender modifies its messages to be acceptable to the receiver, implying that both sender and receiver affect each other (McQuail, 1995).

Revisiting the critique on the sender The traditional definition of instrumentalism sees the legislator as an autonomous, normative-monistic instance that generates unambiguous norms with clear objectives. Let me focus on the three constituting elements of this definition.

First, it is questionable if the policy-maker viz legislator has ever held his autonomy in high esteem. The people in charge of developing legal norms depend heavily on the will of the norms' addressees, in the sense that they form the electorate. The bidirectional aspect of legal communication is quite clear here. Projecting the unidirectional form of communication onto the norm generating process thus does not take the power of the voting mass into account. Second, the presupposition of the exclusivity of the norm construction of the legislator makes abstraction from the fact that policy makers are well accustomed to the tricks of the trades of the political power game. Playing strategy games day in day out throughout their career, they must have gained an insight in the competition that rules the political arena. In addition, the welfare state typically produces compromise legislation, a result of continuing negotiations between political parties and relevant interest groups. Third, and partly as a result of the compromising aspect of policy and law construction, few politicians will walk out of the political arena with the feeling that the resulting law is totally free from ambiguity and states clear objectives.

Revisiting the critique on the transmission of the message According to the analytical deconstruction of instrumentalism, the transmitting process of legal norms is thought of as taking place in a vacuum free of noise and disturbance by other norms. The legal message would reach its audience without interference from outside sources and thus produce the desired effects. In reality, policy makers have developed a more realistic view. The norm constructors must be well aware of the "noise" that distorts their message. That noise falls apart in two categories: first, at the level of acceptance and interpretation by the norm addressees; second, at the level of informal norms that compete with their messages. To overcome these distortions, they traditionally seek refuge in promulgating laws that are not too radical, in accordance with the desires and informal norms that live in society. To impose a law that runs against these societal dynamics would be a brave – or insane – political act.

Revisiting the critique on the receptor The fiction that society is a composition of rational, atomistic, loose individuals has been attributed as an implicit condition to instrumentalism. Nonetheless, it is doubtful that policy-makers disregard the existence of aggregates of people, united as interest groups, families, professional groupings, or any other meta-atomistic unity. In the power game that characterizes politics, politicians are continuously confronted with these aggregates. These groups try to influence the decision-making process, through lobbying, elections and other means, thereby confronting the policy level with customs, habits and attitudes that have often led to the emergence of informal law.

Conclusion In short, the commentaries on instrumentalism relying on untenable theoretical preconditions depart from a strong reduction of the actual political process that generates, in the end, law. This reductionist view holds little affinity with the actual state of affairs in the political arena. I have argued, be it in a concise and tentative way, that instrumentalism can hardly be described as a static, unidirectional S-M-R model. It rather resembles a dynamic transaction process, in which sender and receiver affect each other. However, some of the factors that support the transaction model, such as the emergence of pressure groups, lobbying, the power of the electorate etc., have not always been as predominantly present in the political arena as they are now. A simple example can clarify this: the right to vote has been gradually expanded to all layers of society. Women, e.g., acquired the right to vote no earlier than 1921 on the local level and 1948 on state levels in Belgium. The top-down aspect of legal instrumentalism did thus partly make sense for female norm addressees.[13] This supports the idea that instrumentalism is a dynamic concept, springing from a naive instrumentalism and evolving towards more sophisticated forms. Below, I will elaborate this argument under the heading of an *evolutionary instrumentalism*, a practical paradigm that adapts itself to the societal and political context in which it operates.

On Instrumentalism in Action

A persistent critique on instrumentalism is that it encounters effectiveness problems: a law does not reach the intended effects. This problem has been theoretically elaborated by Teubner (1987), Luhmann (1986) and a host of other authors. Here, I am concerned with the effectiveness of instrumental laws in a "real" setting. The works from Teubner, Luhmann and like-minded theorists excel in the construction of "grand theory", but cannot answer simple questions about facts and figures regarding effectiveness.[14] From an empirical point of view, Vilhem Aubert (1950) conducted a seminal effectiveness study of the Norwegian "Law on Domestic Personnel". This study, empirically and methodologically sound in those days, concluded that the lawmakers' attempt to fundamentally alter the relations between masters and servants was futile.

Unfortunately, this result seems to have cursed the outcome of effectiveness studies ever since. Effectiveness studies seldom show significant effects of a given law on society, or are unable to come to conclusions due to methodological reasons (Griffiths, 2003). This statement demands special caution. First, little unbiased empirical proof exists of ineffective laws, since academics will rather study a law that is not so successful, instead of one that works fine. If all existing laws in effect in a certain area would be examined on the level of effectiveness, the ratio of ineffective over effective laws would be significantly lower than the same ratio as calculated for laws that have actually been subjected to effectiveness research. Second, the methodological knowledge required to conduct these kinds of studies is well beyond the scope of most socio-legal research activities (Van Aeken, 2002). Third, the results of existing studies cannot simply be aggregated to form one general judgment about effectiveness, since the assumptions, research plans, data collections, analyses, and theoretical frameworks employed in each isolated study differ substantially (Cotterrell, 1996).

The bottom line is that more empirical research is needed to reply to the theoretical statements on the domain of effectiveness of instrumental laws. Questions about ineffectiveness and the regulatory crisis in general, must not be answered within a purely theoretical framework, but must be treated on an academic level that values the interplay between empirical investigation and theory construction.

Towards an Evolutionary Instrumentalism

So far, this contribution has aimed at stripping legal instrumentalism from the negative connotations the vast majority of the community of socio-legal scholars attributed to it in the 1980s and 1990s. I have argued that legal instrumentalism and the closely connected social engineering spring from noble, progressive ideas that were badly needed at their time of conception. However, as the welfare state expanded exponentially and the crisis set in, instrumentalism became discredited in many ways. The object of the discrediting was a naive form of instrumentalism, strictly defined through a reductionist perspective. In reality, the instrumental project may never have been that naive. Indeed, the instrumental paradigm has undergone more than one revision so as to align it with the realities of instrumental policy- and law-making. Freed from some of the attributed latent assumptions and the negative aura in general, naive instrumentalism gave way to a sophisticated instrumentalism (Summers, 1980), a critical instrumentalism (Rozemond, 1996) or still, a refined instrumentalism (Bagchus, 1996).

These attempts to shed another light on instrumentalism are certainly worthwhile, since they acknowledge the importance of this perspective. The goal-oriented approach to law (and policy) is flourishing in the political forum (Gribnau, 1999). The demand for instrumental regulation keeps increasing, from the various interest groups in society, and even from the (new) economy, traditionally the first sphere in society to cry for *laissez faire* (Kuttner, 2001). At the same time, many people think we have too many laws. But then again, the emergence of new dangers, new risks and new challenges in society, asks for some kind of regulation. I sum up some phenomena in our current life world that were non-existent or so rare a couple of decades ago that they hardly posed any threat: biotechnology, massive migration, information technology, traffic congestion, chemical and nuclear waste, global terrorism, genotechnology, drug trafficking and abuse, and the disproportional increase of the ageing population.

The developments touched upon above confront instrumentalism with a new problem, which could be formulated as the *regulation paradox*: the demand for regulation increases while the increase of the complexity of the environment, in which the laws have to operate, reduces the chances of reaching the goals of the legislation. This phenomenon forces us to think about the ways we produce laws at the dawn of the 21st century. The development of legisprudence, the scientific study of the creation of laws, can thus only be applauded in this era. Its task is, however, very hard. One of the difficulties with establishing a theory of the norm generating process nowadays is precisely that the creation of norms takes place under ever faster changing societal conditions. Our society becomes more "globally complex" (Urry, 2003), more "liquid" (Bauman, 2000) or more "risky" (Beck, 1992) – the vagueness of these terms already shows how tough it is to grasp current events and the underlying trends, even for renowned social scientists. This inspires an evolutionary approach to things under the banner "all is in flux, nothing abides" (Heraklitus, 5th century BC).

Such an evolutionary approach is very well applicable to the instrumental paradigm: its dominancy in the political arena is only possible through continuing adaptation to a changing context. It is trivial that the naive form of instrumentalism is untenable: if the traditional definitions of instrumentalism would still carry some resemblance to actual instrumental reasoning, one could not explain why the instrumental project has not been blown up decades ago. The instrumental vision thus adapts itself to a changing societal context. Therefore, new "static" descriptions of instrumentalism, as the abovementioned "critical" of "sophisticated" forms, may need revision even in the near future.

At the same time, a radical turning back to the past is neither the most elegant, nor the wisest, way to deal with the regulation paradox or to contribute to a science of legisprudence. Convinced that a *happy medium* generally offers the best possible outcome between extremes, I suggest an evolutionary instrumentalism that embraces the utopian features of traditional instrumentalism on the one hand, and opens up to the pragmatic prerequisites of present day lawgiving on thc other hand. Such an instrumentalism is in constant motion and can therefore hardly be pinned down on some everlasting characteristics. Nevertheless, I will sketch the main conditions that the revisited instrumental project at least has to fulfil to safeguard its future. Some of these conditions may be already (partly) fulfilled in current forms of instrumentalism in western post-industrial nations, a finding that corresponds to its evolutionary nature. Some of the most urgent properties instrumentalism will have to display, are (1) the introduction of the notion of *probability* in instrumental thinking, (2) the systematic *evaluation* of laws and (3) the opening up to *alternatives* in, to and for legal regulation.

Probability

As explained above, the definition of naive instrumentalism includes numerous presuppositions. Since naive instrumentalists are suspected to silently believe that these conditions are fulfilled, they should expect a trouble-free goal attainment. Indeed, according to this scenario, the legal norm that is promulgated travels smoothly from the legislator to the norm addressee that, being an obedient and rational person, immediately complies with the norm. This scenario is in stark contrast with evolutionary instrumentalism that departs from the uncertainty that rules the world and the resulting inability to program the future according to preset parameters.

This uncertainty may not, however, paralyze the lawgiver so that no action at all is undertaken. But what has to be done then in a world where one of the few certainties left is uncertainty? A possible way out may be found in the solutions sought by contemporary architecture. After September 11, 2001, dealing with a highly variable and contingent planning context has become a hot topic in the architectural debate. Indeed, what is the use of drawing high-rise constructions when their realizations may be erased in seconds?

Following the "theory exhaustion" of the 1990s, an era in which the theoretical reflection on architecture was heavily influenced by French post-structuralists such as Foucault, Derrida and Deleuze (Sewing, 2001), a return to Pragmatism[15] took place. As Ockman, director of the Temple Hoyne Buell Center for the Study of American architecture at Columbia University, puts it:

> It is no accident that this distinctively American philosophy, which emerged contemporaneously with modernism and industrial capitalism, has returned at a post-modern, pan-capitalist moment, after the truth claims of other twentieth-century theories and systems have been discredited and at a time when a more supple relationship to a fast changing reality is being demanded. (Ockman, 2001, p. 5)

Some of the features of this rediscovered Pragmatism may offer valuable contributions to architecture, be it an architecture of cities and buildings through the use of concrete and steel, or an architecture of society through legislation. Pragmatists orientate themselves to the "things in the making", to a "living understanding of the movement of reality". Therefore, they remain sceptical about *a priori* truths and judge instead ideas on their consequences in reality, their pay-off in the world. With regard to architecture, Pragmatism is especially relevant in three respects (Ockman, 2001). Two of these show relevancy to both architecture and legal instrumentalism. First, Pragmatism presents itself as a theory of practice. This is a valuable property in the field of architecture in which architectural theory and practice had become polarized since the 1960s. "Constructing" practitioners and "deconstructing" academics stood miles apart. With the "streets" and the "elites" moving closer, 21st century's architecture can "refocus its intellectual energies onto the complex, messy, situational realities of the built environment" (Ockman, 2001, p. 7). Second, contemporary architecture is concerned with experimental forms of inquiry and technological innovation. With the laboratory as the central model for thought or imagination, it is easily understandable that experimentation, action and experience are keywords of the Pragmatic approach.

Now, what does the embrace of Pragmatism by architecture teach us as far as the elaboration of an evolutionary instrumentalism in the framework of legisprudence is concerned? I see three converging elements.

First, Pragmatist architecture acknowledges the importance of a "more supple relationship to a fast changing reality", thus refraining from static "grand theory" and judging ideas in the light of their consequences in reality. This is mirrored in revisiting instrumentalism as an "evolutionary" paradigm: instrumental lawmaking continuously adapts itself to the context in which it operates. Whereas the instrumental use of law may have been rather straightforward at the end of the 19th century, in the sense that a linear relationship between means and goals could rightfully be presumed, this situation has changed drastically over the course of the last decades. The operating context has become more complex, so that many factors may now hinder a linear goal attainment. Consider a simple example: a state introduces higher wages for workers to increase their standard of living. In 1900, such a law could be effective without too many side-effects. In 2000, however, this could lead to the delocalization of some industries to low wage countries, inflicting poverty to the laid-off workers. The complexity factor that intervenes here is globalization. In other words, whereas the law in 1903 would almost certainly reach its goal, this has become questionable a century later. A linear relationship between means and ends must thus be abandoned in favour of *probability*. Evolutionary instrumentalism takes the fluidity of society into account by refraining from a naive, straightforward goal attainment as an *a priori* truth. Instead, it departs from the probability of accomplishing a desired situation by the lawmakers. A law has a probability of reaching its goals. The level of probability of goal attainment is (almost) never 100 per cent, but varies according to a host of factors that may influence its success. In the simple example of increasing wages, one of these factors was globalization. By introducing probability, evolutionary instrumentalism thus expresses the strong sense of realism that is typical for Pragmatism.[16]

Second, Pragmatism presents itself as a theory of practice. In the light of the relationship between politics and law, an evolutionary approach to instrumentalism promotes such a theory of practice. The mere studying of the law from an academic viewpoint, often leading to a detachment of law from its political roots, carries the danger of losing the grip on reality. Contemporary legal science, e.g. as presented under a theory of legisprudence, acknowledges the intimate relationship between the political forum and the law (see, e.g., Eriksson, 2002; Eng, 2002; Tuori, 2002; Winter, 1996). A theory of evolutionary instrumentalism learns from political practice; in turn, it offers a practical tool for politicians who are in one way or another committed to shape society through legislation.

Third, contemporary architecture has inherited the concern with action and experimentation from the classic Pragmatists. They are not paralyzed by unworkable grand theories, which carry the risk of becoming cut off from a fast changing reality, but are still able to act. Here, the idea of "social experimentation" comes close (Campbell, 1999). In the "experimenting society", scientific research is seen as a cornerstone, with a never-ending step-wise improvement of policy in mind (Campbell, 1988). The importance of scientific research was already recognized by the Legal Realists (Duxbury, 1995) and was a main feature of instrumentalism (Summers, 1980). In a theory of evolutionary instrumentalism, it becomes an even more prominent property under the form of the scientific project of evaluation. The picture thus becomes as follows: the lawmaker acts, guided by *ex ante* evaluations, and reflects on what he has been doing by *ex post* evaluations. This acting takes place in a step-wise, incremental way, as opposed to holistic, dictatorial engineering that relies on "great leaps forward". This concept has been elegantly described by Popper in *The Poverty of Historicism*:

> The piecemeal engineer knows, like Socrates, how little he knows. He knows that we can learn only from our mistakes. Accordingly, he will make his way, step by step, carefully comparing the results expected with the results achieved, and always on the look-out for the unavoidable unwanted consequences of any reform; and he will avoid undertaking reforms of a complexity and scope which make it impossible for him to disentangle cause and effects, and to know what he is really doing. (Popper, 1964, p. 67)

The author shows a remarkable sensitivity to evaluation in this quote. Comparing the expected results with the achieved results and disentangling causes and effects, form the central elements of the *ex post* evaluation of effectiveness (Van Aeken, 2002). The carefulness and respect the engineer must display, in addition to the concern about unwanted consequences, mark some of the essentials of the *ex ante* evaluation of effectiveness. These evaluations are necessary, since the piecemeal engineer knows but little, and certainly not what will result from his engineering work. Indeed, it is only with a certain probability that the engineer can "guesstimate" what the effects of his actions will be. This "guesstimation" will be translated into evaluation below. Evaluation is the core element of a living instrumentalism. Before I will embark in a discussion of evaluation, I recapitulate.

By now, I am able to come to a conclusion regarding the first feature of evolutionary instrumentalism. Learning from what physical architecture has learned from Pragmatism, I have gathered the following ideas for legal architecture: the lawgiver must recognize that a law only has a probability of reaching its goals. This probability is determined by a complex interplay of societal conditions. That forces the rulegiving bodies to operate incrementally. The lesser the estimated probability of goal attainment, the more prudently the lawgiver has to act. Cautiousness then means carefully experimenting with laws and policy, which could imply involving fewer people, covering a smaller territory or spending less money. These findings inspire a theory of practice: a theory of evolutionary instrumentalism that theorizes what is going on in the political forum, but offers at the same time guidance to the lawmakers. The connection of politics and law, finally, is in accordance with the realism as displayed in recent writings in the field of legisprudence.

Evaluation

To assess or improve the probability that rules have the desired consequences, evaluation presents itself as an extremely valuable tool in the hands of the rule makers. I will concisely focus on definition, types, purposes, context and tailoring of evaluation research, and top this discussion off by returning to the probability issue.

Evaluation of legal rules offers a means for the operationalizing evolutionary instrumentalism. With the introduction of the concept of probability in lawmaking, the concept of an instrumental paradigm gains more validity and credibility. Evaluation, in turn, can translate the renewed concept in a practical course of action for the rule constructing body. Ideally, evaluation becomes a reflex in the law-producing process, leading to the emergence of an *evaluation culture*.

Definition Evaluation is a daily routine. We evaluate the quality of fresh fruit in the supermarket. We evaluate a football game. We evaluate a potential sister-in-law or son-in-law. In doing so, we adopt certain criteria. Apples may not be bruised or wrinkled. A football game should be exciting. A potential sister-in-law or son-in-law or partner should be reliable and trustworthy.

When legislative evaluation is concerned, we also refer to certain criteria to assess the "quality" of a law (Winter, 1996). In this case, the criteria are of a somewhat different nature, since we aim at a more abstract definition of evaluation. The criteria, by which we make an assessment about some rule, are the criteria used for scientific and juridical research.

What does this mean? First, evaluation studies make use of empirical data and theory in the domain that is researched. Second, since it concerns legislative evaluation, legal studies are involved. It also means that common judgement, based on non-systematic observation, is not a valid evaluation strategy. Furthermore, it means that a purely legistic studying of some rules is not a "full" evaluation, since it lacks empirical content.

Evaluation is thus the judging of regulation based upon specific criteria for scientific and juridical research. It falls apart in different forms, which we will describe in the next paragraph.

Types Simply put, three forms of evaluation research exist. The first and most common is called evaluation *ex post*, and has as its object an existing piece of regulation. Synonyms are product evaluation and retrospective evaluation. Another form deals with regulation that has yet to be put into effect, typically in the stage when negotiations take place in law-making bodies, such as a parliament. This form is called evaluation *ex ante*, plan evaluation or prospective evaluation. A third form relates to regulation that is being implemented, and focuses on the implementation process. Therefore, it is called process evaluation.[17]

Evaluation *ex post* is by far the most developed type of the three; process and prospective evaluation studies are less common. However, the latter types are on the rise. Why has it been so long before the breakthrough of these types took place? In our explanation, we refer to the case of evaluation *ex ante*. Since the lawgiving process is dominated primarily by ideological motivations, rather than by scientific reasoning, the demand for prospective evaluation studies is very low (Van Houtte, 1995). Also, policy makers and legislators are confronted with serious time constraints, so that there often is not enough time to have a regulation evaluated. Another reason for the arrears of *ex ante* evaluation, is the difficulties with the methodology: everyone knows that it is very hard to predict the future, and that is exactly what one wants in this case.

In general, prospective evaluation studies are now catching up with the more common retrospective studies. This is partly due to the insight that is better to prevent a bad law from being implemented, than to cure a bad law that is already into effect, and partly due to the emergence of new methods and techniques that facilitate predictions and simulations. However, countries with a very basic evaluation culture will typically overlook the importance of prospective evaluation research.[18]

Purposes and objectives Good evaluation research starts from a well-defined question. One can ask whether a law that reduces emission of carbon monoxide leads to a cleaner environment. One can also ask whether the benefits of that law outweigh the costs. Another option is to study the legal "quality" of that particular law. Rossi *et al.* (1999) present a structured list of possible objectives of evaluation studies. First, the necessity of a law can be the theme of the evaluation. Is the law, or any other type of regulation, really necessary? Second, objectives can be formulated regarding the validity of a theory that underlies the governmental intervention. In reducing the surface of the ozone hole, e.g., it is of primary importance to know which chemical emissions contribute to the enlarging of that hole. Third, the focus can be put upon the implementation of the regulation. How well do enforcement agencies, e.g., function in maintaining speeding laws? Next, the objective may be the studying of the impact of a certain intervention. Does the intervention create the desired results? What other effects are generated by the intervention? Fifth, one can ask questions about the efficiency of the law. Efficiency assessment answers questions about program costs and cost-effectiveness. Finally, one can also ask questions about the legal status of some regulation, like the compatibility with other regulations, legal security and the principle of the clear objective or right level etc.

Since evaluation of legislation can have very different objectives, it is clear that every individual evaluation study asks for a particular set-up. The object of an evaluation (a new or existent law) and the definition of the objectives (from necessity to legal status) determine in part the form of the study. But there are more factors that shape evaluation research: the methodology and the context involving the relationship between the different actors in the process. The former factor is extremely important, since it determines the quality of the evaluation, but this contribution is not the place to enlarge on a discussion of methods and techniques. The latter I will comment on in the next subsection.

Context This subsection deals with the role of the different actors in the process of legislative evaluation and the institutionalization of that process.

A variety of actors is involved in an evaluation study (Swanborn, 1999). It all starts with the initiator of the regulator, commonly policy makers, lawgiving bodies or groupings thereof. Another major player is the target population. Next to these, a varied group of third parties exists. This group consists of involved pressure- and interest groups, the evaluation sponsor, umbrella organizations, personnel, management within the administration, financing institutions and so on.

One trivial player may not be overlooked: the evaluator. A very important factor for a successful evaluation is a good understanding between the evaluator(s) and the stakeholders. The way the researcher and the stakeholders interact can take on different forms (Rossi *et al.* 1999). If the interaction is intense and frequent, one uses the term participative evaluation. Sometimes, when the group of people with great interests in the legislation has little participation in the legislative process, the evaluation itself can help in boosting their involvement. In this case, we use the term empowerment evaluation. The evaluator stakeholder relationship is participatory and collaborative, as described above, but there is an extra touch of emancipatory support. This means that the evaluation process is not only directed at producing informative findings, but also at enhancing the self-development and political influence of the participants. Opposed to these participatory evaluations stands the independent evaluation. The evaluator then takes the primary responsibility for the conducting of the study.

Now that we have described players and their possible forms of interaction, another important question presents itself: what should the institutional context look like in which these actors operate? If this context is too weak, no incentives will be provided for the systematic conducting of evaluation studies, thus limiting evaluation to ad hoc occasions. Hence there is a need for the institutionalization of the evaluation of regulation, meaning that evaluation takes place under certain organizational provisions. This means that there exist well-defined answers for the following questions: who initiates an evaluation study, who carries it out, how are the results validated? The solutions are captured in an organizational context. As always, different contexts present themselves. On the one hand, the organization and the conducting of the research are consigned to cells or departments that are separated from the legislative work and the governmental administration. These cells often have highly qualified personnel and the required know-how. Nevertheless, some caution is in place. Since their activities are located out of the policy forum, their role in delivering prospective or process evaluations is limited. Also, "in-flight" corrections are hampered, since the isolation from the administrative and policy actors is substantial. Finally, feedback of the results to the political community is not secured, due to that very isolation (Van Humbeeck, 2000).

Another extreme is the positioning of the evaluation activities within the administrative structures that make the laws. While the problems described above can be dealt with, other problems arise. The evaluators are naturally concerned with the incentives and objectives of the regulatory organisms of which their administration depends, thus creating the possibility that evaluation research degenerates in the direction of a formalistic ritual without real content or impact. Another obstacle is the lack of methodological know-how and personnel's skills in the administration (Van Aeken, Jacob, Varone, 2003).

Full centralization or decentralization of the evaluation activities is thus not recommended. Rather, I suggest a "happy medium", meaning that some specialized cells that are counselled and monitored by central units carry out the actual evaluation studies.

Tailoring I have demonstrated above that evaluation research implies making many choices. These choices are related to the type of the evaluation (*ex ante*, process or *ex post*); the objectives of the study (necessity of the regulation, validity of the underlying theory, implementation, impact, efficiency and juridical aspects); the context (actors and organization) and the method. It is thus clear that no "cookbook-strategy" can be followed to conduct an evaluation. Too many options have to be filled in. Therefore, one speaks about "tailoring an evaluation" (Rossi *et al.* 1999). Every evaluation must be tailored to the regulation it examines, taking into account the different choices mentioned above. This implies that the planning of an evaluation requires a thorough investigating of the evaluation situation and the stakeholders involved. In the case of emancipatory regulation, this means that evaluators should get in touch with the administrators of the regulation as well as the main stakeholders (with the emphasis on the group of people that have suffered or are still potentially suffering from discrimination). In doing so, the unique profile of characteristics of the evaluation situation can be taken into account, and translated into a unique evaluation design with a human touch.

Evaluation and probability enhancement Whereas I have been broadening the scope of evaluation research to issues not directly related to the topic of evolutionary instrumentalism and the problems it has to tackle, I now return to the main thesis, the revisiting of instrumental rule constructing. Evaluation takes up a prominent position in an evolutionary instrumentalism, by offering a practical answer to the uncertainties that rule the world and the resulting policy paradox. In the "laboratory language" of the Pragmatists, evaluation would be concerned with the optimalization of the probability of reaching the intended effects of rules. Allow me to clarify this.

Regarding the development of future rules, it is clear that different legislative paths may lead to different outcomes. Evaluation is thus concerned with assessing the probability of these different routes of action. Suppose the rule giver wants to reduce the number of alcohol-related traffic accidents, and the number of alternative ways of regulation is limited to two: passing a new law that lowers the legal intoxication threshold, enforced through heavy policy monitoring; or increasing the price of alcohol. To predict possible outcomes, in order to compare them and opting for the most effective way of policy, *ex ante* evaluation research enters the picture. This research can draw on a variety of sources: simulation, prediction on the basis of behavioural theories, experiences throughout space and time (notably comparable countries or regions or the same geographical area in the past); or results from existing *ex post* studies of equivalent phenomena.

The scope of methodological possibilities is almost unlimited, but it remains very hard to predict the future, due to the complex context. As stated earlier, one way to deal with this unpredictability, is refraining from drastic measures if probability assessment is difficult, or yields meagre results. Low probability demands caution.

As for the evaluation of existing measures, *ex post* evaluation offers the possibility of assessing what has actually become of the good intentions. In case the results achieved do not match the goals expected, some remedy is in place. In the case of piecewise social engineering, the "wrong" done can still be repaired, since effects are not "holistic". This repairing can take place through a revision of the rules under discussion, or through looking for a whole new approach.

Combining the prudent scientific approach as laid down in *ex ante* and *ex post* evaluation, I have arrived at a new feature of evolutionary instrumentalism: comparative probability studies can make clear that traditional legislation is not the best way to intervene in a certain field of society. *Ex post* evaluations can reveal that the legislation at stake was not the best way to act. This will be the theme of the next paragraph.

Metanomism: Opening up to Alternatives in, to and for Legal Regulation

Under the former heading, we described a fictitious case within which the policy maker had to choose between tackling driving under the influence through a restricting law or by means of increasing taxes. Still another possibility would be to change attitudes of people towards drink driving. Yet another approach could depart from infrastructural investments, increasing general traffic safety without regard to the actual drinking and driving behaviour, since alcohol-related accidents are very stochastic in nature (Van Aeken, 2002). The precision of decision making thus depends on *ex ante* evaluation. In most cases – i.e., when the problem is an old one and already "treated" by the government in one way or another – there would be already certain laws in effect. We can then conduct an *ex post* evaluation study, empirically assessing the effectiveness of the policy in effect. In the framework of my doctoral research, I examined the effectiveness of a Belgian law that lowered the legal blood alcohol content limits and enacted stronger penalties for offenders.[19] After overcoming many empirical and methodological bottlenecks, I came to the conclusion that the downward trend in alcohol-related accidents also manifested itself in the time series of non-alcohol related crashes. No statistically significant surplus decrease of alcohol-related accidents in relationship to the general level of accidents could be attributed to the restricting law.

In essence, this evaluation was of an instrumental nature. Some may argue that instrumental evaluations are useless (Griffiths, 1996, 2003). Yet, when reasoning beyond traditional instrumentalism, important conclusions may be drawn. Stronger penalties and stronger enforcement only had a very temporary effect, in this case about a month. The real progression in traffic safety came from elsewhere. While the method employed, univariate time series analysis, could not identify the factors responsible for improved traffic safety, I was able to conclude that classic legal action was not the optimal way to tackle the problem of drunk driving. Feeding back these findings to the political body, it should open up the debate about alternatives to legal regulation. While the evaluation research on driving under the influence was of an *ex post* nature, the results can be transposed to *ex ante* evaluation. The government, always keen on reducing traffic fatalities, can rely on the results of earlier (*ex post*) evaluation studies to shape future regulation. It is clear that the future tackling of the driving and drinking problem must not solely depend on legal rules; the highest probability of reaching satisfying results can be obtained with a blend of non-legal and legal measures. To obtain a more precise idea of the ingredients and their relative weight in this mixture, further *ex ante* research is necessary.

It would lead us too far now to go into details regarding the different possibilities for regulation outside the realm of traditional legislation. Instead, we offer a concise overview of the possibilities, based on Luc Wintgens' (2003) distinction between law as an alternative, alternatives for legal regulation, and alternatives in law.

"Law as an alternative" carries a message that is very similar to what follows from the paragraphs above: law has lost its status as the pre-eminent tool for steering society. In the first instance, society is supposed to regulate itself without interference from a legislator. Only when social communication or social relations are distorted in an unacceptable way, may people resort to law and its ordering capacities. Legal rules are thus not longer regarded as the main tools to shape society; it is society itself that puts its regulatory capacities at the forefront. I would like to call this a shift to "metanomic" thinking: in the political forum, the strong habit to develop a (formal) law to solve a societal problem should be broken. Formal law is but one tool in the toolbox of the contemporary social engineer. That is what I try to express by using the adjective "meta". We must move "beyond" the law to steer society. This does, however, not imply that law is rendered obsolete. On the contrary, I would say. Just as celebrating mass on a daily basis would deflate the intrinsic value of going to church, to come back to the anecdotical illustration I gave earlier, the quasi automatic employment of laws could contribute to a loss of meaning. A conscious, mature use of (formal) law could enrich the underlying policy with very special properties. In this respect, we might think of surplus values inherent to law as expressed by "the morality of law" (Fuller, 1965) or the "integrity of law" (Dworkin, 1986). I leave the discussion of these properties to scholars who are less ignorant in the field of legal philosophy than I am, but I hope I have made my point.

Returning to the alternatives Wintgens suggest, a first option is formulating alternatives *in* law. That means that legal regulation can be "upgraded" to a higher quality level, retaining its status as a law. Different techniques enter into competition for this task, as there are the principles of subsidiarity, collaboration, combination, adequacy or velocity.

If an evaluation suggests that legislation is not the most optimal way of regulating a certain sphere of society, the alternatives *for* law enter the stage. Their number is limited only by our imagination, covering already an amazing variety of approaches. We restrict ourselves to summing up some common forms, relying on Wintgens (2002): self-regulation, deregulation, broad or general law, alternative dispute resolution, licenses, certificates, labelling, convenants, self implementing regulation, information, sunset legislation etc. The alternatives for law are especially in vogue in the world of business: a Google search on the internet for "self regulation in business" yielded 1,990,000 hits.[20] Since the economy is a thriving force in our affluent society, self-regulation will still gain in importance. The application and study of self-regulation will unavoidably lead to a further examination of the construction of traditional law and alternatives, in close connection to the development of an all-embracing theory of legisprudence. I hope that evolutionary instrumentalism, as a theory of practice, may contribute to this new body of theory.

* Koen Van Aeken is co-director of the Centrum voor Rechtssociologie (Centre for the Sociology of Law) of the University of Antwerp, Belgium.

Notes

1 The reference to government does not imply the denial of legal pluralism, but serves as a delineating condition in our framework, mirroring the concern about governmental intervention through legal instrumentalism.

2 "Instrumentalism" sometimes appears as "instrumentality". However, I restrict myself to the use of "instrumentalism" since its meaning is clear, a property that is not completely shared by the term "instrumentality" (see, e.g., Focqué and 't Hart, 1990).

3 For an elaborate commentary, see the doctoral dissertation of Van Aeken (2002).

4 Nazi Germany offers another strong historical bookmark in the discrediting of instrumentalism. The restriction made to (Soviet) Russia is based upon the persistence of instrumental thinking in lawmaking in that area. Even in Russia's imperial legal tradition, i.e. before communism, the belief that law was above all a method for achieving policy goals has been quite dominant. On the other end of the timescale, after the breakdown of communism, the instrumental view on law is not yet obsolete. A rather remarkable example of contemporary naive legal instrumentalism was a bill in the Russian Duma in 2000, which would legalize polygamy. Its main objective was to boost the country's dwindling birth rate (Popova, 2003).

5 Following a discussion with V. Olgiati at the Annual Meeting of the RCSL in Oxford, July 2003, where I presented an earlier version of this contribution. I am grateful to the attendees of the RCSL conference and of the Special Workshop on Legisprudence at the conference of the IVR in Lund in August 2003 for their valuable comments.

6 Some theorists believe that his work may have inspired Franklin Delano Roosevelt's New Deal program in the 1930s. See *The Columbia Encyclopaedia*, Sixth Edition, 2001 (online at http://www.bartleby.com/65/po/Pound-Ro.html).

7 Neil Duxbury's "Patterns of American Jurisprudence" departs from legal formalism, dominating the courts and the legal text books in North America between 1860 and 1930. Formalism can, according to the author, be reduced to two elements: the rise of legal sciences following Langdellian principles and a deeply rooted belief in the principle of *laissez faire* (Duxbury, 1997). While the latter principle originally holds for legal procedures in the courts, it also holds for politics.

8 *Times*, Obituary, 3 July 1964.

9 It should be noted that Roscoe Pound was a prominent botanist as well as a jurist, and spent his early years in Nebraska practising and teaching law, simultaneously serving as director of the state botanical survey (1892–1903).

10 James' quest for adventure and the undertaking of risks is easily extrapolated to Ulrich Beck's Risk Society. Early 20th century, the risks of new technologies were almost unknown. Even then, however, disasters such as the sinking of the Titanic in 1912 must have induced a embryonic awareness of technological risks. But the awareness of risk did not convincingly "trickle up" to the social sciences until the 1980s.

11 This scheme serves analytical purposes only. It stands isolated from the "Law as Communication" movement that has recently been generating a lot of academic attention, following the seminal work by Habermas (1992). A steady flow of publications followed (e.g. Nelken, 1996; Van Hoecke, 2002). In the Netherlands, the communicative approach to law is especially popular at the University of Tilburg. Elsewhere, it faces tough critique. See, e.g., the chapter "Communicatief recht versus de sociale werking van recht" by Havinga a.o. in Van Aeken and Van Loon (2002).

12 Rottleuthner, e.g., attributes the relative success of the thesis of the regulatory crisis in part to "a certain atmosphere in which political clichés constitute a 'plausibility structure' within which assumptions about the (...) crisis and deregulation can be easily framed" (Rottleuthner, 1989, p. 274).

13 This is true for their formal involvement in the lawmaking process. On the other hand, it is very plausible that women exercised control over legal norm constructing before 1948 through informal channels, e.g. through influencing their husbands, male relatives and friends (with the right to vote); through their participation in semi-autonomous social fields such as schools and the family; through interest groups such as associations of nurses, etc.

14 The speculative nature of their work inspired many a heated debate (see e.g., Rottleuthner, 1991 and a reply from Smith, 1991).

15 I use deliberately a capital P in Pragmatism to distinguish from pragmatism, the latter more often than not pejoratively associated with practicality, expediency and naive instrumentalism (Ockman, 2001).

16 The study of legisprudence embraces this realism. See, e.g., Eriksson (2002).

17 Often but incorrectly dubbed as "monitoring". Monitoring is only a part of process evaluation, since its main objective is the gathering of data, needed for the far more fundamental process evaluation.

18 The USA, UK, Canada, Australia and the Netherlands have a well-developed evaluation culture, and pay a lot of attention to "impact studies". Countries with a less developed evaluation culture, such as Belgium, typically overlook *ex ante* studies in their first attempts to institutionalize evaluation research.

19 "Wet van 18 juli 1990 (B.S., 8/11/1990) tot wijziging van hoofdstuk 5 van de wet betreffende de politie over het wegverkeer van maart 1968 (B.S., 27/3/1968)." This law came into effect on December 1st, 1994, through the K.B. of November 21st, 1994 (B.S., 29/11/1994).

20 December 1, 2003.

References

Aristotle (1973), *The Rhetoric*, Arno Press, New York (reprint from the 1877 edition, Cambridge University Press, Cambridge).

Beck, U. (1992), *Risk Society*, Sage, London.

Bagchus, R. (1996), *Waardevolle instrumenten. De totstandkoming van beleidsinstrumenten als plicht, ritueel en zoektocht naar legitimiteit*, doctorale dissertatie, Erasmus Universiteit, Rotterdam.

Bauman, Z. (2000), *Liquid Modernity*, Polity, Cambridge.

Campbell, D.T. (1988), 'The experimenting society' in E.S. Overman (ed.), *Methodology and Epistemology for Social Sciences: Selected Papers*, University of Chicago Press, Chicago.

Campbell, D.T. and Russo, M.J. (1999), *Social Experimentation*, Sage, Thousand Oaks.

Cotterrell, R. (1996), *The Sociology of Law. An Introduction*, Butterworths, Edinburgh.

Deflem, M. (1992), 'De Communicatie-Theoretische Benadering van het Recht', *Recht en Kritiek*, Vol. 18, pp. 235-258.

Durkheim, E. (1983), *Pragmatism and Sociology*, Cambridge University Press, Cambridge (first edition 1914).

Duxbury, N. (1995), *Patterns of American Jurisprudence*, Clarendon Press, Oxford.

Dworkin, R. (1986), *Law's Empire*, Cambridge University Press, Cambridge.

Eng, S. (2002), 'Legislative Inflation and the Quality of Law' in L.J. Wintgens (ed.), *Legisprudence. A New Theoretical Approach to Legislation*, Hart Publishing.

Eriksson, L.D. (2002), 'Making society through Legislation' in L.J. Wintgens (ed.), *Legisprudence. A New Theoretical Approach to Legislation*, Hart Publishing.

Fortson, R. (1999), 'Three Roles for a Theory of Behavior in a Theory of Law. A Commentary on a talk by Lewis Kornhauser', *Stanford Journal of Legal Studies*, Vol 1, pp. 30-34.

Fuller, L. (1965), *The Morality of Law*, Yale University Press, New Haven.

Gribnau, J.L.M. (1999), 'Het instrumentalisme viert hoogtij', *Nederlands Juristenblad*, Vol. 74, pp. 1890-1891.

Griffiths, J. (1978), 'Is Law Important?', *New York University Law Review*, Vol. 54, pp. 339-375.

Griffiths, J. (1996), (ed.) *De Sociale Werking van Recht. Een kennismaking met de rechtssociologie en de rechtsantropologie*, Ars Aequi Libri, Nijmegen.

Griffiths, J. (2003), 'The social working of legal rules', *Journal of Legal Pluralism*, Vol. 48, pp. 1-72.

Habermas, J. (1992), *Faktizität und Geldtung. Beiträge zur Diskurstheorie des Rechts und des demokratischen Rechtsstaats*, Suhrkamp Verlag, Frankfurt.

Havinga, T., van Klink, B., Weyers, H., Schwitters, R., Zeegers, N., Hertogh, M. (2002), 'Communicatief recht versus de sociale werking van recht' in K. Van Aeken and F. Van Loon, F., *De toekomst van de rechtssociologie in het justitieel beleid*, UFSIA, Antwerp, pp. 29-89.

Johnson, P. (1983), *A History of the Modern World. From 1917 to the 1980s*, Weidenfeld and Nicholson, London.

Kuttner, R. (2001), 'Sorry, but the new economy demands new regulations', *Business Week*, July 30, pp. 23.

Le Corbusier-Saugnier (1923), *Vers une architecture*, Collection de l'esprit nouveau, Les Editions G. Cres et Cie, Paris.

Levitas, R. (2000), 'Discourses of Risk and Utopia' in B. Adam, U. Beck and J. Van Loon, *The Risk Society and Beyond*, Sage Publications, London.

Luhmann, N. (1986), 'The self-reproduction of Law and its Limits' in G. Teubner (ed.), *Dilemmas of Law in the Welfare State*, European University Institute Series A Law 3, Walter de Gruyter, Berlin/New York.

Mcquail, D. (1996), *Communication Models for the Study of Mass Communication*, Longman, London/New York.

Moore, S.F. (1978), 'Law and Social Change: the Semi-autonomous Social Field as an Appropriate Subject of Study' in S.F. Moore and M. Chanock, *Law as Process: An Anthropological Approach*, Routledge & Kegan Paul London.

Nelken, D. (1996) *Law as Communication: Constituting the Field*, Dartmouth, Aldershot.

Nehiley, J.M. (1997), *The Role of the Audience in the Communication Process*, AEC 317, Department of Agricultural Education and Communication, Florida Cooperative Extension Service, Institute of Food and Agricultural Sciences, University of Florida.

Ockman, J. (2001), 'Pragmatism and Architecture', *Arquitectura Vivenda Monographs*, Vol. 91, pp. 4-7.

Podgórecki, A. (1996), *Social Engineering*, Carleton University Press, Carleton.

Popova, M. (2003), *Russian objections to the rule of law doctrine*, discussion paper, Department of Government, Harvard University.

Popper, K. (1964), *The Poverty of Historicism*, Routledge and Kegan, New York.

Pound, R. (1942), *Social Control through the Law*, Archon Books, New York.

Rossi, P.H., Freeman, H.E and Lipsey, M.W. (1999), *Evaluation. A Systematic Approach*, 6th ed., Sage, Thousand Oaks.

Rottleuthner, H. (1987), *Einführung in die Rechtssoziologie*, Wissentschaftliche Buchgesellschaft, Darmstadt.

Rottleuthner, H. (1989), 'The limits of Law – The myth of a regulatory crisis', *International Journal of the Sociology of Law*, Vol. 17, pp. 273-285.

Rozemond, K. (1996), 'Pleidooi voor een kritisch instrumentalisme', *Rechtsfilosofie en Rechtstheorie*, Vol. 25, pp. 169-191.

Schuyt, C.J.M. (1985), 'Sturing en het recht' in M.A.P. Bovens and W.J. Witteveen (eds.), *Het schip van staat. Beschouwingen over recht, staat en sturing*, Tjeenk Willink, Zwolle.

Schwitters, R. (1991), *De risico's van de arbeid. Het ontstaan van de Ongevallenwet 1901 in sociologisch perspectief*, Wolters-Noordhoff, Groningen.

Schwitters, R. (2000), *Recht en samenleving in verandering*, Kluwer, Deventer.

Sewing, W. (2001), 'From Deleuze to Dewey?', *Arquitectura Vivenda Monographs*, Vol. 91, pp. 8-13.

Smith, S.C. (1991), 'Beyond "Mega-theory and "Multiple Sociology": A Reply to Rottleuthner', *International Journal of the Sociology of Law*, Vol. 19, pp. 321-340.

Summers, R. (1980), *Het pragmatisch instrumentalisme*, Standaard Wetenschappelijke Uitgeverij, Antwerp/Amsterdam.

Summers, R. (1982), *Instrumentalism and American Legal Theory*, Cornell University Press, Ithaca.

Swanborn, P.G. (1999), *Evalueren*, Boom, Amsterdam.

Teubner, G. (1987), *Juridification of Social Spheres*, European University Institute Series A Law 6, Walter de Gruyter, Berlin – New York.

Tuori, K. (2002), 'Legislation Between Politics and Law' in L.J. Wintgens (ed.), *Legisprudence. A New Theoretical Approach to Legislation*, Hart Publishing, Oxford.

Urry, J. (2003), *Global Complexity*, Polity, Cambridge.

Van Aeken, K. (2002), *Proeven van wetsevaluatie. Een empirisch geïllustreerde studie naar het wat, hoe en waarom van wetsevaluatie, Proefschrift*, Universiteit Antwerpen, Antwerp.

Van Aeken, K. (2003), 'Wetsevaluatie tussen woord en daad', *Tijdschrift voor wetgeving*, Vol. 5, pp. 31-37.

Van Aeken, K. and Van Loon, F. (2002), *De toekomst van de rechtssociologie in het justitieel beleid*, UFSIA, Antwerp.

Van Aeken, K., Jacob, S. and Varone, F. (2003), 'Beleidsevaluatie : een sturingsinstrument voor het overheidshandelen', *Vlaams Tijdschrift voor Overheidsmanagement*, Vol. 8, pp. 29-37.

Van Hoecke, M. (2002), *Law as Communication*, Hart Publishing, Oxford.

Van Houtte, J. (1995), 'Is recht belangrijk? De functies van het recht in de maatschappij: veiligheid, sociale relaties, een humanere samenleving', *Economisch en Sociaal Tijdschrift*, Vol. 49, pp. 141-161.

Van Humbeeck, P. (2000), "Wetsevaluatie vanuit bestuurskundig perspectief" in M. Adams and P. Popelier (eds.) (2000), *Wie waakt over de kwaliteit van de wet? Het wetgevingsbeleid in België*, Intersentia, Antwerp/Groningen.

Van Klink, B. (2002), 'De verhouding tussen symboolwerking en sociale werking van wetgeving' in K. Van Aeken and F. Van Loon (eds.) *De toekomst van de rechtssociologie in het justitieel beleid. Bijdragen voor de jaarvergadering van de VSR*, UFSIA, Antwerp.

Winter, H.B. (1996), *Evaluatie in het wetgevingsforum*, Kluwer, Deventer.

Wintgens, L.J. (ed.) (2002), *Legisprudence. A New Theoretical Approach to Legislation*, Hart Publishing, Oxford.

Wintgens, L.J. (2003), 'Het wetsbegrip anders bekeken. Alternatieven voor en in wettelijke regulering, tevens een inleiding tot de legisprudentie, een nieuwe wetgevingstheorie' in L.J. Wintgens (ed.), *Het wetsbegrip. Handelingen van het Centrum voor Wetgeving, Regulering en Legisprudentie*, I, Die Keure, Bruges.

Chapter 5

How Rational is Rational Lawmaking?

Wojciech Cyrul*

Introduction

Traditionally, two basic approaches to lawmaking can be distinguished in the Philosophy of Law. The first, known here as the transcendental approach, limits the role of the lawmaker solely to discovering, recognizing and recording rules and norms that exist independently of the lawmaker. The second approach, known as voluntarism, assumes that lawmaking is an expression of the will of the lawmaker (Wróblewski, 1985). Such a general distinction explains only the second component in the expression "rational lawmaking", i.e. it provides an understanding of lawmaking, but says nothing about rationality as a concept that would provide a comprehensive distinction between the rational law making process and the non-rational. Obviously the meta-question arises of whether a concept of rational lawmaking adopted by a specific system is actually rational in itself. This compels us to reflect upon the problem of which models of rational lawmaking lie at the basis of the contemporary praxiologically-oriented theory of rational lawmaking and how modern lawmaking processes have absorbed different theories of rationality. Such an approach provides us with a clear view of the ideological function of rationality in lawmaking discourse.

In their professional discourse, lawyers make use of the concept of rationality extremely frequently. It is used both in evaluating the lawmaking process, legal argumentation and interpretations of the law as well as in evaluating the law itself. The question thus arises of what is meant by the term rationality in the context of lawmaking. Does it merely represent a kind of "picklock", which is deprived of any meaning whatsoever, used solely for rhetorical effect and emotively based? Or perhaps, on the other hand, rationality means something more for the lawyer and the legislator? A lack of awareness of the consequences of adopting, consciously or unconsciously, a specific meaning for rationality, leads to great difficulties regarding both the criteria for assessing the law, and the role and the status of lawmaking and law applying processes. This gives rise to an urgent need for an answer to the question: what impact does the choice of a specific meaning of rationality have on the structure of the lawmaking process and how is the selection of such criteria justified?

On account of its limited dimensions, the present article does not claim to be an exhaustive discussion on all aspects of the role of rationality in legal discourse. Its main task is to indicate, which models of rational lawmaking lie at the basis of modern theories and what problems can result from a clash of different concepts of rationality in lawmaking. Out of necessity, neither the historical development of the idea of rationality nor views on the role and status of lawmaking in the legal system are studied in any detail. For the sake of clarity of argument the analysis below is limited to the three concepts of rationality dominant in legal discourse. Although such an approach obviously greatly simplifies the problem, and is open to criticism of being too arbitrary, in the opinion of the author even such a simplified analysis suffices to show the fundamental role played by one dominant concept of rationality in assessing the course and nature of lawmaking discourse. Due to this fact, without overlooking the need for more penetrating research, it can be shown at this level that it is the currently accepted idea of rationality that structuralizes and determines both the model of rational lawmaking and the function of the law. In this way, only through an analysis of different models of rational lawmaking can we establish an external criterion for assessing the rationality of lawmaking processes. This, as a consequence, helps explain why the debate on the role of lawmaking involves a number of competing, mutually exclusive viewpoints, which constantly lay claim to rationality status.

Rationality

The concept of rationality has evolved significantly. Its social meaning and importance has changed not only as a result of a dispute between rationalism and empiricism with regard to scientific rationality (Sady, 2000), but also as a consequence of the process of social development itself.

Three main ideas of rationality are basically distinguished within the framework of the philosophy of science: metaphysical, scientistic and technological (Skarga, 1983). A competing division to that outlined above involves a distinction between into epistemic, instrumental and discursive rationality. Due to the specific characteristics of the legal sciences the dominant role in this discipline is played by metaphysical, argumentative and instrumental rationality (Sarkowicz and Stelmach, 1996). Within the framework of the social sciences, which also includes the science of law, the last of these forms of rationality is usually assigned wide-ranging significance, embracing both scientistic and technological rationality. The concept of argumentative rationality has likewise also gradually undergone change, as is seen in the appearance of essential differences between rhetorical and dialectical theories (Hohmann, 2000; Stump, 1978; Van Der Poel, 2000; Rescher, 1977). Since argumentative rationality can be reduced to instrumental rationality, at least within a rhetorical framework (Goodnight, 1993; Leff, 2000), in the present text we make use of a specific version of this form, i.e., so-called discursive rationality (Habermas, 1997; Van Eemeren *et al.* 1993; Aarnio, 1987).

The metaphysical concept of rationality is based on binding the reason with the Being. As a consequence, such an approach not only excludes any form of chance, but also assumes total determinism in a world that acts in accordance with the rational plan of a divine being. The duty of the rational lawmaker is to reveal this necessary order of things. The goal of the rational procedure is thus to identify universal general truths, moral rules existing beyond time and space, as well as rules and laws flowing from the very essence of God, which constitute an emanation of the perfection of the absolute (Skarga, 1983). Knowledge of these laws is to be based on intuitively obvious truths. Rational intuition becomes a measure of the rationality of the law and the acceptability of inferences and demonstrations of its binding force depends on their logical-mathematical correctness.

With the historical shift in thinking from the metaphysical to the anthropocentric comes a change in our understanding of the concept of rationality. In such an approach, the concept of rationality is reduced to a tool, which allows us to bring together certain groups of facts (Mill, 1962). In the social sciences this has led to an interest in causal relations between intentional actions and their consequences. The aim of research was now to discover the rules of knowledge, which would allow us to gain control over reality. This led to the emergence of the idea of instrumental rationality of intentional human actions. In this approach intentional actions acquire rational status in so far as they perform particular conditions, which justify their rational status. First and foremost, they must be planned and performed on the basis of knowledge in such a way that they would be able to explain why it was possible to achieve a given set goal. In other words, actions which produce a certain effect only accidentally and whose effectiveness we are unable to explain, are not instrumentally rational.

The final form of rationality of interest to us is the conception of discursive rationality. Although to a certain extent it is possible to identify its teleological structure, it differs fundamentally from instrumental rationality. While instrumental rationality is associated with a description of causal relations between events and actions, discursive rationality is based on the concept of ideal communication and communicative actions. In this way, discursive rationality, as opposed to instrumental rationality has a strictly linguistic genesis, and more specifically is based on the idea of communication (Habermas, 1970a, 1999; Thompson, 1982). As a consequence, discursive rationality has two levels. The first involves the assumption that every communicative use of a linguistic expression is based on the desire of the sender of the message to reach an understanding with the addressee. The second level involves the assumption that the content of the message should be such that the addressee could not only understand, but also accept it (Habermas, 1981). In this way, discursive rationality is determined on the one hand by the conditions whereby a speech act can be understandable and on the other by the conditions, which make this act discursively justifiable.

Lawmaking Models

As was pointed out in the introduction, basing our thinking solely on the voluntarism-transcendentalism dichotomy is insufficient on its own. On the other hand, it would be just as unsatisfactory to divide rational lawmaking into a metaphysical current based on the idea of a rational Being, an instrumental current based on the theory of instrumental rationality and a discursive one that refers to the tenets of theory of discursive rationality. Adopting such a distinction leads to the analogous criticism, which can be made of a distinction based exclusively on the criterion of will. While the first approach can be criticized for not appreciating the role of rationality in lawmaking, the second approach fails to consider the problem of the normative will in lawmaking discourse. Thus, to avoid exposing ourselves to accusations of a "mechanical" shift in the discussion from general philosophy to the theory and philosophy of law, both elements must be taken into consideration. It appears that only the introduction of the concept of rationality in any analysis of the transcendental-voluntarist current helps avoid the criticism that such an approach is inadequate. What is more, taking the above into account, the question then arises of whether the domination of any specific concept of rationality assumes a specific model of lawmaking and whether it makes the classification of law as rational dependent on the lawmaking procedure.

The lawmaking models presented in the next parts of the text, which presuppose every idea of rationality, constitute a significant idealization of the problem. In this way, the divisions suggested below tend to show how important the dominance of one concept of rationality is for the concept of lawmaking.

In accordance with the above, in the transcendental current we can distinguish both theories based on the metaphysical idea of rationality and scientistic and technological theories based on the idea of instrumental rationality. The former group embraces theocentrical philosophy of law, classical concepts of natural law, and the views of the German historicist school. The latter group includes sociological, anthropological and psychological concepts of law. Although these approaches differ from one another in an essential way, they do have one feature in common, namely in all the above concepts lawmaking is determined by the effort to discover and record rules that exist independently of the lawmaker, whose role is reduced to confirming their binding power.

In the case of transcendental concepts, therefore, the rationality of lawmaking procedures is not an issue, nor is their outcome, since the "lawmaking" act has a solely declarative character. In this way, the problem of lawmaking is reduced to the question of rational cognition. As a consequence, depending on the prevailing idea of scientific rationality, lawmaking will have metaphysical or scientistic-technological status. In the first case it finds its basis in Being, founded on the principles of divine law, in intuitively necessary laws of nature or in custom. In the second case it is a result of cognizing nature and the biological conditions of man. Although in the second case reason ceases to be treated in metaphysical categories as an attribute of Being and becomes a tool helping explain processes taking place in the reality surrounding us, the law that is created is still *eo ipso* binding and rational. The assumed rationality of the scientific method used by the lawmaker guarantees him *ex definitione* rational status, and thus ensures that the law is not only necessary, but also just in character. The just character of the law resulted from the fact that, as is assumed by scientism, science is free from value judgments (Sarkowicz and Stelmach, 1996). The legitimate status of such an approach was eventually undermined in recent times as a result of questioning the mechanistic current of the natural sciences. It has been universally shown that induction does not lead to causal laws entirely free of exceptions, but only leads to certain statistical regularities, which can be applied until the time of their falsification.

Likewise, two main currents can be identified in voluntarist theories. The first links the ideas of metaphysical rationality with the concept of the lawmaking will. The second combines the normative will with instrumental rationality. The peculiar synthesis of the two constitutes a legalistic current, which also, however, exhibits the increasing influence of the adoption of communicative rationality.

In metaphysical voluntarism, lawmaking appears as the sacral manifestation of the will, which is the source of divine reason. In this current, just as in the case of extreme transcendental concepts, the law is based on metaphysical rationality, whereby it is not discovered but is rather constituted by the sovereign will. The ruler does not discover natural law. Its rationality does not result from seeking reason or an ideal duty. Rather, he/she is the source of such concepts. Such thinking is characteristic of theocentric legal systems, where the ruler is God, as such his/her will is the ideal normative will and his rulings an incarnation of divine wisdom and justice. It is precisely the bestowing of divinity on the lawmaking will, which is the constitutional characteristic of the concepts making up metaphysical voluntarism. This current, however, is not only characteristic of the philosophy of the Old Testament. It likewise played a significant role during the dominance of the Roman Empire, when lawmaking was once more assigned a sacral character, in particular the lawmaking will of the emperor. It also left its mark in medieval and modern philosophy, proof of which is the frequent treatment of the monarchy as a source of reason. In a weaker version it also manifested itself in doctrines, which traced the lawmaking authority of popes, emperors and kings back to the divine origin of their sovereign authority (Grzybowski, 1968; Popper, 1971; Kubes, 1987).

In the historical approach, however, it is instrumental voluntarism that is the prevailing concept. Based on the sovereign authority of the lawmaker, it most frequently refers to autocratic concepts of rational lawmaking. This manifests itself above all in doctrines, which adopt the strictly technical function of the law with regard to regulating social relations. Instrumental voluntarism assumes that the sovereign will is the sole source of the law, and its only boundary is the internal instrumental rationality existing between set goals and their implementation. Lying at the basis of this approach is the idea that the sovereign, who is unlimited by any external circumstances, can arbitrarily choose both his goals and the methods used to achieve those goals within the boundaries of causal relations. In contrast to metaphysical voluntarism, in this approach the concept of sovereignty has a purely political meaning and is not grounded in Being. Theories, which adopt such a current of lawmaking, directly or indirectly assume that the law may have an arbitrary content. Nevertheless, it must also be effective in the context of assumed goals. In this approach, no necessary relationship exists between positive law and morality. At the justificatory level this results in the adoption in instrumental voluntarism of a purely formal legitimating approach to lawmaking. In other words, the law receives justification through the idea of the sovereign will of the lawmaker. Such a solution leads to the suppression of the cognitive role in the sphere of justice, which lawmaking is supposed to play in transcendental currents. In the voluntarist approach these law applying organs are obliged to know and apply the will of the lawmaker.

Instrumental voluntarism is a characteristic feature of the majority of conceptions in which individuals or groups aspire to gain monopoly control of lawmaking functions, while at the same time negating the authority of social representation (Piotrowski, 1988). A sovereign authority does not have to persuade anyone to accept his will and from this perspective is not compelled to seek social consent. Instrumental voluntarism is based above all on power and force. Within the limit in which the sovereign disposes of these resources lawmaking discourse is dominated in its entirety by instrumental rationality. The law is reduced to an instrument that makes it possible to achieve specific goals without the need to take into account the interests of all interested individuals or, more broadly speaking, without taking into account the interests of society as a whole. In accordance with the prevailing idea of rationality, the interest of society or the individual can be taken into account, if it does not stand in contradiction to the aims of the lawmaker (Kustra, 1994).

The voluntarist – instrumental current also has a predominant influence in the modern debate on the state and the law. However, the ideology assumed in modern theories of lawmaking based on the scientific character of the law and its effectiveness in regulating society should not be mistaken for the instrumental effectiveness of the law in resolving social problems. Instrumental voluntarism and its variants are geared towards successful adjudication of problems, and not their solution. Thus, lawmaking activity focuses not on solving problems, but instead, through the introduction of specific regulations, cuts short debate on such problems. Thus social antagonisms are frequently generated, the juridisation of social relations increases and, as a consequence, the law is paradoxically reduced in effectiveness.

A particular variant of instrumental voluntarism is the legalistic current of lawmaking (Kustra, 1994). One feature distinguishing it from classical depiction is the introduction of the idea of the Rule of Law, i.e. an idea based on the theory of communicative rationality. As a consequence, on the one hand, the law ceases to be identified with the order of the sovereign and begins to be linked with a general and abstract text declared and promulgated in accordance with a specific procedure. On the other hand, organs of the executive authority bestowing absolute authority upon a legal text limit the role of communicative rationality as an element structuralizing the system of law as a whole. The special position and function of the legal text is intended to justify the need for centralism in the case of lawmaking and adjudicative legalism. The introduction of the idea of the Rule of Law and the bestowing of absolute authority on a legal text changes the role of instrumental rationality in the lawmaking process. This change is visible in particular at the legislative level, i.e. the process of preparing the texts of normative acts. Regulating social interactions via expanded legal texts containing general norms makes the achievement of the goals of the lawmaker dependent on the quality of the text. As a consequence, as the number and complexity of regulations increases so does the problem both of ensuring that the introduction of new provisions does not clash with existing laws and of predicting their impact on texts which are already legally binding in the system. In the legalistic current, legislation ceases to be purely the art of faithfully recording the will of the lawmaker and becomes instead the art of constructing a coherent system of legal sources. The general character of legal rules faces legislation with enormous challenges, when one realises that it should represent an instrument for achieving thc aims of the lawmaker. The Rule of Law introduces new external limitations on the will of the lawmaker. In spite of this, rights and freedoms are still bestowed on the individual by the lawmaking authority and thus are constantly threatened by a change in the goals of the political game. The weakness of the idea of the Rule of Law in the case of theories in the legalistic current lies in the fact that the judiciary, applying the outcome of the political game recorded in the form of a legal text, cannot act as a check on the designs of the lawmaking authority. One solution supposed to mitigate this danger is that of establishing constitutional rights safeguarded by a tribunal that is independent of the will of the lawmaking authority. However, as long as constitutional rights and freedoms can be changed as a result of the political game, the danger arising from the instrumental side of the lawmaking will remain.

It is particularly difficult to embrace within the above schema discursive theories of lawmaking, which assume an argumentative approach to the law. The difficulty lies in the fact that discursive theories stand, as it were, crosswise to the transcendentalism-voluntarism dichotomy. This becomes particularly evident when the idea of communicative rationality is subjected to analysis. In such an approach, the effectiveness of the law depends on fulfilling not only the conditions of effective communication, which should determine the legislative processes, but also on guaranteeing conditions of discursive validity. In other words, if this approach is to lay claim to acceptability it must be established in particular procedures of social dialogue in which its validity is tested. This leads as a consequence to the need to introduce into the framework of the legal discourse transcendental rules of general discourse. In this approach, the law is not a result of negotiation and economic calculation, but the result of a particular procedure for reaching agreement, achieved through impartial dialogue based on argument and reasoning. In such an approach, instrumental rationality is subordinated to communicative rationality. This results not only with consensual but also rationally acceptable character of lawmaking both with regard to establishing goals and achieving those goals. The lawmaking authority desists from arbitrarily setting and achieving goals on the basis of the instrumental rationality paradigm. Lawmaking competency should thus be decentralized, and to a considerable degree transferred, on the basis of the principle of subsidiarity, to non-governmental institutions. The scope of self-regulation in the case of particular spheres of social activity should be determined by the principle of effectiveness in solving and not adjudicating problems. As a consequence, communication models conceive the law in responsive categories in relation to social needs and expectations (Frank, 1932). The discursive model views lawmaking processes from the perspective of the social context and the relationship between the actions of the lawmaking authority and their social acceptance. Correspondingly, the certainty guaranteed by an autonomous law or the sovereign will of the lawmaker is replaced by the certainty arising from the comprehensive character of a coherent system of dynamic procedures of social order and change (Nonet and Selznick, 1978). However, for discursive concepts to achieve this goal lawmaking should not only be based on impartial procedures of social participation. Discursive theories must also set requirements for the participants of lawmaking discourse which not only provide a guarantee of linguistic competence, but likewise ensure its ability to be rational (Habermas 1970b, 1999).

Conclusions

The analysis of rational lawmaking models carried out above clearly showed that the concept of rationality adopted within the framework of the system of law constitutes not only an internal criterion for assessing the lawmaking system as a rational system, but is also an important component in thinking on its legitimizing function. The above reflections allow us to forward the thesis that rationality of the law in general, and the lawmaking process in particular is not exclusively dependent on its instrumental efficacy. The existing parallelism between historical change affecting the dominant position of a specific concept of rationality and historical change shaping the rationality of lawmaking shows that both the concept of lawmaking and the concept of rationality are relative to the degree of development of society. This at least partly explains why together with the appearance of pluralist democracies classical currents of lawmaking are gradually being supplemented or completely replaced with approaches based on discursive and argumentative elements. This is confirmed by an analysis of modern normative acts regulating lawmaking procedures in *civil law* and *common law* countries. This allows us to identify certain principles of lawmaking common to many legal systems.[1] Although the course of legislative work itself, as well as the stage of voting on and promulgating legal acts sometimes differs considerably in detail from country to country, nevertheless theoretical analysis leads to the conclusion that both at the stage preceding a draft normative act and at the stage when a legal text is drafted, the majority of legal systems adopt similar rules and set themselves similar goals.

Legal acts, which are praxeologically determined by instrumental rationality and regulate the legislative process clearly make a distinction between the stage preceding any decision on preparing a draft legal act and the stage during which the draft is composed. The former usually comes down to establishing the actual state of social relations in the sphere, which is to be the object of the regulation. At this stage legal and extra-legal sources of intervention are usually established. These sources make it possible to achieve established political goals. Extremely interesting is the fact that the dominant role of economic and social analysis of proposed solutions is already clear at this stage. Lawmaking organs are faced with the need to specify the expected social, economic and legal effects of all the submitted alternatives. They are usually obliged to determine which method of intervention is the most economically efficient method for achieving the planned results. On the other hand, in a different dimension, at this stage of the work lawmaking organs are also obliged to sound out the opinions of entities, which may be interested in the method of regulation. Obviously, such actions are undertaken not only to reduce the costs of enforcing the law, but also with the aim of achieving the requirements of justice, i.e. an equal distribution of rights and burdens. In this way, we can observe that modern regulations of the lawmaking process introduce elements postulated by discursive theories. At the same time, however, this leads to an increase in tension between the instrumental treatment of the law and the axiological element justifying its binding force. The instrumental element prevails, however, for consensual elements or popular lawmaking initiatives, if they are at all acceptable, still lie on the margin, at least at the state level.

The very fact of the appearance of normative acts regulating legislative processes allows us to reach conclusions on how important the problem of drafting and composing the text of a legal act has become. This stage of work in the lawmaking process is particularly interesting from the point of view of our own reflections. Comparative analysis of the principles of lawmaking technique, in force in different countries, shows that at this stage the attention of lawmaking organs are focused above all on the effects of introducing new provisions into a system of law. It is precisely at the stage of drafting a legal act that the effects of hitherto regulations are determined and decisions are made on whether or not to improve them. At this stage, lawmaking organs are usually obliged to establish alternative legal solutions capable of effectively ensuring the achievement of set goals and specifying the expected costs and benefits of their introduction. In this way the final decision on choosing the optimal regulation depends not only on the costs and effectiveness of a selected solution but likewise on its constitutionality and legality in the context of the legal system as a whole.

Taking into account the above-mentioned requirements, lawmaking organs in the lawmaking process can reach the conclusion that instrumental rationality is the dominant conception of rationality in lawmaking discourse. Such a conclusion is, however, mistaken, for the principles of lawmaking technique, refer not only to the effectiveness and economical value of draft regulations. This is because another major element in rational lawmaking is a concern over the form of the legal act and the quality of the language used in a legal text. In a large majority of cases the texts of normative acts are expected to be concise, synthetic and free of excessive casuistry. Legislators are obliged to phrase legal texts in a way that is understandable for addressees of the norms contained within, in so far as this is possible in accordance with universally adopted semantic rules and the constituents of everyday language. The requirements set for the phrasing of legal texts together with the methods and ways employed in the promulgating of legal acts show that besides such clearly evident instrumental rationality there is also the problem of communicative rationality, which imperceptibly imposes a number of limitations on the former. If we observe the lawmaking process still more closely we see that this takes place in a specific context. First of all, by referring to scientific, technical and economic achievements, the discourse of lawmaking becomes subordinated to the idea of scientific and technological rationality that prevails in normal science (Kuhn 2001, p. 33ff.). Secondly, by referring to the requirements of formal and material cohesion in the legal system, lawmaking discourse is introduced in limitations both of universal requirements of logic and rationalist, empirical and constitutional justification of the rights of the subjective entities of the law. It thus turns out that at the basis of lawmaking discourse function are various implicitly assumed, competing ideas of rationality, and that the rationality of rational lawmaking consists in the optimal balancing of claims raised by different concepts, employing them simultaneously to strengthen the legitimating role of the lawmaking procedure itself for established rights.

* Wojciech Cyrul Ph.D, LL.M (EATL), The Theory and Philosophy of Law Department, Faculty of Law and Administration at the Jagiellonian University.

Note

1 US President Executive Order 12866, 58 FR 51735 (9/30/93) as amended by Executive Order 13258, 67 FR 9385 (2/26/02), Ordinance of the Prime Minister of 20 June 2002 with regard to "Principles of Lawmaking Technique" Dz.U. No 100 item.908

References

Aarnio, A. (1987), *The Rational as Reasonable. A Treatise on Legal Justification*, D. Reidel, Dordrecht.

Frank, J. (1932), 'Mr. Justice Holms and Non – Euclidanian Legal Thinking', *Cornell Law Quarterly*, Vol.17, pp. 568-603.

Goodnight, G.T. (1993), '"A New Rhetoric" for a "New Dialectic": Prolegomena to a Responsible Public Argument', *Argumentation*, Vol. 7, pp. 329-342.

Grzybowski, K. (1968), *Historia doktryn politycznych i prawnych (The History of Legal and Political Doctrines)*, PWN, Warszawa.

Habermas, J. (1970a), 'Toward a Theory of Communicative Competences' in H. S. Dreitzel (ed.), *Recent Sociology*, nr. 2., Macmillan, New York.

Habermas, J. (1970b), *Zur Logik der Sozialwissenschaften*, Suhrkamp, Frankfurt/M.

Habermas, J. (1981), *Theory of Communicative Actions. Reason and Rationalisation of Society*, Bacon Press, Boston.

Habermas, J. (1997), 'Pojęcie racjonalności komunikacyjnej w świetle teorii aktów mowy' in T. Buksiński (ed.), *Rozumność i racjonalność (The Communicative Rationality in the Light of the Speech – Act Theory)*, Wydawnictwo Naukowe IF UAM, Poznań.

Habermas, J. (1999), 'What is Universal Pragmatics' in M. Cook (ed.), *On the Pragmatics of Communication*, Polity Press, Cambridge.

Hohmann, H. (2000), 'Rhetoric and Dialectic: Some Historical and Legal Perspectives', *Argumentation*, Vol. 14, pp. 223-234.

Kubes, V. (1987), *Theorie der Gesetzgebung*, Springer-Verlag, Vienna/New York.

Kuhn, T.S. (2001), *'Struktura rewolucji naukowych'(The Structure of Scientific Revolutions)*, Aletheia, Warszawa.

Kustra, E. (1994), *Polityczne problemy tworzenia prawa (The Political Problems of Lawmaking)*, Wydawnictwo UMK, Toruń.

Leff, M. (2000), 'Rhetoric and Dialectic in the Twenty-First Century', *Argumentation*, Vol.14, pp. 241-254.

Mill, J.S. (1962), *System logiki (A System of Logic)*, PWN, Warszawa.

Nonet, Ph. and Selznick, Ph. (1978), *Law and Society in Transition, Towards Responsive Law*, Harper and Row, New York (NY).

Piotrowski, R. (1988), *Spór o model tworzenia prawa (A Dispute About the Model of Lawmaking)*, PWN, Warszawa.

Popper, K. R. (1971), *The Open Society and Its Enemies*, Princetown University Press, Princetown. Volume I

Rescher, N. (1977), *Dialectics. A Controversy-Oriented Approach to the Theory of Knowledge*, State University of New York Press, Albany.

Sady, W. (2000), *Spór o racjonalność naukową. Od Poincarégo do Laudana,(A Dispute about the Scientific Rationality. From Poincaré to Laudan*, Wydawnictwo Funna, Wrocław.

Sarkowicz, R. and Stelmach, J. (1996), *Teoria prawa, Monografie Wydziału Prawa i Administracji UJ*, Wydawnictwo UJ, Kraków.

Skarga, B. (1983), 'Trzy idee racjonalności', *Ruch filozoficzny*, Vol. 5-6, pp. 87-117.

Stump, E. (1978), *Boethius's De topicis differentiis*, Cornell University Press, Itaca, New York.

Thompson J.B. (1982), 'Universal Pragmatics' in J.B. Thompson and D. Held (eds.), *Habermas Critical Debates*, The Macmillan Press, London/ Basingstoke.

Van Eemeren, F.H., Grootendorst, R., Jackson, S. and Jacobs, S. (1993), *Reconstructing Argumentative Discourse*, The University of Alabama Press, Tuscaloosa, London.

Van Der Poel, M. (2000), 'Comments on 'Meeting in the House of Callais', Rhetoric and Dialectic', *Argumentation*, Vol. 14, pp. 219-222.

Wróblewski, J. (1985), *Teoria racjonalnego tworzenia prawa*, Ossolineum, Wrocław.

PART II

CONSTITUTIONALISM, LEGALISM AND DEMOCRACY

Chapter 6

Two Models of Democracy: How to Make Demos and Hercules Collaborate in Public Deliberation

Tatsuo Inoue*

Introduction: Liberalism and Deliberative Democracy

"Deliberative democracy" has become a prevailing catchword in the recent discourses on the reinvigoration of democracy (Sunstein, 1993, pp. 133-145; Habermas, 1996, pp. 287-328; Gutmann and Thompson, 1996; Elster, 1998; Bohman and Rheg, 1997). The underlining motivation is this. Promoting people's participation in political process is necessary but not sufficient for the establishment of democratic practices. The quality of this process matters. The democratic process must be something higher than the kind of negotiations and bargaining among interest-groups that the so-called "pluralists" hold to be the core of democratic politics. It must be a forum of deliberation where each participant transcends her naked interests and idiosyncratic belief system and seeks for publicly justifiable decisions through the endeavour to give such moral reasons for her political claims as her opponents cannot reasonably reject.

Contemporary "communitarians" and "civic republicans" tend to claim that deliberative democracy as characterized above is a distinctive feature of their standpoints and that liberalism is antagonistic to this conception of democracy because its commitment to individual rights and neutrality blinds us to the possibility and necessity of public deliberation that shapes the common political values higher than the sheer procedural justice for interest-group rivalry (Sandel, 1996). But this is not a fair assessment of the liberal project. Such a classical liberal thinker as J. S. Mill, for example, emphasized the vital role of public-spirited deliberation in democracy as passionately as any (Mill, 1975). Even his notorious proposal to give plural votes to the well educated class is part of his attempts to enhance the deliberative quality of democratic politics under the condition of the scarcity of civic virtue. Ironically enough, Carl Schmitt, one of the arch-enemies of liberalism, vividly witnessed the deliberative perspective of liberalism inherent in the classical parliamentarism when he declared its death. He depicted the "dead" liberal paradigm of legislature as "das in öffentlicher Diskussion die vernünftige Wahrheit und die gerechte Norm findende Parlament [the parliament that finds the rational truth and just norms in public discussion]"

(Schmitt, 1993, pp. 315-319). Among contemporary liberals, John Rawls gave a central place to the notion of public reason in his conception of political liberalism (Rawls, 1993, pp. 212-254). Although his conception of public reason based on the idea of overlapping consensus has invited searching criticism, even his critics are led to reconstruct liberalism on a basis of their own alternative conceptions of public justification (for a remarkable example, see Gaus, 1996). The liberal concern for public justification is not confined to the hypothetical situation for choosing principles of justice constructed in theory. It penetrates into actual democratic politics.

To be sure, liberals do not indulge in wishful thinking by assuming that democratic deliberation will never go wrong. They are aware that democratic process, even if it is a deliberative one, has the danger of degenerating into the tyranny of majority. They warn that Demos may become demonic. Accordingly, liberals recognize the need to protect the basic rights of individuals and minorities by reinforcing them as constitutional constraints upon democratic process. They turn to judicial review for a standard means of implementing these constraints. This liberal trust in the judiciary as the protector of fundamental rights against the danger of democratic process seems to be the main reason why liberalism is now often castigated as undermining democratic deliberation. But I think it is misguided for the advocates of deliberative democracy to criticize liberalism this way.

The first reply to be made to this criticism is that such advocates also require the court to exercise its power of judicial review to override a democratic decision when it falls short of the standard of public deliberation. They expect the judiciary to play the role of "the custodian of deliberative democracy." (Habermas, 1996, pp. 238-328). They say that they accept judicial interference not to impose external and substantive value-constraint upon democratic process, but to make deliberative process work well. It is questionable, however, whether their distinction between the substantive outcome-oriented and the deliberative process-oriented constraints on democratic process is anything more than a difference in *façon de parler*.

J. Habermas, for example, smuggles in independent substantive principles such as universalistic justice and basic human rights under the disguise of procedural reason. (Habermas, 1996, pp. 282, 304, 388-446, 463-490). Some recent proponents of deliberative democracy explicitly recognize that substantive values like liberty, equality and fair opportunity are constitutive of democratic deliberation (Gutmann and Thompson, 1996, pp. 26-51, 199-229; Cohen, 2003, pp. 17-38). This is not surprising. We cannot distinguish the deliberative process from non-deliberative ones such as the bargaining process of interest-group politics and strategic compromises reached through mutual threats unless we see whether participants in the democratic process adduce in support of their political claims the kind of reasons that can be appropriately used in public justification and whether the final decision falls within the ambit of public justification.

Of course it is a very controversial issue what constitutes the criteria for public justifiability. For that very reason, however, the proponents of deliberative democracy must specify and defend their own conceptions of public justification in terms of the substantive values that they hold to be indispensable to any fair scheme of political society. They cannot shift their own responsibility for such substantive value judgments on to the process of democratic deliberation, because these judgments are needed to identify the democratic deliberation that they look for. They would simply beg the question if they said that the answer to the question about what is public deliberation should also be given by public deliberation. They must "impose" a certain set of their own substantive value judgments upon the democratic process as the preconditions of its public and deliberative status. If they avoid doing so by assuming that the actual political practice of a given democracy has the final authority to decide what constitutes public deliberation, then the deliberative democracy as they conceive it will lose its normative edge that cuts it off from the pluralist or other pre-deliberative conceptions of democracy that prevail in contemporary industrial democracies.

I will not push this point any further here. In this paper I want to develop another reply: liberal commitment to the role of the judiciary as the protector of the fundamental rights of individuals and minorities is not only compatible with, but also conducive to the democratic deliberation. If we use the Dworkinian metaphor of "Hercules" to refer to the Judiciary that conducts a thoroughgoing constitutional scrutiny of political power, my claim may be put this way: Demos needs Hercules as an indispensable collaborator in carrying out its task of public deliberation. In order to show this I will present and contrast two models of democracy: reflectional and critical democracy. Reflectional democracy gives primacy to consensus and power sharing among different political actors that represent different social interests. It protects minorities by giving them a collective veto on political decision making. By contrast, critical democracy seeks to promote the self-critical learning process of democracy by activating competition among alternative policy systems and sifting out them on a trial and error basis and so requires mutual criticism and power change rather than consensus formation and power sharing among competing political actors. As for minority protection, it adopts judicial implementation of constitutionalized fundamental rights not just as a compensation for, but also as a better alternative to the collective veto power which it denies the minorities in the political decision making. I will argue that it is critical democracy that fosters democratic deliberation in a principled way. To understand the contrast between the two models of democracy, however, we have to consider the role, or virtues and vices, of consensus in democracy first. I will discuss the problems of consensus in democracy in the next part and present and evaluate my two models of democracy in the last part of this paper.

The Virtues and Vices of Consensus in Democracy

Is Democracy Government by Consent?

Democracy is sometimes characterized as "government by consent." Democratic government is said to depend for its legitimacy on the consent given by the ruled, or in a looser form of speech, on social consensus. "The identity of the ruler and the ruled" is another way of expressing the same idea. But this is nothing more than a fiction. There is no universal consensus among, nor identity of, the ruler and the ruled in democracy. Like other regimes, democracy is a form of political domination where part of society imposes its will upon the rest. The believers in the iron law of oligarchy say that even in democracy the effective leverage of power is monopolized by a minority of political elite, especially those who can manage the organized votes and election machine. We may object that this is a pathological form of democracy. But even in a sounder form of democracy where popular participation in politics is more than rhetorical, the majority dominates the minorities. The political decisions that reflect the will of the majority are enforced on all including the minorities who made strong objections to them.

Those who want to defend democracy as based on consensus may reply that the democratic decision-making procedure where minorities have equal right to participation is accepted by even those minorities who object to the specific outcomes of the democratic process where they are defeated. This may be true of the tentative minorities whose minority status is contingent on the distribution pattern of political opinions at a given time and who have a fair chance of constituting the majority in the future. But the "structural minorities" who have no hope of winning in the democratic decision making cannot be expected to accept the democratic procedure. Moreover, this reply misfires because it shows the legitimacy of democracy only to those who already accept the democratic decision procedure. But democracy must be justified to none other than those who object that the democratic decision making process is not fair for them.

If consensus fails to be a positive justification for democracy, then what role can it play in democracy? Two functions are worth considering here: consensus can work as a negative constraint on democracy or as its regulative idea. Let me discuss the problems involved in these two functions respectively in the next and last sections of this part.

Internal and External Vetoes

Although consensus fails to be a positive justification for democracy, there are alternative candidates for positive justification available: the utilitarian maximization of social welfare, or the republican aspiration to cultivate civic virtue, or populist doctrine that "*vox populi, vox Dei*," or what you like. But whatever argument may be adopted as positive justification for democracy, consensus can be resorted to as the negative constraint on democracy. The idea of consensus involves giving a veto on democratic decision to those who are vulnerable to the tyranny of the majority that democracy has the inherent danger of degenerating into, and that the positive justificatory theories as mentioned above may permit or even require. Consensus cannot legitimatize democracy, but it can delegitimatize the latter when it becomes unbearably oppressive for minorities. This philosophical role of consensus is indispensable for critical examination of every form of political power. The fiction of social contract as a conventional formula of the idea of consensus in political theories is deceptive (or redundant at best) if it is used to give positive justification for government, but it is defensible if used as a metaphoric expression of the idea that people reserve the right to resistance against their government whatever origin or whatever form it may have.

The veto that the minorities have on the democratic decision making is a corollary of the right to resistance reserved for people.

But this idea of veto involved in consensus has ambiguity, which is reflected in the two ways of institutionalizing it in democracy. One way is to give the minorities a collective veto that they can exercise within the democratic decision making process; the other is to confer the power of veto on an independent organ outside the democratic political process to which the individuals and minorities helpless in this process can turn for rescue. Let me call the former internal veto and the latter external veto. Internal veto is secured by rejecting the majoritarian decision making principle in favour of the consensual principle: unanimity or semi-unanimity (strongly weighted majority) principle. The consensual principle may prevail not just as a formal decision making rule but as informal decision making practice of political actors. External veto takes the form of constitutionalized fundamental rights implemented through judicial review. In this system the individuals and minorities whose constitutional rights are infringed by democratic decisions can seek remedies through the judicial process that is insulated from the influences of the political forces dominating the democratic process. External veto finds its typical philosophical expression in the Dworkinian concept of individual rights as trumps over the collective goals (like utilitarian maximization of the aggregate social interests) that are pursued in the democratic political process (Dworkin, 1978).

Let me make one conceptual note here. It may be indicated that an external veto can be reduced to an internal veto because constitutional rights are normatively reinforced usually by the weighted majority rule for constitutional amendment. Here I want to make two replies. First, this paper is concerned with how to foster deliberative process in the "normal politics" as distinguished from the "constitutional politics." (For this distinction, see Ackerman, 1991, pp. 3-33.) The distinction between internal and external veto is crucial at least in the context of normal politics that goes on within the given constitutional framework.

Secondly and more importantly, external veto cannot be reduced to internal veto even in constitutional politics if we accept the "entrenchment" of fundamental constitutional rights by setting them beyond the limits of a legitimate constitutional amendment process. B. Ackerman who proposed the distinction between normal and constitutional politics rejects the entrenchment of constitutional rights in order to give the sovereignty of "We the People" primacy over the individual rights. Thus he holds that the fundamentalist-populists (such as the Moral Majority) can lawfully abolish the First Amendment of the US Constitution and impose their faith on all the citizens as the state religion if they win in the constitutional politics (Ackerman, 1991, pp. 13-16). Such an absolutist interpretation of popular sovereignty, however, would undermine rather than reinforce the public normative authority of "We the People." The structural minorities who are deprived of their constitutional shelter in the current round of constitutional politics while lacking the political resources for winning it back in a future round cannot accept the current outcome of constitutional politics as the choice of "We the People" that they can identify themselves with. They cannot but feel that they are denied the equal membership of the political community that constitutes "We the People." As a result, constitutional politics would lose its public nature and degenerate into the arena of the conflict of private factions that seek power to realize their own idiosyncratic goals. To keep the public legitimacy of constitutional politics, we have to entrench at least the core constitutional rights such as religious liberty and freedom of speech, conferring on the court the power of external veto to strike down as unconstitutional the constitutional amendments that attempt to abolish such rights. To be sure, this is a very controversial issue. But the point is this. Whatever position we may take about the issue of the normative limits of constitutional politics, we need the conceptual distinction between internal and external vetoes as the terms of discussion on this issue. With this point confirmed, let me get back to the main line of my discussion.

An internal veto protects the minorities endowed with it more powerfully than the external veto system would. But I think that this protection is too powerful in its force and too restrictive in its recipients to be justified. It runs counter to fairness in the distribution of political influence, and erodes the discipline of public justification essential to democratic deliberation.

First, it is observed that organized interest groups can exercise greater political influence than the unorganized general public who are depicted as a "silent majority" or "floating votes" in contemporary democracy. It is the case even in a democracy with the majoritarian decision making rule. But under the consensual principle the organized minorities can enjoy even far greater political leverage by exercising their institutionalized veto power in the democratic decision making process, so that the sense of political powerlessness and the resultant apathy prevail among the unorganized majority, whose retreat from politics helps organized minorities to enjoy further enhancement of their political influence. An internal veto is meant for the "vulnerable" minorities, but ironically it turns them into a powerful kingmaker with a decisive casting vote.

Secondly, the consensual principle gives an internal veto only to those minorities who have organized votes beyond a certain threshold. This clearly holds in the case of a semi-uniformity rule or weighted majority rule. Even if the full unanimity rule is adopted, however, it cannot be the case that any minorities or any individuals can exercise internal veto. If an internal veto were universally distributed and exercised this way, it would be impossible for us to make collective decisions given the fact of persistent conflicts of our interests and values. Accordingly, the effective political actors who can participate in the formation of "unanimity" must be formally or informally delimited to make the unanimity rule work. All this means that the "discrete and insular minorities,"[1] or those minorities who are unorganized or whose votes are below the threshold of political effectivity, are not protected by internal veto. The consensual principle gives the effectively organized minorities far more political power than they deserve, while aggravating the political marginality of the marginal minorities who need protection against the majoritarian tyranny more desperately than the former.

Thirdly, the consensual principle gives an internal veto to the minorities whenever they can organize the votes beyond the threshold. They can exercise it not only when the majority attempt to violate their fundamental rights that the majority must respect to retain the public legitimacy of democratic decision making, but also when they want to secure their naked special interests that cannot be publicly justified. They may offer a specious rationale for their exercise of veto, but they can act as the judge of their own case when they can exercise internal veto. The lack of independent constraint on the reasons for exercising internal veto cannot fail to erode the minorities' moral motivation to seek for public justification, and their power of securing their naked interests is sure to make the majority angry at, and intolerant of, them. Deliberative processes cannot be expected to prosper under these conditions.

In contrast with these defects of internal veto, we can appreciate the merits of external veto. External veto can be exercised only when the court (considerably if not perfectly) insinuated from the pressures of political actors in the democratic process judges that its exercise is justified by virtue of the constitutional principles of fundamental rights that even the majority cannot reasonably reject. There is a strong normative constraint on the reasons for its exercise, and the access to the remedies that it offers is independent of the political influences and resources of the given minority. Even the politically powerful minorities cannot exercise it when they fail to give principled constitutional argument for their rights-claims that they want to protect by this veto. For the same reason, however, even the marginal minorities and politically helpless individuals can exercise it when they successfully offer such arguments.

To be sure, this is the ideal that the actual constitutional practice may fall short of. For example, constitutional litigations often involve such a cost that they are accessible only to people with politically organized support. But this is a reason to improve the practice so as to approach the ideal (by the legal aid to facilitate the access to constitutional remedies, for example), not a reason to cast off the ideal. If the practice approaches the ideal to some decent extent, the discipline of public justification can be more effectively enforced and minorities are more fairly protected by external veto than by internal veto. To forestall misunderstanding, I must hasten to add that I am not making an unfair comparison between the perfect form of external veto and imperfect form of internal veto to show the superiority of the former. My point is that the full implementation of the ideal of internal veto gives the minorities endowed with it such an absolute power that it absolutely tends to get corrupt, according to the Lord Acton's axiom of politics, and that an external veto can prevent this corruption in proportion to the extent that its ideal is implemented.

The Wrong Way to Seek Consensus in Democracy

Now it may be objected that it is not fair to estimate the consensual principle only in terms of its veto conferring function. We have to realize, so goes the objection, that this principle has another important function: setting consensus formation as the regulative idea of democratic process. It is true that there are severe political conflicts and moral disagreements in democracy, but it does not follow that we should not endeavour to form consensus as far as possible. The endeavour for consensus formation is indispensable to democratic deliberation because what constitutes the public justification that should be sought in the deliberative process is not just the "morally right reason" for a specific political actor but the reasons that are "morally and mutually acceptable" for competing political actors.

I do not deny that consensus formation should be sought as far as possible in democratic deliberation. But consensus formation should not be sanctified as *the* regulative idea, because it is just one of the two competing ideals for democratic deliberation: moral acceptability and mutual acceptability. There is a persistent tension between the two ideals, and we have to accept the tension. If we seek for consensus for its own sake, we will regress to unprincipled strategic compromises characteristic of interest group politics. To be sure, we should try to transcend our own special interest and idiosyncratic belief and seek for public reasons that we believe to be morally acceptable for our opponents as well as for us. But there is no guarantee for convergence between what we believe to be publicly justifiable and what our opponents believe to be so even if both are sincere in seeking for public reasons. So we need a decision making rule. If we stick to the consensual principle for the decision making and institutionally force the political actors to form consensus to make a collective decision, the deliberative quality of the democratic process will be gravely vitiated by the following defects that the majoritarian principle can repair.

First, under the consensual principle, the dissenting minorities are subject to strong social pressure for conformity. They are treated as troublemakers because their dissent is regarded by the mainstream group as the cause of a failure of collective decision making and social discord. If the dissenting minorities have sufficient resources for resisting this pressure, they can exercise internal veto and obtain concessions from the mainstream majority. But the helpless individuals and marginal minorities who lack such resources are prone to succumb to this pressure and conform to the majority. They are forced to hide their dissent under the surface. Given the majoritarian principle, however, the dissenting minorities do not prevent the majority from making the collective decision that the latter want, so there is no need for conformity pressure. The minorities need not be pressed to say yes. They can rather say to the majority, "We said no. You said yes. Put it on the record. And remember that it is you who will have to take full responsibility for the decision when it proves to have a devastating consequence as we said it would." Although it may sound somewhat paradoxical, the right to dissent that is a prerequisite for democratic deliberation is more effectively and more fairly protected under the majoritarian principle.

Secondly, political responsibility is blurred by the consensual principle. This principle creates the partially fictitious perception that the political decision reflects the will of all the participants in the political process. Those who believe in it would say, "We made this decision all together, so we are all responsible for it." But to say that all are responsible for the decision is to say that there is no one specifically responsible for it. Universal responsibility is tantamount to universal irresponsibility. To look at the other side of the same medal, all the political actors feel, not totally unjustifiably, that the decision is not fully their own. No wonder that the helpless minorities who are forced to hide their dissent cannot identify themselves with the decision. Even the majority and the effectively organized minorities, however, may well refuse to take full responsibility for the decision because they feel that they were forced to make more concessions than due, and shift the blame on to each other. If political responsibility is blurred in this way, democratic deliberation is sure to get corrupt. People cannot be sincerely motivated to give public justification to the political decision that they refuse to take a clear responsibility for. Moreover, they cannot be expected to learn from their own mistakes if they can shift the blame to the others. The corrosion of the self-critical learning process undermines the integrity of democratic deliberation. By contrast, the majoritarian principle is far less likely to have these effects because, as is shown above, it makes it far clearer who is to blame for the political decision if it turns out to be wrong.

Thirdly, the consensual principle undermines the critical learning process necessary for democratic deliberation by spoiling the coherence in the principle of the policy mix adopted in a political decision. Given the sharp and deep difference in principle between the competing policies of the different political actors, the consensual principle often obliges them to make a patchwork compromise to conjure up an agreement. Such a compromise cannot be justified by any principled argument but by the fact that it makes agreement possible. It may be functionally contradictory, with its policy mix components spoiling each other's merits. Naturally this unprincipled compromise has a consequence that does not please anybody; it can even have a catastrophic consequence owing to its failure to give any effective solution to the urgent problem. But when the product of such a compromise is put in practice and proves to be a failure, it is as hard to see what is wrong as it is to see who is wrong. Not just agent responsibility ("Who is to blame?") but policy responsibility ("Which policy is to blame?") is blurred because the patchwork compromise deprives each of the competing policies of full and fair opportunity for trial. A critical learning process on the basis of trial and error fails here. Certainly, the need for making a compromise is not obviated even under the majoritarian principle. But this principle mitigates the pressure for making unprincipled compromise. It makes it more likely for the political actors whose policies are similar or reconcilable in principle to form a majority by themselves and to give a thorough trial to their own coherent policy set. Not just who is wrong but what is wrong becomes clearer. The majoritarian principle thereby facilitates the trial-and-error learning process about the relative merits of alternative policy systems.

These considerations on the virtues and vices of consensus in democracy show that the majoritarian principle constrained by external veto, which is typically expressed in the liberal commitment to judicial review, protects minorities and fosters democratic deliberation more adequately than the consensual principle. I will reformulate this point by constructing two competing models of democracy in the last section of this chapter.

Toward Critical Democracy

What is Wrong with the Lijphart Models?

Before presenting my models of democracy I want to make a brief comment on A. Lijphart's influential model building of democracy in comparative politics (Lijphart, 1984). He contrasts the Majoritarian Model and Consensus Model. The majoritarian democracy is said to be historically originated in the British parliamentarism, and thus also named the Westminster Model, although its more thoroughgoing exemplification was found in New Zealand before its recent political reforms. He characterizes the majoritarian democracy as based on the majority rule and presents the following elements as a means to carry out the majority rule: one-party and bare majority cabinets (concentration of executive power), fusion of power with cabinet dominance, unicameralism (or asymmetric bicameralism), two-party system, one-dimensional party system (divided mainly in terms of socioeconomic issues), plurality system of elections (single .member district method), unitary and centralized government, parliamentary sovereignty with unwritten constitution (lack of judicial review), and exclusively representative government. In a word, this is the political system that enables one party to form a majority in the parliament and exercise concentrated sovereign power without effective constitutional constraint. The only safeguard against the danger of the ruling party becoming tyrannical is the possibility of power change with the opposition party.

In contrast with this rather dire picture of the majoritarian democracy, he depicts the consensus democracy as "a democratic regime that emphasizes consensus instead of opposition, that includes rather than excludes, and that tries to maximize the size of ruling majority instead of being satisfied with a bare majority" (Lijphart, 1984, p. 23). Using the regimes of "consociational democracy" in Belgium and Switzerland as illustrative examples, he presents the following majority-restraining elements as its constitutive features: executive power sharing (grand coalitions), separation of powers, balanced bicameralism (equal powers of the two chambers), multiparty system, multidimensional party system (involving not only socioeconomic but religious, cultural, linguistic or other lines of cleavage), proportional representation system of elections, decentralization and territorial or non-territorial federalism, minority veto secured in written constitution. This is the system where political power is shared by a variety of social forces that make political decisions through consensus formation within the constitutional framework that constrains the majority's dominance by separating and decentralizing political power and giving minorities strong veto.

Lijphart's aim is to relativize the British parliamentarism that used to be regarded as the historical archetype of representative democracy by indicating that the Westminster model is applicable only to homogeneous societies, whereas the consensus model works better in culturally and religiously divided societies with a greater danger of mutual intolerance. He also suggests that it is the Westminster model that is exceptional and that even Britain is diverging from it. I think he is right in urging that democracy must be sensitive to minority protection if it is to be applicable to plural societies with deeper cleavage between heterogeneous groups. But I do not think that the way he characterizes the majoritarian and consensus models is fair. He depicts the majoritarian model too darkly and the consensus model too brightly. Let me mention just two points that are important in the context of the discussion in this paper.

First, he fails to see that the merits of the majoritarian principle and demerits of the consensual principle in terms of the effects on deliberative process as I pointed out above are reproduced respectively in his majoritarian and consensus models. He is unaware of this issue because the deliberative perspective has no place in his perception of democracy underlying his model building. This is shown in his following remark on the *Leitmotiv* of his analysis: "An ideal democratic government would be one whose actions were always in perfect correspondence with the preferences of all its citizens. Such complete responsiveness in government has never existed and may never be achieved, but it can serve as an ideal to which democratic regimes should aspire. It can also be regarded as the end of a scale on which the degree of democratic responsiveness of different regimes may be measured" (Lijphart, 1984, pp. 1-2). By setting the responsiveness to people's preferences (which may involve a variety of naked special interests) as the democratic ideal, he disregards the fundamental role of deliberation in democracy that consists in transforming people's preferences. In the deliberative perspective, people's preferences as exogenous variables should not be the exclusive or dominant criteria for estimating the quality of democratic process. What counts as much or even more is the endogenous variable of this process, namely, whether and to what extent people can cultivate the public-spirited and well considered judgments within this process.

His lack of deliberative perspective can also be seen in specific features of his model building. For example, he regards bicameralism simply as a means of giving minority veto and thus as inconsistent with the Westminster model. In the deliberative perspective, however, bicameralism is an institutional device for requiring the political actors to "stop to think again" before making a final decision and to form a well considered judgment concerning the public interest. Bicameralism so conceived can be seen as indispensable to the Westminster model if we fairly appreciate the deliberative orientation of the latter.

Secondly, Lijphart fails to distinguish between internal and external veto. He regards the constraint of constitutional rights implemented by judicial review as just another form of minority protection that is characteristic of the consensus democracy but inconsistent with the majoritarian democracy. He thus sees one of "the British deviations from the Westminster Model" in the fact that "Britain's membership in the European Community has also introduced a potential right of judicial review both for the Community's Court of Justice and for British courts" (Lijphart, 1984, p. 15). But it is an internal veto that is inconsistent with the majoritarian model. An external veto is not just compatible with this model but is required by it as indispensable compensation for the rejected internal veto. Unless coupled with an external veto, the majoritarian model is doomed to lose legitimacy in plural societies. Accordingly, it is not fair to uncouple both unnecessarily just in order to show the inadequacy of the majoritarian model for plural societies.

Moreover, the external veto that, as I have shown above, is a fairer and more principled method of minority protection than the internal veto should be coupled with the majoritarian rather than with consensus model if its merits are not to be spoiled by the countervailing effect of an internal veto built into the consensus model. We have also seen that an external veto helps to facilitate democratic deliberation because it imposes constitutional constraint on the justificatory reasons for exercising the veto and thereby prevents the effectively organized minorities from seeking their naked special interests in the political process. In other words, the majoritarian model needs an external veto not just to protect minorities against the corruption of majority rule but also to protect the deliberative quality of majority rule against the corruption of minority powers. Lijphart fails to see not only the compatibility but also the interdependence of the majoritarian model and external veto.

These difficulties with the Lijphart models lead us to develop alternative models that are more coherently characterized and differentiated in terms of philosophical basis and political function.

Reflectional Democracy versus Critical Democracy

The alternative models that I want to propose are Reflectional Democracy and Critical Democracy. Let me sketch and contrast their basic features. (Hereafter I refer to them respectively as RD and CD for short.)

The regulative idea The difference in the regulative idea between the two models of democracy can be expressed by the following two symbolic imperatives. RD posits "Follow the will of the people" as the axiom of democratic government whereas CD sets forth "Behead the bad ruler" as the basic political responsibility that democracy imposes on the people. Namely, RD finds the *raison d'être* of democracy in reflecting or mirroring the people's preferences in political decisions to the maximum extent, because it denies the validity of values irreducible to the popular preferences. On the other hand, CD holds that the fundamental role of democracy is to subject the political power (including people's own power) to critical control and searching revision. CD requires democratic control of political power not because there is no independent values constraining the popular will but because whoever enjoys absolute power will absolutely get corrupt. Philosophically, RD is congenial to, if not logically derivable from, value relativism, while CD rejects value relativism and the resultant decisionism of the popular will in favour of fallibilism that ascribes fallibility even to the popular will and thus urges the need to open the democratic process to incessant critical self-examination. This fundamental difference in the understanding of the *raison d'être* of democracy underlies the difference between RD and CD in the following respects.

Political process Given the great diversity of people's preferences in the large-scale modern states, RD has to solve the problem of how to maximize the reflection of those preferences in political decisions by imposing the consensual decision-making principle on the democratic process and thus making this process function as the stage for consensus formation through bargaining among competing interest groups that represent different preferences given in society. The underlining value relativism leads RD to deny the existence of any public values independent of, and substantively constraining, this consensus formation process. So this process is endowed with the normative authority as "pure procedural justice" in the sense that the process legitimates the outcome, not vice versa.

On the other hand, CD regards democratic process as the competitive venture of trial-and-error searching for public values that cannot be reduced to an admixture of exogenously given popular preferences. CD responds to the diversity of value-perceptions in contemporary society by promoting the thoroughgoing and open critical debates between alternative political positions that compete for public support, subjecting them alternately to experimental test and enabling people to learn about their merits and demerits on a trial-and-error basis. CD adopts the majoritarian decision-making principle not because it recognizes the absolute authority of the majority will but because the majoritarian principle facilitates such critical learning process by mitigating the need for unprincipled compromises and making political responsibility clearer. Accordingly, CD regards the normative status of democratic process as "imperfect procedural justice" in the sense that the process guarantees not the infallibility of the outcome but its tentative acceptability open to critical re-examination.

Political agency Democracy is not just "government for the people." To distinguish it from a benevolent dictatorship, it must be understood to be "government by the people." Both RD and CD recognize the importance of the idea of self-governance for democracy. Of course, this idea is more or less fictitious because no feasible democracy is completely free from heteronomous elements. Self-governance is an ideal of democracy, not its reality. RD and CD interpret this ideal differently. For RD it means the sovereign authority of people's preferences as the ultimate standard for political decision making; for CD it means the final responsibility of the people for searching for public values through critical deliberation. This implies the different perceptions of political representation and participation.

RD understands political representation to require that the representatives should seek maximum satisfaction of the preferences of their constituencies in the political decision-making process. The preferences of their constituencies are given as exogenous variables independent of the deliberative process in the parliament and are supposed to bind the representatives as an imperative mandate. But CD understands representation to mean that the representatives are entrusted by the people with the task of searching for public values through critical deliberation. The policy choice of the representatives is expected to be based on their own well considered judgment, which is the endogenous variable of this deliberative process. The responsibility of a representative for her constituency is not to mirror their preferences but to involve them in the deliberative process by explaining to them the reasons for her judgment and responding to their objections. She will be dismissed in the next election if her constituency find her inadequate to her task, but CD requires that this *ex post facto* control should be conditioned on the public assessment of her deliberative performance, not on the organized votes of naked special interests.

Both RD and CD recognize the need to couple representative democracy with participatory democracy. But they understand the significance of popular participation in political process in different ways. RD holds that the essence of the participatory principle is to give the people the power to make political decisions directly. People have the right to participation in this sense as the sovereign authority for political decision making. It must be added, however, that out of concern for maximum inclusion of popular preferences, RD prefers localized and consensus-oriented grass-roots decision making to the majoritarian plebiscitary politics at the national level. By contrast, CD holds that the core of participatory principle is not just to give people the power to make a political decision directly but also to impose on them the responsibility to participate in the deliberative process before exercising this power. People can legitimately exercise their direct decision making power provided they carry out their deliberative responsibility. If this proviso is met, even the national plebiscitary politics is acceptable; if not, even the local grass-roots politics is unacceptable. Like RD, CD normally prefers local participatory politics to national plebiscitary politics. CD does so, however, not because it seeks for maximum inclusion of popular preferences but because the deliberative proviso is usually harder to be met by a huge mass of people at the national level than by small communities at the local level. This does not mean that CD excludes national participatory politics as impossible. It just reminds us of its legitimacy condition that populist passions sometimes make us neglect.

Institutions The institutional designs for RD and CD depend on their perceptions of the regulative idea, process and agency of democracy as shown above. The main considerations for RD are, on the one hand, to facilitate maximum inclusion of popular preferences through consensus formation and, on the other, to keep the resultant enormous political "transaction costs" within the limits of feasibility; those for CD are, on the one hand, to facilitate democratic deliberation through a critical trial-and-error learning process by a majoritarian decision-making system that promotes competition and power change among alternative coherent policy systems and, on the other, to secure minority protection by a means coherent with such a deliberation-oriented majoritairian system. To show what specific institutions are appropriate for RD and CD for these purposes, we have to consider some empirical questions that I cannot fully discuss in this paper. But my preceding discussions of the merits and demerits of the consensual and majoritarian principle and critical considerations on the Lijphart models show that the institutional features of his consensus and Westminster models can be respectively adapted to RD and CD, provided the following important "*mutatis mutandis*" conditions are met.

First, concerning institutions for minority protection, an external veto secured by judicial review for constitutional rights should be distinguished from an internal veto inherent in the consensual principle, as I have emphasized in my criticism of Lijphart. The latter is constitutive of RD, but the former coheres better with CD.

Secondly, as I have suggested, bicameralism as a device of internal veto should be distinguished from bicameralism as a deliberation facilitator. In deliberative bicameralism the upper house may be constituted in such a way that its members are more immune from turbulent mass passions and special interests than the members of the lower house. Long tenure, ineligibility for re-election and guaranteed economic independence may be part of the conditions that serve the purpose. Such a deliberative bicameralism is suitable for CD whereas veto bicameralism with the upper house representing specific minority groups belongs to RD.

Thirdly, separation of powers should not be interpreted simply in terms of the consensus orientation of RD. Separation of powers can have a deliberation-facilitating function favourable for CD. For example, the independence of the judiciary is needed to make judicial review effective and to prevent the executive from failing to enforce or violating the law as the product of democratic deliberation; separation of the legislature and the executive helps to prevent the principled argument required for deliberative process of law making from being eroded by the influences of the administrative considerations of expediency and to prevent legislators from influencing the administrative enforcement of law to the advantage of their political clients.

Lastly, we must consider the Tocquevillian distinction between the governmental and administrative centralization (de Tocqueville, 1969, pp. 87-98) in the institutional design. Governmental centralization that covers only the public affairs of the national community is necessary for making political responsibility clear, but administrative centralization that permeates local matters is erosive of political responsibility because it subjects local residents to the regulation by the "distant power" that they cannot effectively control. CD requires governmental centralization but rejects administrative centralization. RD does not make much of this distinction. It is ready to weaken even governmental centralization in order to mirror divided popular preferences in national politics.

For a summary of my presentation of the two models of democracy, please see the table at the end of this paper. I hope I have said enough to clarify the distinctive features of my two models of democracy and to show that they are philosophically more discerning and functionally more coherent than the Lijphart models. I also hope my model of critical democracy helps to remove, or at least to allay, the misunderstanding and misgivings about the majoritarian decision-making system that Lijphart's characterization of the Westminster model has disseminated. But critical democracy is not just "not too bad." I think that it is a better model than reflectional democracy. I want to conclude this paper by summing up the main reasons for this assessment, which have been already shown in my preceding comparative analysis of the majoritarian and consensus principles.

First, critical democracy facilitates democratic deliberation by promoting a critical trial-and-error learning process and by preventing the effectively organized minorities from exercising their internal veto to seek special naked interests. Reflectional democracy has the defects of the consensual principle in this respect: it blurs political responsibility (not just agent responsibility but policy responsibility) and lacks principled constraint on the political veto power of the organized minorities.

Secondly, an external veto system secured by critical democracy offers a fairer means of minority protection than the internal veto constitutive of reflectional democracy. The former protects minorities irrespective of their differentiated political power resources if their claims are justifiable in terms of the constitutional principles of fundamental rights, whereas the latter protects minorities irrespective of public justifiability of their claims if they have political power resources sufficient to obstruct the formation of the required level of consensus.

Lastly, critical democracy integrates "liberal" commitment to judicial protection of fundamental rights with "republican" commitment to deliberative democracy that attempts to curb factional interests and to rehabilitate public legitimacy of politics. To be more precise, critical democracy throws light on the deliberative perspective of liberal politics of rights and shows that the republican politics of civic virtue have the inherent need to be coupled with the former. On the other hand, reflectional democracy spoils both liberal and republican projects by inflating them excessively: it spoils the liberal concern for minority protection by rendering minority power undisciplined, and spoils the republican search for the public interest by replacing a sound form of political competition with all-inclusive unprincipled compromises.

In a nutshell, the model of critical democracy as opposed to reflectional democracy shows why and how Demos can be a responsible agent of public deliberation only if it collaborates with Hercules. I am aware my arguments are sketchy and ambitious. Even if they may not sound terribly convincing, however, I hope they are provocative enough to invite critical responses. Even that would be a thrilling success for me.

Two Models of Democracy

	REFLECTIONAL DEMOCRACY	CRITICAL DEMOCRACY
The Regulative Idea		
Symbolic imperative	"Follow the will of the people."	"Behead the bad ruler."
The *raison d'être* of democracy	Maximum reflection of popular preferences in political decisions	Critical control and reformation of government
Epistemological stance	Value relativism	Fallibilism
Political process		
The function of democratic process	Consensus formation for maximum inclusion of competing preferences	Competitive search for public values by trial and error
The mode of decision making	The consensual principle	The majoritarian principle
The normative status of democratic process	Pure procedural justice	Imperfect procedural justice
Political Agency		
The meaning of self-governance	The sovereign authority of popular preferences	People's primary responsibility for improving the government
The status and accountability of representatives	Imperative mandate; representing the constituency's interest	Entrusted with deliberative role; fostering deliberation in the constituency
The essence of participation	People's right to exert political decision making power directly	People's responsibility to participate in the deliberative process
Institutions		
The main guide for institutional design	Maximum inclusion of political actors and control of inflated political transaction cost (proportional representation, grand coalitions etc.)	Promotion of competition and power change among political actors with alternative coherent policy systems (plurality election system, one-party administration etc.)
Minority protection	Internal veto	External veto
Separation of powers	For balancing powers	For securing deliberation
Bicameralism	Veto bicameralism	Deliberative bicameralism
Distribution of powers	Governmental and administrative decentralization	Governmental centralization and administrative decentralization

* Professor of Legal Philosophy at Graduate Schools for Law and Politics, the University of Tokyo.

Note

1 This phrase is borrowed from Justice H. Stone's famous statement of the conditions for legitimate judicial review in footnote 4 of the US Supreme Court's decision in the *Carolene Products* case. For a discussion of Stone's view, see Ely (1980).

References

Ackerman, B. (1991), *We the People: 1. Foundations*, Harvard University Press, Cambridge (Ma).

Bohman, J. and Rheg, W. (eds.) (1997), *Deliberative Democracy*, The MIT Press, Cambridge (Ma).

Cohen, J. (2003), 'Procedure and Substance in Deliberative Democracy' in T. Christiano (ed.), *Philosophy and Democracy: An Anthology*, Oxford University Press, Oxford.

de Tocqueville, A. (1969), *Democracy in America*, G. Lawrence (tr.), J.P. Mayer (ed.), Anchor Books, Garden City (NY).

Dworkin, R. (1978), *Taking Rights Seriously*, 2nd ed., Harvard University Press, Cambridge (Ma).

Elster, J. (ed.) (1998), *Deliberative Democracy*, Cambridge University Press, Cambridge.

Ely, J. (1980), *Democracy and Distrust: a Theory of Judicial Review*, Harvard University Press, Cambridge (Ma).

Gaus, G. (1996), *Justificatory Liberalism: An Essay on Epistemology and Political Theory*, Oxford University Press, Oxford.

Gutmann, A. and Thompson, D. (eds.) (1996), *Democracy and Disagreement*, Harvard University Press, Cambridge (Ma).

Habermas, J. (1996), *Between Facts and Norms: Contributions to a Discourse Theory of Law and Democracy*, W. Rheg (tr.), The MIT Press, Cambridge (Ma).

Lijphart, A. (1984), *Democracies: Patterns of Majoritarian and Consensus Government in Twenty-One Countries*, Yale University Press, New Heaven.

Mill, J.S. (1975), *Three Essays on Liberty, Representative Government, the Subjection of Women*, R. Wollheim (ed.), Oxford University Press, Oxford.

Rawls, J. (1993), *Political Liberalism*, Columbia University Press, New York.

Sandel, M. (1996), *Democracy's Discontent: America in Search of a Public Philosophy*, Harvard University Press, Cambridge (Ma).

Schmitt, C. (1993), *Verfassungslehre*, 8th ed., Duncker & Humblot, Berlin.

Sunstein, C. (1993), *The Partial Constitution*, Harvard University Press, Cambridge (Ma).

Chapter 7

The Paradox of Democratic Representation. On Whether and How Disagreement Should be Represented

Samantha Besson*

> The paradox is that representative democracy may help, by its insidious educative power, to sustain and promote a culture that is, in sectors and particulars, more directly democratic, more constitutionally delicate, and more beautifully illustrative of moral indeterminacy than the political system itself; while in the encouragement given to independence of spirit in the twofold sense, it may attain its highest justification. (Kateb, 1981, p. 368)

Introduction

If it is right, as many argue nowadays[1] (Dryzek, 2000; Elster, 1998; Habermas, 1998; Benhabib, 1996; Gutmann and Thompson, 1996; Cohen, 1989; Manin, 1987), that deliberation can be seen as a response to pervasive and persistent reasonable disagreement about justice and hence as a way of legitimizing political and legal decisions in conditions of reasonable pluralism,[2] a difficulty remains: who is deliberating (Gargarella, 1998, p. 274)? Theories of deliberative democracy typically conceive of deliberators as representatives and not as citizens.[3] The question that arises then is how to make sure our representatives' deliberation can represent our deliberation, how to make sure their disagreement can represent our disagreement. Similarly, when political equality is invoked to justify majority decisions and explain their authority in the face of disagreement[4] (Waldron, 1999, pp. 114, 165; Singer, 1972, p. 32ff.; Besson, 2003a, pp. 237-240), the appeal is to the equality of citizens; it is they who will be bound by decisions they disagree with and should therefore be able to regard themselves as these decisions' authors. The difficulty is that most of the time majority decisions are not made by those who are subjects to the law, but by their representatives.

There is, in other words, a *prima facie* problem of *political equality*[5] and *lack of inclusion* contrary to one of the basic tenets of democracy[6] (Aristotle, 1988, III: 1275b13-b21, VI:1317a40-1318a10; Habermas, 1998 and Dryzek, 2001, pp. 651,

662): when representatives are the ones to deliberate and take decisions, not all those affected by these decisions, and who might be in disagreement with them, can take part in the deliberation and in the vote that leads to the final decisions, although these decisions are meant to settle their disagreements.[7] True, as some deliberative democracy theorists have argued, more deliberation in more institutional and non-institutional forums will help constitute a stronger public sphere and hence ensure more implication of the citizenry in their representatives' decisions and hopefully more responsiveness on the part of those representatives as well. It will not, however, elude the present difficulty:[8] what matters here is who takes part in the final deliberation and the final vote[9] (Goodin, 2003b, pp. 1-2), and hence who gets a hearing rather than just a voice.[10] Since all matters are only rarely exhaustively discussed in the public sphere before being transferred for deliberation to representatives (Phillips, 1995, p. 43) or at least hijacked by parties,[11] it is the legitimacy of representation that should be sought and not only the legitimacy of deliberation itself;[12] any consideration of deliberative democracy is incomplete without consideration of how inclusive deliberation and hence representative structures are (Saward, 2000, p. 10).

This is no doubt an old chestnut. The tension between direct participatory and indirect representative democracy has been a recurrent theme in the history of political theory. Still, the conditions of widespread and persistent reasonable disagreement about justice which prevail in contemporary politics exacerbate its difficulty (Gargarella, 1998, p. 270; Kymlicka, 1995, pp. 129-130). Some authors even contend that disagreement can be adduced against representative institutions and justify the adoption of a purely participatory model of democracy.[13] While Rousseau's views have for long been disparaged as idealistic and bizarre, a number of thinkers have recently begun to resurrect these views and to challenge the substitutability of representation for direct participatory democracy[14] (Barber, 1984, pp. 145-146). This approach is now under revision, however. Representation is not only an inescapable and necessary dimension of contemporary politics and thus, for pragmatic and prudential reasons, related to the size of the polity or to the division of labour. What recent proponents of direct participatory democracy also ignore is that representation is a desirable and justifiable mode of government (Young, 1997; Urbinati, 2000 and 2002; Kateb, 1981; Plotke, 1997). It is more than a second-best approximation or substitute for direct democracy or even for democracy *tout court.*[15] In fact, more and more voices can be heard every day in favour of the democratic legitimacy of representation, and not only, as until recently, on the part of neo-Schumpeterian theorists of electoral democracy[16] (Kateb, 1981; Plotke, 1997, p. 18; Young, 1997, p. 352; Urbinati, 2000 and 2002).

The problem is, however, that a systematic and comprehensive defence of the democratic legitimacy of representation has not been provided yet.[17] The general, and mostly pragmatic, adhesion to representation does not mean that the democratic legitimacy of representation can be taken for granted. Representation cannot simply be associated with the exact "reflection of the underlying ideal of debate, deliberation and voting among the members" of the polity, as Waldron would have it[18] (Waldron, 2002, p. 7 fn. 3). This all the more so given all the misgivings democratic representation commonly provokes in our political systems.[19] Demands for more presence of members of minority or disadvantaged groups among representatives become more insistent every day (Young, 1990, 1997; Phillips, 1995; Williams, 1998; Gargarella, 1998). It has become more difficult nowadays in the face of pervasive moral and political conflicts to argue that a few representatives who represent fixed interests can determine what is good and right for everyone than it was in thc 17th century[20] (Burke, 1899; Hamilton, 1961, n. 35, pp. 220-221). As Mansbridge rightly argues, the more conflicts and disagreements there are, the more the demand for political equality grows within representation mechanisms.[21] Representing the whole of society does not yet mean full political equality and inclusion in the modes of representation itself.[22].

As a result, an argument for the democratic legitimacy of representation and hence of representatives' decisions in the face of reasonable disagreement has become a missing link in recent "legisprudential"[23] accounts. It is the case, for instance, of Waldron's *jurisprudence of legislation*, which rightly claims that democracy, and participatory majoritarianism in particular are the only ways of taking legitimate legal decisions in conditions of widespread reasonable disagreement.[24] Without an argument for the democratic legitimacy of representation, however, these theories of legislation are bound to attract, and have already attracted critiques of their idealization of democratic participation (Eisgruber, 2002, p. 41ff.; Kavanagh, 2003, p. 470) and objections based on the commonplace view of representation *qua* perverted, purely interested, elitist and over-politicized mode of decision-making (Setala, 1996, p. 40; Müller, 1992, p. 156ff.). It is crucial therefore, on the one hand, to present arguments for the democratic legitimacy of representation in the context of conflict-ridden conditions of decision-making and, on the other, to suggest institutional reforms of current modes of representation that take reasonable pluralism more seriously.[25] This is what one may refer to as the *challenge of disagreement*.

To take up this challenge, the present essay is structured as follows. In the first section, I will present some elements of a plausible conception of democratic representation. In the next section, I will examine the challenge disagreement raises for representation, by first posing the challenge itself and then by presenting one of its most common answers: descriptive group representation. In the third section, I will discuss two counter-challenges one may raise against the challenge of disagreement: the paradox of democratic representation and the counter-challenge of diversity. In the fourth section, I will develop a revised conception of representation that takes both the challenge of disagreement and the two counter-challenges seriously and argue that this revised account of representation is in fact necessary for the relationship of representation to take place. Finally, in a last section, I will discuss the consequences of this revised account of representation both for the protection of deliberation and political equality and for the justification of representation itself. A *caveat* is in order at this stage. For reasons of scope, the present argument will largely remain at a theoretical level despite the difficulties this raises.[26] It should be clear, however, that the test of such a disagreement-based account of representation lies in the institutional measures one may take to implement it in practice (Pitkin, 1972, pp. 239-240; Müller, 1992, pp. 158-159; Scanlon, 1977, p. 98; Beitz, 1983, pp. 69-70).

The Contours of Democratic Representation

Before examining the challenge disagreement sets for representation, and discussing ways of meeting it and of justifying democratic representation in the face of reasonable pluralism, it is important to present briefly the notion of representation as well as its scope, before introducing its five main constitutive elements.

Notion and Scope

Representation is a normatively laden and heavily contestable concept of which there can be many different plausible conceptions[27] (Ragowski, 1981, p. 395ff.). This is because, as Arendt elegantly puts it, "the question of representation, one of the crucial and most troublesome issues of modern politics ever since the revolutions, actually implies no less than a decision on the very dignity of the political realm itself" (Arendt, 1970, p. 239).

The *general* idea that democratic decision-making revolves around the deliberation and decision of a few representing the many has now become one of the major creeds in democratic theory. As I explained in the introduction, representation is not only an inescapable and necessary dimension of contemporary politics, but also a desirable mode of decision-making. First of all, representation is regarded as *necessary* and this mostly for pragmatic and efficiency reasons[28] related to the size of the polity[29] or to the division of labour (Sieyès, 1963; Manin, 1997, p. 3). No person can be present at all the decisions or in all the decision-making bodies whose actions affect her life, because there are so many and they are so dispersed. Besides, these bodies could not hold all those affected with all the conflicting opinions, interests and perspectives they might have. Secondly, representation is also, however, a *desirable* and justifiable mode of government in contemporary pluralistic conditions (Young, 1997; Urbinati, 2000 and 2002; Kateb, 1981; Plotke, 1997). This has to do mainly with the channelling and resolution of conflicts (Hobbes, 1999; Sieyès, 1963; Dunn, 1999; Ankersmit, 1996 and 2002; Loughlin, 2003) and hence with the facilitation of deliberation (Arendt, 1973, p. 226ff.; Pitkin, 1972, pp. 212-213; Young, 1997, p. 353). Representation eases deliberation by reducing the number of discussants and hence the number of conflicting opinions, interests and perspectives in conflict (Müller, 1992, pp. 155, 157-158; Müller, 2002, p. 109; Habermas, 1998, pp. 210ff., 222ff.; Young, 1990, p. 263; Young, 1997, p. 353), but also by establishing a gap between representatives' deliberation and citizens' decision or vote, and hence by granting more time for reflection and deliberation among citizens, among representatives and among citizens and representatives (Urbinati, 2000; Kateb, 1981; Young, 1997). More arguments will be presented for the justification of representation in the course of this essay[30] (Pitkin, 1972, p. 86).

Despite the general adhesion to the principle of representation, democratic representation remains a *complex ideal* with a variety of forms. Although it is a significant and widely used concept, its precise meaning remains contested (Pitkin, 1972, Introduction, and Pitkin, 1989, pp. 132-133; Manin, 1997, Introduction).

What I reconstruct here as the standard case of representation is based on the convergence in the writings of a wide range of theorists, not all of whom may subscribe to every aspect of the definition I give. Representation, broadly defined, is a *process according to which some people, the "representatives", usually only a few, stand for and act so as to bind the "represented", usually more or even all those affected people who cannot be physically present* (Pitkin, 1972, pp. 8-9; Urbinati, 2000; Müller, 2002, p. 107). More precisely, one may summarize the core phenomena that count as representation as the process (i) according to which the constituency, first, authorizes the representative to stand and act for it, mainly through elections, (ii) according to which, then, the representative stands and acts for the constituency so as to bind it and (iii) according to which, finally, the representative is held accountable[31] by the constituency, mainly through re-elections,[32] but also through other modes of periodical or even constant control.[33]

According to this definition, the relationship of representation is best described as a process[34] (Young, 1997, p. 358ff.). Representatives and their constituency should be in constant dialogue about the deferred political decision from the moment of authorization to the moment of accountability. They should indeed all act as agents in order for true and democratic representation to take place; representatives should represent and be held accountable, while represented should authorize and then hold accountable. Without an active constituency which holds representatives accountable, there is no representation *stricto sensu* but mere domination (Kuper, 2004, Ch. 3; Plotke, 1997, p. 27ff.; Pitkin, 1972, pp. 231-232). This explains the importance of the impulse to political participation and to the development of a rich public sphere which, in sufficient deliberative conditions,[35] should be generated by the spatial and temporal gap opened by representation between deliberation and decision.[36] Representation is indeed "deferred democracy" (Young, 1997, pp. 355-357) according to Young, that is to say a democracy in which the moment and location of deliberation (by representatives) are distinct from the moment and location of the decision or electing vote (by constituents).[37] It is in this democratic deferral and spatio-temporal gap therefore that the "indirectness" of the relationship of representation resides rather than at the level of active participation of citizens, which is an essential element of representation as well (Urbinati, 2000). The relation of mutual agency and dialogue thus created then leads to the differentiation and mutual constitution of represented and representatives.[38] By becoming an agent of the representation relationship it establishes, the constituency constitutes itself as a political entity and participant (Ankersmit, 1996, p. 56). This initial self-constitution then becomes mutual constitution and hence progressive differentiation in the course of the representation relationship and of the dialogue thus initiated.[39]

Five Constitutive Elements

If representation is a matter of persons choosing other persons to represent them, the identification of the relationship of representation can be broken into five independent questions:[40] Who is represented?; Who are the representatives?; How are they chosen?; What do they represent?; and How do they represent?.

Who is represented? Usually, representatives represent *citizens*, i.e. the individual members of the political entity at stake.[41] They can represent them as a whole people or else represent them as sub-groups of the whole people in different political entities. Two interesting issues are worth discussing in this context.

First, the relationship between *individual and group representation*. Although representatives usually represent individuals who elect them, i.e. their constituency, it is not rare to encounter the representation of groups *qua* constituency. It is the case for party representatives, but also of the representation of groups of interest or of other social groups. Besides, most of the time, representatives represent many different layers of individuals or groups within their constituency; a socialist woman will represent socialist voters and women socialist voters.[42]

Second, the relationship between *one's constituency's interests and the people's as whole*[43] (Pitkin, 1972, p. 215ff.). A further difficulty relates to the choice that has to be made by a representative, in case of a conflict of interests, between her constituency's interests, on the one hand, and the people's as whole, on the other. According to Burke, representatives represent the people as a whole rather than those who elected them (Burke, 1899). In practice, however, things are never that clear. In the European Parliament, for instance, some MPs claim they represent Europeans as a whole, whereas others claim to represent their own constituency, i.e. voters in their own European country (Schmitt and Thomassen, 1999).

Who are the representatives? This is certainly one of the most contested questions in theories of representation. One usually opposes the descriptive model of representation, according to which representatives should represent their constituency by resembling those represented as much as possible, preferring the substantive model of representation, according to which, on the contrary, representatives should represent their constituency symbolically only[44] (Pitkin, 1972, Ch. 4 and 5). In the descriptive model, representatives should mirror their constituency ("Darstellung" in German) and *not only* stand and act for it as in the substantive model ("Stellvertretung" or "Repräsentation" in German).

Of course, it is impossible for a small group of representatives to mirror the entire diversity of the wider population in every detail of their individuality (Müller, 1992, p. 156). Some proposals have been made, especially in the 18th century, for *microcosmic representation* of this kind (Adams, 1951, p. 205; Mirabeau, 1834, I, p. 7; Mansbridge, 2000, pp. 105-107; Pitkin, 1972, Ch. 2). The problem is, however, partly one of size of the representative assembly (Goodin, 2003a) and partly one of costs (Mansbridge, 2000, p. 107). The most that can realistically be intentionally described in practice are broadly distributed common characteristics,[45] such as a person's life experience, identity or activity where she has affinity with others (Young, 1997, p. 362). What is usually meant by descriptive representation is therefore *group representation*, such as representation of women or ethnic, religious or cultural groups.[46]

It is interesting to note that according to Pitkin and others, descriptive representation is purely passive and aims at gathering information rather than at deliberating and decision-making (Pitkin, 1972, pp. 61, 81, 90; Parkinson, 2003a, p. 189). Although this view may hold purely theoretically, it does not have any practical relevance. Usually, indeed, descriptive representatives actively promote the interests of those they represent, both in a creative manner when new circumstances arise and in a manner responsive to them[47] (Mansbridge, 2000, p. 107). Representation is a constitutive relationship through which identities and opinions are mutually forged rather than merely mirrored and then defended (Saward, 2003; Ankersmit, 2002). Descriptive representation does not therefore exclude substantive representation, but merely adds onto it[48] (Mansbridge, 2000, p. 101; Parkinson, 2003b).

How are the representatives chosen? This third question is intrinsically related to the first one – or at least was in ancient times.[49] One usually distinguishes three modes of selection of representatives: election, lot and random sampling. While it should be clear how an election and its different variants work, selection by lot or sampling is less evident.

Whereas in an election, people choose their representatives, the selection of representatives by lot or random sampling shares the characteristic of submitting the determination of representatives to others than those represented. While the selection of representatives by lot leaves it to chance to determine who should be representative among all or some of the represented, selection by sampling is the task of a few citizens who choose randomly from samples of the population.[50] All three modes can therefore be ordered in a decreasing order of democratic legitimacy: the more choice the citizen has in the determination of her representatives, the more influence she can be said to have in the final deliberations and vote[51] (Manin, 1997, p. 83). Although selection by lot is somehow more legitimate than arbitrary sampling, it only makes sense in a homogeneous society in which all citizens have very similar interests and perspectives and in which the political equality that matters is the equal chance of holding office rather than equality in consenting to power (Manin, 1997, pp. 34-41).

What do the representatives represent? At first sight, representatives represent the people affected by their decisions. The difficulty is that given the extreme diversity of all individuals constituting the citizenry, it is impossible to represent them in all their individual features. All it is possible to represent therefore are common aspects of citizens' individualities (Müller, 1992, p. 156; Young, 1997, p. 362). One usually finds mention of the representation of people's interests, opinions or perspectives, but there may be many others.[52] Although all these characteristics are related to one another in some ways[53] and are often inseparable at the particular level,[54] they are conceptually distinct.

Before anything, two *caveats* are in order. First, although the object of descriptive representation can be different from the object of substantive representation, it is not necessarily the case.[55] There is a difference indeed between the object and the agent of representation. Second, if the object of representation amounts to the constituency's opinions, there is not much the representative can do beyond following a mandate, but things are different when the object of representation consists in the constituency's best interests or in its general perspectives, as then both dependent and independent approaches of representation may apply.[56] There is a difference indeed between the object of representation, i.e. what a representative stands for, and the activity of representation, i.e. what the representative does when she stands for those represented.

It is worth examining each of the potential objects of representation in turn. The presentation will be brief, however, as these elements will be addressed again later in the essay.

First of all, people's *interests*. This is the most common object of representation which is often simply described as "acting in the interest of the represented" (Pitkin, 1972, p. 209; Kuper, 2004, Ch. 3). The concept of interest stems from the objective theory of values. It amounts to what is in the objective interest of a person, i.e. what is important to her life prospects, rather than to her subjective interests, choices, desires or preferences. In the representation context, what is at stake are the interests of many people, i.e. the nation's or the constituency's public interests. As such, it is important to distinguish these interests from three other things. First, the interests of the public ought to be distinguished from the *common good*, that is to say the amalgam of standards that has priority over individual interests because it is fundamental to the way of life of the group.[57] Second, what is in the public interest differs from what is *good for all*, i.e. whose benefits can be shared by all constituents. Third, public interests are different from the *aggregate of subjective individual goods* as in the utilitarian calculus of what produces the most preference-satisfaction overall, regardless of the distribution of satisfaction. Although it remains contested, the benefit to a numerical majority of people is to date the least contestable indicator of the interests of the public (Kuper, 2004, Ch. 3; Mansbridge, 1981, p. 468), provided all perspectives are somehow given a voice in official and non-official deliberations (Müller, 1992, pp. 156-57).

Second, people's *opinions* or *ideas*. They amount to any judgement or belief about how things are or ought to be, and the political judgements that follow from these judgements or beliefs (Young, 1997, p. 364). They are based on principles, values and priorities, since these bear on a person's judgement of what ends should be pursued. Opinions may be about what one takes to be one's objective interests and the means to achieve them, but they should not be confused with them; there may be opinions over other principles or values than objective interests and the representation of objective interests need not depend on the opinions of those whose interests it is, although they will have to depend on the opinions of those who defend these interests. Contrary to interests, which can become public through the game of the majority, and to perspectives which usually stem from social and hence shared structures, opinions and ideas remain individual. Of course, they can be affected by social perspectives and hence become more common, but it is rarer. This fact makes them relatively indeterminate and their individual representation more complex (Arendt, 1973, p. 227). Besides, according to Arendt, it is often difficult to represent opinions because most of the time they are the result of a political confrontation and expression which does not always take place before the representatives' deliberations (Arendt, 1973, p. 268). Opinions which can be represented therefore are those rare ones which have been expressed in the public before representatives' deliberations and those which are usually held commonly by many people.[58]

Finally, people's *perspectives* or *standpoints*. Perspectives involve the ways people interpret issues and events and produce judgements and beliefs, because of their structural social locations and experiences (Young, 1997, p. 365). These structural locations result from group differentiations and collective cultural attributions, such as age, gender, race, religion, etc. Perspectives affect one's opinions and interests, but should not be confused with them. It is possible to share a common perspective without having the same opinions, the same interests or even the very same perspectives on particular issues. Perspectives are worth representing, because they are not necessarily shared by all representatives and often need to be present for fair and balanced decisions to be taken. They are easier to represent than individual opinions as they are usually part of a social being and attitude, that is to say something that need not be expressed to be recognized and that is usually collective and less indeterminate.

How do the representatives represent? This last question should be carefully distinguished from the first one; once we know who the representatives are with respect to their relationship to the represented, it is important to establish how they should represent them. Of course, both issues are often related, but their relationship is not a necessary one.[59]

One usually opposes representation *qua* delegation (representation as mandate) to representation *qua* trusteeship (representation as independence).[60] When representatives are regarded as delegates, they are bound by the instructions of those represented as in a mandate relationship. When, on the contrary, representatives are associated with trustees, they are given free rein to make decisions according to their best judgement, within the limits of course of the object represented (interests, opinions or perspectives) and their accountability to those represented. One of the main difficulties with these two models is that they describe the representation relationship in a manichean way. It is rare indeed to see either representatives or those represented as the only ones responsible for a decision (Pitkin, 1972, pp. 154-155). Part of the problem is that representation is not so much a matter of agency as one usually understands it. There is indeed no principal and agent, but two groups of political agents so to speak (Kuper, 2004, Ch. 3; Plotke, 1997, p. 31; Young, 1997, p. 358ff.); both sides of the relationship of representation are needed to ensure that all interests and perspectives are taken into account, on the one hand, and thoroughly discussed and hence understood, on the other. The relationship of representation may indeed be, as I explained earlier, divided into a relationship of authorization, first, and of accountability, second.[61]

The Challenge of Disagreement

Now that I have presented the main elements of the conception of representation that constitute this essay's starting point, it is time to turn to the challenge that persistent and widespread reasonable disagreement raises for democratic representation. To do so I would like, first of all, to restate and develop this challenge and, secondly, to present the main answer it has been given so far: descriptive group representation.

The Challenge

As I explained in the introduction, deliberation and majority rule are usually seen as the solutions to widespread and persistent reasonable disagreement about justice and matters of principle. The problem, and the challenge this sets to our current conceptions of democratic representation, is that those who deliberate and vote to settle our conflicts are representatives and not those who disagree in the first place. True, some degree of exclusion is inherent to representation, but the challenge retains its sting: if representation is a necessary and desirable way to deliberate and vote, then the disagreements we would have deliberated and voted on, had we not been interrupted or had we been able to start deliberating at all, should be represented. This is what I have called the *challenge of disagreement*. Of course, this intuition is not entirely new and disagreement is already partially represented in practice.[62] The point is, however, to unpack and rationalize this practice and understand whether and to what extent exactly disagreement should be represented.

Why should disagreement be represented? There are different reasons for requiring sufficient representation of our disagreements and more generally of our diversity in our representatives' deliberations and votes.

First of all, *representatives' horizontal disagreements.*[63] Our disagreements are very rarely exhausted before the buck is passed on to our representatives. Since most of our disagreements are not settled before representation takes place (Phillips, 1995, p. 43) or even only arise alongside representatives' disagreements as some topics only appear in parties' packages or once representatives have started to deliberate,[64] there is no one crystallized opinion, principle or interest to be represented but a multitude of conflicting perspectives about what this opinion, principle or interest should be (Mansbridge, 2000, p. 100). According to some authors, our disagreements are suppressed by our electoral choices and translated into horizontal disagreements among representatives; the latter's settlement should therefore be taken to solve our disagreements.[65] True, representatives tend to disagree reasonably as much as citizens (Pitkin, 1972, p. 212ff.) - and there is no reason why they should not, since disagreements about objective interests or among opinions are inescapable among reasonable people, whether citizens or representatives (Pitkin, 1972, p. 212). Their disagreements can, however, be very different from ours (Manin, 1997, p. 204; Pitkin, 1972, pp. 212-213). One may therefore question their legitimacy in deciding for all citizens on that basis.[66] It is important, in other words, that all points of view in conflict be represented both in further deliberations among representatives, on the one hand, and in the voting process, on the other.[67] First, all points of view should be represented in the deliberative process to ensure full information and insights on the issues discussed. Second, they should also be represented in the aggregative process so that the resolution of conflicts can take all interests and perspectives into account.

Second, *representatives' and citizens' vertical disagreements*. Citizens often disagree reasonably with their representatives, for instance about the setting of the agenda, and this disagreement constitutes an intrinsic part of their relationship of representation. It is indeed through this constant dialogue that the dialectic between authorization and accountability can take place and that both representatives and represented can be agents of representation.[68] Since the quality of representatives' deliberation and decisions depends on this vertical exchange and dialogue between representatives and citizens (Pitkin, 1972, p. 212; Kateb, 1981, p. 361), the more informed and complete the latter is, the better it is. It follows therefore that the more citizens' horizontal disagreements are represented within their representatives' horizontal disagreements, the more constructive their vertical disagreements will be. Vertical disagreements that feed into representatives' horizontal disagreements will in turn stimulate citizens' horizontal disagreements.

How should disagreement be represented? Now that I have clarified why disagreement should be represented, it is important to establish more clearly what it is that should be represented in order to represent disagreement. "Representing disagreement" sounds indeed more like a slogan than like a practical form of representation.

First of all, then, the *particulars*, *sources* or *fact* of disagreement. To say that disagreement should be represented means that those people who disagree should be represented. As I explained earlier, however, we know that we cannot represent people in all their particulars and it is the same with disagreement: we can represent it in general, but cannot actually stand for all their particulars. The three potential objects of disagreement representation, i.e. the particulars, sources and fact of disagreement, correspond to a decreasing degree of specificity of the object represented.[69] *Particulars* of disagreement include interests and opinions in conflict. As it is difficult, however, to represent all interests and all opinions in conflict, some authors have argued, albeit in other words, for a representation of some of the *sources* of disagreement, i.e. the different perspectives or standpoints on the basis of which people forge their opinions and conceive of their interests (Young, 1997, p. 365ff.). Perspectives can be regarded as sources of disagreement in the sense that perspectives influence the development of opinions and interests that conflict. True, there may be other sources of disagreement than social pluralism and the plurality of perspectives, such as moral pluralism in particular. However, social perspectives can be said to be the most easily describable and representable source of disagreement. Besides, as perspectives tend to be socially forged, there are less perspectives to represent than conflicting opinions, in order to represent the same disagreements. Another benefit of representing perspectives is that the disagreements need not have been completely spelled out to be represented. Although standpoints are fewer than opinions in conflict, they remain very numerous. Some authors have therefore argued that what should be represented is the sheer *fact* of disagreement rather than the exact parameters of that disagreement.[70] This can be done by representing some but not all interests, opinions or perspectives in conflict so that the fact of disagreement is made present.

Second, *individual* or *group disagreement*. When representing either of the three elements distinguished before, it is important to know whether it is individual or group disagreement one wishes to represent (Gould, 2000, p. 185). Disagreements may indeed result from conflicts of individual interests, opinions and perspectives, but also - and the two are often related as they usually take place among individuals - from conflicts of group interests, opinions and perspectives.[71] In fact, individual disagreements are rarely, and maybe sadly so, isolated from group disagreements in practice. Of course, to concentrate on group disagreement tends to dangerously simplify the grounds of disagreement and even to acknowledge the existence of pre-constituted constraints on individual opinions and perspectives.[72] It remains, however, that in the context of democratic representation, group disagreements are the most relevant disagreements. First of all, group disagreements are easier to represent than individual disagreements given the extreme individual diversity one would have to represent in the latter case.[73] Secondly, when disagreement representation is reduced to the representation of conflicting perspectives rather than opinions, the relationship to group representation becomes clearer, since individual perspectives are in large parts determined by individuals' belonging to social groups (Young, 1997, p. 365; Phillips, 1995, p. 6).

A Common Response: Descriptive Group Representation

All this explains why group representation and descriptive group representation is the most common response to the challenge of disagreement. In the following, I will, first of all, argue in favour of the descriptive representation of disagreement. I will then discuss three different dimensions of the implementation of the descriptive representation of disagreement in practice.

From disagreement representation to descriptive representation. While it should be clear that disagreement representation can only realistically occur in practice through the representation of group disagreements, it remains to be established why the representation of disagreement is better ensured by descriptive representation, albeit not exclusively so.[74] In other words, what is it that requires, for instance, that the representation of the difference of perspectives between men and women is ensured by having both male and female representatives deliberate and vote over these matters? Some of the reasons for this overlap with reasons for descriptive group representation *tout court*, but a second group of reasons are specific to the issue of disagreement representation.[75]

First of all, *descriptive representation* tout court. Different arguments have been made for descriptive group representation. Primarily, it is a concern for presence, memory or voice which has been proposed (Young, 1997; Phillips, 1995; Williams, 1998; Mansbridge, 2000). The recognition of distinct groups' interests and standpoints is indeed facilitated by the presence of members of these groups among the representatives (Mansbridge, 2000, pp. 119-122). This is also sometimes referred to as the *consciousness-raising function* of descriptive representation (Phillips, 1995, p. 176). Secondly, descriptive representation also increases the visibility of diversity thus stimulating deliberation (Goodin, 2003a and 2003b; Gargarella, 1998; Urbinati, 2000 and 2002). This is also sometimes referred to as the *perspective-expanding function* of descriptive representation (Phillips, 1995, p. 53).

Second, *descriptive disagreement representation.* The two arguments for descriptive group representation *qua* disagreement representation are related to the two prongs of the justification of the disagreement challenge discussed before. First of all, *horizontal disagreement among representatives.* When representatives are members of the different groups whose different standpoints and differences of opinion lie at the origins of horizontal disagreements among citizens, they can represent these different standpoints and opinions better than members of other groups (Mansbridge, 2000, p. 100). Some groups cannot indeed even realize what other standpoints could be and how to get to them (Young, 1997, pp. 366ff., 369ff.). This applies to the deliberative as much as to the aggregative functions of representation (Mansbridge, 2000, pp. 103-105). Second, *vertical disagreement among representatives and citizens.* The presence of descriptive group representatives eases the representation of the points of view at stake in horizontal disagreements among citizens and hence the vertical communications between representatives and citizens, as well as the settlement of their vertical disagreements (Mansbridge, 2000, p. 99).

The implementation of descriptive disagreement representation. Now that the grounds for descriptive group representation in the context of the representation of disagreement have been clarified, it is important to turn our attention to the implementation of descriptive disagreement representation.

First, *the groups to be represented.* Not all groups of affinities can be descriptively represented given the issue of size that underlies representation (Phillips, 1995, pp. 46, 171; Young, 1990; Young, 1997, p. 362). Besides, not all groups have reasons to be represented either. Authors usually mention historical disadvantage, political marginalization or some kind of political relevance of the groups at stake (Young, 1997, p. 349; Tully, 1995, pp. 4-6). The issue arises then of how to identify these groups. All we have are the groups' claims (Phillips, 1995, p. 169) combined with a certain degree of collective recognition. In the context of the representation of disagreement, however, the groups selected for representation should be those whose members' perspectives provoke differences of opinions and disagreements relevant to the issues the representative system must solve[76] (Mansbridge, 2000, p. 103; Mansbridge, 1981, p. 474; Williams, 1998, pp. 50-51). The identification of those groups therefore relies on the visibility of disagreement and hence on the factual observation of differences of opinions and/or perspectives among groups, thus reducing the level of indeterminacy.

Second, *the dimensions of disagreement to be represented.*[77] Once we know which groups should be represented, it is important to determine which dimensions of disagreement should be represented.[78] Within the context of descriptive group representation, it is impossible to represent not only all the individual particulars of disagreement, but even all the collective ones. What they can represent by virtue of their difference, however, is of course the sheer fact of disagreement, but also more interestingly, the sources of disagreement and in particular conflicting group perspectives[79] (Young, 1997, p. 365ff.). In this respect, it is important to emphasize that group representation cannot and should not be associated with essentialism.[80] Women should be represented by women in the context of disagreement representation, not so much because there are allegedly purely and essentially feminine interests and opinions which any *one* woman and only a *woman* can represent. Ideas are not necessarily gendered and when they are, they are too diverse to all be represented and this through descriptive representation in particular. The reason for having women representing women is, as Young argues, that women represent other women's standpoints or perspectives and a shared experience of marginalization (Young, 1990, p. 184; Young, 1997, p. 369ff. See also Williams, 1998, pp. 5-6). As Phillips explains, it is indeed possible to share an experience without having the same experience (Phillips, 1995, pp. 52, 176).

Finally, *the amount of descriptive group representatives*. One often speaks of statistical or proportional representation to identify descriptive representation, thus indicating that, in order to mirror the wider population, group representatives should be elected in proportion to the importance of the group in the entire population.[81] However, according to some authors, descriptive group representation does not require proportional representation, but only a threshold presence in the deliberation (Phillips, 1995, pp. 47, 67ff.; Kymlicka, 1995, p. 147). Such a presence is, indeed, sufficient to comply with many of the reasons for descriptive representation and in particular the consciousness-raising and perspective-expanding functions of descriptive representation. What it underestimates, however, is the importance of having as many representatives as possible of the same group to achieve the best representation of as many facets as possible of group membership and hence of perspectives. It also neglects the importance of having a critical mass of representatives of one group of perspectives for deliberative synergy to take place and hence to convince others.[82] Finally, it is at odds with the necessity to have a proportional number of representatives for the conditions of legitimacy of the final vote to be fulfilled (Mansbridge, 2000, pp. 104-105).

The Counter-challenge

After presenting the challenge of disagreement and one of its most common responses, descriptive group representation, it is now important to assess two of the obstacles which seem, at first sight at least, to limit both the desirability and the possibility of representing disagreement:[83] the paradox of democratic representation and the counter-challenge of diversity.

The Paradox of Democratic Representation

One of the justifications often given to representation is diversity and the need to overcome political conflicts (Sieyès, 1963; Loughlin, 2003; Dunn, 1999) or at least to channel them in order to facilitate or even enable democratic deliberation

(Arendt, 1973, p. 226ff.; Pitkin, 1972, pp. 212-213; Young, 1997, p. 363; Habermas, 1998, pp. 210ff., 222ff.; Müller, 1992, pp. 157-158). Some have even called this element of facilitation of deliberation the great *opportunity of representation* (Müller, 1992, p. 157; Müller, 2002, p. 109; Habermas, 1998, pp. 210ff., 222ff.). In these conditions, it would make no sense, at first sight at least, to try to make deliberation totally inclusive and to aim at full equality by mirroring diversity and thus freezing disagreement.[84]

This position is instantiated at one extreme end of the spectrum by reference to Hobbes' first examination of representation in political theory; according to him, the sovereign should be the only representative of a divided people, which can only thereby be considered a political unit (Hobbes, 1999, Ch. 19, pp. 129-130 and Ch. 30, pp. 114, 121). This conception of representation was then adopted and expanded by Sieyès who saw representation as a fundamental fact of modern society and political representation as a permanent necessity in any large and populous country in which it was virtually impossible to unite the voice of the people directly (Sieyès, 1963; Loughlin, 2003). More recently, many authors have revived this position and developed it further; representation is regarded as a cultural phenomenon (Saward, 2003) which constitutes the represented *qua* political entity as much as the representative (Plotke, 1997, p. 30). Some also speak of representation as differentiating those represented into a true and unified "people" or a "constituency" as opposed to merely mirroring them (Young, 1997, p. 359; Ankersmit, 2002; Loughlin, 2003; Ankersmit, 1996, p. 44).

The puzzle thus generated may be referred to as the *paradox of democratic representation* (Young, 1997, p. 353): the *democratic* element requires that all subjects be given full and direct participation in the deliberation and decision-making process (Aristotle, 1988, III: 1275b13-b21, VI:1317a40-1318a10; Dryzek, 2001, p. 651), while the *representative* element is the institutional response to the impossibility of entirely respecting the latter when organizing democratic deliberations (Müller, 1992, p. 155). The more representation aims at imitating direct participation and full inclusion, the more disturbing the paradox therefore becomes (Young, 1997, p. 353; Ankersmit, 1996, p. 347; Loughlin, 2003).

The Counter-challenge of Diversity

Even if the concept of representation were to tolerate the expression of any diversity and full inclusion in principle, it would be impossible (Goodin, 2003a; Young, 1997, p. 353), or at least too costly (Mansbridge, 2000, pp. 105-107) in the present conditions of widespread and extremely complex diversity to represent all the dimensions of the disagreements at stake. This objection was Hamilton's, but it has been put forward again recently (Hamilton, 1961, n. 35, p. 218). As Goodin argues, indeed, it would be paradoxical if the problem of size, which is often used to justify representation (Pitkin, 1972, p. 87; Mill, 1991a; Urbinati, 2000 and 2002), was not to become in turn a problem for descriptive group representation itself (Goodin, 2003a). Hence what I will refer to as the *counter-challenge of diversity*.

There are different facets to this counter-challenge. First, beyond the important individual differences, there are in the context of group differences too many distinct groups requiring representation (Goodin, 2003b, p. 188; Sunstein, 2002, p. 175). Second, these groups are too heterogeneous internally (Goodin, 2003b, pp. 186-188; Phillips, 1995, pp. 145, 176, 52, 55-56). Finally, the dimensions of difference are cross-cutting and multiple (Goodin, 2003a; Gargarella, 1998, pp. 270-271; Phillips, 1995, p. 9). Not all of these three facets of the counter-challenge cut some ice, however.[85] Whereas the first issue may be conceded in the context of representing all politically pertinent conflicting perspectives in a society, the next two difficulties are not as important as they seem. It is indeed a consequence of my account of the objects of representation in general that the representation of disagreement should be limited to the representation of collective perspectives. As a consequence, both the amount of internal heterogeneity and of cross-cutting dimensions of difference are much more reduced than claimed.

The Representation of Disagreement Reconceptualized

Despite the gravity of these counter-challenges, it is important not to fall into the opposite trap and to see representation as a purely substantive and independent function entirely cut off from the represented. Even authors like Sieyès or Burke, who emphasize the unity-producing role of representatives, assume that representatives need to demonstrate a certain heterogeneity (Burke, 1899; see also Manin, 1997, p. 186). Disagreement can and should therefore be represented, but it must be reconceptualized in view of the paradox which affects the relationship between disagreement and representation (Arendt, 1973, p. 236; Young, 1997; Urbinati, 2000 and 2002; Mill, 1991a; Phillips, 1995; Williams, 1998). In this effort to reconceptualize the representation of disagreement, I will, first of all, discuss this second paradox in the relationship between disagreement and representation. I will then present a multidimensional and mixed model of representation which reconciles the differentiating requirement of representation with the requirement of inclusion and presence of diversity.

The Paradoxical Relationship between Disagreement and Representation

Reconceptualizing the representation of disagreement is not only a matter of finding a way out of the paradox of democratic representation and hence of striking a compromise between two conflicting demands of democracy, i.e. deliberation and inclusion. It is also, paradoxically, about enabling the basic functions of representation and hence of deliberation. In fact, without the descriptive representation of disagreement, the very deliberations and questioning within and outside main institutions, which representation is claimed to enable or at least improve by channelling conflicts and deferring democracy, cannot take place.[86]

The deferring and differentiating relationship of representation through the dialectic of authorization and accountability cannot be constituted without the stimulation of a certain interest and participation on the part of those represented

(Urbinati, 2000 and 2002; Young, 1997, p. 358ff.). This active participation of citizens depends in turn on the quality and perceived legitimacy of the horizontal disagreements among representatives and hence of vertical disagreements among representatives and citizens. The latter is necessarily related to the descriptive representation of citizens' horizontal disagreement for two reasons. First of all, citizens will only be interested in taking part in representation's exercise in mutual learning and civilization if their conflicting opinions, interests and perspectives are taken into account before being debated further by their representatives, and hence only if they feel part of their representatives' disagreement.[87] Secondly, it is only if their disagreements are part of their representatives' disagreements that they will engage actively in vertical disagreements and deliberations with them.[88] Vertical disagreements that feed into representatives' horizontal disagreements will then stimulate citizens' horizontal disagreements, thus creating a virtuous and reinforcing circle of disagreement and deliberation (Kateb, 1981, pp. 360-361; Kuper, 2004, Ch. 3; Ankersmit, 1996, p. 56).

Disagreement, which is to be channelled by representation and deferred in order to further deliberation, turns out therefore to be required by representation and deliberation themselves (Arendt, 1973). But how can one paradox reply to another?[89] Williams, one of descriptive representation's most recent advocates, mentions two opposed approaches of representation depending on whether they are more expressive or suppressive of disagreement (Williams, 1998, pp. 9, 50-54, 243). Given the resolutely discursive and expressive orientation of the account of representation defended here, disagreement can be turned into a resource for representation itself (Williams, 1998, p. 243).

The Revised Model of Disagreement Representation

Despite the crucial role of diversity in representation, the identity and mirroring objection remains untouched. Since representation is to create unity out of diversity and to contribute to the constitution of its own constituency through differentiation and mutual learning, the more representation aims at imitating direct participation and full inclusion, the more acute the paradox becomes (Young, 1997, p. 353; Ankersmit, 1996, p. 347; Loughlin, 2003). There are at least[90] two ways, however, of institutionalizing and organizing the descriptive representation of disagreement so as to reduce the amount of identification between representatives and represented and hence to circumvent the paradox, without, however, giving up disagreement's descriptive presence:[91] on the one hand, a balance of descriptive and substantive representation and, on the other, a balance of the models of representation *qua* trusteeship and *qua* delegation.

A balance of descriptive and substantive representation. A mixed model of descriptive and substantive representation, or more precisely a minimally descriptive model of representation,[92] can provide representation with the necessary degree of diversity to represent disagreement, without, however, aiming at mirroring existing social segmentations and hence undermining representation's differentiating effect. There are two alternative ways of reaching this result.

First of all, *representing the sources rather than the particulars of disagreement.* As I argued earlier, the representation of disagreement should focus on the *sources* of disagreement, and more particularly on *group* or *collective sources* of disagreement such as conflicting perspectives or standpoints which influence individual and collective opinions and hence induce disagreements (Young, 1997, p. 369ff.). Very different individuals with very diverse opinions and interests can share common perspectives and hence be part to the same disagreements. Besides, since conflicting perspectives lie at the origins of disagreements rather than constitute their outcomes, representing them does not equate to mirroring people's opinions and identities (Young, 1997, p. 366). On the contrary, it leaves sufficient leeway to the differentiating and constitutive effect of representation (Young, 1997, p. 369) and to genuine and unconstrained deliberation among representatives, among representatives and citizens and in turn among citizens themselves.[93] Conceived in this way, the descriptive representation of disagreement distances itself from the search for identity between representatives and represented and hence meets the first counter-challenge. The difficulty is, however, to meet the counter-challenge of diversity.[94]

Second, *representing the fact rather than the sources of disagreement.* Rather than represent the sources of disagreement thanks to the descriptive representation of group perspectives, the representation of disagreement could be reduced to the representation of the *fact* of disagreement, as Goodin argues (Goodin, 2003a). This could be done, for instance, by reducing the requirement of proportional representation to a mere presence threshold of one representative *per* group[95] (Phillips, 1995; Kymlicka, 1995). It could also be achieved by only descriptively representing some groups and some perspectives.[96] This is already the case in many countries in which the most relevant groups, and not all, are represented.[97] Finally, representing the sheer fact of disagreement could be done by representing some dimensions, opinions or perspectives of individual disagreements rather than group disagreements.[98] Thus, representing the fact of disagreement presents the advantage of dealing not only with the puzzle of democratic representation, but also with the counter-challenge of diversity (Goodin, 2003a).

This minimalist account of the descriptive representation of the sources or the fact of disagreement could not only complement ordinary substantive representation, but it could also usefully be associated with what one could call *reflexive* representation.[99] This mode of internal representation corresponds to Kant's idea of "enlarged mentality" (Kant, 2001, p. 216) and to Arendt's idea of "representative thinking" (Arendt, 1973; Arendt, 2001; Beiner, 1983); it requires from each representative that she projects herself in her own internal deliberation into the place of others (Arendt, 2001, pp. 19-20), rather than leave the confrontation with diversity to external and interactive deliberation.[100] Without some kind of minimal descriptive representation, however, reflexive representation cannot be as diversified as required by the representation of disagreement (Goodin, 2003a and 2003b, pp. 186-188; Eckersley, 2000, p. 128; Gargarella, 1998, pp. 261-262). Besides, it might also be necessary to give representatives the impetus for making other perspectives imaginatively present (Goodin, 2003b, p. 171; Gargarella, 1998, p. 262; Eckersley, 2000, p. 128). Ideally, then, it is a mixture of both the modified descriptive and reflexive forms of representation that should be used to represent disagreement. This is what Eckersley calls *diverse representation* (Eckersley, 2000, pp. 128-129).

This mixture of descriptive and substantive representation in the context of the representation of disagreement offers another advantage. As Sunstein has recently argued, too much diversity in a deliberative body may induce polarization and hence less deliberation (Sunstein, 2002; Goodin, 2003a). However, as I argued earlier, some descriptive representation of diversity may help enhance mutual questioning and curiosity and thus improve deliberation (Sunstein, 2002, pp. 186, 192). Furthermore, as Goodin argues, it might be better for the quality of deliberations not to have a full descriptive representation of disagreement as people tend to cut deals in such circumstances (Goodin, 2003a; Sunstein, 1988, p. 1587; Phillips, 1995, pp. 24-25). If, on the contrary, they realize the existence of disagreement through its descriptive representation, but also realize at the same time that not all perspectives in conflict are represented, they will be inclined to be more cautious and respectful of others' interests (Goodin, 2003a). Finally, the fluidity ensured by this mixed model of representation tends to prevent the danger of "balkanization" most critiques of descriptive representation have emphasized (Phillips, 1995, p. 21ff.; Mansbridge, 2000, pp. 122-123; Young, 1997, pp. 349-351; Williams, 1998, pp. 5-8; Squires, 2000).

A balance of trusteeship and delegation. As I explained earlier, one usually opposes representation *qua* delegation to representation *qua* trusteeship. One of the main difficulties with these two models is that it is actually very rare to see either the representatives or those represented as solely responsible for a decision. Usually, all are to a certain extent, as they must be able to influence and convince each other in open conditions of deliberation (Pitkin, 1972, pp. 154-155; Kuper, 2004, Ch. 3; Plotke, 1997, p. 31; Young, 1997, p. 358). This is what Urbinati refers to as *advocacy* in the representation relationship (Urbinati, 2000 and 2002), in order to distinguish this model from pure delegation without authorization and pure trusteeship without accountability.

It is crucial that representatives have a certain autonomy and can act as they judge best in new circumstances, while also taking citizens' relevant perspectives and interests sufficiently into account. It is indeed through this link that representatives can stimulate the participation of citizens and the dialectic of representation without, however, mirroring too exactly their constituents' opinions and hence hindering the mutual differentiation and civilization which the enhanced participation and deliberation are to achieve. Disagreements among citizens should be able to influence the deliberations of representatives, but the latter's disagreements or the disagreements they cause among citizens or among representatives should also be able to influence citizens' disagreements in return.[101] In fact, representatives' decisions should amount neither to mere compromises of their constituents' conflicting perspectives and interests[102] (Urbinati, 2000 and 2002, p. 83), nor to the recognition of a common good beyond conflicting perspectives, by reason of the cognitive virtues of representative deliberation.[103]

The Implications of the Revised Conception of Representation

Adequate modes of representation, which take disagreement on board, not only succeed in reconciling representation and disagreement. They also, paradoxically enough, provide an even *better protection of political equality and deliberation* in some cases than direct democracy alone.[104]

First of all, *the enhanced amount and quality of participation and deliberation.* The quality of deliberation increases through the distance that representation establishes between the deliberation and the decision. By interrupting disagreements and deliberations and deferring decisions until later, representation increases the quantity and quality of deliberations (Urbinati, 2000 and 2002; Young, 1997, p. 358ff.). This is of course only as long as deliberations include most points of view in conflict among citizens (Williams, 1998, pp. 8-9). As I argued earlier, indeed, it is only when disagreement is represented that citizens will develop sufficient interest to disagree further on these issues among themselves and then to disagree with their representatives, thus triggering the participation and deliberation that representation requires. Then, in turn, vertical disagreements that feed into representatives' horizontal disagreements will stimulate citizens' horizontal disagreements, thus intensifying the effect of disagreement and deliberation. This revised conception of representation enables more disagreement within and outside the institutional forums to arise from the representation of disagreement.[105] This contributes in turn to solving the issue of citizens' chronic apathy[106] (Kuper, 2004, Ch. 3) and circumventing representation's depoliticizing effect (Arendt, 1973). With their disagreements represented, citizens feel involved in debates and start disagreeing afresh among themselves and with their representatives on the basis of the new opinions thus produced. This then extends the scope of disagreement to all the agents of representation and thus changes the nature of disagreement (Manin, 1997, p. 222). Once disagreements are adequately represented, representation therefore becomes *disagreement-generative*, an outcome which Kateb celebrates,[107] and thus induces more and better deliberation.[108] One may say therefore that thanks to the adequate representation of disagreement and hence to the triggering of citizens' involvement *qua* agents of representation, the deferred effect of representation can be stimulated and the degree and quality of democratic deliberation increased. This way, representation gains in legitimacy by comparison to direct democracy alone.[109]

Second, *the enhanced political equality.* The protection of equality is also increased through the different degrees of political deliberation and control introduced by representation (Urbinati, 2000 and 2002), provided of course disagreement is adequately represented. Simple majorities cannot exclude minorities as easily as in a direct democracy; it takes a majority to elect and authorize representatives, another for these to act and still another to make them accountable. The deferred nature of the decision and the increased scope of deliberation also leave more time and space for diverging opinions and perspectives to make themselves heard and maybe to convince and change majorities until decision-making. Although the descriptive representation of disagreement cannot be as inclusive as the direct participation of all, the lack of complete inclusion is compensated by the correctives representation provides to the excesses of majoritarianism. One may say therefore that representation may become more consistent with political equality in some cases than direct democracy alone (Urbinati, 2000 and 2002).

It follows therefore from what I have said of the enhanced protection of participation, deliberation and political equality that the revised account of representation provides additional arguments for the *democratic legitimacy of representation* itself. This is particularly important as there has not been a complete normative justification of representation and of its intrinsic democratic value to date (Urbinati, 2000 and 2002; Young, 1997; Plotke, 1997; Kateb, 1981 and 1992, pp. 36-56). Reassessed and revised as suggested, representation becomes more than a necessary and inescapable mode of government; it constitutes a desirable and justifiable model of democratic decision-making in conditions of reasonable pluralism. In the proposed model, representation increases participation and deliberation by deferring democratic decision and thus by establishing a gap between representatives' deliberation and citizens' decision or vote; this provides more time for reflection and deliberation among citizens, among representatives and among citizens and representatives[110] (Urbinati, 2000; Kateb, 1981). This is what gives representation, what Kateb calls, its own *moral distinctiveness* (Kateb, 1981). As Plotke rightly contends, "representation is democracy" and "the opposite of representation is not participation" (Plotke, 1997, p. 19) but exclusion; true representation requires inclusion and participation to increase the quality of democratic deliberation. Participation and representation are two necessary dimensions of modern democracy and should be understood as intrinsically related in the complex constellation of democracy (Arendt, 1973, pp. 236, 278). In these conditions, representation's democratic legitimacy may be said to have been redeemed by the very phenomenon it aimed at dealing with: disagreement.

Conclusion

For a long time, democratic representation has been regarded as a default and pragmatic solution to the difficulties of practical democratic governance. In fact, it has become such an inescapable part of the political landscape that people simply take its legitimacy for granted. The constant reference to a non-inclusive model of decision-making to settle our reasonable disagreements ought, however, to have been *accounted for and justified* in current theories of legislation, on the one hand, or at least *institutionalized* in such a way as to ensure sufficient representation of our conflicting perspectives, on the other.

This is what I referred to in this essay as the *challenge of disagreement*. To meet this challenge, I argued that disagreements, or more precisely the conflicting perspectives that induce disagreements, should not only be represented, but that they should be descriptively represented through group representation. This is not only a matter of presence and visibility of the diversity of perspectives in conflict, but also of effective communication and deliberation among representatives and among representatives and citizens. Of course, the challenge of disagreement was not as straightforward as expected and its discussion raised many paradoxes and puzzles. To start with, given the conception of representation *qua* deferred relationship used in this essay, representation cannot afford to mirror constituents' identities and full diversity. This is what I have called the *paradox of democratic representation*. Besides, a second *counter-challenge of diversity* has also been put forward that relates to the practical impossibility of representing all particulars of disagreement descriptively.

My response to these two counter-challenges has been to present another paradox. Representation itself requires sufficient descriptive representation of disagreement to stimulate the dialogue and participation through which only the relationship of representation can be launched. Paradoxically, then, adequate descriptive representation of disagreement amounts not only to a requirement of political equality, but also of representation itself. Of course, any descriptive representation of disagreement will not be able to comply with the differentiating requirement of representation, on the one hand, and the counter-challenge of diversity, on the other. In response, the proposed account conciliates both descriptive and reflexive elements and adopts a half-independent mode of representation. What is represented is the sheer fact of disagreement rather than its particulars, and at the most some of the main group perspectives at the origins of the relevant disagreements.

In fact, this revised model of representation not only reconciles the differentiating and constitutive dimensions of representation with the requirement of inclusion and diversity. The challenge of reasonable disagreement has also provided us with the occasion to *relegitimize representation democratically*. Thanks to the stimulation of participation and deliberation ensured by the descriptive representation of some dimensions of disagreement, the proposed account of representation guarantees a better protection of political equality and deliberation in some cases than direct and purely participatory democracy. Of course, this essay's argument should not be understood as a disavowal of direct democracy. The point of my argument was to show the inescapable necessity of representation, and as far as possible try to legitimize it in the context of reasonable pluralism. The point was not, however, to do this by contrast to direct democratic participation, which retains a *prima facie* advantage in terms of the guarantee of political equality and inclusion. In fact, I would suggest, both forms of governance should be *combined in a semi-direct system*, so that the benefits of representation and deferred democracy can be complemented by those of direct democracy and full inclusion. This is what one should hope to achieve in the European context in particular. The indirectness of representation does not reside in the lack of participation of citizens, but in the spatio-temporal deferral it creates between deliberation and decision. The time has come to go beyond the sterile distinction between participation and representation and, to borrow Plotke's words, to "try to improve representative practices and forms to make them more open, effective, and fair" (Plotke, 1997, p. 19).

* PD (Bern), Dr. iur. (Fribourg), M. Jur. (Oxon.), Lic. iur. (Fribourg and Vienna). SNF Research Professor, Law Faculty, University of Fribourg and Lecturer, Law Faculty, University of Geneva. A more extensive version of this paper is due to be published as a chapter of my forthcoming book *The Morality of Conflict – Reasonable Disagreement and the Law* (Hart Publishing, Oxford, 2005). Many thanks to Thomas Pogge for an enlightening discussion on the general outline of this paper and to Roberto Gargarella for raising my interest in this question in the first place and for his interesting comments on the last version of this paper. An earlier draft was delivered at the IVR World Congress, Lund, August 2003; I would like to thank all participants in the working group for their comments and criticism, and in particular Tom Campbell and Vlad Perju. Many thanks also to Luc Wintgens for organizing this publication. Last but not least, I want to express all my gratitude to Jose Luis Marti Marmol for his invaluable comments and our numerous discussions on this issue. All mistakes remain mine, of course.

Notes

1 See also Besson, 2003b on the legitimacy of deliberation and especially voting after deliberation.

2 In this essay, I understand reasonable disagreement about justice as a consequence of reasonable pluralism, i.e. the pluralism of opinions about justice and matters of principle that flows from the burdens of reason generated by different social and cultural backgrounds (social pluralism) or the plurality of values (moral pluralism).

3 Of course, ideally, all those subject to a decision should have a say in the decision-making process and hence in deliberation (Dryzek, 2001, p. 651; Habermas, 1998), but in practice, most deliberative democracy theories target forums where all citizens are rarely present and where representatives are the ones taking decisions (Goodin, 2000, p. 82). See Parkinson, 2003a for a discussion of the legitimacy problem this raises for deliberative democracy theories.

4 Note that, for reasons of space, I am assuming that both the argument of deliberation and the argument of political equality are correct.

5 It is the equality to participate rather than the equality to vote and elect one's representatives, and hence to consent to power, which is at stake here. See Manin, 1997, pp. 34-41.

6 Note that I am assuming in this essay that democracy understood in this way is a desirable ideal. I distance myself, however, from the deliberative view according to which the outcome of a *procedure to which all agree* may be regarded as a sufficient *ersatz* to the participation of all to that procedure and hence as sufficiently democratically legitimate (see e.g. Müller, 1992, pp. 155, 158 on the representative procedure).

7 I am concentrating in this essay on legislative or parliamentary representatives, although my argument could also apply *mutatis mutandis* to other political representatives, to the exception, of course, of judges who cannot be said to represent *stricto sensu*. This choice stems from the general *legisprudential* orientation adopted in this book.

8 Deliberative democracy theorists seem to have underestimated the issue of the legitimacy of representation as they have concentrated most lately on extending the scope of deliberation in non-institutional forums such as the public sphere in particular: see e.g. Dryzek (2000, 2001); Mansbridge (1999); Habermas (1998); Müller (1992, p. 155ff.). See, however, Parkinson (2003a, pp. 190-191) who addresses

the issue of representation in conjunction with the extension of the spheres of deliberation. See also Squires (2000, p. 104) and Saward (2000) who argue that representation in official and institutional forums not only requires, but also nurtures deliberation. Note that I take Goodin's (2003b) proposal of "democratic deliberation within" or "reflexive democracy" to apply to representatives (see also Dryzek, 2001) and as such I will discuss his proposal in the context of my reconceptualization of representation in conditions of reasonable disagreement.

9 It is important to recall that there is more to democracy than deliberation and in particular the issue of determining who deliberates, but also who votes. See Besson (2003b) on the importance of developing a deliberative voting ethics. Contra: Dryzek (2001, p. 665).

10 See Goodin (2003b, p. 178) criticizing Dryzek (2001); Habermas (1998); Bohman (1996). Paradoxically, some authors, like Pettit (2004), propose to "depoliticize" democratic deliberation even more, mainly for epistemological reasons. See, however, on the limitations of such arguments, see Waldron (1999); Gaus (1996).

11 See Manin (1997, Ch. 6) on the further level of complexity added to representation by the emergence of parties. For reasons of clarity, I will not dwell on this issue in detail in this essay and will concentrate on the relationship of representation itself. See for the same move, Young (1997); Urbinati (2000 and 2002). In short, parties represent one form of disagreement stimulated by commonly held opinions and perspectives dictated by party membership; some people will disagree on a new social statute, for instance, along the lines dictated by party membership. It is important, however, to keep in mind that these disagreements do not exhaust political disagreements, although they have become omnipresent and tend to encompass or even replace other disagreements (see Manin, 1997, on the setting of the agenda by parties in so-called "audience" democracy).

12 See Gargarella (1998, p. 274) on the complementary relationship between deliberation and representation and the absurdity there is to wanting to fix issues of democratic legitimacy through deliberation only. (See also Parkinson, 2003a, p. 186.) As we will see, deliberation and representation are complementary; although it is important to address the issue of the democratic legitimacy of deliberative representation separately from the legitimacy of deliberation itself, I will argue that the legitimacy of representation requires and in fact nurtures deliberation (see Mill, 1991a, pp. 241-242, 247-248, and more recently Urbinati, 2000, and Mansbridge, 1999, on the necessity to conceive representation as surrounded by deliberation). Note, however, that some of the underlying assumptions of deliberative democracy still need to be reassessed in the light of the specificities of disagreement and group representation; the very notions of reasonableness and impartiality may indeed already exclude some of the group perspectives (Williams, 2000; Young, 1996).

13 See e.g. Rousseau (1997, III:15) who contends that the only legitimate form of representation is fully descriptive. See, however, Wintgens (2001, pp. 274-276) for a representative reinterpretation of Rousseau.

14 See also Hirst (1990); Pitkin (1989, pp. 150-151). See Urbinati (2000); Plotke (1997, pp. 25-27) on this growing interest for direct participatory democracy as opposed to indirect representative democracy. Note that I refer to "direct participatory" and "indirect representative" democracy to quote the use of these terms in this context; as we will see, later, however, the indirectness of representative democracy does not lie in the absence of participation, but in the spatio-temporal gap between deliberation and decision.

15 Representation was not democratic from its origins (Manin, 1997, p. 1ff.; Manin, Przeworski and Stokes, 1999, p. 4; see e.g. Hobbes, 1999) and is not democratic *per se* (Pennock, 1968). In any case, it has been associated for a long time with democracy – hence the title of this essay. It is important therefore to see whether the "principles of representative government" which apply unchanged in contemporary democracies (Manin, 1997, p. 236) can really be regarded as democratic, especially with respect to political equality and deliberation as stated in the disagreement challenge discussed in this essay. In what follows, therefore, I will use "representation" and "modes of representation" to refer to democratic representation, unless otherwise stated.

16 As we will see later in this essay, this increased interest for representation should not be confused with a disparagement of democratic participation; both dimensions are important in modern democracy and representation cannot be thought of without participation.

17 Note that I am not concerned in this essay with other forms of legitimacy than democratic legitimacy (see also Urbinati, 2000 and 2002). As such, I will not discuss epistemological modes of legitimization of representation in general and of descriptive representation in particular, such as those founded on impartiality (e.g. Gargarella, 1998, pp. 261-262; Arendt, 1968, pp. 241-242). In the same line, my interest for the descriptive representation of disagreement is led by a concern for political equality and democratic inclusion rather than by a rationalistic concern for the truth and impartiality of political decisions; the inclusion of diversity matters *per se* even if, as Phillips argues, "it proves to have no discernible consequences for the policies that may be adopted" (Phillips, 1995, p. 20). In fact, it is because we disagree about moral but also epistemological issues that procedural legitimacy and in particular equal participation are even more important.

18 See also Waldron (1993, p. 49) in the context of his right-based critique of judicial review by contrast to democratic participation: "We should distinguish between a court's deciding things by a majority, and *lots and lots of ordinary men and women deciding things by a majority*" (emphasis added).

19 I am concentrating in this essay mainly on the representative system at work in many modern Western democracies and in particular in European democracies. See on the contemporary crisis of democracy, Manin, 1997, Ch. 6.

20 See Gargarella (1998, pp. 270-271) on the increase of pluralism.

21 See Mansbridge (1981, pp. 466, 469-470) who argues against Kateb's (1981) apology of representation.

22 This is where I think Gargarella (1998, p. 262ff.) errs, when he argues that Burke and the American Founders shared the idea of "full representation" with promoters of descriptive representation. The most they shared was the democratic ideal that all those affected should be represented, independently of the ways to represent them.

23 On the new jurisprudential approach that concentrates on the legitimacy of legislative law-making and calls itself *legis*prudence by contrast to *juris*prudence, see the essays collected in Wintgens (2002).

24 See e.g. Waldron (1999 and 2002b) where the representative issue is only very rarely directly addressed, although it is omnipresent in the background. The only exception is Waldron's (2000) article on the disagreement-related importance of the size of legislative assemblies. Note that, although the amount of representatives is related to their ability to represent disagreement, I will concentrate here on the relationship between represented and representatives itself.

25 Note, however, that I lack the space in this essay to get into the detail of these institutional reforms. See on such attempts, the contributions in Manin *et al.* (1999).

26 It is important to remember in particular that other elements of the political system contended might affect the representative practice and hence the implementation of the proposed model of representation. For instance, the Swiss consociational model of democracy influences the way in which disagreement may be represented and this even though the Swiss representative model is proportional (see Lijphart, 1984, pp. 22-23). The consociational model encourages compromises and cannot easily accommodate nor benefit from disagreement. For the same concern in the European context see Magnette (2003). Note that this essay's argument concentrates mostly on national representation and cannot encompass all the fascinating dimensions the revised account of representation could have in the post-national sphere (see e.g. Kuper, 2004, Ch. 3).

27 See also Pitkin (1989) for a detailed presentation of the history of political representation.

28 Note that some add the refinement of ideas to this list on the model of the Federalist Papers' argument for representation: Madison (1961, p. 82). See e.g. Arendt (1973, pp. 226-227) who contends that representation in politics will pass opinions "through the sieve of an intelligence which will separate the arbitrary and the merely idiosyncratic, and thus purify them into public views." The idea is not an elitist assumption about the lack of deliberative capacities of ordinary people (see Schumpeter, 1947), but rather the view that ordinary citizens are not given the chance to develop those deliberative capacities, a point that goes back to Mill (see Pateman, 1970). Others, however, add to the list of reasons to adopt the representative model of democratic decision-making the Burkean and elitist argument that some people are simply epistemologically more able to recognize and protect objective public interests: Burke (1899) and (Hamilton, 1961, n. 35, pp. 220-221) (see Manin, 1997, p. 94ff. and Gargarella, 1998, pp. 263-264 for a critique of this Burkean epistemological approach of representation).

29 See Arendt (1973, p. 236): "obviously direct democracy will not do, if only because the rooms will not hold all". See also Hamilton *et al.* (1961, n. 35, p. 218). See also Young, 1997, pp. 352-353; Pitkin (1972, p. 87); Dahl (1989, Ch. 13) on the inescapability of the scale problem in a democracy, even in a very small polity. See on the same point, Urbinati (2000) on the *de facto* representation known even in the Athenian allegedly direct democracy for reasons of time and space in the democratic interaction. See also Goodin (2003a and 2003b, pp. 4-5) who contends that new technologies cannot mend the difficulty created by the number of people who are to deliberate and vote.

30 See, however, Urbinati (2000 and 2002); Young (1997); Plotke (1997); Kateb (1981 and 1992, pp. 36-56).

31 Note that in this essay I will use the terms "accountability" and "responsiveness" interchangeably. Strictly speaking, however, accountability is a property of institutional structures, whereas responsiveness is a consequence of interaction within such structures. See Ferejohn (1999, p. 131).

32 See Manin (1997, p. 175ff.) on the retrospective character of elections and the anticipation this creates among representatives. Provided this were true, however, the points of view taken into account would be the majority's and not all those perspectives in conflict (see Gargarella, 1998, p. 272). The same difficulty applies to other non-electoral means of ensuring more responsiveness on the part of representatives.

33 See on accountability through the public sphere, Müller (1992, pp. 156-157); Urbinati (2000); Mansbridge (1999); Parkinson (2003a, pp. 190-191). See Kuper (2004, Ch. 3) for proposals of alternative modes of ensuring responsiveness among representatives

both at the national and post-national levels. See, finally, the contributions in Manin *et al.* (1999) for a more detailed discussion of different means of ensuring accountability including but not only through elections.

34 See also, although in other terms, Kuper (2004, Ch. 3); Urbinati (2000 and 2002). See also Harlow (1985, p. 81) on the idea of representation *qua* "buckle between power and people".

35 It remains to see what these conditions for participation to the relationship of representation are, as I will in the fourth section of this essay.

36 See Urbinati (2000) by reference to Mill's (1991a, p. 413) *agora* which encompasses representation, but also a rich public sphere and forms of direct participation and public duties. See also Mansbridge (1999, pp. 227-228) and Parkinson (2003a, pp. 190-191) on a broad "deliberative system" which includes representation forums but also deliberation between such forums and in the public sphere.

37 In this sense, deferred democracy can be summarized by three differentiated elements : deliberation and decision take place in *different places*, at *different times* and are handled by *different people*.

38 See on the idea of representation *qua* creative source of unity and constitution of the represented, e.g. Young (1997, pp. 354-358); Young (2000); Plotke (1997, p. 30); Ankersmit (2002); Saward (2003); Loughlin (2003).

39 As such, it is important to distinguish this conception of representation from a widespread conception based on Pitkin's influential definition of representation. The latter conceives of representation as a mere replacement for what cannot be present without further interaction between the absent and passive constituent, on the one hand, and the present and active representative, on the other. See Pitkin (1972, p. 9); Pitkin (1989, p. 142).

40 Contrary to Pitkin (1972, pp. 90-91), I hold that there are more than two main questions about representation, and, more importantly, that it is possible to reply to each of those questions independently from the answer given to the other ones. According to Pitkin, indeed, it is only possible to discuss what representatives should do, if one chooses a substantive as opposed to a descriptive account of representation. I argue, on the contrary, that it is possible to have either models combined with a delegation or with a trusteeship model of representation. See also Saward (2003) on the importance of understanding representation as both an active and passive phenomenon.

41 An interesting question to raise and which I will have to leave aside in this essay is the extent to which resident aliens should also be represented. They should be, but this cannot be done through the issue of representation, but through extending the franchise of political rights in general.

42 Of course, one may wonder whether she has the choice to represent women or not; the issue is usually approached from the end of the voters rather than from the representatives' view. One may contend, anyway, that given her woman's standpoint, a woman representative cannot avoid representing women.

43 It is important not to confuse this distinction with another contrast between representation *qua* delegation and representation *qua* trusteeship; in both cases, the constituency's interests might have to be represented, but in one case according to a mandate and in the other without any.

44 See since then, Mansbridge (2000). By contrast, see Phillips (1995) who speaks of "politics of presence" by opposition to "politics of ideas"; Williams (1998) who speaks of "self-representation"; Young (1990, 1997) who speaks of "group representation"; Gargarella (1998) who speaks of "full representation"; Ankersmit

(1996, p. 347) who opposes "aesthetic" or symbolic representation to "mimetic" or descriptive representation.

45 Of course, minor and more personal characteristics can also be descriptively represented, but not intentionally and on a large scale. I will return to this issue in the context of the descriptive representation of disagreement.

46 Note that, contrary to what its denomination seems to indicate, the descriptive character of the representative can therefore be more or less *visible* depending on how much the common element to the membership to one group depends on visible characteristics. See Mansbridge (2000, pp. 100-101) on this point. One may think of the representation of classes when they lie at the origins of some of our disagreements; class-based disagreements are as visible and hence as identifiable as any disagreements, but the descriptive representation of classes, by political parties for instance, does not rely on visible characteristics.

47 Part of the problem with Pitkin's evaluation of descriptive representation may be explained by the fact that she concentrates on a microcosmic form of representation which aims at representing all individual specificities and group differences present in society, and this mostly through sampling rather than through election. The same applies to Ankersmit's (1996, p. 28) critique of what he refers to as "mimetic" representation.

48 As a consequence, while descriptive representation implies substantive representation, the reverse need not be true. In this sense, the opposition between substantive and descriptive representation is not entirely logical: while descriptiveness really refers to a *personal quality* of the representatives, substantiveness refers to their *activity* rather than to their personal qualities. See Phillips (1995, p. 5) on the subordination of the "who" represents to the "what" is represented.

49 See Manin (1997, p. 8ff.) on the relationship between the selection of representatives by lot and the dominant type of representation in ancient Athens.

50 See e.g. Fishkin (1991 and 1997) on deliberative opinion polls made of sampled representatives. See also Mansbridge (2000, pp. 105-107) on microcosmic representation by randomly sampling representatives from the population.

51 See also, however, Manin (1997, Ch. 4) on the deficiencies and in particular the aristocratic nature of elections in the selection of representatives.

52 I am excluding, for instance, preferences, desires and subjective interests.

53 It is difficult indeed to distinguish someone's ideas or opinions from her interests, since, although they differ in nature, the ideas or opinions represented will usually be about her interests, i.e. about which should be her personal ends and how best to achieve them. Similarly, a person's perspectives will influence her opinions and her conceptions of her interests.

54 It is difficult to defend someone's interests without thereby acting according to her perspectives. This is actually even an intentional outcome in the case of descriptive representation where representatives should be able to act in their constituency's interests through sharing their perspectives.

55 It is possible to imagine a descriptive representative who represents the interests of her constituency and not necessarily its members' opinions as well, although it is difficult to imagine a descriptive representative not judge from her own perspectives thus not represent her constituency's perspectives (see Young, 1997, pp. 369-373). The reverse is more difficult to imagine, however: how indeed could a substantive representative be trusted to represent her constituency's perspectives or standpoints as well as a descriptive representative? There are possibilities, however, as we will see later and in particular reflexive representation, i.e. substantive representation which stands for

diverse standpoints thanks to the faculty of "enlarged mentality" to quote Kant (see Goodin, 2003a and 2003b).

56 It is worth distinguishing these two groups of issues, however, as there is a difference between what you stand for, on the one hand, and how you stand for it, i.e. what you do when you stand for it, on the other.

57 See Mansbridge (1981, pp. 467-468) on the evolution to an adversary conception of the representation of a balance of conflicting interests rather than of a common interest.

58 This is the case, for instance, of the representation by *parties*, which usually represent conflicting perspectives or conflicting opinions which are commonly held by the members of a party.

59 It is important not to confuse these two issues, as it is possible to conceive of a descriptive representative who acts as a trustee and vice-versa. It is true, however, that it helps being a delegate to also be a descriptive representative. It is not, however, because the representation of disagreement is in part descriptive, that it is limited to the collection of information or to the mere application of a mandate; descriptive representatives also act in the best interest of their constituents and this with or without a precise mandate. See Phillips (1995, p. 56) on the necessary alliance between politics of ideas and politics of presence. See also Mansbridge (2000, p. 101) on the relationship between substantive and descriptive representation.

60 Some authors, like Pitkin (1972, Ch. 7) identify this distinction with the distinction between representation *qua* authorization and representation *qua* accountability. These denominations might become confusing, however, since even representatives *qua* delegates are authorized and even representatives *qua* trustees are accountable. This is particularly important in the context of descriptive representation where Pitkin and other authors after her simply assume that what is at stake is a mandate and that when there is a mandate, there need be no accountability. See Phillips (1995) and Williams (1998) on the importance of providing descriptive representation with means of accountability.

61 See Young (1997, p. 358ff.); Urbinati (2000 and 2002) on representation *qua* advocacy.

62 It suffices to think of political systems like the Swiss or Belgian ones in which proportional representation applies.

63 On this opposition between horizontal disagreement among citizens, vertical disagreement among citizens and representatives and vertical disagreement among representatives, see Postema (1982).

64 See Manin (1997, Ch. 6) on "audience" democracy and the setting of the agenda of disagreement by parties and representatives only. Disagreement among citizens amounts, in this context, to a consequence of representation rather than the reverse. It remains important, however, to represent it, since what matters is that as many conflicting perspectives as possible are present in the deliberative and aggregative phases of representation.

65 See Dunn (1999) according to whom, in order to avoid conflicts, we transpose the "horizontal danger" of killing each other into the "vertical danger" of being coerced by governments.

66 This argument is analogous to Waldron's (1999) argument against the legitimacy of judges in disagreement to decide for citizens in disagreement, since there is no coincidence of their disagreements and no dialogue among them.

67 On the importance of representing disagreement in both the deliberative and aggregative moments of the decision-making process, see Mansbridge (2000, p. 103).

68 See even Pitkin (1972, p. 212). See also Ankersmit, 2000 who argues that disagreement among citizens and their representatives ensures that they remain attentive to each other's opinions and decisions.

69 Of course, those represented remain people, but what matters here is what it is exactly in those people that is to be represented and more particularly what it is in their disagreements that should be represented.

70 See Goodin (2003a) who, however, only distinguishes between the particulars and the fact of disagreement and does not envisage the third option I have discussed here: representing the sources of disagreement, or at least one of its sources: perspectives.

71 Note that I am assuming that groups pre-exist disagreements among group perspectives. Of course, the existence of groups may be reinforced or undermined by disagreements among their members or disagreements with other groups, but this is not my concern here.

72 See Urbinati (2000) according to whom Mill does not associate proportional representation with group representation. This is an important *caveat* that should be kept in mind. Individual disagreements should be represented as much as possible within the increasingly restrictive limits of descriptive representation, but also of course through more substantive means of representation such as reflexive representation, as we will see.

73 I explained this earlier in relation to the opposition between "microcosmic" and mainstream descriptive group representation. See Mansbridge (2000, pp. 105-107) on this point.

74 This section should not therefore be taken to exclude other modes of representation of disagreement, as we will see in the fourth section where I discuss a revised and complex account of disagreement representation.

75 The representation of disagreement can therefore provide descriptive representation with additional arguments and justifications in that specific context. The present argument should not, however, be taken to provide descriptive representation with an exhaustive and complete argument, which is proof to all critiques and objections to the general idea of descriptive representation. (See on the costs of descriptive representation, Phillips (1995, p. 21ff.); Mansbridge (2000, pp. 122-123); Young (1997, pp. 349-351); Williams (1998, pp. 5-8); Squires (2000).) See more generally Besson (1999, 2001 and 2002) on the importance of the flexibility of seat and list quotas and other affirmative action measures.

76 Of course, there is a *time factor* to take into account when disagreement has been observed and before identifying the groups at the origins of those disagreements. It is only through the recurrence of some divisions that we can identify their origins.

77 Note that other forms of non-descriptive disagreement representation may represent other dimensions of disagreement. Purely substantive and reflexive representation may indeed concentrate more on individual opinions and perspectives when representing disagreement. I will return to this point in the fourth section where I reconceptualize representation in view of the different challenges raised in this essay.

78 Perspectives need not therefore be identified independently from the groups to be represented.

79 In fact, most advocates of descriptive representation are aware of the difficulty there is of representing the particulars of disagreement and would tend to fall into the group of perspectives' representation (see e.g. Phillips, 1995, p. 52, 176; Williams, 1998, pp. 5-6; Young, 1990, p. 184; Kymlicka, 1995, p. 138).

80 See Pennock's (1979, p. 314) famous phrase: "no one would argue that morons should be represented by morons".

81 See e.g. Urbinati (2000) who speaks of "proportional representation" to refer to descriptive representation.

82 See Waldron (2000) on the importance of the number of representatives for deliberation in assemblies and the representation of disagreement.

83 Note that this paradox is similar to the one Pettit (2004) argues is allegedly created by some of the depoliticizing trends recognizable in our political practice, which are, however, not contrary, but necessary to deliberative democracy itself. This is because, according to Pettit, the deliberative and the democratic elements in deliberative democracy tend to pull apart. One could draw an interesting parallel here and deduce a *second-order paradox* for democratic representation that would not so much apply to the choice of representation over participation, but to the choices of representative modalities: not only does democratic deliberation require a limitation of full participation by the instauration of representation, but within representation, it calls for a limitation of full descriptive representation.

84 See e.g. Goodin (2000, p. 82) and Goodin (2003a) by reference to the Federalists' Papers and in particular Hamilton (1961, p. 218). See also Ankersmit (1996, p. 44). See already Mill, 1991a as discussed by Urbinati, 2000 and 2002, on the dangers and advantages of reintroducing diversity in representation through proportional representation.

85 Note that Young (1997); Phillips (1995); Gargarella (1998) defend descriptive accounts of representation, but do not assume it is possible to ensure full representation and hence the inclusion of all individual particularities.

86 This is the link missing from Young's (1997) argument whose conclusions are, however, similar to mine: representation is a justified mode of democratic decision-making by virtue of its differentiating effect, but group representation is still desirable in these circumstances.

87 See already Mill (1991a, p. 370) as discussed by Urbinati (2000 and 2002, p. 81): "A symbolic presence would make up for physical attendance, *while expanding political debate beyond the parliament and allowing citizens to feel more identified with their representatives, and finally with the political institutions*" (emphasis added).

88 See Kateb (1981, p. 361) on the importance of representing diversity as the source of regulated contest and competition.

89 See Kateb (1981, p. 368) on this last paradox. See Mill (1991a) on both the advantages and the dangers of reintroducing diversity into representation. See Urbinati (2000 and 2002) for a discussion of Mill's views.

90 Note that none of the hereby discussed ways of accommodating the paradoxical constraints of representation in conditions of diversity should be taken as excluding the others. See also Kuper (2004, Ch. 3) on different suggestions as to non-electoral means of ensuring representatives' responsiveness and in particular "advocacy agencies" or "channels of dissent" which keep representatives informed of citizens' opinions and require feedback when necessary. See also the contributions in Manin *et al.* (1999). Of course, other institutional correctives than democratic representation should also be targeted to ensure full equality of participation, such as minorities' veto rights or the decentralization of power from national parliaments to regional ones. In fact, one may contend that democratic representation alone, even with the correctives and reforms suggested here, might not suffice in ensuring complete equality in conditions of reasonable pluralism.

91 On such mixtures and alternative models of representation, see Goodin (2003a and 2003b); Eckersley (2000, p. 128-129); Young (1997); Urbinati (2000 and 2002).

92 As I argued earlier, descriptive representation implies substantive representation. Hence the idea of a mixed model can only be taken in a figurative sense.

93 See Manin (1997, p. 222) on the new shapes disagreement may take once represented.

94 This does not mean that a special argument for the descriptive representation of *one* group in particular, e.g. women, is needed. What is at stake here is the descriptive representation of *all* groups whose pertinent perspectives conflict.

95 Contra: Mansbridge (2000, p. 104).

96 Note that the distinction between representing the fact or the particulars of disagreement should not be confused with the distinction between substantive and descriptive representation; it is possible to represent descriptively and substantively both the fact and some particulars of disagreement.

97 It is the case in Switzerland and Belgium with respect to representatives of different linguistic areas and it is the case in some European countries like Germany with respect to female and male representatives. Note that I am not discussing in this essay the costs and dangers of the different means of ensuring descriptive group representation: see Mansbridge (2000, pp. 108-111); Young (1997, pp. 372-373); Besson (1999, 2001 and 2002).

98 This is particularly important given the *caveat* I mentioned earlier with respect to the independence of many individual disagreements from group disagreements. See Urbinati (2000) about Mill's distinction between proportional and group representation.

99 I borrow this expression from Goodin's (2003b) concept of "reflexive democracy".

100 Hence Goodin's (2003b, p. 169ff.) idea of "democratic deliberation within".

101 See Manin (1997, p. 222) on the change of nature of disagreement through the relationship of representation.

102 In this respect, it is important to distinguish representatives' judgements that take citizens' perspectives into account, from their judgements *qua* officials which should cohere with other officials' judgements and lead in some cases to compromises of principle: see e.g. Besson (2003a).

103 See Mansbridge (1981, pp. 475-476) criticizing Kateb (1981) for straddling these two approaches.

104 See also Urbinati (2000, 2002); Mill (1991a, p. 165) on representation as a device that can help actualize the normative content of democracy.

105 See Manin (1997, p. 186ff.) on disagreement in representation *qua* school of citizenship.

106 This is particularly important as many authors have criticized Waldron's (1999) "jurisprudence of legislation" for not taking the lack of interest and participation of citizens sufficiently into account.

107 See Kateb (1981, p. 361) on the importance of diversity in representation as the source of further democratization and regulated contest and competition.

108 The entrenchment of disagreement at the end of representative deliberation is not excluded therefore, but this is a positive outcome rather than a negative one as Gargarella (1998, p. 274) seems to fear. My account of deliberative democracy is indeed an *agonistic* one which is not founded on the rationalistic presumption of agreement and impartiality as Gargarella's, but on the generative and desirable nature of disagreement and as such it concentrates on conflict and discussion as these are part of the legitimacy of deliberation, i.e. voicing all opinions in conflict and discussing them before taking a vote and hence respecting the basic principle of equality. See also Kateb (1981, p. 361); Urbinati (2000 and 2002).

109 See Plotke (1997, pp. 25-27) on the false opposition between representation and participation.

110 This can be exemplified by the Swiss case; the spatio-temporal gap between representatives' deliberation and citizens' decisions on a referendum or in elections stimulates people's participation and deliberation on issues over which they might not have deliberated otherwise. All this depends of course on the proportional representative system that guarantees a good representation of disagreement.

References

Adams, J. (1951), 'Letter to John Penn' in *Works of John Adams*, Vol. 4, Princeton University Press, Princeton.

Ankersmit, F.A. (1996), *Aesthetic Politics: Political Philosophy beyond Fact and Value*, Stanford University Press, Stanford.

Ankersmit, F.A. (2002), *Political Representation*, Stanford University Press, Stanford.

Arendt, H. (1968), *Between Past and Future: Six Exercises in Political Thought*, 2nd edn, Viking, New York.

Arendt, H. (1970), *On Violence*, Allen Lane, London.

Arendt, H. (1973), *On Revolution,* Penguin, Harmondsworth.

Arendt, H. (2001), 'The Crisis in Culture: Its Social and Its Political Significance' in R. Beiner and J. Nedelsky (eds.), *Judgment, Imagination and Politics, Themes from Kant and Arendt*, Rowman & Littlefeld, Lanham.

Aristotle (1988), *The Politics,* Cambridge University Press, Cambridge.

Barber, B. (1984), *Strong Democracy: Participatory Politics for a New Age*, University of California Press, Berkeley.

Beiner, R. (1983), *Political Judgement*, Methuen, London.

Beitz, C. (1983), 'Procedural Equality in Democratic Theory: A Preliminary Examination' in J. Pennock and J. Chapman (eds.), *Liberal Democracy*, Nomos XXV, New York University Press, New York.

Benhabib, S. (1996), 'Toward a Deliberative Model of Democratic Legitimacy' in S. Benhabib (ed.), *Democracy and Difference: Contesting the Boundaries of the Political,* Princeton University Press, Princeton.

Besson, S. (1999), 'Mesures positives: le nouvel équilibre asymétrique. Perspectives pour le droit suisse', *Pratique Juridique Actuelle,* 4, pp. 390-404.

Besson, S. (2001), 'Paritary rights for women in Switzerland: what can one learn from a negative popular verdict?', *Jus Gentium*, pp. 55-85.

Besson, S. (2002), 'Plus d'égalité pour les femmes dans les faits – quel rôle pour la nouvelle Constitution cantonale?', *Revue Fribourgeoise de Jurisprudence*, pp. 3-18.

Besson, S. (2003a), 'Four Arguments against Compromising Justice Internally', *Oxford Journal of Legal Studies*, 23:2, pp. 211-241.

Besson, S. (2003b), 'Democracy and Disagreement – From Deliberation to Vote and Back Again. The Move towards Deliberative Voting Ethics' in M. Iglesias and J. Ferrer (eds.), *Globalization, Democracy and Citizenship*, Duncker & Humblot, Berlin, pp. 101-135.

Bohman, J. (1996), *Public Deliberation: Pluralism, Complexity and Democracy,* MIT Press, Cambridge Mass./London.

Burke, E. (1899), 'Speech to the Electors of Bristol at the Conclusion of the Poll' in E. Burke, *The Works*, Nimmo, London, vol. 3, pp. 89-98.

Cohen, J. (1989), 'Deliberation and Democratic Legitimacy' in A. Hamlin and P. Pettit (eds.), *The Good Polity*, Blackwell, Oxford.

Dahl, R. (1989), *Democracy and Its Critics*, Yale University Press, New Haven.
Dryzek, J.S. (2000), *Deliberative Democracy and Beyond*, Oxford University Press, Oxford.
Dryzek, J.S. (2001), 'Legitimacy and Economy in Deliberative Democracy', *Political Theory*, 29:5, pp. 651-669.
Dunn, J. (1999), 'Situating Democratic Political Accountability' in A. Przeworski, S. Stokes and B. Manin (eds.), *Democracy, Accountability and Representation*, Cambridge University Press, Cambridge.
Eckersley, R. (2000), 'Deliberative Democracy, Ecological Risk and "Communities of Fate"' in M. Saward (ed.), *Democratic Innovation: Deliberation, Association and Representation*, Routledge, London.
Eisgruber, C.L. (2002), 'Democracy and Disagreement: A Comment on Jeremy Waldron's *Law and Disagreement*', *Legislation and Public Policy*, 6:5, pp. 35-47.
Elster, J. (1998), 'Introduction' in J. Elster (ed.), *Deliberative Democracy*, Cambridge University Press, Cambridge.
Ferejohn, J. (1999), 'Accountability and Authority: Toward a Theory of Political Accountability' in A. Przeworski, S. Stokes and B. Manin (eds.), *Democracy, Accountability and Representation*, Cambridge University Press, Cambridge.
Fishkin, J. (1991), *Democracy and Deliberation*, Yale University Press, New Haven.
Fishkin, J. (1997), *The Voice of the People*, Yale University Press, New Haven.
Frankena, W. (1968), 'Two Notes on Representation' in J. Pennock and J. Chapman (eds.), *Representation*, Nomos X, New York University Press, New York.
Gargarella, R. (1998), 'Full Representation, Deliberation and Impartiality' in J. Elster (ed.), *Deliberative Democracy*, Cambridge University Press, Cambridge.
Gaus, G. (1996), *Justificatory Liberalism: An Essay in Epistemology and Political Theory*, Oxford University Press, Oxford.
Goodin, R.E. (2000), 'Democratic Deliberation Within', *Philosophy and Public Affairs*, 29, pp. 81-109.
Goodin, R.E. (2003a), 'Representing Diversity', http://eprints.anu.edu.au/archive/00001451/01/Represent_Diversity.pdf.
Goodin, R.E. (2003b), *Reflexive Democracy*, Oxford University Press, Oxford.
Gould, C. (1996), 'Diversity and democracy: representing differences' in S. Benhabib (ed.), *Democracy and Difference*, Princeton University Press, Princeton.
Gutmann, A. and Thompson, D. (1996), *Democracy and Disagreement*, Belknap, Cambridge Mass./London.
Habermas, J. (1998), *Faktizität und Geltung, Beiträge zur Diskurstheorie des Rechts und des demokratischen Rechtsstaats*, Suhrkamp, Frankfurt/M.
Hamilton, A., Jay, J. and Madison, J. (1961) in J. Cooke (ed.), *The Federalist Papers*, Wesleyan University Press, Middletown Conn.
Harlow, C. (1985), 'Power from the People? Representation and Constitutional Theory' in P. McAuslan and J. McEldowney (eds.), *Law, Legitimacy and the Constitution: Essays Marking the Centenary of Dicey's Law of the Constitution*, Sweet & Maxwell, London, pp. 62-81.
Hirst, P. (1990), *Representative Democracy and Its Limits*, Polity, Cambridge.
Hobbes, T. (1999) in R. Tuck (ed.), *Leviathan*, 2nd edn, Cambridge University Press, Cambridge.
Kant, I. (2001), *Kritik der Urteilskraft*, Meiner, Hamburg.
Kateb, G. (1981), 'The moral distinctiveness of representative democracy', *Ethics*, 91, pp. 357-374.
Kateb, G. (1992), *The Inner Ocean: Individualism and Democratic Culture*, Cornell University Press, Ithaca.

Kavanagh, A. (2003), 'Participation and Judicial Review. A Reply to Waldron', *Law and Philosophy,* 22, pp. 451-486.

Kuper, A. (2004), *Democracy beyond Borders: Justice and Representation in Global Institutions*, Oxford University Press, Oxford.

Kymlicka, W. (1995), *Multicultural Citizenship*, Clarendon, Oxford.

Lijphart, A. (1984), *Democracies: Patterns of Majoritarian and Consensus Governement in Twenty-One Countries*, Yale University Press, New Haven.

Locke, J. (1999) in P. Laslett (ed.), *Two Treatises of Government,* Cambridge University Press, Cambridge.

Loughlin, M. (2003), 'Representation and Constitutional Theory' in P. Craig and R. Rawlings (eds.), *Law and Administration in Europe*, Oxford University Press, Oxford, pp. 47-66.

Magnette, P. (2003), 'European Governance and Civic Participation: Beyond Elitist Citizenship?', *Political Studies*, 51:1, pp. 1-17.

Manin, B. (1987), 'On Legitimacy and Political Deliberation', *Political Theory,* 15:3, pp. 338-368.

Manin, B. (1997), *The Principles of Representative Government*, Cambridge University Press, Cambridge.

Manin B., Przeworski A. and Stokes S. (1999), 'Introduction' in A. Przeworski, S. Stokes and B. Manin (eds.), *Democracy, Accountability and Representation*, Cambridge University Press, Cambridge.

Mansbridge, J. (1980), *Beyond Adversary Democracy*, Basic Books, New York.

Mansbridge, J. (1981), 'Living with Conflict: Representation in Adversary Democracy', *Ethics*, 91, pp. 466-476.

Mansbridge, J. (1999), 'Everyday Talk in the Deliberative System' in S. Macedo (ed.), *Deliberative politics, Essays on* Democracy and Disagreement*,* Oxford University Press, Oxford.

Mansbridge, J. (2000), 'What does a Representative Do? Descriptive Representation in Communicative Settings of Distrust, Uncrystallized Interests, and Historically Denigrated Status' in W. Norman and W. Kymlicka (eds.), *Citizenship in Diverse Societies*, Oxford University Press, Oxford.

Mill, J.S. (1991), *Considerations on Representative Government,* Prometheus Books, Amherst.

Mirabeau, H.G. (1834), *Œuvres*, Paris.

Mouffe, C. (2000), *The Democratic Paradox*, Verso, New York.

Müller, J.-P. (1992), *Demokratische Gerechtigkeit,* Deutscher Taschenbuch Verlag, München.

Müller, J.-P. (2002), *Die demokratische Verfassung*, Neue Zürcher Zeitung Verlag, Zürich.

Parkinson, J. (2003a), 'Legitimacy Problems in Deliberative Democracy', *Political Studies*, 51, pp. 180-196.

Parkinson, J. (2003b), 'Hearing Voices: Negotiating Representation Claims in Public Deliberation', Paper presented to the ECPR Joint Sessions 2003, http://www.essex.ac.uk/ECPR/events/jointsessions/paperarchive/edinburgh/ws14/Parkinson.pdf.

Pateman, C. (1970), *Participation and Democratic Theory*, Cambridge University Press, Cambridge.

Pennock, J.R. (1968), 'Political Representation: An Overview' in J. Pennock and J. Chapman (eds.), *Representation*, Nomos X, New York University Press, New York.

Pennock, J.R. (1979), *Democratic Political Theory*, Princeton University Press, Princeton.

Pettit, P. (2004), 'Depoliticizing Democracy', *Ratio Juris*, 17:1, pp. 52-65.

Phillips, A. (1995), *The Politics of Presence*, Clarendon, Oxford.
Pitkin, H. (1972), *The Concept of Representation,* University of California Press, Berkeley.
Pitkin, H. (1989), 'Representation' in T. Ball, J. Farr and R. Hanson (eds.), *Political Innovation and Conceptual Change*, Cambridge University Press, Cambridge.
Plotke, D. (1997), 'Representation is Democracy', *Constellations*, 4:1, pp. 19-34.
Postema, G. (1982), 'Coordination and Convention at the Foundations of Law', *Journal of Legal Studies,* 11, pp. 165-202.
Rogowski, R. (1981), 'Representation in Political Theory and Law', *Ethics*, 91, pp. 395-430.
Rousseau, J.-J. (1997) in V. Gourevitch (ed.), *The Social Contract and other later Political Writings,* Cambridge University Press, Cambridge.
Saward, M. (ed.) (2000), 'Introduction' in *Democratic Innovation: Deliberation, Association and Representation*, Routledge, London.
Saward, M. (2003), 'The Representative Claim', Paper presented to the ECPR Joint Sessions 2003, http://www.essex.ac.uk/ECPR/events/jointsessions/paperarchive/edinburgh/ws14/Saward.pdf.
Scanlon, T. 1977, 'Due Process' in J. Pennock and J. Chapman (eds.), *Due Process*, Nomos XVIII, New York University Press, New York.
H. Schmitt and J. Thomassen (eds) 1999, *Political Representation and Legitimacy in the European Union*, Oxford University Press, Oxford.
Schumpeter, J. (1947), *Capitalism, Socialism and Democracy*, 2nd edn, Allen & Unwin, London.
Setala, M. (1996), *Referendums and Democratic Government*, Macmillan, Basingstoke.
Sieyès, A. (1963), *What is the Third Estate?*, Pall Mall Press, London.
Singer, P. (1974), *Democracy and Disobedience*, Clarendon, Oxford.
Squires, J. (2000), 'Group representation, deliberation and the displacement of dichotomies' in M. Saward (ed.), *Democratic Innovation: Deliberation, Association and Representation*, Routledge, London, pp. 93-105.
Sunstein, C.R. (1988), 'Beyond the Republican Revival', *Yale Law Journal,* 97, pp. 1539-1590.
Sunstein, C.R. (2002), 'The Law of Group Polarization', *Journal of Political Philosophy,* 10:2, pp. 175-195.
Tully, J. (1995), *Strange Multiplicity: Constitutionalism in an Age of Diversity*, Cambridge University Press, Cambridge.
Urbinati, N. (2000), 'Representation as Advocacy', *Political Theory,* 28:6, pp. 758-786.
Urbinati, N. (2002), *Mill on Democracy: From the Athenian Polis to Democratic Representation*, University of Chicago Press, Chicago.
Waldron, J. (1993), 'A Right-Based critique of Constitutional Rights', *Oxford Journal of Legal Studies,* 13, pp. 18-51.
Waldron, J. (1999), *Law and Disagreement*, Oxford University Press, Oxford.
Waldron, J. (2000), 'Legislation by Assembly', *Loyola Law Review,* 46/3, pp. 507-534.
Waldron, J. (2002), 'Introduction: Disagreement on Justice and Rights', *Legislation and Public Policy*, 6:5, pp. 5-10.
Williams, M. (1998), *Voice, Trust and Memory*, Princeton University Press, Princeton.
Williams, M. (2000), 'The Uneasy Alliance of Group Representation and Deliberative Democracy' in W. Norman and W. Kymlicka (eds.), *Citizenship in Diverse Societies*, Oxford University Press, Oxford.
Wintgens, L. (2001), 'Sovereignty and Representation', *Ratio Juris*, 14, pp. 272-280.
Wintgens, L. (ed.) (2002), *Legisprudence: A new Theoretical Approach to Legislation*, Hart Publishing, Oxford.

Young, I.M. (1990), *Justice and the Politics of Difference*, Princeton University Press, Princeton.

Young, I.M. (1996), 'Communication and the Other: Beyond Deliberative Democracy' in S. Benhabib (ed.), *Democracy and Difference,* Princeton University Press, Princeton.

Young, I. M. (1997), 'Deferring Group Representation' in I. Shapiro and W. Kymlicka (eds.), *Ethnicity and Group Rights*, Nomos XXXIX, New York University Press, New York.

Young, I.M. (2000), *Inclusion and Democracy*, Oxford University Press, Oxford.

Chapter 8

On the Descriptive and the Prescriptive Nature of the Constitution. Constitutionalism and the Legitimisation of the Constitution in the Practice of its Implementation

Pasquale Policastro*

Introduction: A Brief Description of the Problem and of my Thesis

At the beginning of this contribution we would like first of all to underline that our approach is concentrated on the function of the constitution as a way to provide a democratic rationalisation of political power. With this conception we refer to the fact that a significant contribution of constitutionalism has been to organise societies characterised by inequalities, within a project to reduce the inequalities themselves, in the measure in which they are a cause of discrimination in the full exercise of rights. In our approach, then, legal norms contained in the constitution may not be seen only as a means to trade off between different legal interests. Indeed, the constitutional construction includes the concept of fundamental rights, to be related with the political expectations of individuals and groups. The fulfilment of these expectations legitimates the constitution in front of the society. Constitutional rules contain indeed, values, political and ideological principles, programmatic principles, public and individual duties, as well as different kind of sanctioned commands and permissions. For these reasons, as we can see from the history of constitutions, constitutional rules deal not only with the regulation of the present situation, but they also aim to support given patterns of social, political and economic evolution.

According to our approach, in constitutional interpretation it is not only the balancing of arguments that really matters. It is important to find legal reason supporting the process of subsumption of the dynamical principles and values, included in the constitution, within the activity of the legislator. For this reason it is important, among others, that there is a public debate permitting the joining together of the different approaches to the mentioned operation of subsumption. In presenting evidence for this thesis, we aim to show how our approach may be consistent with the challenges of multilevel constitutional systems and the efforts to found a multilevel democracy.

The Production of Legal Rules must be Considered a Science: Indeed, as Many Sciences deal with the Dichotomy 'Being-Becoming'

The object of many sciences is the study of the processes of transformation. Also, in physical sciences, we may find a 'dichotomy' between the static, deterministic, approach, which can be related to the physics of 'being' and the thermodynamic description, dealing with irreversible processes, which can be connected with the 'becoming' (Prigogine, 1978-1986, p. 24). What is important to point out is that in the first approach the equations are symmetrical with respect to time, whilst in the second case they are not. Still, the different approaches ought to coexist in the measure in which any of them specifically complies with different attempts to reconstruct and to describe the reality. But here it comes a first point that may be related with the relationship between physical reality and the social reality, whose complexity is the object of constitutional science. Indeed, whether we want to acquire some knowledge of the reality or we want to deal with it, making experiments or otherwise making use of physical properties of the matter, we need to have a description of the reality. This description is functional to the kind of phenomena we want to operate with. This holds true also for legal science, provided that it aims to operate within a social context. In this way we may find a first aspect of the relationship existing between physical science and the science of the constitution. A second point is related with the fact that the science of the constitution as well as jurisprudence deal with phenomena that are characterised by a high degree of irreversibility. In law, time matters and the changes that occur within time transform in an irreversible way the person and the society. When the European Court of Human Rights affords just satisfaction to the injured party (art 141 ECHR), in many cases it cannot possibly restore the original state or condition. Still, the aim of the ECHR and of the activity of the Court is to lead to a change in the legal practices in the different member states, which prove to lead to undesirable infringements of the human rights. The aim of ECHR is to produce a transformation addressed to achieve a more desirable state, in order to deal with undesired irreversible changes by means of the introduction of new changes, compatible with the Charter. As another example, we may say that, in the period of the constitutional transition, the Polish Constitutional Tribunal has been dealing with the rights legitimately acquired by the citizens, prohibiting the derogation from them.

The purpose of the legal activity, including jurisprudence, cannot be said to deal uniquely with irreversibility. When dealing with contracts, its aim is to guarantee that the values of the mutual promises or obligations may balance, in a way that may be measurable or accountable. Still, when we deal with public law we are confronted with irreversible phenomena, and with the inequality of the social actors. The rule of law, if it has to deal only with the balancing measure of different obligations, may not be politically accountable within the field of the purposes of a given society. Still, the legitimisation of the political power rests also upon some optimisation of the dissipation that may occur in achieving a given purpose. Therefore, the science of constitution and of legislation deals with irreversible processes in time, as well as with the confrontation between values and the objective reality within the different periods of time. Indeed, between the end of the 18th century and the first part of the 19th century the study of the 'science of administration' was denominated 'statistics' (Vincenzo Cuoco, 1990, reprint). The authors that have been studying the latter concept have been stressing the relationship between statistics and constitutional, legislative and administrative policies (Sofia, 1988, passim).

The science of constitution, dealing to a significant extent with irreversible processes, is, in our approach, a science of the 'being-becoming'. The importance given to budget law as a political tool and to the question of its legal accountability may show from another angle what we aim to say. Indeed, the discipline in the public finances, that has been characterising the process of implementing a common currency in Europe, shows the necessity of making use of the public finances in a way not to distress the relations between the states in an integrating system. We shall remember that an important contribution to the process of rendering political power accountable was given from the debate on whether budget law may be understood only as a formal statute or also a substantive statute, submitted to judicial control (Heller, 1927-1987, pp. 340-341).

The Need of an Approach to Being-Becoming and the Constitutional Rules: The Problem of the Dual Nature, Prescriptive and Descriptive, of Constitutional Rules

Determining patterns of social evolution has been a fundamental task of public law from the very beginning of the reflections on politics and jurisprudence. The difficulty of directing the system to predetermined transformations allowing a better implementation of political values, such as freedom, equality or justice has been leading to reserve a special interest in the normative formulations of the principles of distribution, of the social expectations and of the ideological values, which ought to set the framework and the direction in which a political society may develop. The problem related with the rules of transformation lies in the relationship between the objective situation of a given society and the implementation of a satisfactory evolutionary pattern. The principles of distribution are the first to appear in the contractualistic tradition, and are related to distribution of political power, of social power and economic resources (Hobbes, 1651, Chapter XXIV, passim). Later on, starting from the French constitution of 1848, as we can see, especially on the debate in the constituent assembly, the content of the constitutions started to attempt to embody a wider range of social expectations then they did formerly. It became necessary to relate expectations with rights and programmes concerning the legal activity of the state. Already from the debate that developed from that occasion, we see that the attempt to discuss the question of the 'economic calculation of the reforms became related with the question of the 'irreversible' transformation that may have been caused. Some members of the constituent assembly mentioned the dangers of socialism, some others the dangers that people may lose their entrepreneurship when sure of the state help. Other voices mentioned the importance to preserve the confidence of the workers in the new constitution (Craveri 1985, passim; Policastro, 2002). From the juridical point of view, this question may be formulated as saying that the problem was that the 'principles of distribution' at the initial moment not satisfying for the masses, but surely satisfying for a certain part of the society and many representatives. A new and better order ought to have been characterised by a path, starting from a given distribution of power and health, and leading to another pattern of distribution. The question of the formulation of such a path, by means of law, is related to the clear consideration of what is the initial state, and which 'principles' ought to be respected. This approach to legal principles that does not seem to be anymore compatible with the contractualistic tradition, characterised the future developments of the European constitutions, markedly the ones approved after World War I and the ones approved after World War II. These conceptions can be partly found in the approach to the legal principles supported by Emilio Betti, according to whom legal principles, with respect to other norms, are characterised by a superabundant normative content: "*un'eccedenza di contenuto logico* (*o assiologico...*" (italics in the text: Betti 1990, reprint, p. 849 passim; see also Cerri, 1987, passim). Within this conception the 'principle of distribution' may be considered within an approach to constitution as a form to achieve a democratic rationalisation of the political power, aiming to eliminate discrimination and overcome inequalities (Policastro 2000, passim). The said superabundant normative content ought to support the (irreversible) political, economic and social transformations envisaged by the constitution. Also the conception of Robert Alexy (2003, pp. 771-772 passim), relating the legal principles with the rules of optimisation, is extremely important for our reflections, since it concentrates on the legal framework in which the transformation envisaged by the constitution ought to take place.

Rules of Different Kinds are Characterized by Different Rules for their Production, both Formal and Substantive

A substantive definition of the concept of constitutional rules requires the definition of the legal relationships that are covered by constitutional rules and of the legal relationships that are covered by other kinds of rules. In the development of the reflections on law and politics an important role has been claimed by the development of the concept of higher law (see Brick, 1999, pp. 13-18 passim). The concept of higher law, which we may refer to as 'constitutional law' in its substantive meaning (Arnold, 2004, passim), shows the following characteristics: a) to be selective, namely centred on the determination of the elements that have to be the object of higher regulations. In this way it is made a choice of elements that are relevant for a political organisation; b) to the comparative, namely to refer, explicitly or implicitly, the system of the higher law to some patterns, in which a given model of evolution has been produced, or to rational arguments supporting the above mentioned pattern (Cervati, 1999, pp. 30-34 passim); c) to be accountable, namely setting responsibilities for the achievement of a given pattern of evolution.

The fact that constitutions have been dealing to a significant extent with the dichotomy being-becoming, with the social tensions related to the application of principles leading to irreversible transformations, but also with the necessary relationship between constitutional rules and social expectations, has been leading to a wider and generalised approach to constitutional rules by means of documents that have been involving ideological principles, rights, tasks to be achieved, sources of law, political functions, and rules of adjudication. The refusal to accept the coexistence of principles of distribution and principles of change within the normative framework of a constitution (Forsthoff, 1953-1973, passim, Policastro, 2002, p. 93 passim) represents in itself the choice of rules of change that privilege given classes and interests with respect to the totality of the interests involved in a political society.

From the above-mentioned reflections, there comes the general problem of descriptivity-prescriptivity in public law or, namely, in the 'science of constitution'. This problem is related to the initial situation in which a society is at the point of having its constitution approved and to the purposes of the constitution itself, namely the changes it aims to implement. Such a question affects, in a significant way, the questions related to the 'science of legislation', since the latter has the task to 'interpret' constitutional law (Cerri, 1999, passim), leading to the gradual implementation of the transformations envisaged in the constitution itself. The problem cannot be considered only by means of choices of methods of constitutional interpretation as well as of criteria that make the process of constitutional implementation correct or acceptable. It is a problem that relates politics with law (Neumann 1957-1973, passim), and that highlights the 'obligation' of each interpreter to implement the constitutional rules. Indeed, as has been studied with a particular interest in relation to Weimar's constitution, the refusal of the interpreters of the constitution to recognise the system of values carried by it, led to deep substantive distortion in its application (Rigaux 1997-2001, pp. 107-135 passim). It may also be worth mentioning the Italian example in the period between the approval of the Republican Constitution of 1848 and the coming into force of the Constitutional Court in 1956, when the majority party attempted to give an interpretation of the Constitution absolutely limiting the freedoms and the social rights embodied in the Constitution. Furthermore, looking at the whole history of the interpretation of the Italian Constitution, a critical author has been claiming that, in all its lifetime, the Italian Constitution has never been truly functioning, at least never in its entirety (Negri, p. 167 passim).

The normative character of a constitution rests upon the fact that the constitution embodies different, somehow conflicting, interests and expectations, and that only the guarantee of the application of the different constitutional principles may generate a virtuous circle in which all the interpreters take the risk of a full interpretation of the constitution itself. The danger that the constitution, and that law in general, may be interpreted simply according with the will of the interpreter has been leading some present exponents of the legal realism to stress that this phenomenon is somehow related to the 'nature of the things' in the legal interpretation, or anyway in the legal process, since in the end "Judicial review by a constitutional court is justified by the argument that it is merely formal" (Troper, 2004, passim). The point is that many actors participate in constitutional interpretation, although with different intensity, and not only the judges: we have the different levels of legislators and governments, the political parties, and private subjects. This is the reason why the constitutions have been searching for different institutional means to verify whether or not a constitution has been applied in all its parts, and why legal doctrines have been stressing the dangers coming from the fact that judges may become the arbiters or the meaning of law (Rigaux 1997-2001 p. 293 passim), as well as to claim the need to "Take the Constitution away from the Courts" (Tushnet, 1999 passim). The need to control the growing interaction of different actors in the process of constitutional interpretation may also be observed in the tendency to develop different levels of constitutions, such as at the European level, the one given by EU-EC law and the ECHR, that influence, both vertically and horizontally, the interpretation of the national constitutions (Arnold, 2004 passim), setting political constraints to be followed, among others, by the legislator and the government(s), under the responsibility of the state.

In our opinion, the special object of constitutional rules, that regulates the development of irreversible processes, leads not only to a fundamental difficulty if we want to reconstruct its normative content on the basis of a theory of norms that may reduce all kinds of norms to a single 'genus'. Indeed the special object of constitutional rules deserves not only a study based mainly upon duties and rights (Kelsen, 1979-1985, p. 208 passim: chapter XXXII: "Diritto, dovere, sanzione" – right, duty, sanction), but requires an analysis of the obligation to implement the constitutional rules. To this task is not only needed a deep evaluation of the political aspects related to this matter, but also a clear analysis of the relationship between constitution and legislation.

The Legal Relationships that are Covered by Constitutional Rules ought to be taken into Consideration Observing that, the Historical Evolution of the Norms of Higher Law, has been Characterised by the Expression of Legal Constraints for the Legislator. We can find for example constraints for the legislator in the formulation of the fundamental rights of the citizens, reserving to the legislator certain matters, and setting some rules for the correct exercise of the public functions. For the above-mentioned reasons, higher law sets rules for the production and/or the interpretation of other legal rules. We will concentrate on the rules of production of other rules, hereafter called 'legislation'. We will distinguish legislation from adjudication using the concept of legal prescription. The legal prescription does not relate only to the achievement of a future state, but it is connected also with the protection of certain goods related to given situations that are relevant for the higher law. Therefore, the higher law legitimates an order and sets the ways in which to achieve a given order. An essential aspect of the higher law can be seen in the limitations and the constraints given to the legislator. This system of constraints may permit to check: a) if and in which way a system of law corresponds to the institutional framework characterising in a given moment a certain society; b) the priorities that have to be set in the achievements of the goals of the society in the postulated order. Since the constitutional order makes it possible to set goals characterised by a noteworthy degree of discrepancy from the actual state of a given society, the concept of validity may not be enough in order to control whether the legal order is leading to social developments according to the purposes set in the higher law (Policastro, 2004a).

The Concept of 'Higher Law' and its Relation with Reason

In our conception, the concept of constitutional interpretation is not only related with the judicial review of legislation. Indeed, as has been observed (Cerri, 2004), the political process can be seen as somehow similar to a succession of experiments by which a consensus is slowly found. Indeed, according with this conception, "the majority-principle, such as the entire constitutional framework (preserved by the courts), is a rule of legitimisation to verify". Instead, according to this conception, the activity of a court is not insuperable and is of a measurable and limited force, "but it is also not insignificant". In this approach we may envisage the necessity of an interpretation of the constitution supported by political and democratic processes, together with a more limited role of the constitutional interpretation supported by the judges. This approach not only poses strong requirements to the text of the constitution, namely to describe sufficiently well the model of social transformation suitable to the needs and expectations of the society. It also requires that, its interpretation through the activity of the legislator permits defining how a polity has been advancing from the starting point when it approved its own constitution, to the desired social transformation. Furthermore, the interpretation of the legislator ought to describe the necessary steps needed to achieve the desired transformations. Now, there emerges once more a necessary relationship between the fundamental constitutional principles, through which is defined the direction of the transformation suited in the constitutional design, and the means needed to achieve the transformations that the constitution wishes to achieve, granting the normative value of its parts. The latter means may be the object of interpretation leaving a discretional power to the legislator. Their application, or the difficulties of this process, may also lead to undertaking constitutional revisions. The relative rigidity of the constitutional principles refers instead to the need of a coherent design in the achievement of transformations within a polity (see Pfersmann, pp. 373-374 *passim*). For this reason, it is extremely important to refer to the constitution as a 'system'. Therefore, the relationship between the constitutional principles, having to pilot the polity to given transformations and the means foreseen in the constitution to achieve these goals, may be very tight. In this light we can understand the criticism of different authors to the actual project of reform of the Italian Constitution (approved by the Senate of the Italian Republic on March 25th 2004 and by the Chamber of the Deputies, with changes, on October 18th, 2004 – retransmitted to the Senate for the continuation of the procedure of constitutional revision). Indeed, this project may not seem to interfere with the fundamental constitutional principles, but in practice it transforms the system of government in a way that any attempt to fully bring into life the normative content of the fundamental constitutional principles, among others, through the means specified for the legislation within the system of the fundamental rights may be jeopardised (see Bevere, 2004, passim). Such a constitutional reform, enhancing, the role of the prime minister (see Stammati, 2003, p. 15), sets limits to the possibility of the democratic principle to constantly exercise a political pressure on the government directed, for example, to the implementation of the constitutional principle concerning the elimination of the substantive discriminations within the society (art. 3.2 It. Const.). This lack of coherence of the present reform with the original design of the Constitution may deserve some more reflections. Indeed, we do not aim to support here the thesis that the interpretation of the constitution ought to be based uniquely on the original design of its founders. For us, the process of interpretation of the constitution ought to make sure that the constitution maintains its democratic legitimisation in the practice of its implementation, in the process of constitutional interpretation. Indeed, to abandon the requirement of the coherence with the principles having to lead to given economic, social and political transformations, it means leaving to the ruling forces in a given moment the power to 'pronounce the constitution'. The extreme danger of this eventuality may be seen by taking into account that concepts of 'people's sovereignty' or 'general will' mask the fact that power is not exercised through the making of a common 'homogeneous' will. It is the result of tensions between interdependent actors, individual and collective, characterised by mutual differences and inequalities. We may find a support in our statements from the results developed by the philosophical school of Frankfurt, starting from Horkeimer and Adorno, that have been highlighting that in the contemporary age the domain of the economic and political forces is exercised on the masses through the means of communications, the cultural industry and publicity in a more efficient way than through the use of the force and the coercion. In this way, technology may render impossible the critical self-reflection of the individual (Volpe, 2000, p. 239). The remarks of the members of the school of Frankfurt seem to anticipate the reflections concerning freedom in the process of globalisation as well as in the age of the "Governance Without Government" (Rosenau and Czempiel, 1992, passim, especially the contribution of Rosenau), where the increase becomes evident of the number of actors influencing the life of the individuals and the complexity of their relations.

The relationship between the coherence in the constitutional interpretation and the rationality of the interpreter is indeed a matter of democratic rationalisation of the political power.

The Question: 'Is the Interpreter of Law Rational?' is Connected with the Question: 'Is the Producer of Legal Norms Rational?'

Both the production and the interpretation of law can be seen as hermeneutic activities. Reason is one of the elements used in order to adjudicate legal relations. As we have been saying above, the tendency to acknowledge to the legislator a role embodying a collective reason, leads to the necessity to control the rationality of the legislator. It may also lead to the acknowledgement of a creative role of the adjudication that may potentially be without limitations (Rigaux, 1997, p. 321

passim), although different schools of thought try instead to see the role of the jurist as more even than that, because it is related to some 'platitudes' that are stable across cultural divergences (Peczenik 2002, section 8). In the search for criteria needed to define the patterns to be followed in order to consider in which substantive framework we may conceive the concept of 'rationality', we may point out first of all that the approach to 'higher law' in terms of a hierarchy of rules is not able to give an univocal answer to the problem of the rationality of the interpretation processes, due to the problems related with the interdependence of the interpreters and the inequalities in the society, including the interpreters. Also the jurists may become in this process an active subject for the transformation of the legal systems according to the interests of a given class of subjects, such as the big corporations (Dezalay, 1992-1997, p. 223 passim). In this context, constitutionalism can be seen as a sort of 'historical reason', that may be able to consider the way in which the relationship between different social actors have been legally defined, by means of legal principles and rules, through public debate and social conflict. In different contributions, we have been denoting the said relationships by means of paradigms such as: the relationship between the formulation of human rights and the approaches to their achievement, the relationship between participation and representation, as well as the relationship between norms and hermeneutics (Policastro, 2001, 2002, 2004a, passim). The substantive expression of each of these paradigms has been evolving with time, according to the quality which the concrete specification of these relations manifests in a given constitutional system, both in the formulation of the constitutional rules and in their interpretation. For this reason, the paradigms themselves can be used to check the process of constitutional implementation and interpretation, as well as to verify if the pattern of evolution of a given polity responds to the criteria developed by constitutionalism intended as a 'historic reason'.

Therefore we argue that, in order to characterize the nature of the constitutional rules in terms of the prescriptive-descriptive dichotomy, in interpreting and producing legal rules we have to take into account the necessary duality,k constitutionalism-constitution. Constitutionalism, as a mean to conceive a certain 'historical reason', may be seen as a way to permit the production of a virtuous circle between the development of a political rationality, in the majoritarian tendency, but structured in a way to take into account the different needs and the different kinds of inequalities that characterise a society, and the development of a critical process of adjudication.

The Descriptive Character of a Constitution: A Way to 'Recognize' Constitutional Rules

Therefore, the descriptive character is a criterion to 'validate' constitutional rules in the processes of micro-production and micro-interpretation of constitutional rules, legitimating the hermeneutic processes that, as a result, give rise to certain rules. Our approach to the constitutional interpretation is based upon two dualisms: the dualism 'being-becoming' characterising the object of the constitution, to which corresponds the dualism 'descriptivity-prescriptivity' characterising its rules. In a theory of interpretation centred upon the process of implementation of the constitutional rules by the public powers, starting from the legislative, as well as upon the process of 'reception' of the constitutional rules in the activity of the private subjects, the normative strength of the constitution has to be seen in relation to its overall legal fitness to gradually generate the transformations envisaged by the political interpretation of its text. Since the transformations we deal with are characterised by their irreversibility, the task of the constitutional rules is to apply to the different situations that will be produced in the different parts, as well as in the overall process of transformation envisaged by the constitution. In the process of constitutional interpretation, the question of the 'choices' of the public interpreters such as the legislative, the government(s), the judges that on a micro-analysis may be seen as related to 'independent' acts of will, with different consequences according to the theoretical approach followed, will be the object of a general political 'accountability' of the public bodies with respect to the implementation of the constitution: from this it will depend the democratic legitimisation of the implementation of a constitution, that has not to be seen as a form of institutionalised consensus generated in a given moment, but as a process. The democratic legitimisation of the implementation of a constitution depends on the development of the following levels of coherence: a) between the fundamental principles of the constitution and the policies implementing the constitutional rules; b) between the social expectations, manifested through the democratic debate and the fundamental principles of the constitution.

The democratic legitimisation of the process of implementation of a constitution depends to a larger extent on the possibility of 'subsuming' the events characterising the development of the life of a polity, in the positive constitutional framework. The latter process, takes necessarily place within the social confrontation. The relationship between subsumption and balancing adopted in concrete, embodied in the choices of the constitutional interpreter(s) (see Alexy, 2003, p. 771-772) is indeed the result of the confrontation between the interested social actors having different views on the normative content of the constitutional rules. Therefore, apart from their use in order to control the judicial activity, the rules of subsumption may be an important means for the development of principles that may make the legislator(s) and the government(s) substantively accountable for their activity. Also, for this reason we are convinced that the descriptive character of the constitutional norms helps the constitution to gain normative strength, in the measure in which it relates the process of implementation of a constitution with a theory of democracy (Habermas, 1992-1996, p. 316).

The Descriptive Character of the Constitution is also a Way to Consider the Relationship between the Constitutional Rules and the Institutional Constraints Characterising a Certain Society

The relationship between the constitutional rules and the institutional constraints characterising a given society, affects the activity of the legal interpreters, and of the lawyers in general. The institutional constraints mentioned above form the burden and, at the same time, permit defining the tasks of a 'lawgiver' having to achieve, as a result of the process of constitutional implementation, some social transformations. The strict relationship between the programmatic purposes of the constitution and its descriptive character is evident in the constitutions that try to ground the political consensus needed to produce social transformations. Therefore, we may describe the relationship between the constitution as a political document and the constitution as a legal document in the attempt to set norms that relate to a specific social situation. In this approach, the political character of the constitution does not seem to be in opposition with its legal character. This is the reason because the processes of rationalisation of constitutional law, which are often related to the reception of models that have been working in other systems, may not guarantee the desired normative strength, without a clear political awareness and participation.

The attempt to find a solution to the problems related to political conflicts by means of a higher degree of social integration (Smend, 1928-1988), which risk appears also nowadays when the market is understood as a dominating principle in constitutional interpretation, does not seem to be able to eliminate those other risks for democracy related to the work of hegemonic forces within the political sphere.

The Problem of Communication and the Crisis of Contemporary Constitutionalism

The communication patchwork can be considered as a critical issue in the whole history of constitutionalism. Constitutionalism postulates not only the possibility to claim for public rights, but also the need to create the individual and collective possibility to develop an opinion on the individual and the social situation. The interaction between individual needs and expectations and collective interests, which is often shown within an unequal distribution of the social power, has been leading to the need to give an institutional form to the instruments of mass participation to policy-making. This in turn has been leading to the risk that an institutionalised logic may prevail over the expectations and the need to participate of the individuals and of the social groups. In this sense we may reflect on the sense of the approach to political power proposed by Massimo La Torre (1999, p. 204 passim). Indeed, this author points out that political power appears related to a system of rules, whilst 'domain' and 'hegemony' (see Gramsci, more recently Amirante, 2003, p. XXI; for consideration about 'hegemonic international law' see Picone, 2003, p. 331) show when 'social rules' lose contact with the social framework, namely, as we would say, with people's needs and expectations, especially embodied in the constitutional rules. The conception of law of this author seems, in addition, aware of the possibility to gradually implement social, economical and political transformation through law (La Torre, 1999, p. 205). But when the communication context seems to be dominated by different actors, the use of the relationship between constitutional law and legislative policies may be put in danger by the influences of the different actors on the communication framework. Here, the pluralistic approach seems to be useful. We will limit ourselves here to discussing the role of some of the actors in the process of developing a sphere of communication, and the question of their interaction.

For what concerns political parties – the criticism that has been addressed to mass parties, namely that they have been gradually acting according to a logic responding to their own interests, keeping somehow apart from the expectations of their own constituency – is only a part of the dangers related to the political meaning of the communication process. The political uses of the mass-media industry, the growth of big corporations and the development of public monopolies have been other factors leading to different spheres of legal understanding. This has been due to the peculiar role played by the interaction of a plurality of 'institutional' orders in contemporary societies. We can find these institutional orders, for example in the one produced by the interaction of the language of the mass political parties on the public life, or in the public influence of the trade unions. The above-mentioned patterns of interaction are indeed affecting the means of producing and interpreting law. Significant attention ought to be reserved to the role of the jurist, seen as a factor influencing the interpretation of law. Here we can mention the opinion of Dezalay, according to whom the mobilisation of the 'elites' of the lawyers at the service of the entrepreneurs, as is taking place under the development of the organisation system and the methods of activity characterising the big law firms, may lead to the formation of a dualistic system of justice: one applying to the holders of the economic power, the other to consumers. This fragmentation of the legal sphere may be solved by a factual mediation of the jurists and the legal interpreters that may 'recognise' the rules applying to the different situations (Hart, 1961-1965, p. 155: more recently, with special reference to the role of the legal culture see the approach of Cervati, 2001, pp. 31-38) or by supporting an interaction of the different subjects that may render 'of public domain their reasons'.

Indeed, concentrating on the language of the legal interpretation, which tends to stress the role of the different subjects that determine the meaning (Troper, 2004 passim) or interpret law, but given the due attention to the descriptive character of constitutional norms and to the descriptivity-prescriptivity relationship, we may find that the constitution itself is productive of language and of flows of communication, that must be accounted for by the subjects that determine the sense and the concrete meaning of the constitution in different situations. This language may permit the development of a consistent and understandable interpretation, when it produces a flow of information, that becomes the object of discussion within the different subject and individuals interacting in the public sphere. A good descriptive character is therefore needed in order that the process of interpretation of the constitution may remain consistent, notwithstanding the plurality and the difference of purposes and viewpoints of the subjects participating in it. In this way, the language of the subjects interpreting the constitution may become the representation of the expectations and the needs of the subjects and the institutions participating to the public sphere.

The Process of Globalisation has been Increasing the Possibilities to Communicate, but in the Same Time has been Enhancing the Possibilities of some Actors to influence the Process of Communication. An Irremediable Crisis of the Constitution?

The interaction of the flows of communication in the sphere that is produced with the advent of globalisation produces two kind of forces, the one directed to create a spontaneous legal system, the second is addressed to developing a dialogue about the needs and the expectations of the people expressed within the different constitutional systems, including the ones that are created through the superposition of different levels of substantive constitutional relations, as is taking place in Europe. In the first case, there are developed almost opposite approaches, the ones stressing the formation of a new 'ius commune' and the others claiming the possibility of development of spontaneous forms of democracy through the 'multitudes' (Hardt and Negri, 2000, especially pp. 43-46 passim) or in any case through non-formalised political actors, such as NGOs. Concerning the role of NGOs, their importance has been stressed for the development of a supra-national public opinion (Habermas, 1998-1999, passim). It has also been stressed that the activities of an NGO may be supportive for a peaceful debate among nations and peoples, since they operate outside the network of inter-state relations (Kimijima, 2004, Urata, 2004, passim). Although an NGO can be considered as a form to develop a more direct contact between citizens and allow a wider form of consciousness on their common problems, the implementation of people's expectations as described in the constitutional rules (both formal and substantive) requires the activity of representative bodies vested with public powers. Any extension of the concept of the public body poses the problem policying their activity, and therefore the problem of their constitutional acknowledgement, through a reference to the public tasks which ought to be pursued by them. We think that despite the new problems that appear, national constitutions are still to be seen as an important means to achieve a democratic rationalisation of the political power. But the constitutions ought to describe and take into account the new sources of inequality that appear.

Multi-level Constitutionalism and Multi-level Democracy. Descriptivity of the European Constitution and the Question of Communication

The description of the new problems that appear in the national constitutions may also take place through the mutual interaction of different levels of substantive constitutional norms, as it is taking place in Europe, where we have vertical and horizontal influences between different levels of substantive constitutional rules, namely the ECHR, the EU-EC law (which substantively embrace constitutional relations) and the national constitutions. The relations between the different levels of constitutional rules may overshadow the descriptive content of the national constitutions, and so they need to be analysed with a special attention. Indeed, the ECHR and its interpretation may be seen as a strong element stressing the need of a common interpretative language concerning human rights, with binding effects, following the tendency to the international codification of human rights that has been taking place, starting from the Declaration of S. Francisco. As we have already stressed (Policastro, 1999, 2002, passim), the ECHR is originally based upon the connection of the different elements composing the theory of rights in the countries that jointly gave rise to its formulation. This legal construction has then been enriched by protocols and a rich collection of jurisprudence. In itself, the Charter may be seen then as a document acknowledging the initial situation concerning the conceptions of human rights in the different countries that undersigned the Convention, and aiming to achieve a joint clarification of the different aspects related to the legal meaning of the single rights and the possibilities to limit them. So it might be understood as a substantive constitutional document in the sense that it aims to jointly direct the constitutional interpretation of the member states in the field of human rights towards common patterns. But it does not replace, in our opinion, the need for a theory of rights expressed in each national constitution, acknowledging the given situation of each country and the need of given patterns of evolution to be implemented through the public activity. The problem has arisen when these patterns have been considered 'standards', whose respect was needed, among others, in order to admit new countries to EU. Indeed, many countries of Central Eastern Europe have limited themselves to a reception of the standards of the ECHR without promoting a deep debate concerning the task that had to be achieved through the regulation of human rights in the specific conditions of a given country (Policastro, 2002, pp. 362, 363 passim). This has been generating a deficit of descriptivity of some national constitutions that is showing in the difficulty of the democratic legitimisation of the process of their implementation.

For what concerns the vertical relationships between the EU-EC law and the national constitutions, we may say that the principle of supremacy has been allowing, from the beginning of its jurisprudential enunciation, the application of community freedoms escaping the dangers of double standards. The importance of this approach to the application of the community law, has been giving rise to a new legal order within the field of international law, by means of a limitation in limited fields, of the states' sovereign rights. This order has been including not only the states, but also its nationals, conferring "upon them rights which become part of their legal heritage" (ECJ 26/62 van Gend & Loos). Here we see the development of a superposition in the 'legal heritage' of the citizens, including the contents of Community law and the contents of the national constitutional rules. In this superposition, we find the attempt to achieve at the Community level a situation in which it is forbidden to leave in force or to approve any "discrimination between nationals of member states" within the field of application of the Treaty. Taking into account the political and economic history of the relations between European countries, especially for what concerns the whole range of the causes that led to World War II, such legal principles have been giving a definite legal form to the principle of peaceful coexistence (Policastro, 2004a, 2004b, passim). Still, the implementation of the different European policies has been gradually leading to the formation of a sort of European 'material constitution' concerning the economic field. Without aiming to enter in the details of the question, we may say that the supremacy of European law over national law has been a key issue for the development of a binding law of peaceful coexistence. As a matter of fact, the general and fundamental principle of EC law of equal treatment or of non-discrimination (Tridimas, 2000, p. 4), clearly shows that the European construction leads to the achievement of a third dimension of the constitutional principle of equality, not any more related to the national system, as the principle of 'formal equality before law' and the 'programmatic principle of substantive equality supporting social policies. The principle of non-discrimination, understood in the system formed by the national constitutions and the European legal order, tries to achieve a form of equality between legal subjects having a different nationality, and therefore may be taken as an example of the tension of the different national polities to achieve a peaceful coexistence after World War II.

The critical issues emerging in the legal doctrine concerning the production of a material constitution 'of the market' at the European level (Amirante, 2001, p. XXII; Castiglione, 2002, p. 3 passim) may be seen in this light, showing that the development of European law has been creating a certain tension between the description of the relevant matters and the legal tools needed for the implementation of the constitutional rules and the relevant matters for EU-EC legal order.

The interest of the European Community in the increase of the range of its policies, the interest shown for social matters, and last but not least the decision of the ECJ, show the need to take into account the difference of the specific aim of the EC law and the aims pursued from national law (such as C-267/91 and C-268/91, Keck-Mithouard or C-185-91 Reiff).

A remarkable effort in order to acquire a higher degree of systematic order between the EU law and the national law can be seen in the project of the Treaty Establishing a Constitution for Europe and its components, especially The Charter of Fundamental Rights of the European Union. Indeed, as it has been stressed (Castiglione, 2002) the development of the Treaty has been taking place within a political context characterised by factors that were calling for a reorganisation of the relationship between European policies and national policies, and finally among national constitutional goals and the finalities of the EU. Among these factors, we can mention the question of the enlargement and the related issues, the introduction of the common currency, as well as the delicate problems related to the international order under the dangers of terrorism and the difficulties of the UN. The tendency of codification of the European achievements within the Charters of the European Union ought to be analysed taking into account that, already in the Nice Charter, there is formed grounds for a statutory reservation for the limitation of fundamental rights (II-112). This aspect, shows the attempt to lead to a democratic rationalisation of the political power embodied in the EU legal order. Apart from that, we can see that the Charter gives rise to a dialectic relationship between European statutes and national ones. We can see this, for example, in art. II-76 of the Charter, where the freedom to conduct a business is recognised in accordance with European law, national laws and practices. A similar reference to the relationship between European law and national law can be found for example when the Charter deals with the right to collective bargaining and action (art. II-88), the protection in the event of unjustified dismissal (II-90), the social security and social assistance (II-94), the right to health care (II-95), and the right of access to services of general economic interest (II-96). It is worth also noticing the reference to the general principles common to the laws of the Member States (II-101), in relation to thc liability of the European Union for the institutions or civil servants. The attention shown to the relationship between European law and domestic law acknowledges that there has been produced a centre of political power at the European level, through the gradual increase of the range of policies of the CE-UE. The democratic rationalisation of this power, which appears characterised by the development of a 'Governance Without Government' or a multi-level governance (on this latter subject see, for example, Rubino, 2004), may need a coordination of the different levels of public power. In this case the question of the institutionalisation of the political debate appears extremely important for the development of a concept of constitutional law that may form, on a multi-level base the ground for a mediation concerning the implementation of the different principles embodied in the national constitutions and in the European (constitutional) law. For this reason the concept of European laws and European framework laws jointly approved by the European Parliament and the Council acting on a foot of equality (I-34) appears extremely interesting. It indeed creates a ground for a debate between national governments represented within the Council and people's representatives. This is surely an attempt to understand the 'European Constitution' in juridical terms, as an element of mediation between the governments and the European peoples. The fact that the European laws and European framework laws are excluded in certain matters, and in other matters are not adopted by the Parliament and the Council on an equal footing, shows beyond any reasonable doubt that there are spheres of power related to the implementation of the European legal principles that hardly can be said to be democratically rationalised on multi-level grounds. As an example, we may mention that in the field of common security and foreign policy, European law and framework laws are excluded (II-40.6). We may also mention that the guidelines and the conditions necessary to ensure the necessary progress in the field of internal markets are adopted by means of regulations issued by the Council on a proposal of the Commission (III-130.3). We see that from one side the states together keep a bulk of exclusive political power in the field of foreign policy and internal affairs. From the other side, an important aspect shall be pointed out: the obligation of the states to act in a spirit of loyalty and solidarity and to refrain from action contrary to the interest of the Union or impairing its effectiveness. Furthermore, it required, among others, the achievement of an ever-increasing degree of convergence of the action of the member states (I-40). One may see that, in a field such as foreign policy, there is still a lack of descriptivity of all the different issues that may relate to the 'relevant' 'species facti' for the relationships between European policy and national policies. Indeed, we may say that the new Treaty shows the formation of a European law of the 'interdependence' (see Picone, 2003, p. 334). The problem is that the democratic rationalisation of the power produced within the 'governance' of this interdependence is still open and depends, on a large extent, on the description of the relevant juridical 'species facti'. In this way the legal sphere may take the role of mediating and rationalizing the political power in a way that tends to eliminate inequalities among the subjects involved (in this case the states). For what concerns the internal market, although the constitutionalisation of the principles relating to its functioning appears to be consolidated in the new Treaty, is that the development of the European economic governance has been producing a bulk of power, which has not been yet transferred to democratic debate.

In the context of the new European Treaty, within the process of implementation of the national constitutions, the joint interpretation of the different levels of constitutional rules ought to lead to the elimination of the inequalities between individuals and groups. The new form of European legislation, and the co-operation between national parliaments and European institutions, such as in the case related to the principle of subsidiarity and proportionality, as well as the participation of the national parliaments for the determination of the resources of the UE may be an important element in order to involve the national representative institutions in the debates concerning the implementation of the different levels of the constitution in Europe.

Responsibility, Reason, Ethic and Constitutional Interpretation

The approach to the relationship between the prescriptive and the descriptive character of the constitution, that we have been following so far, stresses the link between the elements that relate to 'subjective' reality and 'legal' reality in the interpretation of law. In our work we consider description as related to the expression of different expectations, both individual and collective. These expectations are founded on the present situation, and not only with respect to the moment at which the constitution is approved but also successively, as well as in the aims of a given society. In our approach, these aims, mainly embodied in the fundamental constitutional principles, form the substantive ground for the democratic rationalisation of the power. On the basis of their analysis we may answer to the question: 'Which democracy do we deal with?' These principles determine indeed the potential patterns of evolution of a society, starting from a given point of departure. The possibility of implementing these principles depends firstly on the legal means set in the constitution for this purpose, namely by the model of fundamental rights and the legal means established for their achievement, as well as by the pattern of political government, considered within the framework of the relationship between participation and representation. It depends also from the relationship between the normative content of the constitution and the hermeneutic approach of its interpreters.

The need to produce formal norms and to determine – ahead of the consideration of the present situation and of the needs and the expectations of the society – normative principles and constitutional rules, is indeed the consequence of the juridical role of the constitution to balance, to reciprocally limit and temper the subjective expectations, supporting a public political debate on the reasons of the different expectations. It is related to the presence of inequalities in the society and with the attempt to develop a public debate on the related matters. For example 'a significant part of the people in Poland and in Italy are not at the present moment sure of their job', permits delimiting the concept of the 'nature of the things' (for example with respect to 'the need of the good functioning of the production and the exchanges'), arguing that certain objective processes ought to be corrected and ruled by means of law. As an example we may refer to the following argument: 'the market is useful provided that in the long run it may produce a tendency to the full employment. But in the short term its mechanisms ought to be corrected whenever it may produce undesirable social effects'.

Through the need to develop a public debate and to take into account the reasons of the choices undertaken in interpreting law, legal science – the science of the production and interpretation of norms – becomes a moral science. The particular aspect of constitutional law is that the question of the social, political and economical transformations following its application, takes a paramount importance. The science of constitutional law can be said to be a science of the transformations.

The Juridical Sphere as the Element of Mediation Between Subjective Expectations, Objective Law and Reality

So far, then, we have been considering the reasons why the normative character of the constitution may be seen, within the developments of constitutionalism, as significantly related with its role leading to the democratic rationalisation of political power. We considered, in this light, the relationship between the descriptive character of the constitution and its normative character. Democratic rationalisation of political power leads to underlining the juridical role of the constitution connected with its role of mediation. Indeed, as we have pointed out, an essential aspect of the democratic legitimisation of the constitution is related to the fact that its implementation responds to the expectations of the society. For what concerns the role of the legal science in this process – the concept of mediation, characterising the juridical sphere in the process of democratic legitimisation of the constitution, achieved through the democratic rationalisation of the political power – leads us to underline that, under these conditions, the task of legal science may not be limited to the description of existing law. Indeed, it ought also to describe the reasons and the political, social and economical grounds on which legal rules came to exist, and the reasons that permit maintaining the democratic legitimisation of the constitution within the process of its implementation. Here, the descriptivity of the constitution, under the specification that legal science ought to consider the reasons that led legal norms to exist, as well as the potentiality of the existing legal norms for the accomplishment of the social needs, includes terms of reference to the objective situations as well as to the social expectations and to the social needs. The descriptivity of the constitution also includes a reference to the relationship between constitution and constitutionalism. The requirement that law ought to respond to the social needs, leads us to point out, that legal production and interpretation may not be referred to a rational parameter responding to the social expectations in a given moment, but ought also to be referred to historical parameters. Therefore in this context legal science becomes a science of the evaluation. Its object is indeed the change, and the question of the (ex ante and ex post) possible legitimisation of such a change.

In this sense we may see that the juridical sphere ought to be analysed in a different way with respect to the other social sciences. In particular, we ought to say that the separation of the paradigm of descriptivity from the paradigm of prescriptivity (normativity) such as applied to the knowledge of other social sciences, among other economics (Baranzini and Scazzieri, 1986, p. 5 passim), does not respond to the particular object of legal science; that is, dealing with facts, both physical and normative, related to expectations, needs and (irreversible) transformations. There does not exist a privileged viewpoint to observe law: anyway, since the study of the juridical sphere includes law, which is known through its interpretation, as well as the expectations and needs of individuals and the society, we may say that the study of the said phenomena requires methods adequately designed. In particular, we believe that the need to describe the conditions, in which a given society is, as well as its needs, is very important for the process of legal subsumption.

This aspect ought to be treated through a method enabling us to confront law with society. To deal with the social transformations through law, as well as with the expectations, both individual and collective, is extremely important for the process(es) of balancing. The latter question presents a twofold nature. One facet is related to the interpretation of the expectations of the subjects to which law is addressed. It requires the use of generally accepted principles, involving the use of public reasonableness. Looking at the question from the other viewpoint, in order to take into account the above-mentioned expectations, it is needed to deal with the intentionality expressed by the subjects interpreting law (Brentano: see Huemer, 2002, pp. 5-6; for the question of beliefs in economic science see Bacharach, 1986, p. 177 passim; for the possible influence of Brentano on the approach of Petrażycki, see Biernat 2001, p. 15). The difficulties related to the operation of balancing, are indeed linked with two levels of intentionality: i) the one concerning the expectations of the subjects to whom the law is addressed; ii) the other dealing with the preferences and the political belief of the interpreters (for an approach to the balancing in terms of principles and ideals, that appear related with questions of subjectivity, see Peczenik, 1999).

The Importance of the Construction and the Reconstruction of a Juridical Sphere within the Processes of Transition

For the reasons stated above, we believe that, when we deal with the methods needed in order to develop a knowledge of the juridical sphere, which involves both objective and subjective elements, the statement of the legal scholars relating to the similarity between jurisprudence and science, may be read requiring a consistency between the three levels mentioned above, namely: a) the starting situation of a society, the social needs and the level of general political purposes that ought to be achieved by means of the constitution; b) the expectations of individuals and groups; c) the political preferences and the commitments of the legal interpreters. Although each of these levels may be described through synthetic models, the consistency between the above-mentioned levels ought to confront levels of legal knowledge based upon descriptivity from one side, and behavioural assumptions from the other. The difficulty to reconcile synthetically these levels of understanding has been widely acknowledged with reference to economic science.

The first level of knowledge may be approached through an input-output model of analysis, which may be descriptive, but not predictive and may be said to be somehow consistent with an approach of the kind followed by the "Pure Theory of Law", with the limitations envisaged in the "General Theory of Norms" (Kelsen, 1979-1985; Losano, 1985). Indeed, looking at the arguments developed in different chapters (especially chapters 28, 30, 31, 36, 38, 41, 42, 58) of the posthumous work of Kelsen, we have the impression that, the approach of the Austrian author in his last contribution to the study of law, may acknowledge that, although legal science does not produce norms, the results obtained by legal science cannot be replaced by a mere activity of the judge and of the legislator. The judge(s), the legislator(s), and the government(s) are indeed politically responsible to explain the sense of the commands they set, but even if not, they will be responsible in front of the science. They have to rationally ground their decisions. This call to responsibility makes this method compatible with the attempt to find a dynamic framework for those scholars that study the economic systems with descriptive analytical tools (Pasinetti, 1981, passim) and arrive to determine a framework of reference for the dynamic equilibrium, or the constitutional law scholars (Amirante, 2003, passim; Cervati, 1999; Policastro, 2002, 2004a) that approach the study of the constitutional interpretation, by means of the achievements of constitutionalism.

The second level of knowledge may be approached by means of the interaction of preference curves and resource constraints (see Alexy, 2003, with reference to the question of Pareto optimality; on this subject see also Peczenik, 1999, p. 184). But the problems related to the substantive role of the legal interpreters (for example, the ones presented in the 'New Interpretative Realism', see Troper, 2004, passim; see also Troper, 1994-1998) lead to the creation of levels of interaction between expectations and preferences that are difficult to be confronted through closed trade-off interactions. Indeed, the comparison of the legal effects of the balancing (evaluation) performed by the subjects to whom the law is addressed, with the balancing performed by the legal interpreters, is made difficult since the representation of the political effects of the balancing may be different from both sides.

For this reason, we believe that the historical analysis of constitutionalism ought to be seen as a framework of reference supporting the debate leading to making a full use of the possibilities of each constitution to find a process of mediation and of democratic rationalisation of the political power. In this way, the legal doctrine addresses the call for a responsible and accountable use of the power and the achievement of a democratic legitimisation in the process of implementing, making or reforming the constitutional rules (see, for example, Bevere, 2004, in particular the contribution of Amirante, passim).

Transitions, Bifurcations and the Evolution of Legal Systems. Conclusions

Trying to present some of the results of this paper that may be considered as questions for further inquiry, we point out that it is too simplistic to deal with the transformation of the legal system through the 'continuity' – 'discontinuity' dichotomy. A theory of jurisprudence, able to confront the different components of the process of constitutional interpretation and the question of the democratic rationalisation of the political power, ought to take into account the problems of time change. In constitutional law, in particular, we find a dichotomy between the attempts to conquer wider spaces of freedom by the social classes and groups (which characterised, through their role, the different phases of development of contemporary constitutions), and the tendency to constrain the legal system within the existing relationships of influence prevailing in the society (Policastro, 2004). In particular, the big juridical revolutions that happened to take place in the history of western civilisation, were intended to overcome the problems caused by the constraining of the legal system within the existing relations of power (see Berman, 1983-1998, passim; Stolleis, 1990-1998, passim). The juridical revolutions have therefore been allowing the legal system to escape from an approach to the logic of the legal interpretation characterised by a very high degree of 'self-referentiality', which may have lead to a juridical 'stationary state'. In order to allow the system not to consist of a mere crystallisation of power (see Policastro, 2002, pp. 217-218 passim; Trzciński, 1978, p. 30 passim) the rule of law must be opened to a hermeneutic of the fundamental constitutional principles supporting the social transformations that may open wider spaces of freedom. These conclusions are not related to the constitutions at the level of the nation state only. They apply in a multilevel and manifold system of substantively and/or formal constitutional rules, and support the idea that an institutional framework is needed, which may consent to the development of a multi-level democracy, allowing the juridical mediation of the constitutional law, both formal and substantive, in a context characterised by strong inequalities, between individual, groups and states.

Summing up, the scientific characteristics of the process of implementation of constitutional law, through which constitutional law deals with irreversible transformations and through which it undergoes the process of democratic legitimisation 'in practice' are strictly related to the fact that it deals with an 'objective sphere' and a 'subjective sphere': the first one includes the rights and the interests guaranteed and protected within the existing relations of power, whilst the second one includes the sphere of social expectations, social preferences and social needs. The above-mentioned characteristics of constitutional law make necessary both descriptive elements and prescriptive elements: descriptive elements are needed in order to make clear what is the particular political, social and economic situation that constitutes the status quo, and that ought to be transformed through the constitution; prescriptive elements are indeed necessary to make sure of the normative strength of the constitution.

The normative strength of the Constitution lies therefore on the relationship between the descriptive and the prescriptive elements that it includes: it is therefore different for each particular constitution or for each particular level of constitution or of constitutional relations. The international courts, especially at the regional level, including the European one, have so far been helping to harmonize, among other things, the different normative strengths of the constitutions involved, but alone, they cannot guarantee the democratic legitimisation of the constitutions in practice. For this purpose, they need an adequate process of implementation of the (different levels of) constitution, and an institutional system to guarantee in practice the democratic rationalisation of the power. The descriptive and the prescriptive elements are both necessary elements for a constitution if constitutional law and constitutional rights are to be considered the expression of power that, in order to exist within the time, needs a democratic legitimisation. And so it must play a role of mediation. It must also confront the need to implement the expectations of the different subjects and the question of whether it leads to implementing economic, political and social transformations, addressed to eliminate discrimination and overcome inequality. The construction of different constitutional levels, or of different legal spheres aiming to regulate a constitutionally relevant situation also needs an adequate expression of descriptive elements, together with the necessary prescriptive elements. Political activity and people's participation and representation to the exercise of power, which involve their adequate interaction with the institutions approving and implementing law, are therefore necessary elements for making and interpreting law also when we deal with distinct levels of a constitution and various constitutionally relevant spheres of legal relations. In the case in which this process may be difficult to achieve, legal doctrines as such, through the reconstruction of the principles concerning the general obligations of the subjects participating to the exercise of power, may play an important role for the democratic rationalisation of power.

* The Catholic University of Lublin; University of Szczecin; University of Salerno.

References

Amirante C. (2001), 'Unione Monetaria e Unione Politica: Contraddizioni e prospettive del processo di integrazione Europea', in C. Amirante, *Unioni sovranazionali e riorganizzazione costituzionale dello stato*, Giappichelli, Torino.

Amirante C. (2003), *Costituzionalismo e costituzione nel nuovo contesto europeo*, Giappichelli, Torino.

Arnold R. (2004), 'The Different Levels of Constitutional Law in Europe and Their Interdependence' in J. Nergelius, P. Policastro and K. Urata (eds.), *Challenges of Multi-Level Constitutionalism*, Proceedings of IVR 21st World Congress, Lund 2003, Polpress Publisher, Ratio Book Series, Kraków.

Bacharach M. (1986), 'The problem of Agents' Belief in Economic Theory', in M. Baranzini and R. Scazzieri (eds.), *Foundations of Economics*, Basil Blackwell, Oxford.

Baranzini M. and Scazzieri R. (eds.) (1986), 'Knowledge in Economics: A Framework', in *Foundations of Economics*, Basil Blackwell, Oxford.

Berman J. (1983), *Law and Revolution. The Formation of the Western Legal Tradition*, Harvard University Press, Cambridge, Ma.; It. ed. (1988), *Diritto e rivoluzione. Le origini della tradizione giuridica occidentale*, Il Mulino, Bologna.

Betti, E. (1990), *Teoria generale dell'interpretazione*, ed. G. Crifó, Giuffré, Milano.

Biernat A. (2001), *Poglądy filozoficzne Leona Perażyckiego i ich interpretacje (The philosophical conceptions of Leon Petrażycki and their interpretation)*, Wydawnictwo Adam marszałek, Toruń.

Bevere A. (ed.) (2004), *La democrazia riformata. Analisi del progetto di revisione costitutionale*, Edizioni Scientifiche Italiane, Napoli; contributors: A. Bevere ('Introduzione'), G.U. Rescigno ('La forma di governo nella legge di revisione costitutionale proposta dal governo Berlusconi'), G. Rizza ('La revisione della forma di governo nella «bozza di Lorenzago»'), S. Stammati, ('A proposito del nuovo dimensionamento del ruolo e dei poteri del Presidente della Repubblica'), C. Amirante ('Per la storia del processo di erosione di un sistema costitutionale democratico'), A. Cerri ('Conclusioni').

Bryk A. (1999), *The Origins of Constitutional Government. Higher Law and the Sources of Judicial Review*, Wydawnictwo Uniwersytetu Jagiellońskiego, Kraków.

Castiglione D. (2002), *From the Charter to the Constitution of Europe? Notes on the Constitutionalisation Process in the EU*, : "Queen's Papers on Europeanisation" No 5, http://ideas.recep.org/s/erp/queens.html: visited, 10/11/2004.

Cerri A. (1987), 'Il principio come fattore di orientamento interpretativo e come valore privilegiato: spunti ed ipotesi per una distinzione', *Giurisprudenza costituzionale*, vol. I, pp. 1806-1830.

Cerri A. (1994), 'Ragionevolezza delle leggi', in *Enciclopedia giuridica*, updates, III vol., Treccani, Roma.

Cervati (1999), 'A proposito dello studio del diritto costitutzionale in una prospettiva storica e della comparazione tra ordinamenti giuridici', *Diritto romano attuale. Storia, metodo, cultura nella scienza giuridica*, vol. 2: Le costituzioni e la storia, pp. 15-48.

Cervati A. (2001), 'Il diritto costituzionale europeo e la crisi della dogmatica statualistica', *Diritto romano attuale. Storia, metodo, cultura nella scienza giuridica*, vol. 6: Il giurista europeo, pp. 21-47.

Craveri P. (1985), *Genesi di una costituzione. Libertà e socialismo nel dibattito costituzionale del 1848 in Francia*, Guida, Napoli.

Cuoco V. (1991 repr.), *La statistica della Repubblica Italiana*, Archivio Izzi, Roma.

Dezalay Y. (1992), *Marchands de droit. La restructuration de l'ordre juridique international par les marchands du droit*, Librairie Arthem Fayard, Paris; It. ed. (1997), *I mercanti del diritto*, M. Raiteri (ed.), Giuffré, Milan.

Forsthoff E. (1953-1954), 'Concetto e natura dello Stato sociale di diritto', in E. Forsthoff (1964), *Rechtstaat im Wandel*, Kohlhammer, Stuttgart; It. ed. (1973), *Stato di diritto in trasformazione*, C. Amirante (ed.), Giuffré, Milano.

Habermas J. (1992), *Faktizität und Geltung*, Suhrkamp, Frankfurt a. M.; It. ed. (1995), *Fatti e norme*, L. Ceppa (ed.), Guerini e associati, Milano.

Habermas J. (1998), *Die postnationale Konstellation*, Suhrkamp, Frankturt a/M; It. ed. (1999) *La costellazione post-nazionale*, L. Ceppa, Feltrinelli. Milano.

Hardt M. and Negri A. (2000), *Empire*, Harvard University Press, Cambridge (Ma).

Hart H.L.A. (1961), *The Concept of Law*, Oxford University Press, Oxford; It. ed. (1965), *Il concetto del diritto*, Einaudi, Torino.

Heller H (1927), *Der Begriff des Gesetzes in der Reichsverfassung*, Berlin-Leipzig; It. ed. 'Il concetto di legge nella Costituzione di Weimar'; in H. Heller (1987), *La sovranità ed altri scritti sulla dottrina del diritto e dello Stato*, ed. P. Pasquino, Giuffré, Milano.

Hobbes T. (1651), *Leviathan*, London, (reprint 1968); It. ed. (1996), *Leviatano o la materia, la forma e il potere di uno stato ecclesiastico o civile*; ed. A. Pacchi in collaboration with A. Luppoli, Laterza, Roma-Bari.

Huemer W. (2002), 'Franz Brentano', *Stanford Encyclopedia of Philosophy*, http://plato.stanford.edu/entries/brentano/.

Kelsen H. (1979), *Allgemeine Theorie de Normen*, Manzsche Verlags- und Universitätsbuchhandlung, Wien; It. ed. (1985) *Teoria generale delle Norme*, M. Losano (ed.), Einaudi, Torino.

Kimijima A. (2004), 'The Peace Vision in Japanese Constitution. How Can Peace Be Achieved in West Asia?' in J. Nergelius, P. Policastro, K. Urata (eds.), *Challenges of Multi-Level Constitutionalism*, Proceedings of IVR 21st World Congress, Lund 2003, Polpress Publisher, Ratio Book Series, Kraków.

La Torre M. (1999), *Norme, istituzioni, valori. Per una teoria istituzionalistica del diritto*, Laterza, Rome-Bari.

Negri A. (1999), 'Tra conflitti e rapporti sociali. La Costituzione e l'immaginazione costituzionale, nel secolo breve', *Diritto romano attuale. Storia, metodo, cultura nella scienza giuridica*, vol. 2: Le costituzioni e la storia, pp. 167-183.

Neumann F. (1957), *The Change in the Function of Law in Modern Society*, in F. Neumann, *The Democratic and the Authoritarian State*, Free Press, New York, It. ed. (1973) *Mutamenti della funzione della legge nella società borghese* in *Lo Stato democratico e stato autoritario*, N. Matteucci (ed.) , Il Mulino, Bologna.

Pasinetti L. L. (1981), *Structural Change and Economic Growth - A Theoretical Essay on the Dynamics of the Wealth of Nations*, Cambridge; It. ed. *Dinamica strutturale e sviluppo economico. Un'indagine teorica sui mutamenti nella ricchezza delle nazioni*, UTET, Torino, 1984.

Peczenik A. (1999), 'The Passion for Reason' in L.J. Wintgens (ed.), *The Law in Phikosophical Perspective. My Philosophy of Law*, Kluwer Academic Publishers, Dordrecht, Boston, London.

Peczenik A. (2002), 'Pluralism, Common Ground in the Law and Legal Doctrine'; It. ed., forthcoming, 'Pluralismo, fondamenti comuni del diritto e dottrina giuridica' in A. Peczenik, *La passione per la ragione*, A. Cerri, P. Policastro (eds.), Il cigno Galileo, Roma.

Pfersmann O. (2003), 'De L'impossibilité du changement de sens de la Constitution', *Mélanges Pierre Pactet*, Dalloz, Paris, 2003.

Picone P. (2003), 'La guerra contro l'Iraq e le degenerazioni dell'unilateralismo', *Rivista di diritto Internazionale*, vol. II, pp. 329-393.

Policastro P. (1999), 'Libertà, diritti fondamentali e doveri costituzionali nella nuova costituzione polacca', in C. Amirante, A. Cerri, Z. Czeszejko-Sochacki, V. Cocozza, L. Garlicki, M. Granat, R. Granata, C. Mirabelli, V. Onida, A. Pace, P. Policastro, F. Rymarz, M. Scudiero, S. Staiano, J. Trzciński, M. Vari, B. Wierzbowski, *Diritti di libertà e diritti sociali tra giudice costituzionale e giudice comune*, Jovene, Napoli.

Policastro P. (2000), *La Costituzione di Weimar e la razionalizzazione democratica del potere politico tra metodo storico, paradigmi evolutivi del costituzionalismo e metodo giuridico*, in E. Amato A. Capo D. Viscido (eds.), *Weimar, le letterature classiche e l'Europa del 2000*, Helios Editrice, Salerno.

Policastro P. (2001), *Political Parties, Participation and Representation Face to Globalisation, European Integration and Democratic Transition* in M. Granat, P. Policastro and J. Sobczak, (eds.), *Partie polityczne we współczesnym konstytucjonalizmie*, Morpol, Lublin.

Policastro P. (2002), *Prawa podstawowe w demokratycznych transformacjach ustrojowych. Polski przykład* (Fundamental Rights and Democratic Transitions. The Polish Example), Wydawnictwo KUL, Lublin.

Policastro P. (2004a), 'On The Reconstruction of the Legal Strength of the Constitution in a World in Transition. Multi-Level Constitutionalism towards Multi-Level Democracy', in J. Nergelius, P. Policastro and K. Urata (eds.), *Challenges of Multi-Level Constitutionalism*, Proceedings of IVR 21st World Congress, Lund 2003, Polpress Publisher, Ratio Book Series, Kraków.

Policastro P. (2004b), 'Constitutionalism, Multi-Level Democracy and Fundamental Values', preface to J. Nergelius, P. Policastro and K. Urata (eds.), *Challenges of Multi-Level Constitutionalism*, Proceedings of IVR 21st World Congress, Lund 2003, Polpress Publisher, Ratio Book Series, Kraków.

Prigogine, I. (1978), *From Being to Becoming. Time and Complexity in the Physical Sciences*, W.H. Freeman & Co., San Francisco, 1980; It. ed. (1986), *Dall'essere al divenire*, Einaudi, Torino.

Rigaux F. (1997), *La loi des juges*, Editions Odile Jacob, Paris; It. ed. *La legge dei giudici*, Naples 2001.

Rosenau J.N. (1992), 'Governance, Order and Change in World Politics', in *Governance Without Government*, Rosenau J.N. and Czempiel E.-O. (eds.), Cambridge University Press, Cambridge.

Rosenau J.N. and Czempiel E.-O. (eds.) (1992), *Governance Without Government*, Cambridge University Press, Cambridge and New York.

Rubino F. (2004), 'Multi-Level Governance as a Process of Development of a Supranational Institutional Framework', in J. Nergelius, P. Policastro, K. Urata (eds.), *Challenges of Multi-Level Constitutionalism*, Proceedings of IVR 21st World Congress, Lund 2003, Polpress Publisher, Ratio Book Series, Kraków.

Sofia, F. (1988), *Una scienza per l'amministrazione. Statistica e pubblici apparati tra età rivoluzionaria e restaurazione*, Carucci, Roma.

Smend R. (1928) *Verfassung und Verfassungsrecht*, Duncker & Humblot, München-Leipzig, It. ed. (1988), *Costituzione e diritto costituzionale*, G. Zagrebelsky (preface), F. Fiore, J. Luther (translation), Giuffré, Milano.

Stammati S. (2004), 'Osservazioni concise sulla nuova forma di governo (maggioritaria e personale)' in A. Bevere (ed.) (2004), *La democrazia riformata. Analisi del progetto di revisione costituzionale*, Edizioni Scientifiche Italiane, Napoli.

Stolleis M. (1990), *Staat und Staatsräson in der frühen Neuzeit: Studien zur Geschichte des öffentliches Rechts*, Suhrkamp, Frankfurt; It. ed. (1998) *Stato e ragion di stato nella prima età moderna*, Il Mulino, Bologna.

Troper M. (1994), *Pour une théorie juridique de l'Etat*, Presses Universitaires de France, Paris; It. ed. *Per una teoria giuridica dello stato*, A. Carrino (ed.), Guida, Napoli.

Troper M. (2004), 'The Influence of Judicial Review of Statutes on Substantive Law', in J. Nergelius, P. Policastro and K. Urata (eds.), *Challenges of Multi-Level Constitutionalism*, Proceedings of IVR 21st World Congress, Lund 2003, Polpress Publisher, Ratio Book Series, Kraków.

Tridimas T. (2000), *The General Principles of EC Law*, Oxford University Press, Oxford.

Trzciński J. (1978), *Funkcja prawna konstytucji socjalistycznej* (The Juridical Function of the Socialist Constitution), Acta Universitatis Wratislaviensis, n. 69 Wrocław.

Tushnet M.V. (1999), *Taking the Constitution Away From the Courts*, Princeton University Press, Princeton N.J.

Urata K. (2004), Reflections on a Global Constitutionalism: In Search for Democracy and Peace, in J. Nergelius, P. Policastro and K. Urata (eds.), *Challenges of Multi-Level Constitutionalism*, Proceedings of IVR 21st World Congress, Lund 2003, Polpress Publisher, Ratio Book Series, Kraków.

Volpe G. (2000), *Il costituzionalismo del Novecento*, Laterza, Roma-Bari.

Chapter 9

The Theory and Practice of Constitutional Review in the Civil Law: The Case of Belgium

Maurice Adams and Dirk Vanheule*

Introduction

On 11 August 1988, the President of the District Court of The Hague (The Netherlands), sitting in summary proceedings, gave a ruling in a case which in The Netherlands has achieved a certain measure of fame. The case related to the so-called Harmonisation Act. This Act retrospectively limited the educational rights of students, and thus constituted an infringement of the principle of legal certainty. Section 20 of the Dutch Constitution of 1983 states that the courts may not review the constitutional validity of statutes and treaties. Constitutional review in The Netherlands is therefore the preserve of the legislature. The President in question did, however, take the view that it was permissible for legislation to be reviewed in the light of the so-called Basic Law ("Statuut") of the Kingdom of The Netherlands, and of general legal principles, which are not referred to in Section 120 of the Dutch Constitution. The Basic Law – which dates from 1954 and stipulates that The Netherlands, the Netherlands Antilles and Aruba are equal partners within the jurisdiction of the Kingdom – constitutes the supreme system of rules governing the state of The Netherlands. As such, it also takes precedence over the Dutch Constitution. This Basic Law did not, according to the President of the District Court of The Hague, exclude the possibility of assessing legislation in the light of the Basic Law. Since Section 43(1) of this Basic Law lists the principle of legal certainty, the judge regarded the Act on Harmonisation as being contrary to the Basic Law, and declared it invalid.

Several months later the *Hoge Raad,* i.e. the Supreme Court of The Netherlands, overruled this decision (Hoge Raad, 14 April 1989). The Supreme Court took the view that the Dutch Constitution excluded any possibility of reviewing legislation in the light of any higher rule whatsoever. The Court also pointed out that, on the occasion of the parliamentary revision of the Dutch Constitution in 1983, the Dutch Parliament had discussed the question whether it was desirable or not to abolish the rule prohibiting constitutional review, and that no fundamental objections had been raised against its undesirable nature. The Court went on to conclude that a generally applicable rule prohibiting such review would be entirely consistent with the "traditional position" occupied by the courts in the institutional structure of the Dutch state. The ultimate judgment on the meaning of the constitution must therefore be entrusted to the democratically-elected legislature.[1]

Constitutional review comes in various forms and degrees (Brewer-Carias, 1989). In the context of this article, it is understood as a special type of judicial review, more particularly the opportunity for the courts to set aside the statutes adopted by the legislature on the basis that they are contrary to the constitution. This "outlawing" process can take place by annulling, either wholly or in part, the legislation under review (as is the case in Belgium following an action for annulment before the Belgian Court of Arbitration) or by declaring the statute in question wholly or partially inapplicable (as is currently the case in the US).

From a democratic point of view, however, this type of judicial review remains controversial. The well-known American judge Learned Hand was of the opinion that such review should only be allowed in a very limited form:

> For myself it would be most irksome to be ruled by a bevy of Platonic Guardians, even if I knew how to choose them, which I assuredly do not. If they were in charge, I would miss the stimulus of living in a society where I have, at least theoretically, some part in the direction of public affairs. Of course I know how illusory would be the belief that my vote determined anything; but nevertheless when I go to the polls I have the satisfaction in the sense that we are all engaged in a common venture. (Learned Hand, 1958, pp. 73-74; Dworkin, 1996, p. 322)

Although this somewhat vague statement on the part of Learned Hand, who actually describes little more than a feeling, is open to a multitude of interpretations, the crux of his argument appears to be twofold. On the one hand he seems to believe that, as the influence exercised by the electorate on court decisions in constitutional matters will always be minimal, there should likewise be little scope for such decisions. Thus he writes that "if they were in charge, I would miss the stimulus of living in a society where I have, at least theoretically, some part in the direction of public affairs". He therefore takes the view that constitutional review at least lacks *substantive* democratic legitimacy. On the other hand, Learned Hand also appears to be claiming that it is unacceptable for the people to be governed by an organ which has not been elected by them. As a consequence, the *personal* democratic legitimacy of judges is much less direct than that of the parliamentary delegates: "For myself, it would be most irksome to be ruled by a bevy of Platonic Guardians, even if I knew how to choose them, which I assuredly do not". In Learned Hand's comment, two sides of the democratic coin, namely election and accountability, come together. According to this view, the most essential aspect of a democracy consists in respecting the will of the people.

It is definitely a fact that these two aspects, election and accountability (which cannot be neatly separated from each other) are infringed in the most spectacular fashion when legislation is subjected to constitutional review. However, the question arises as to whether this practice is therefore necessarily undemocratic.

Can democracy be exclusively associated with election and accountability? Is that all there is to say?

In this article, we will examine what role constitutional review may have in a democracy. First of all, we ask whether there are practical reasons *today* which can justify an additional check on the constitutional compliance of legislation. We will next examine which method of constitutional review is best suited to guaranteeing democratic values, following which the question of whether constitutional review can be reconciled with democracy will be answered. Finally, we will consider the manner in which the Belgian constitutional court, i.e. the Court of Arbitration ("Arbitragehof"*)*, acquits itself of its task.

The Role of Constitutional Review in the Welfare State: A Relational Approach

In effect, the view expressed by Learned Hand fits in perfectly with a traditional conception of the *trias politica*, namely the *trias politica* conceived on the basis of the *separation of powers* as supposed to be expressed by Montesquieu (Montesquieu, 1748, especially Section 6 of Book 11. Critically on the idea of *trias politica* as *separation of powers*, Stewart, 2000). It is supposed that with this doctrine Montesquieu advocated that state power be divided into a legislative, an executive and a judicial power and that these three should be kept separate. As a result, each power will be vigilant that the other two powers will remain within the bounds of their constitutional authority.

Behind this allocation of responsibilities lies a certain assumption on the distinction between law and politics, between applying law and creating law as constituting two separate spheres. As a result, judicial adjudication is an independent and emphatically non-political activity. Courts and judges are expected to apply the existing law objectively and impartially, as if they were some kind of robot. The enactment of legislation, on the other hand, is in its essence definitely a political activity, since the legislature is not bound to seek the same degree of impartiality or neutrality as is incumbent on the courts.

However, this conception is not a very convincing one. In the first place, it is remote from reality: a clear dividing line between the application and the creation of law cannot be drawn. Secondly, it does not provide a satisfactory present-day picture of what the father of the *trias politica,* i.e. Montesquieu, sought to achieve.

As to the first point, one of the basic assumptions behind the notion that the courts have no creative role to play seems to be that the courts actually have a choice whether to be creative or not, and whether or not to use their potential discretionary powers. Any such claim is untenable in principle because, contrary to the prevailing theories, the courts *necessarily* create law. Interpreting the law also inevitably entails creating it, for the reason that the law is to a certain extent indeterminate in both semantic and normative terms. This does not mean that the creative role of the courts is identical to that of the legislator. Nevertheless, the courts do engage in law creation. This means that courts will also make "political" decisions, since by creating law they direct society and impose rules on it. This is a political act. Those who deny this seem to confuse an institution's *supremacy* in law creation with its *monopoly* in this area.

As to the second issue, what Montesquieu desired was not so much the separation of powers. More than anything else, he focused on the principle of "moderate governance" (*gouvernement modéré*), whereby the exercise of power proceeds along levels that keep each other's power sufficiently in balance to avoid arbitrariness and the excessive exercise of state power. Ultimately, what is at stake here is the question of whether adequate guarantees exist for the citizen against excessive exercise of state power. What counts is not so much separation of powers, but balance of powers. Hence, arguments that are based on the separation of powers are not very useful against constitutional review.

Nevertheless, this does not paint the full picture. Significantly, these arguments run parallel to those which are used against the courts playing a creative role in the law-making process. However, constitutional review involves special considerations, since, as has been mentioned earlier, it enables the enactments of an elected parliament to be set aside. Constitutional review thus allows the popular will not just be circumvented, as is the case where the ordinary courts engage in law creation, but also to *expressly* set it aside. Therefore, constitutional review by the courts comes close to involving itself in parliamentary politics. This could prompt the view that, in exercising constitutional review, the courts risk venturing too far into the political arena. In any case, the ability to assess legislation in the light of, for example, the equality principle, as well as other rights and freedoms, constitutes an *express* invitation to assess the relevance and proportionality of the distinctions made by the legislator.

This is an argument that has some mileage in it. The question that must therefore be answered is not whether or not courts should be allowed to create law, but whether constitutional review involves the courts too much in politics. The answer to this question cannot be given in abstract terms, because in our opinion it will depend on the societal context in which constitutional review takes place. This observation goes some way towards invalidating the view of the Dutch Supreme Court, which, as was mentioned in the Introduction, found that a generally applicable prohibition on constitutional review was perfectly consistent with the traditional position occupied by the courts in the institutional system of The Netherlands. This type of abstract approach does not indicate an awareness that the arguments for and against constitutional review are to a large extent relational. In other words, the question of whether constitutional review is necessary or not depends at least to some extent on the manner in which the legislature goes about its business.

It is precisely with this perspective in mind that there appear to be reasons for accepting that at least today's European welfare states provide sufficient scope for constitutional review. This can be illustrated by the circumstance that the present-day courts are, almost involuntarily, having an increasingly important role assigned to them. To put it differently: it has become increasingly necessary for the courts to act as a counterweight to an increasingly overbearing bureaucratic machinery. This proposition is clarified below.

In this context, it is first of all necessary to mention the increasingly intensive legislative and regulatory action on the part of the public authorities. Legislation is viewed today mainly as an instrument of direction and policy, and as a way of achieving change at the social, economic and cultural levels. The rise of the welfare state, as well as various developments in the realms of science and technology, have even compelled the authorities to intervene. The latter have come to take on a more active role not only out of choice, but also out of dire necessity. The growth of legislation governing the environment, casual work, the multicultural society, new social risks or biotechnical developments are all examples of this trend. It has given rise to new and functionally defined legal disciplines such as consumer protection law, welfare law, educational law, media law, public health law, IT law, insurance law and the law relating to refugees. This growing legal dimension of society is, moreover, an inevitable consequence of a more active and directive approach by the authorities towards their responsibilities. More particularly the principle of legality produces a negative and restricting effect on the activities of the authorities, because the latter should, in order to be consistent with this principle, ideally refrain from any intervention affecting the citizen which is not guaranteed by legislation. Therefore, if the authorities, under the pressure of events, increasingly experience the need to intervene in society, this will in the majority of cases be done by means of legislation. In relation to the subject under review it is important to note that this trend also has implications – as is the case virtually everywhere in the Western world – for the quality of the rule-making process. Social justice and technological developments, as well as the large number of detailed rules aimed at specific groups and situations which this entails, give rise to legislative complications. The need for policy-oriented legislation leads to complex chains of rules which usually come at the expense of quality, sound legislative technique and a systematic or coherent approach towards law-making. Instead, nowadays welfare states have legislation that is constantly evolving and has lost its stability, with all the dangers that this entails in terms of lack of coherence, uncertainties and contradictions, which could threaten the general applicability of legal rules and the equality principle. It is precisely this type of problem that the courts will often be called upon to resolve.

As regards the role of Parliament in this context, it is perhaps a truism to state that the latter also no longer corresponds to the ideal picture of representing or controlling the will of the people. It is increasingly the executive which lays down the rules, and the influence exerted by the elected delegates on the rule-making process diminishes accordingly. In other words, the parliamentary legislature has also come to suffer a legitimacy problem. People's sovereignty is less and less represented exclusively in parliament. This trend demands, in our view, that the role of the courts be reinforced. It is the latter, rather than parliament, which is increasingly being called upon to assess the legality of state intervention, including various forms of substantive rule-making.

Moreover, these trends take place in interaction with the courts themselves. Influenced by the increasingly intensive intervention by the authorities in society, the courts are experiencing the need to develop a number of overarching quality standards which need to be met, such as the general principles of law, principles of good administration, rules of reason and fairness, social justice requirements, etc. It is, *inter alia*, this development which serves to explain the rise of a relatively young legal discipline such as administrative law. The opportunities given to citizens of entering in discussion with the authorities and with each other are constantly growing. This gives rise to what could be described as a self-fulfilling prophesy. The courts have increasingly a role to play as troubleshooters. In addition, however, as Hirsch-Ballin correctly and aptly observes, the law itself is increasingly linking complex sets of interests. The courts can no longer confine themselves to applying the legal rule which gives expression to the weighing up of interests which is sought by the legislator, but are themselves increasingly expected to weigh up the interests in question (Hirsch Ballin, 1991, pp. 296-302). Increasingly, the courts can merely derive from the available rules the standards such as legal principles, principles of good administration, demarcations of responsibilities, discretionary powers, vague rules, rules of reason and fairness, social justice requirements on the basis of which they are able to assess the extent to which the interests shaped in other relationships are being protected. One needs only to consider the court decisions relating to strikes, closures of businesses, or disputes concerning environmental and consumer protection. The standards referred to above can serve to guarantee the supremacy of the law. The resulting lawmaking by the courts is an essential element in enabling the legal system to operate satisfactorily as a forum for organising social trends and relationships and as a mechanism for the resolution of the conflicts to which these can give rise.

Naturally the increasing demands being made on the courts have given rise to new problems – including those of an organisational nature. One needs only to consider the way in which the courts are, at least in Belgium, being overloaded. This is at the same time an expression of the fact that citizens and organisations do not appear to see other ways of channelling conflict than by calling upon the courts to act as referees. However, it is important to stress that this trend is almost inevitable because of the increasingly prominent dimension assumed by the "bureaucratic machinery" in our society. In these circumstances, it is essential to be able to turn to an independent judiciary. In essence, what has happened here is that this machinery has evolved from an institution guaranteeing that the law is upheld towards what is potentially one of the greatest threats to exercising one's rights. This explains the increasing importance of judicial protection not only against the actions of the executive, but also against those of the legislator. To a considerable extent, the task of a constitutional court fits in with this perception. Constitutional courts can act as referees in clashes of interests. They attempt to control or restrict the negative implications of the increasingly active role of the legislator for the citizen.

Let us conclude this section with the following observations. The Dutch constitutional scholar Kortmann has pointed out that it cannot be maintained *on logical grounds* that the courts should have the last word in assessing the constitutionality of legislation – for who in turn shall supervise the judiciary? (Kortmann, 2001, p. 357). Why should courts be in a better position to assess the constitutional validity of legislation than the legislature? More particularly, who will protect us against unconstitutional decisions by the courts? Once again, it is impossible to reply to this question in abstract terms. Courts are not necessarily in a better position to review constitutional compliance, because that in turn depends on the manner in which they actually make such assessments. At the same time, however, it cannot, for the same logical reasons, be maintained either that it is the legislature which is in the best position to engage in constitutional review. Other arguments will therefore have to be found to entrust this task to the courts or the legislature. It is at this point that it becomes possible to maintain that the courts can as such act as a counterweight against an overbearing legislature. This approach sits well with the perception of the *trias politica* which was set out at the beginning of this section. Thus constitutional review becomes a compensating strategy, which can make good an imbalance that has arisen in the relationship between the citizen and the state. In this context, however, the constitutional court remains nevertheless bound by a certain degree of reticence, because it may only act in the wake of the legislature. Therein also resides an essential and permanent difference between these two bodies – the legislature takes the initiative, and the courts follow. Whatever the case may be, the question whether the courts should be allowed to engage in constitutional review is posed in the wrong way by the logic referred to above. The advantage that constitutional review entails resides not only in the fact that the courts will possibly be better at performing such a review – even though this may or may not be the case – but especially in the fact that this review assumes a different or in any case an extra dimension. An attractive conception of the *trias politica* is for power to be exercised over several levels and for power to become visible in this manner. This gives rise to a system of weight and counterweight, checks and balances. It is this aspect that it is all about. As has already been pointed out, additional checks are not a superfluous luxury in our present time. Constitutional review as such can also be regarded as a dialogue, in that a ruling which declares a statute to be unconstitutional invites the legislature to re-examine the legislation in question as well as the underlying policies it was intended to achieve by means of this legislation, and can thus be a stimulus for democratic debate. This is also related to the fact that, unlike the courts, the legislator wears two hats, being both a threat to fundamental rights and their guarantor. In many cases, fundamental rights may only be restricted on the basis of formal legislation (i.e. by the parliament); on the other hand, it is precisely this parliament which has the duty to guarantee the citizen's fundamental rights by means of legislation. This dual capacity can cause tensions and requires an additional check. Accordingly, the courts can also have a certain advantage over the legislature.

The foregoing also serves to a certain extent to reject the Aristotelian argument that the "many" know more than the "few". In the *Politica*, Aristotle states that

> the principle that the multitude ought to be supreme rather than the few is one that is maintained, and, though not free from difficulty, yet seems to contain an element of truth. For the many, of whom each individual is but an ordinary person, when they meet together may very likely be better than the few good, if regarded not individually but collectively (….). (Aristotle, 1973, Book III, Chapter 11, 1281b. See on this also: Waldron, 1999, pp. 136-138)

Aristotle's conception was that the diversity of the perspectives afforded by the multitude (in our case the members of parliament) gives rise to a kind of cumulative wisdom, the whole being greater than the sum of its parts. However, it must be pointed out that constitutional review is not intended to reduce the cumulative wisdom of the parliament, since the latter is not being sidelined from the outset, and retains the ability to gather together and to externalise this collective wisdom. All that is involved is that an *additional check* can be placed on this collective wisdom through the medium of constitutional review.

Models of Constitutional Review

Having examined the reasons why there could be a place for constitutional review in the welfare state based on the rule of law, we must now consider the question of how this review can take place in the best possible conditions, namely in the most democratic manner possible. In other words, we must examine the following issues: how can constitutional review best be reconciled with an attractive perception of democracy, and what is the best way to guarantee democratic values through constitutional review? The answers to these questions will obviously depend on the view one takes of democracy. This then expresses itself in theories on the scope for interpretation and intensity of assessment involved in constitutional review. In fact we have already lifted the veil on this issue slightly in the previous section. When stating our opinion that there is some room for constitutional review because in today's welfare state there are reasons to fear infringements of fundamental rights, we have already pointed in the direction of a conception of democracy in which the protection of rights and freedoms is one of the central tenets. Seen in this light, democracy is about more than just elections, accountability and majority decisions; it is also about the protection of fundamental rights and freedoms, and therefore about going against majority opinion on certain types of issues. In the remainder of this article, we will subject this conception, as well as the questions raised above, to closer scrutiny. For this purpose we will use arguments taken from the extensive literature on this subject in the United States (US), because they illustrate very well the various conceptions of democracy and the position which the legislature and the courts occupy in it.

Three models of constitutional review used in US constitutional theory are helpful to illustrate the points we want to make: *originalism*, *democratic proceduralism* and the *fundamental rights model*.

According to the doctrine of originalism, the courts are strictly bound by the text of the constitution or by the intentions of the authors of this constitution. Only where the original meaning of the constitution and/or the intentions of the constitution's authors are clear will the courts be allowed to correct the legislator and leave aside legislation because it is unconstitutional. The courts themselves are not allowed to make choices between conflicting values when interpreting and applying the constitution. If they were, there would be a risk that the judges would allow their personal value judgments to be relied upon in their decision-making. This would be in fundamental contradiction of democracy conceived as embodying people's sovereignty, since the people have expressed their sovereign will, as represented in the parliament, in the statute law. And it is this will that must take precedence. Where it proves to be impossible to gauge the intentions of (the authors of) the constitution, this sovereignty principle assumes that the court will give precedence to (the text of) the constitution as such. According to Bork, a prominent originalist, the implication of this conception is that, for the courts, an unclear constitutional rule is equal to a non-existent constitutional rule. He explains:

> The judge who cannot make out the meaning of a provision is in exactly the same circumstance as a judge who has no Constitution to work with. There being nothing to work with, the judge should refrain from working. A provision whose meaning cannot be ascertained is precisely like a provision that (...) is obliterated past deciphering by an ink blot. No judge is entitled to interpret an ink blot on the ground that there must be something under it. (Bork, 1990, p. 166)

The possible confusion between law and politics, between applying law and creating law, also appears to be a major argument against constitutional review for the originalist. Although, institutionally speaking, the courts are superior to the legislature and the government, because they may refuse to carry out decisions of the latter two on the grounds that they infringe the constitution, they do not have the same freedom of discretion and powers as the two other state authorities. Courts may only assess the constitutional compliance of a statute, and not its political, social or ethical desirability. The latter are questions that must be entrusted to the judgment of the people and their elected representatives.

We will not concern ourselves any further with the originalist doctrine. Quite apart from its methodological and heuristic problems – for example: how is it possible to gauge the intentions of the constitution's authors – this doctrine is based on a number of dubious propositions. It is based on the outdated notion that a clear dividing line can be traced between the spheres of politics and law, as well as on a strict interpretation of the separation of powers. We have already pointed out above that these assumptions are neither desirable nor tenable. Applying the law cannot be separated from creating it. Doctrines such as originalism confuse the *supremacy* of law creation with the *monopoly* of law creation, and are based on the notion that the parliament is the sole and ideal forum for exercising power in a state. To this must be added that the outcome of the originalist approach at its most extreme can no longer fit in with the established constitutional case law of the US. To depend on the outdated vision of the framers of the constitution would merely amount to turning back the clock.

In the two other models, namely democratic proceduralism and the rights model, it is possible to discern two conceptions of democracy. Advocates of these models accept that the courts have a role to play in guaranteeing the proper functioning of a democratic society. The anti-majoritarian nature of judicial action against the legislature is not necessarily inconsistent with a democratic form of governance. More particularly where the actions of the majority are themselves no longer reconcilable with the essence of democracy, they will lose the legitimacy which they derived from majority rule, and will be open to corrective action by the courts. This raises the question as to what is the essence of democracy according to these doctrines. In the approaches adopted by John Hart Ely and Ronald Dworkin, which are briefly discussed below, we can find two different conceptions of the essence of democracy.

J.H. Ely's Proceduralism

Democracy can be perceived in purely procedural terms. Here, a central position will be assumed by the people, whose will is expressed through the majority in the legislative assembly. Present-day political reality, however, shows that the citizen's will being expressed through representative delegation cannot invariably be guaranteed in practice. Nevertheless, distortions in the process of parliamentary law-making have to be avoided as much as possible, since its proper functioning is an essential democratic value. Only where this is the case may the legislature itself, taking account of the interests of all those who are represented in the legislative assembly, engage in democratic decision-making. Constitutional review has a role to play to the extent that it can serve to guarantee the proper operation of the procedures required under democratic rule.

This approach differs from the originalist perception of constitutional review, in the sense that the democratic proceduralist seeks recognition that the parliament is not necessarily the ideal legislature. Accordingly, the American constitutionalist J.H. Ely also accepts the principle of constitutional review, and sees in judicial supervision over the legislature a mechanism for improving the functioning of the democratic procedure. However, he shares the originalists' concern that the judge should not make any value judgments that are based on his own moral perceptions. This does not, however, detract from the active role which should be conferred on the courts in a democratic society. In the author's view, an essential characteristic of a democracy is the participation by the citizen in the legislative process through representation, and the principle of equality. Where either of these principles is under attack, it becomes legitimate for the courts, in the interests of democracy, to intervene. In this context, Ely puts forward the view that the most controversial period in constitutional review in the US, which consisted of the active interventions by the US Supreme Court under Chief Justice Warren, could be described as legitimate. The Court advanced not only values such as constitutional priorities, but was motivated by two concerns. In the first place, there was the desire to keep the political decision-making process – which is the forum where the ultimate decisions need to be made on which values to adopt – accessible to all on an equal basis (what he describes as "clearing the channels of political change") (Ely, 1980, p. 74). Secondly, constitutional review was a method of enabling the traditional minorities in the US (ethnic groups, foreigners, the poor) to enjoy equal treatment without requiring the courts to decide whether a certain asset or value is so fundamental that its award is deserving of protection ("correcting certain kinds of discrimination against minorities") (Ely, 1980, p. 74).

Ely regards a constitution less as a document that determines the fundamental values and their substance than as a set of rules regulating the decision-making process. Since the majority does not normally go against its own interests, the framers of the US Constitution attempted to prevent that majority from systematically subjecting others to less favourable treatment. In order to achieve this, the interests of all citizens must be represented, actually or virtually, when substantive decisions are being taken. When these are being applied to individual cases, the system may not be manipulated to the extent that there arises a kind of discrimination which is not reconcilable with these fundamental notions (Ely, 1980, pp. 100-101).

It is this element that brings the courts into play. In a representative democracy, it is inconceivable that the courts should be able to make substantive value choices. This is, according to Ely, part of the essential task entrusted to the elected people's representatives who may only be judged on these choices at election time. The courts are well placed to invigilate the equal representation of all citizens in the decision-making process. Just as a referee in a sporting contest merely intervenes where one of the teams has unjustly acquired an advantage, regardless of the team's ranking order, the courts will similarly only intervene where the political "game" functions defectively (Ely, 1980, pp. 102-103).

This is more particularly the case where a majority that has acquired power, closes off the channels of political change with the intention of retaining power and preventing others from obtaining a majority. For this reason, the courts will exercise strict supervision over any restrictions of, or impediments to, the freedom of expression, press freedom, rights of political association and electoral rights, since these are essential for the functioning of an open and truly democratic decision-making process. However, the manner in which the legislative authority is exercised must also be correct. According to Ely, democratic decision-making also involves disclosure of the true reasons on which a legislative enactment is based, so that the citizen may judge legislative policy at election time with full knowledge of the facts. The object of the exercise is to improve the voters' ability to react. Participation through representation is, moreover, only possible where the elected representatives themselves exercise their legislative powers. Legislation which allows its essential substance to be determined by the executive cannot be reconciled with this principle. This is why the courts have a duty to ensure not only that the executive follows the directions issued by the legislature, but also that the legislature itself imposes criteria for this purpose that are sufficiently clear.

The other major distortion in the legislative process occurs when the representatives who find themselves in the majority systematically victimise a minority, whether merely out of enmity or out of a refusal, born out of prejudice, to acknowledge their interests. Free and equal access to the decision-making process does not in itself contain a guarantee that the interests of all will actually be taken into account. However pluralist the democratic system may be in its conception and execution, in practice there can be no escape from concentrations of power and from the inequalities that arise between various groups. Ely sees an illustration of this in the treatment of the black population of the US, even after the latter were given access to the decision-making process (Ely, 1980, p. 135).

The equality principle has a major role to play in this regard. An unequal allocation of rights can be regarded as unconstitutional by the courts where it appears that the process by which this allocation was arrived at was defective. In other words, such constitutional review will be based on an assessment of the decision-making process and its history, and not on an assessment of the final result (Ely, 1980, pp. 135-136). Accordingly, the courts will examine the legislative process on the basis of the reasons that motivated the legislature on the one hand, and the classification used on the other hand. Thus the courts will also need to consider the grounds on which a distinction was introduced. Choices which are based on ethnic origin, religion, political proclivities or personal preference indicate that the decision-making process was defective and that due process was not observed in the legislative procedure. Even where the reasons behind legislation appear to be neutral, a more intensive degree of judicial supervision will remain acceptable in the event of "suspicious classifications" of groups which occupy a minority position in society. In historical terms, these concern classifications based on ethnic and national origin, but they can be extended to "discrete and isolated minorities", minorities that are incapable of having their interests safeguarded by means of existing interaction processes, such as the building of coalitions and mutual respect for each others' interests, and that are feeling increasingly isolated. The legislation in question will therefore be more strictly reviewed in the light of the equality principle. The legislature will not only need to demonstrate a substantial objective that may justify the difference in treatment – this difference will also need to be perfectly consistent with the achievement of this objective if its review is to stand the test of the equality principle.

Through his democratic proceduralism, Ely seeks to present an approach towards constitutional review which advocates value-free intervention on the part of the courts but which, contrary to originalist theory, remains consistent with the major constitutional decisions of the Supreme Court since the 1950s. The question, however, remains whether he has succeeded in this endeavour. For how can the courts distinguish "discrete and insular minorities" from ordinary minorities that simply failed to obtain a majority at election time? Society does not consist of social groups that can be separated on objectively perceptible lines. Tribe points out that these lines have precisely been drawn by humans themselves:

> people *draw* lines, attribute differences, attribute differences, as a way of ordering social existence – of deciding who may occupy what place, play what role, engage in what activity. (Tribe, 1980, p. 1074)

The recognition of a group as such, whether it be "discrete and insular minorities" or ordinary minorities, is the outcome of an assessment made of a group by outsiders, but results also from the actions of the group members, in the sense of them consciously acceding to, or separating themselves from, the group. With his choices between various minorities, the democratic proceduralist becomes guilty of that of which he accuses activist judges. He too makes value-laden choices, since any prejudice that may exist in relation to a group will be based on *a value assessment* of that group's behaviour.

Dworkin's Rights Model

A major current in the American debate on constitutional review adopts, in the wake of the criticisms made of the Ely model referred to above, a more substantive approach towards the manner in which the principle of democracy should be carried out by constitutional courts. The idea on which this current is based thus transcends the merely procedural. Neither equal political participation by the citizens nor the power wielded by the majority within the legislative assembly are by themselves capable of guaranteeing that the values that are regarded as fundamental in western democratic society, and that are translated into individual rights and freedoms in the constitution, remain intact. True democracy must also offer certain substantive guarantees. This follows from the intention behind opting for democracy as a way of constituting the state, namely the safeguarding of the citizen's fundamental rights and freedoms. Certain rights and freedoms are essential in order to maintain the autonomy and independence of each individual, as expressed in freedom of conscience and thought, freedom of association and of profession, and freedom as to one's person. These are all rights and freedoms implicit in the notion of the rule of law. Once these have been abandoned, the citizen in question loses his moral independence and equal status. From this perspective, democracy definitely has a substantive function. Freeman formulates this as follows:

> [W]hat makes a constitution democratic is not equal consideration in majority procedures, but that it specifies rights and procedures devised to promote the good of each citizen and maintain the equal rights that constitute their democratic sovereignty. (Freeman, 1990-91, p. 350)

Under this model it would appear that the role of the courts when engaging in constitutional review amounts to more than merely acting as a watchdog over the respect of the original *contrat social* or of the democratic decision-making procedures. The courts have to ensure that the legislature, and the majority represented in it, respect democratic *values* in a constitution that evolve in step with social developments.

This kind of model naturally gives rise to potential problems, since the practical expression given to the values referred to above could depend on the personal political, ideological and philosophical proclivities of the judge. Therefore, in order to prevent judicial arbitrariness it is necessary to objectivate these values. The work of R. Dworkin contains a model to that effect.

Dworkin seems to admit that there are good arguments for and against constitutional review (Dworkin, 1996, p. 34). However, where the legislature is subject to judicial review, the question must be answered as to how the courts can best apply such review. In an attempt to find such an answer, Dworkin bases himself on his general approach to law, which he regards as a set of legal rules and principles. The difference between rules and principles cannot always be derived directly from their form. The decisive question for distinguishing between both legal standards, is whether or not the standard gives rise to a concrete result. Where this is indeed the case, we are dealing with a rule (since rules apply in an "all-or-nothing"-fashion). Principles, on the other hand, tend to be couched in relative terms; they point in a certain direction and constitute a kind of context for interpretation, but do not point directly to a specific result. Instead, they impose a standard that needs to be observed in law, as a condition for justice, fairness or some other moral dimension. Dworkin understands the notion of principles thus as propositions of political morality which confirm, and even support, the existence of individual rights and freedoms (Dworkin, 1977, p. 22).

This approach by Dworkin also has a more general political significance. Dworkin enshrines individual rights – rights which are based on principles – as trump cards, in such a way that the citizen may, in principle, always be able to play them against the authorities or against others, where they are breached, or threaten to be breached. The message is clear: neither the authorities nor one's fellow-citizens may restrict individual rights for the sake of what the majority would regard as a "common good". This kind of considerations, which Dworkin calls policy considerations, may not be allowed to restrict the rights and freedoms enjoyed by individuals. Therefore, the courts may not in principle base their decisions on policy considerations, but just on individual rights and freedoms, as well as on the principles which support these rights. Formulating or using policy considerations by courts invariably involves considerations of political expediency, which is something which must be left to the democratically elected legislature.

In so doing, Dworkin makes a plea for the courts to engage in a moral interpretation of the constitution. More particularly he maintains that the morality which is relevant for the courts is not a purely personal or subjective morality, but more particularly the "institutional" morality of the law. The courts need to apply the "institutionalised morality", i.e. morality that can be found in the law (the constitution, case law) and constitutes the background to it. This is the morality that expresses itself in the principles that support the law, the "propositions that describe rights".

At this point, it is legitimate to ask as to why these individual rights seem for the courts to be of much more importance than policy considerations. Would it not be better for the courts simply to follow the policy consideration that the legislature sought to introduce, even where it came into conflict with certain notions of individual rights and freedoms, as well as their scope? Surely this would be to give expression to the legislator's will? However, Dworkin considers that those who suggest so have no understanding of the essence of a constitutional state based on the rule of law, since there is something special about individual rights and their protection. Such protection complies with the self-image of society as this has developed in the course of time. It is the self-image in which present-day Western law, as well as the American Constitution, is located. It represents the most essential political theory (i.e. political morality), which supports and characterises the law as a whole. This political theory is based on the assumption that there are a number of fundamental and intuitively shared notions or principles which either implicitly or expressly are present in society's political culture and legal system. They are notions that have been derived from, or developed on the basis of, major historical events, certain documents (for Dworkin as an American this will be documents such as the American Declaration of Independence and for us the Declaration of the Rights of Man and of the Citizen of 1789), court decisions, but also notions about society as a "fair system of co-operation" (to use Rawls's terminology). This self-image is therefore the outcome of many centuries of democratic thinking and the development of a body of legal and constitutional practice which conforms to this thinking. This gave rise not only to a public perception of such democratic practice and values, but also to a certain sense of loyalty to them.

The question then arises as to how the courts must involve this self-image when reviewing legislation and interpreting the law. According to Dworkin, the courts, should at all times refer to the said principles, which form part of the "*network* of political structures and decisions of [its] community" (Dworkin, 1986, 245). The courts must at all times ask themselves the question of whether their interpretation of this network

> could form part of *a coherent theory justifying the network as a whole.* No actual judge could compose of anything approaching a full interpretation of all of his community's law at once. (…) But an actual judge can (…) allow the scope of his interpretation to fan out from the cases immediately in point to cases in the same general area or department of law, and then still farther, so far as this seems promising. (Dworkin, 1986, p. 245, emphasis added)

What is at stake here is that the principles justify the law as a whole. According to Dworkin, principles are themselves an integral part of the law and therefore need to be applied when engaging in adjudication. In other words, the law, is sensitive to the value we attribute to it, and this is precisely why we wish, or even must, attempt to achieve these values as best we can. Those who take part in adjudication do therefore much more than merely refer to positivistic conventions as expressed in positive rules. They attempt not only to link the facts of a particular case to the language – whether clear or not – of the positive law, but also to interpret the law in the light of a certain intention, i.e. a general normative justification or moral aspect, which they ascribe to it and which finds expression in the said legal principles. As Dworkin puts it:

> A participant interpreting a social practice, according to that view, proposes value for the practice by describing some scheme of interest or goals or principles the practice can be taken to serve or express or exemplify (Dworkin, 1996, p. 52).

Dworkin is able to argue all this because he assumes that every stable Western legal system is an expression of the political philosophy described above, in the shape of principles, individual rights and freedoms, and that this philosophy brings unity and coherence to the legal system. In this conception, the legal system is regarded as being not only logically consistent, but also coherent. The requirement of coherence goes a good deal further than that of logical consistency. Because from the point of view of coherence, legal standards (rules and principles) are understood not only to contain no mutual contradictions, but also to be mutually supportive. Viewed in relation to each other, they provide a more solid and reliable entity than if they are considered separately. Applying the institutionalised moral dimension of the law gives thus direction to the best interpretation of it. It is precisely for this reason that those who interpret a legal text in the light of these notions put forward by Dworkin will not make decisions on the meaning of the law in all freedom. A Dworkinian interpretation of the law merely makes explicit that which was actually already present in the law. Judicial decision-making

> will depend, that is, not only on [the judges'] belief about which of these principles is superior as a matter of abstract justice but also about which should be followed, as a matter of political fairness, in a community whose members have the moral convictions his fellow citizens have. (Dworkin, 1986, p. 249)

What an individual is legally entitled to therefore depends to a large extent on the manner in which the political institutions have included political morality in the law. And in Western liberal law, this means that

> [l]aw insists that force not be used or withheld, no matter how useful that would be to ends in view, no matter how beneficial or noble these ends, *except as licensed or required by individual rights and responsibilities flowing from past political decisions about when political force is justified.* (Dworkin, 1986, p. 249, emphasis added)

Phrased in constitutional terminology:

> Judges may not read their own moral convictions into the Constitution. They may not read the abstract moral clauses as as expressing any particular moral judgment, no matter how much that judgment appeals to them, unless they find it consistent in principle with the structural design of the Constitution as a whole, and also with the dominant lines of past constitutional interpretation by other judges. They must regard themselves as partners with other officials, past and future, who together elaborate a coherent constitutional morality, and they must take care to see what they contribute fits with the rest. (Dworkin, 1996, p. 10)

In this sense, legal claims are interpretative judgments that look to the past as well as to the future. Dworkin's legal philosophy therefore has a retrospective ("fit") and an anticipatory ("justification") aspect. When making their decisions, the courts need to locate moral principles in the tradition that covers the law, and subsequently have to improve the law with a view to the future. Thus, a constitution represents a guideline for opinions about the best way in which to continue the law in the shape of new court decisions. The law thus becomes an unfolding narrative, and develops, as does a chain novel, not arbitrarily, but as an expression of an underlying aspiration towards making explicit the coherent legal consciousness of society. The quest for this moral dimension which characterises the law, gives a sense of direction to the interpretation of the legal narrative. Thus, the principles not only buttress the law by implicitly forming part of it and constituting the background to its interpretation. They also rise above that law and at the same time constitute a critical standard for assessing the law.

From the foregoing it is possible to discern, more or less expressly, the conception of democracy advocated by Dworkin. According to Dworkin, democracy is all about self-government, in the sense of government by and for the people. Nevertheless collective decisions are, in a democracy, binding not so much because the majority of citizens as represented in parliament advocate them, but because

> collective decisions be made by political institutions whose structure, composition, and practices treat all members of the community, as individuals, with *equal concern and respect.* (Dworkin, 1996, p. 17, emphasis added)

And:

> Democracy means government subject to conditions – we might call these the "democratic" conditions - of equal status for all citizens. When majoritarian institutions provide and respect the democratic conditions, then the verdicts of these institutions should be accepted by everyone for that reason. But when they do not, or when their provision or respect is defective, there can be no objection, in the name of democracy, to other procedures that protect and respect them better. (Dworkin, 1996, p. 17)

"Equal concern and respect" is the general phrase Dworkin has chosen in order to define his views on the importance of the principles that describe individual rights and freedoms. Where this equal respect, and the enjoyment of individual rights and freedoms that comes with it, is not guaranteed, the majority imposes comprehensive ethical notions on a minority which does not subscribe to these notions and which infringes on the self-image of Western society. In Dworkin's conception, therefore, what characterises democracy is the manner in which minorities and their concerns are dealt with. Individual rights present the opportunity to be different, where possible even against the wishes of the majority. Dworkin expresses all this as a neutrality requirement:

> [P]olitical decisions must be, so far as is possible, independent of any particular conception of the good life, or of what gives value to life. Since the citizens of a society differ in their conceptions, the government does not treat them as equals if it prefers one conception to another, either because the officials believe that one is intrinsically superior, or because one is held by the more numerous or more powerful group. (Dworkin, 1985, p. 191)

In this sense, equality means taking everyone equally serious and ensuring that no-one is discriminated, so that it becomes possible to live in accordance with one's personal convictions. It means to bring about a state of moral independence, in the best possible liberal meaning of the term. Where the authorities should disapprove or even prohibit certain lifestyles on purely majoritarian grounds, this could constitute a discrimination towards those who act in accordance with a lifestyle that is actually permitted.

It would appear therefore that Dworkin rejects the majority theory as the sole basis for US governance. Majority decision-making is important but qualified, since the constitution seeks to protect individual citizens and groups against certain decisions made by the majority of citizens, even if that majority acts in the belief that this decision serves the public interest. The framers of the constitution were thus of the opinion that certain limitations of majority rule were justified by the institutionalised moral rights which the individual has against the majority. These fundamental rights against the state are therefore rights in the strongest sense of the term: the state may not restrict these rights for the sole reason that such a restriction can, in general terms, work to the advantage of society. This is why, where the majority fails to take account of fundamental rights, there can be no objection on democratic grounds against attempting to have this remedied by means of constitutional review. When the courts engage in constitutional litigation they will start from the assumption that what is stated in the constitution is the expression of a political system that is sufficiently just and has to be regarded as established on grounds of fairness. All this does not, moreover, mean that the said rights or claims against the state are absolute. Restrictions are possible, but cannot be imposed solely on the grounds that they serve the public interest. Only where others can also plead moral rights, or when a societal catastrophe must be prevented, may a right be restricted.

We conclude this section with one observation about Dworkin's views. The foregoing illustrates the attempt at substantive interpretation of the notion of democracy that goes beyond the procedural aspect (participation in elections, participation through the majority rule, etc). The model designed by Dworkin is attractive because it indicates that the law amounts to more than merely rules that have been adopted by, for example, the legislature. In the context of constitutional law, with its vaguely worded rights and freedoms, an approach based on principles is attractive. Dworkin's model could prevent arbitrariness on the part of the courts *up to a certain point*: court decisions must be capable of being encapsulated in existing legal developments and in the principles and ideals of justice and fairness, which are the expression of what can be regarded as standards in Western society and which, as underlying moral values, buttress and support the legal system.

However, the question arises how to implement all this in practice. What does "equal concern and respect" amount to? Solving complex problems that arise in practice requires a yardstick on the basis of which the scope of this phrase can be measured. When does the exclusion of a person from access to certain goods amount to unequal treatment? What can, and what cannot, be regarded as actual or relevant differences between persons? These are essentially moral questions, of which people judge very differently. Dworkin's model is quite an abstract one and by itself gives little guidance to the courts when faced with the prospect of applying it to constitutional disputes. Dworkin's position nevertheless expresses an ideal that is a worthy aspiration for the courts. The fact that the notion of "equal concern and respect" is a vague one does not deprive it of its philosophical meaning. Dworkin indeed provides no criterion which can at all times objectively identify what "equal concern and respect" amounts to, but that does not in any way detract from the philosophical meaning of the phrase. Dworkin is, more than anything else, seeking to emphasise that the courts adopt a democratic approach where they make a serious effort to accommodate their beliefs in the self-image of the society in which the law as such is located, a self-image that takes the ideal of "equal concern and respect" for each individual as a fundamental aspect of it.

Is Constitutional Review Consistent with Democracy?

The question whether constitutional review is consistent with democracy deserves to be answered in the affirmative, albeit not unconditionally.

It should be answered in the affirmative because democracy amounts to more than having decisions made by the majority (of, for example, a representative assembly). The legislator is also bound by the value choices which are contained in the constitution. Moreover, this constitution is not a static concept but is subject to development, which also reflects trends in society. Both the legislator and the constitutional court must bear this in mind. This also entails that the constitution should be interpreted in a substantive (value-laden) manner. The model sketched by Dworkin is an attractive one from this point of view because it gives rise to substantive reflection on that which democracy stands for. This task is incumbent in the first place on the legislature itself, which may not allow purely policy considerations to take precedence over essential and moral rights which we all have towards the state. If the legislature fails to respect these values, it can no longer hide behind the majority principle in order to plead that the (unconstitutional) rule has legitimacy. In countries such as Belgium, where a specific court has been specifically given this responsibility of constitutional review, that court in a certain sense even occupies a position that is superior to that of the legislature, as was explained by Delva, the former president of the Constitutional Court, in the following terms:

> The court is not in any way part of any of the three state authorities. It acts as a watchtower at the top of the federal construction. Being linked to the constitutional function without being a part of it, it is automatically involved in the process of exercising national sovereignty. The court is a derivative of the constitutional authority and at the same time its empowered agent. It guarantees compliance with the Constitution and penalises its infringement in relation to the established authorities of the sovereign state. (Delva, 1991, p. 80)

The answer to the question of consistency with democracy cannot, at the same time, be unconditionally affirmative. The constitutional judiciary definitely is not given *carte blanche*, but must accommodate itself in the constitutional model in which the other state authorities are also supposed to act. In this sense, Dworkin's fundamental rights model gives direction to the courts, but its practical interpretation will invariably be a difficult exercise in which the courts can only attempt the complex assessment which Dworkin imposes on judges. In any case, the judge must refrain from reading his own value judgments in the constitution or from applying non-legal policy considerations. This is also why constitutional review must be conducted with the necessary degree of caution.

The Practice of the Belgian *Arbitragehof* (Court of Arbitration)

In Belgium also, the idea of *separation* of powers has for a long time prevented constitutional review of legislation by the judiciary. The Belgian Constitution of 1831 did not attribute this power of review to the courts. However, this vision came under increasing pressure from a principle-based approach towards the relationship between constitution and legislation on the one hand, and the gradual development of the Belgian federal state model on the other hand.

At the principle level, the Belgian *Hof van Cassatie* (*Cour de Cassation* - Supreme Court), which is the highest court for issues of private, social and criminal law, had to a certain extent undermined the immunity of legislation to judicial review by courts as early as 1971. In its *Franco-Suisse Le Ski* decision, the Court ruled that when Belgian legislation conflicted with international rules of law which had direct effect, the court should give precedence to the latter (Hof van Cassatie, 27 May 1971). Although in so doing the Court did not pronounce itself on the relationship between legislation and constitution, it conceded that legislation could be subordinated to higher (international) rules, and that the courts had the duty to compel respect for the highest rule, even on the part of the legislature.

Three years later, in the *Le Compte* case, the Advocate-General with the Belgian *Cour de Cassation*, whose task it is to make reasoned submissions to the *Cour* in cases pending before it, put forward a similar position as regards the relationship between legislation and the constitution (Hof van Cassatie, 3 May 1974). He pointed out that, in Belgium, the separation of powers doctrine does not coincide with the theory of the very strict separation of powers as it was supposedly proclaimed in Montesquieu's *L'esprit des Lois.* On the contrary, each of the three state authorities does intervene in the exercise of other powers without distorting relations between these authorities:

> The principle of the separation of powers is merely a way of dividing public authority in such a way that those who hold these distinct powers may restrain each other within the limits of their respective responsibilities. (...) [This principle] does not prevent that, in the absence of a constitutional rule, the courts are given the power to review, under certain conditions, the constitutionality of legislation. (Hof van Cassatie, 3 May 1974, p. 979)

The *Cour de Cassation*, however, did not follow this argument. Reacting to the Attorney General's opinion, a number of Senators tabled a draft piece of legislation that would expressly have denied the courts the right to engage in constitutional review. From the principle of the separation of powers they drew precisely the opposite conclusion:

> The legislature exclusively adopts legislation, and this legislation applies to all. The judiciary exclusively assesses whether and how legislation should be applied to the disputes which are submitted to it. It does not have the task of "assessing legislation itself", any more than the Executive, which also exercises exclusive powers in its area, may refuse to enforce judicial decisions or legislation which it could deem to be "unconstitutional".[2]

Ultimately, the reform of the Belgian state, which transformed it from a unitary structure into a more federalised structure in the 1970s and 1980s, would lead to acceptance of constitutional review as a method of solving conflicts of jurisdiction between various levels of government. Belgium contains two language communities that are virtually equal in size, namely the Dutch-speaking part in the North and the French-speaking part in the South. They are separated by a "linguistic frontier", which is also enshrined in the Constitution: whereas Dutch is the official language in the North, French is the official language in the South. There is in addition the bilingual area of Brussels, where Dutch and French speakers reside and are as such constitutionally recognized, as well as a smaller German language area near the border with Germany. Within these linguistic communities, there also burned a desire for more self-rule in cultural, personal, social and economic matters. As from 1969, this desire has found expression in a reform of the Belgian state, as a result of which two decision-making levels were established – the Communities (which had jurisdiction in cultural, person-based and educational matters) and the Regions (which had jurisdiction in location-based and economic matters). Gradually, the Communities and Regions also acquired legislative and executive powers. As is the case in every federal state, this allocation was capable of giving rise to conflicts of jurisdiction and required the constitutional establishment of a conflict-solving organ. Rather than entrusting this task to the courts, the framers of the constitutional amendments in question opted for the creation of a special court, namely the Court of Arbitration (*Arbitragehof, Cour d'Arbitrage*).

This creation was in accordance with the traditional reluctance to entrust constitutional review to the ordinary courts. This reluctance finds expression in, for example, the fact that the provisions relating to the Court of Arbitration are contained in a separate chapter of the Constitution. The composition of the Court also expresses this reluctance. In addition to ensuring that there was a balance between Dutch and French speaking Belgians amongst the 12 judges, which was thought particularly important for the purpose of assessing issues of federal allocation of powers, the framers of the legislation on the Court of Arbitration also paid considerable attention to the background of these judges. Within every language group, half of the judges are former politicians who have been members of a legislative assembly for at least five years. These judges are supposed to be able, on the basis of their parliamentary experience, to contribute their knowledge of political sensitivities in Belgium. The other judges are lawyers appointed from among the judges of the *Cour de Cassation* and the Supreme Administrative Court (*Raad van State-Conseil d'Etat*), referendars with the Court of Arbitration and professors of law. This mixed composition, seeking a balance between theory and practice, was to make the principle of constitutional review more acceptable to the politicians in the legislature. In addition, these judges are appointed by the King on proposal by one of the chambers of the federal parliament. This was intended to partly resolve the democratic problem presented by constitutional review, namely that unelected judges should be able to review legislation adopted by the democratically elected representatives of the people (Velaers, 1990, para. 559). The requirement of a two-thirds majority for such appointment proposals, seeks to ensure that the Court of Arbitration should be as representative as possible of the political and ideological currents in the country.

The creation of such a specific Court was therefore deemed to be consistent with the principle of the separation of powers and removed the fear of a *gouvernement des juges*. The term "constitutional court" instead of Court of Arbitration would nevertheless, both in legal and in factual terms, give a more accurate description of the true nature of the Court.

Initially, only the governments and legislative assemblies of the state, the Communities and the Regions, were allowed to seize this Court by means of an application for annulment, so that the latter may pronounce itself on infringements of the distribution of powers laid down in the Constitution. Ordinary courts which, in a case before them, consider that an applicable statute could contain an infringement of these rules on distribution of powers were also authorised to apply to the Court for a decision on this, by way of a preliminary ruling.

The scope of the Court's powers of review has been gradually extended. Since 1989, the Court may also give rulings confirming infringements of the equality and non-discrimination principles (Sections 10 and 11 of the Belgian Constitution) and of the freedom of education (Section 24). This extension of powers was accompanied by the ability, conferred on the citizen with an interest in the matter, to initiate annulment proceedings before the Court of Arbitration, thus enabling these citizens to challenge every new piece of legislation before the Court during a period of six months. In concrete disputes they may also plead the unconstitutional nature of applicable legislation before the regular courts, after which the court in question may, or shall, refer a request for a preliminary ruling to the Court of Arbitration.

The broad interpretation which the Court of Arbitration has made of the equality principle has ultimately, in 2003, led to a formal extension of its powers of review to include violations of all rights and freedoms, which are stated in Title II of the Belgian Constitution.

During the period from 1989 to 2003, litigation involving infringements of the equality and non-discrimination principles in Sections 10 and 11 of the Constitution, developed into the key responsibility of the Court of Arbitration.[3] However, the Court does not appear to regard its ability to review legislation in the light of the equality principle as a *carte blanche*, but has attempted to give a coherent interpretation to the Constitution.[4]

In its interpretation of the equality principle, the Court sought inspiration from the case law that exists at the European level by adopting the assessment criteria that apply in the decisions of the European Court of Human Rights, namely an assessment based on comparability and accountability (see the *Belgian Linguistics Case*). In so doing, the Court acknowledged the major importance of equality, as a principle that is inherent in the Belgian legal order. It regards Sections 10 and 11 of the Constitution as adequate assessment criteria that contain a general prohibition on discrimination, regardless of its origin. These constitutional provisions are applicable to the enjoyment of all rights and freedoms, including those which are derived from international treaties having direct effect (Arbitragehof No. 4/96). Even discrimination in protection offered by institutional or procedural provisions in the Constitution, is prohibited by Sections 10 and 11 of the Constitution.[5] Moreover, the Court also assesses whether a disputed measure does not unlawfully infringe the principle of equal enjoyment of the protection which derives from general principles, the fundamental principles of the Belgian legal order and general legal principles (Arbitragehof No. 18/90, No. 6/94 and 24/96). The Court applies the equality principle and the prohibition of discrimination also to the equal enjoyment of rights and freedoms, which are recognised by the legislator itself and which do not find their basis in a constitutional provision, treaty rule or general legal principle.

By thus reading a general prohibition of discrimination in Sections 10 and 11 of the Belgian Constitution, the Court of Arbitration has brought within its scope every type of discrimination at the level of the enjoyment of rights, fundamental rights and freedoms. Where the Court, when assessing whether Sections 10 and 11 of the Constitution have been violated, decides that a fundamental right has been infringed, it will conclude that the category of persons whose fundamental rights were infringed has been discriminated against.

As regards the comparability test – the equality principle is only made applicable to groups of persons who are sufficiently comparable – it must be conceded that the Court of Arbitration does not make reference to any clear criteria on the basis of which it can conclude that certain groups are comparable and that therefore the equality principle should apply. An example of this can be found in the Abortion case, in which the most fundamental right to respect of life was at stake (Arbitragehof No. 39/91). Section 350 of the Criminal Code makes it an offence to perform an abortion even with the consent of the pregnant woman. However, a 1990 amendment provides that no offence is committed where the pregnant woman, whose situation has caused her to be in a "state of necessity", requests a doctor to terminate her pregnancy. The termination of pregnancy must be carried out under the conditions stipulated by law, as regards the moment of termination, the medical circumstances, the prior information given and an assessment of the resolute will on the part of the woman. Women who intentionally commit an abortion outside these conditions may also be penalised (Section 351 Criminal Code). Opponents of abortion have requested the Court of Arbitration to set aside the 1990 Law on abortion. The arguments they adduced from the point of view of the unequal treatment of the child were based on the principle that the continuity of human life entails unbroken and identical protection as from the moment of conception. These arguments therefore assumed that Sections 10 and 11 of the Constitution contain the prohibition of giving unequal treatment to the unborn child, or various categories of unborn children. In this respect the comparable category is the child as from its moment of conception.

The Court however found that the born and the unborn child are not entitled to identical rights:

> These provisions do not by themselves confirm that mankind enjoys the protection which they guarantee from the moment of conception. From the provisions of the international law relied upon by the applicants it cannot be concluded that the consent with these provisions intimated by the Belgian state carries the constitutional guarantee

> of identical rights for living persons and unborn children. Admittedly some of the provisions which are featured in several of the treaties relied upon by the applicants impose on the contracting parties the obligation to adopt measures ensuring that a pregnancy can develop normally in the best possible conditions. Moreover, there exist, more particularly in Belgian civil and social legislation, rules which protect the interests and health of the unborn child as from the moment of its conception. Although the obligation to respect human life compels the legislator to adopt measures also to protect human life, it cannot be concluded from this that the legislator, under penalty of infringing the Sections [10 and 11] of the Constitution, is obliged to give equal treatment to the born and unborn child. (Arbitragehof No. 39/91, para. 6.B.3)

The Court concluded:

> The Court has no jurisdiction to assess whether a provision is consistent with rules other than the equality principle and the prohibition of discrimination or the rules on jurisdiction which have been laid down in or on the basis of the Constitution. Since Sections [10 and 11] do not contain the obligation to give the unborn child the same regard, in legal terms and in every respect, as a born and living person, the arguments which are based on an infringement of this provision should only be considered to the extent that they seek to prevent discrimination between born and living persons. (Arbitragehof No. 39/91, para. 6.B.4)

This part of the grounds of judgment can be interpreted in several ways (Van Nieuwenhove, 1992, p. 354). The grounds of judgment could, on the one hand, be regarded as an application of the comparability test (Rimanque, 1992-93, p. 9: born and unborn persons are not comparable). The Court does not say so in so many words, but neither does it deny it. This passage could, on the other hand, also be regarded as an assessment of the objective and reasonable justification for the difference in treatment. In this interpretation, the difference in treatment is not disproportionate because the principles under review in the dispute do not go so far as to impose an absolute prohibition on terminating the life of the unborn child. Against this interpretation, there is the argument that the Court does not examine in greater detail the question of whether the termination of life, under the conditions stipulated by the legislator, is justified and still proportionate to this lesser protection that is given to the life of the unborn child (Van Nieuwenhove, 1992, p. 354). Under both interpretations, the Court has, through this general form of words, circumvented the question of the status and rights of the unborn child.

Should this decision nevertheless be interpreted as the outcome of applying the comparability test, it follows that Sections 10 and 11 of the Constitution are not applicable to a comparison between the treatment of an unborn child and that of the born child. In other words, as far as the right to equal enjoyment of the rights pleaded by the applicants is concerned, the born and unborn child are not comparable, since the unborn child does not enjoy the guarantees that are conferred on born children. The comparability test therefore results in an important decision on the scope of the rights and freedoms that have been the subject of discrimination as to their enjoyment. Only the comparable group of born and living persons enjoy these rights. By failing to regard these situations as being sufficiently comparable, the Court has eluded the obligation to assess the justification of this distinction (Theunis, 1997, para. 163).

The Court thus exposes itself to the criticism that it allowed itself to circumvent legal issues that are very difficult to assess from a political and ideological point of view on the pretext that the discrimination complained of concerns situations that are not comparable. If the Court of Arbitration is to achieve a principle-based demarcation of similar situations, it will need to find a definition of the notion of comparability. Such criticism should, however, be tempered by the consideration that, *de facto*, the Court hardly ever dismisses complaints on the basis that the various categories are not comparable.

When applying the accountability test – Can the difference in treatment be accounted for? - the assessment can be divided into two types of assessment: a coherence or functional assessment on the one hand, and a proportionality assessment on the other hand. If a Law fails on one of these assessments, the distinction created by that Law will be tantamount to discrimination, in violation of Sections 10 and 11 of the Belgian Constitution.

For a statute to meet the test of Sections 10 and 11 of the Constitution, it may not be marked by functional defects or incoherence. Supervising such incoherence is a form of constitutional review whereby the Court is not compelled to substitute its own value judgment for that of the legislature. It is the expression of the principle that, in a democratic society consisting of free and equal persons, membership of this society is only possible where each of its members is regarded as each other's equal. This expresses itself in, *inter alia*, the obligation to take account of each person's interests when legislating. Accordingly, within the framework set by the legislature itself, the legislative rule must be capable, taking account of these interests, of reaching the appropriate category of persons which the legislature, in the light of its objectives, intended to reach and thus achieve the objective set by the legislation. Here, the Court fully assesses the objective nature of the distinction and the adequacy of the legislative measure.

This kind of functional assessment is therefore somewhat technical in character and is aimed at improving the democratic decision-making process. The Court of Arbitration has thus come to play a corrective, rather than a substituting, role in relation to the legislature. This enables the Court also to expose the "passive" discrimination that results from gaps in the applicable legislation and to compel the legislature to take action. The equality principle therefore includes a coherence requirement, in the sense of a requirement to adopt proper legislation that can also compel the legislature to take action:

> The legal subject may expect a coherent system of rules from the legislator (…). Where a system of rules appears to be inconsistent with the underlying rules, the legislator needs to act in order to adjust the system appropriately. It will not suffice merely to repeal the infringing rules. (Popelier, 1996-97, p. 1250).

This technique enables the measure itself, to the extent that it is constitutionally valid and appropriate for the party that has not been discriminated against, to remain in force. Yet, at the same time it implicitly invites the legislator to apply the measure equally to those left out (Arbitragehof No. 31/96).

However, when engaging in proportionality assessment, the Court is definitely obliged to make a value judgment between the pursued objective of the Law and the general interest on the one hand, and the inequality which expresses itself by restricting the free enjoyment of rights and freedoms on the other hand. On this issue, it is possible to discern a difference in intensity of assessment by the Court of Arbitration. Any difference in treatment which distorts the equal enjoyment of fundamental rights and freedoms will have a discriminatory effect where a solution is being sought at the expense of an infringement of fundamental rights and freedoms. The Court itself makes reference to a "particularly stringent assessment" where a fundamental right has been infringed (Arbitragehof No. 74/92). In this respect, the Court allows itself to be led by the case law of the European Court of Human Rights. However, whenever possible the Court will give precedence to an interpretation that is consistent with the Constitution. Where the infringement is merely the result of the practical application of a statutory provision, the Court will not rule that provision to be unconstitutional as such. The same reluctance to review is noticeable where the alleged infringement is the result of inaction on the part of the authorities.

A review based on proportionality will also be strict where a statutory provision infringes "fundamental principles", "basic principles of the legal order", or "basic principles of the Belgian legal order" (Arbitragehof No. 78/98). Here the Court is particularly vigilant where the legislation in question has repercussions for the legal protection of the citizens such as access to legal professions or to assistance by a lawyer (Arbitragehof No. 6/94), for legal certainty (Arbitragehof No. 24/96) or for procedural due process.

Where there are no fundamental rights and freedoms or principles involved in the dispute, the Court is extremely reticent in its review. In a number of decisions involving social, fiscal or environmental policy, the Court has engaged in hardly any proportionality assessment. Here, proportionality assessment almost always coincides with functional assessment: the Court assesses whether a statutory provision has a certain finality and whether there is a reason why a certain category of persons has been made subject to different treatment. Where the Court confirms that such a rational relationship is present and the system of rules is not, moreover, affected by inconsistencies, the review often goes no further. This applies particularly where the disputed statutory provision is the expression of a political project on which there is a broad social consensus or one which has been difficult to achieve, or where a balance between the linguistic communities is being sought. An example for the latter was, for instance, the Court's judgment in 1990 where it upheld the distribution of the "Belgian" seats in the European Parliament between Dutch- and French-speaking MEPs. That distribution did not correspond with the population numbers in the Dutch- and French-speaking areas of Belgium respectively. The distribution was announced as a temporary measure, awaiting a future application of the proportional distribution principle (Arbitragehof No. 26/90).

The brief opinions of the Court's decisions, and the absence of possible dissenting opinions on the part of individual judges, make it difficult to gain an insight into its inner thoughts. Although there are decisions where the Court, by reviewing legislation on the basis of Sections 10 and 11 of the Constitution, in conjunction with the European Convention on Human Rights, painstakingly examines the objectives set by the legislature, there are other decisions where the Court confines itself to the mere statement that the statute in question is an intervention that is authorised by the same Convention.[6] Whether this intervention is inspired by an objective that is necessary for "the interests of the national security, public safety, or the economic well-being of the country, for the prevention of disorder or crime, for the protection of health or morals, or for the protection of the rights and freedoms of others", is never expressly explained.

However, the Court does appear to seek to interpret the equality rule in a principled manner. This does not mean that the case law of the Court is free from criticism. It has major political implications and will for this reason alone be capable of criticism. The vague and general nature of the equality principle, even as reworded at the "European" level, definitely does not exclude the possibility of arbitrariness or political manipulation, in which extra-judicial considerations determine the decisions made.[7] Anyone who believes that the equality principle can be mastered in its entirety and can lead to predictable results when subjected to review is mistaken. Similarly, no decision by the Court of Arbitration can answer all the questions that arise in connection with a statutory provision. Indeed, there are times when the Court's decisions give rise to new questions. The Court thus enters into a dialogue with the legislature and the ordinary courts, in order to achieve an acceptable position between the majority decision-making principle and that of individual freedom.

* Both authors are professor of law at the University of Antwerp in Belgium.

Notes

1 This gave rise to the somewhat paradoxical situation whereby, in The Netherlands, legislation may not be reviewed in the light of such principles as the fundamental rights and freedoms contained in the Dutch constitution, but may be judged on its consistency with treaties such as the UN Covenant on Civil and Political Rights and the European Convention on Human Rights, since Section 120 of the Dutch Constitution does not appear to exclude the possibility of reviewing legislation in the light of treaties.

2 *Parliamentary Documents* Senate, 1974-75, No. 602/1, 1. The proposal was never voted.

3 Section 10: "There is no distinction between orders in the State. All Belgians are equal before the law; they alone are acceptable for civil and military posts, with some exceptions which may be established by law in particular cases." Section 11: "Enjoyment of the rights and liberties to which Belgians are entitled must be safeguarded without discrimination. To this end, laws and decrees shall guarantee the rights and liberties of ideological and philosophical minorities." In the Court's first 1.000 decisions, rendered until 2000, 67 per cent concerned discrimination claims,

against 7.8 per cent freedom of education claims and 25.2 per cent federalism claims. (Leysen *et. al.*, 1999-2000, p. 1386).

4 This paragraph is based on research on the case law of the Court of Arbitration in Vanheule, 2001.

5 Such provisions are, for instance, the distribution of judicial functions between courts (Arbitragehof No. 14/97 and No. 26/2002), the reserved legislative powers in taxation (Arbitragehof No. 64/95, No. 21/97 and No. 105/99) and in military and police matters (Arbitragehof No. 81/95 and No. 134/99).

6 An example of an explicit reference to the Strasbourg case law can be found in Arbitragehof No. 45/96 where the Court upheld criminal law that made it punishable to deny, minimise, justify or approve genocide committed by Nazi-Germany in the Second World War. In Arbitragehof No. 4/96, the Court was on the contrary very brief on the compatibility between the obligation for aliens, in immigration law, to live together for family reunion purposes, and Section 8 of the European Convention on Human Rights.

7 The Court's decision to declare the ban on advertising tobacco products discriminatory is an example of such controversy, given its consequences for the (sponsoring of) car racing sport in French speaking Belgium. See Arbitragehof No. 102/99.

References

Aristotle, (1973), *Politica*, B. Jowett (tr.), Clarendon Press, Oxford.

Bork, R. (1990), *The Tempting of America. The Political Seduction of The Law*, The Free Press, New York.

Brewer-Carias, A. (1989), *Judicial Review in Comparative Law*, Cambridge University Press, Cambridge.

Delva, J. (1991) 'Staatsrechtelijk profiel van het Belgisch Arbitragehof (Constitutional profile of the Belgian Court of Arbitration)', *Tijdschrift voor Bestuurswetenschappen en Publiekrecht*, Vol. 47, pp. 69-99.

Dworkin, R. (1977), *Taking Rights Seriously*, Harvard University Press, Cambridge (Ma).

Dworkin, R. (1985), *A Matter of Principle*, Harvard University Press, Cambridge (Ma).

Dworkin, R. (1986), *Law's Empire*, Fontana Press, London.

Dworkin, R. (1996), *Freedom's Law. The Moral Reading of the American Constitution*, Harvard University Press, Cambridge (Ma).

Ely, J.H. (1980), *Democracy and Distrust: A Theory of Judicial Review*, Harvard University Press, Cambridge (Ma.).

Freeman, S. (1990-91), 'Constitutional Democracy and the Legitimacy of Judicial Review', *Law and Philosophy*, Vol. 9, pp. 327-370.

Hirsch-Ballin, E.M.H. (1991), 'Onafhankelijk rechtsvorming (Independent law-creation)' in *Rechtsstaat & Beleid*, Tjeenk Willink, Zwolle.

Kortmann, C.A.J.M. (2001), *Constitutioneel Recht (Constitutional Law)*, Kluwer, Deventer.

Learned Hand (1958), *The Bill of Rights*, Harvard University Press, Cambridge (Ma).

Leysen, R., Paty, B. and Rasson-Roland, A. (1999-2000), 'Een kaap overschreden: het duizendste arrest van het Arbitragehof' (The 1.000th Judgment of the Court of Arbitration), *Rechtskundig Weekblad*, Vol. 63, pp. 1385-1397.

Montesquieu (1748), Montesquieu, *De l'esprit des lois* in D.Oster (ed.), *Œuvres completes de Montesquieu*, Seuil, Paris, 1964, pp. 527-795.

Popelier, P. (1996-97), 'De beoordeling door het Arbitragehof van het ontbreken van een wettelijke regeling' (Evaluation by the Court of Arbitration of the absence of legal provisions), *Rechtskundig Weekblad*, Vol. 60, pp. 1249-1252.

Rimanque, K. (1992-93), 'De paradoxale werking van het gelijkheidsbeginsel' (The paradox of the equality principle), *Rechtskundig Weekblad*, Vol. 56, pp. 6-15.

Stewart, I. 'Montesquieu in England: his "notes on England", with Commentary and Translation'. At: http://ouclf.iuscomp.org/articles/montesquieu.shtml

Theunis, J. (1997), 'Het gelijkheidsbeginsel. Juridisch interpretatiekader, met bijzondere aandacht voor "corrigerende ongelijkheden" en doorwerking in private rechtsverhoudingen' (The equality principle. Legal interpretation scheme, with special attention for corrective inequality and application in private relations), in *Publiekrecht. De doorwerking van het publiekrecht in het privaatrecht (Public Law: The Application of Public Law in Private Law)*, Mys & Breesch, Ghent.

Tribe, L. (1980), 'The Puzzling Persistence of Process-Based Constitutional Theories', *Yale Law Journal*, Vol. 89, pp. 1063-1080.

Vanheule, D. (2001), *Amerikaanse modellen van grondwettigheidstoetsing toegepast op de rechtspraak van het Arbitragehof over de artikelen 10 en 11 G.W. (American Models of Constitutional Review Applied to the Case Law of the Court of Arbitration on Equality and Non-Discrimination)*, University of Antwerp Ph.D. thesis, Antwerp.

Van Nieuwenhove, J. (1992), 'Zwangerschapsafbreking: afweging van rechten door hoge gerechtshoven' (Abortion: balancing of rights by supreme courts), *Tijdschrift voor Bestuurswetenschappen en Publiekrecht*, Vol. 48, pp. 352-358.

Velaers, J. (1990), *Van Arbitragehof tot Grondwettelijk Hof* (*From Court of Arbitration to Constitutional Court*), Maklu, Antwerp.

Waldron, J. (1999), *Law and Disagreement*, Clarendon Press, Oxford.

Case Law

European Court of Human Rights, Belgian Linguistic Case, Judgment of 23 July 1968, Series A, No. 6, 1 E.H.R.R. 252.

Hof van Cassatie 27 May 1971, *Pasicrisie belge* 1971, I, 886, also commented in "Conflicts between Treaties and Subsequently Enacted Statutes in Belgium: Etat Belge v. S.A. «Fromagerie Franco-Suisse Le Ski»" (1973-74), *Michigan Law Review*, vol. 72, p. 118.

Hof van Cassatie 3 May 1974, *Arresten van het Hof van Cassatie* (*Case law of the Belgian Supreme Court*) 1974, 967, conclusions W.J. Ganshof van der Meersch.

Hoge Raad 14 April 1989, *Nederlandse Jurisprudentie* (*Dutch Case Law*) 1989, 469.

Arbitragehof No. 18/90, 23 May 1990, www.arbitrage.be (text in Dutch, French and German).

Arbitragehof No. 26/90, 14 July 1990, www.arbitrage.be.

Arbitragehof No. 39/91, 19 December 1991, www.arbitrage.be.

Arbitragehof No. 74/92, 18 November 1992, www.arbitrage.be.

Arbitragehof No. 6/94, 20 January 1994, www.arbitrage.be.

Arbitragehof No. 90/94, 22 December 1994, www.arbitrage.be.

Arbitragehof No. 29/95, 4 April 1995, www.arbitrage.be.

Arbitragehof No. 64/95, 13 September 1995, www.arbitrage.be.

Arbitragehof No. 81/95, 14 December 1995, www.arbitrage.be.

Arbitragehof No. 4/96, 9 January 1996, www.arbitrage.be.

Arbitragehof No. 24/96, 27 March 1996, www.arbitrage.be.

Arbitragehof No. 31/96, 15 May1996, www.arbitrage.be.

Arbitragehof No. 45/96, 12 July 1996, www.arbitrage.be.

Arbitragehof No. 14/97, 18 March 1997, www.arbitrage.be.

Arbitragehof No. 21/97, 17 April 1997, www.arbitrage.be.
Arbitragehof No. 78/98, 7 July 1998, www.arbitrage.be.
Arbitragehof No. 105/99, 6 October 1999, www.arbitrage.be.
Arbitragehof No. 102/99, 30 September 1999, www.arbitrage.be.
Arbitragehof No. 134/99, 22 December 1999, www.arbitrage.be.
Arbitragehof No. 26/2002, 30 January 2002, www.arbitrage.be.

PART III

POLITICS, LEGISLATION AND LEGITIMACY

Chapter 10

Legislating Human Rights

Tom Campbell*

Even the most ardent advocates of constitutional bills of rights see that there is a place for human rights legislation, that is for legislation that is aimed primarily at the protection and implementation of human rights. A constitutional bill of rights would not, for instance, do away with the need for a Racial Discrimination Act or Equal Opportunity or Land Rights legislation. For those who have serious doubts about bills of rights, especially those bills that are used to override democratically enacted legislation, but who are, nevertheless, fully committed to human rights objectives, human rights legislation takes on even greater significance, for it becomes the state's core contribution to the protection and furtherance of human rights.

By "human rights legislation" I do not mean legislated (or statutory) bills of rights, that is statements of general moral principles enacted for the purpose of guiding judicial interpretation,[1] or setting up a system of judicial review of other legislation.[2] By "human rights legislation" I mean legislation that promotes human rights in a legislative manner, that is by the enactment of a body of clear and specific rules that can be followed and applied without using broadly based moral reasoning.[3] This normative model of legislation, and the virtues of rule-governance associated with it generally, are derived from a democratic theory of prescriptive legal positivism (Campbell, 1996).

Assuming, for the purpose of this chapter, that there is good reason either to do without or to tightly constrain bills of rights, I explore the idea of giving special status to human rights legislation, a status that reflects the heightened priority that an interest acquires by being identified as a human right. The objective is to provide a quasi-constitutional role for human rights that goes some way towards meeting the rationale for having bills of rights, namely providing some constraint on the immoralities that occur when democratic procedures, which are intended to provide decision-making mechanisms that manifest and serve the wishes and interests of all citizens, are distorted in ways that promote the illegitimate self-preferences of statistical majorities or privileged and powerful minorities.

The sort of constitutional role for human rights legislation I have in mind includes the relatively mild device of giving human rights legislation interpretive priority when it conflicts, or appears to conflict, with other pre-existing or later legislation, or with the common law. Thus the presumption that a parliament does not intend to legislate to the detriment of fundamental principles of the common law would be supplemented, or displaced, by the assumption that a parliament does not intend to legislate in a way that diminishes the force and application of existing human rights legislation. Such a presumption would be rebutted only if the later legislation clearly and unequivocally displaces existing human rights legislation. In the case of human rights legislation it might be appropriate to require that it can be repealed or amended only through the use of a particular form of words comparable to the "notwithstanding" clause of the Canadian Charter of Rights and Freedoms.[4]

This form of constitutionalization is equivalent to the suggestion of Laws LJ and the logic of *Factortame* (Laws, 1991) that the UK European Communities Act 1972 is a "constitutional statute" in that it cannot be "impliedly repealed". According to Laws "Ordinary statutes may be impliedly repealed. Constitutional statutes may not. For the repeal of a constitutional Act or the abrogation of a fundamental right to be effected by statute, the court would apply the test: is it shown that the legislature's actual – not imputed, constructive or presumed – intention was to effect the repeal or abrogation? I think the test could only be met by express words in the later statute, or by words so specific that the inference of an actual determination to effect the result contended was irresistible. The ordinary rule of implied repeal does not satisfy this test. Accordingly, it has no application to constitutional statutes."[5] A similar approach may be taken to the UK Human Rights Act 1998, and even to particular statutory rights in ordinary legislation that are held to be in some way fundamental.[6]

Going much further, we might give human rights legislation a procedurally distinctive constitutional status by having it enacted and repealed or amended only by special procedures comparable to constitutional amendment. Such special procedures could either make it more difficult or easier to change human rights legislation. The rationale for making it more difficult, for instance by requiring more than a simple majority of votes cast, is that this protects rights from selfish or ignorant majorities. The rationale for making it easier to change human rights legislation is to make it possible for vulnerable minorities to have privileged control over human rights legislation. For instance, a second chamber, elected on the basis of proportional representation, might be empowered to pass human rights legislation without the consent of a first chamber elected on a first-past-the-post basis.

Another possibility is to require human rights legislation to be endorsed by referendum. It would depend on knowledge of many demographical, political and legal variables to know whether such a procedure would provide better protection against powerful minorities or selfish majorities, but this approach has the potential to give human rights legislation the sort of preferred constitutional status that would warrant using it to trump ordinary legislation even where there is a clear incompatibility between the constitutional statute and the later legislation.

In fact there are many less dramatic procedural requirements that could be entrenched or "constitutionalized" in such a way as to encourage majoritarian political processes to give less partial and more empathetic consideration to human rights and provide better protection to vulnerable minorities. Some of these can be adapted from the UK Human Rights Act 1998, such as a requirement for government ministers to provide statements in relation to the compatibility of proposed legislation with existing human rights legislation when presenting new legislation to the Parliament.[7]

In particular, there are many variations on the institutionalized role of a human rights committee of a legislature whereby such a committee, perhaps composed in such a way as to give statistically disproportionate representation to vulnerable minorities, has powers to require governments not just to provide reasons for apparent threats to human rights in proposed legislation, but actually to bring forward specified types of human rights legislation or propose amendments to existing human rights legislation in order to meet a perceived human rights deficit, or, less dramatically, to delay the enactment of legislation that they deem to be in potential violation with enacted human rights.

Such constitutional mechanisms may be viewed as extensions of the inquisitorial and de facto delaying powers of Parliamentary committees, as exemplified by the Australian Senate Standing Committee for the Scrutiny of Bills whose terms of reference require it to draw to the attention of the relevant Minister and subsequently of the Senate if any proposed legislation seems to them to be in conflict with "personal rights and freedoms". Thus in its Second Report of 2003, that committee records that it drew the attention of the Minister for Immigration and Multicultural and Indigenous Affairs to the fact that, in the Migration Legislation Amendment Bill (no 1) 2002, no reason is given for certain retrospective clauses and that it sought "the Minister's advice as to why these provisions apply retrospectively and whether they will disadvantage any person" adding that "Pending the Minister's response, the Committee draws Senators' attention to these provisions as they may be considered to trespass unduly on personal rights and liberties, in breach of principle 1(a)(I) of the Committee's terms of reference."[8]

In the same report, a similar process is recorded relating to the abrogation of the rules of natural justice in relation to another bill: "The rules of natural justice have been developed over many years to ensure fairness in the application of law. It is unusual to see them cast aside simply to avoid 'operational difficulties'. The Committee, therefore, seeks the Minister's advice as to the deficiencies in the existing provision and why such an extreme amendment is seen as necessary to deal with them".[9] Clearly not satisfied by the Minister's response: "The Committee thanks the Minister for this response and accepts that there may be substantial reasons in this case to abrogate the rules of natural justice. However, those rules are central to personal rights and should be excluded only in exceptional circumstances. The absence of procedural fairness in these provision is a beach of such rights, but the Committee leaves to the Senate to decide whether, in the circumstances, it is an undue breach".[10]

In another matter the Committee takes up a concern over the extension of strict liability in criminal law. A proposed new subsection in a bill which "makes it an offence for a person to make arrangements that make it look as if two people are de facto spouses for the purposes of the regulations where the person knows or reasonably believes that they are not de facto spouses", appeared to them to make a change in the law in a way that introduced strict liability in so far as it would not be necessary for the prosecution to prove knowledge of a difficult and technical piece of law in this respect.

Going beyond the function of commenting on the rights implications of particular bills, the Committee also sought to bring about changes in the form of presentation of legislation by inserting a requirement that all bills provide a full and clear explanation of proposed legislation, especially where this has a potential impact on personal rights and democratic procedures : "The Committee emphasises that an Explanatory Memorandum should include a full explanation of the background of the bill and its intended effect. This is particularly the case where it includes provisions which may affect personal rights or parliamentary propriety. An Explanatory Memorandum should be more than a brief introduction followed by notes on clauses that largely reproduce the clauses themselves. The purpose of the Explanatory Memorandum is to assist parliamentarians during the passage of the bill and to be a guide for all those affected by it proposed provisions. This would usually include a substantial discussion of these issues in addition to the notes on clauses". This matter was taken up by the Committee with the Acting Parliamentary Secretary to the Prime Minister and to the First Parliamentary Counsel.

Such devices, actual and imagined, have a variety of objectives, particularly (1) to improve the quality and direction of debate so as to reduce the impact of partisan and ill-informed majoritarianism and the capture of parliaments by privileged minorities, (2) to protect the interests of identified vulnerable minorities and individuals by providing mechanisms for questioning or delaying legislation that, perhaps inadvertently, threatens important rights or to promote the passage of human rights legislation designed to further such interests, and (3) to provide an institutionalized way of justifying the prioritization of human rights legislation.

Such mechanisms do not displace the need for a political culture, which is deliberative in that a sincere and good faith commitment is made by the majority of those involved as leaders, activists and voters in seeking to arrive at decisions that are believed to be either in the equal interests of all citizens or represent morally justifiable departures from that standard. However, they may be seen as helping in the promotion of such a culture without undermining democratic rights in the way that court-centred bills of rights tend to do.

In particular, the oversight role of legislative committees could be enhanced by the existence of comprehensive human rights legislation that could be taken as an authoritative and specific expression of what constitutes the "personal rights and freedoms" that are left unspecified in the terms of reference of the Senate Standing Committee for the Scrutiny of Bills. Indeed the terms of reference of such committees and the political force of their comments and recommendations could be strengthened by enacting a non-justiciable bill of rights that identifies in a brief and eloquent manner the rights that they are charged to protect and enhance. Where there is also in place provision for the judicial review and invalidation of ordinary legislation, such scrutiny becomes a matter of predicting what courts might say rather than an independent assessment of the best legislative instantiation of abstractly formulated rights, but the process is capable of adaptation to a less legalistic and more moral form of reasoning and debate as to what abstract human rights are to mean in practice. In this context, there is room for what might be called a "Democratic Bill of Rights", that is a non-justiciable abstract statement of fundamental rights that is deployed in various ways to affect the agenda and outcome of legislative process so as to achieve closer attention to human rights issues without having to empower judiciaries to use overrule or radically reinterpret enacted legislation.

Human Rights Legislation

With these thoughts in mind we can explore further the idea of human rights legislation. What might human rights legislation be? What are its distinctive characteristics? What marks it out from other human rights instruments? How might the concept be institutionalized?

Such questions present us with a number of fluid concepts that require some stipulated clarification in order to render the above questions answerable. With respect to "legislation" itself, we should note that the term can be taken as referring either to a type of law-making, or to a type of law. As a type of law-making, legislation is a complex process whereby an authorized individual or collective, the legislator(s), produce a bundle of interconnected rules and principles according to a process whose outcome is recognized as creating authoritative law in the jurisdiction in question. Legislation typically involves a formally defined process whereby policy decisions and commitments are turned into justiciable rules in a constitutionally recognized way. In democracies (the only type of government in which the idea of human rights legislation has any resonance), this is the work of a large representative elected assembly, or assemblies.

As a type of law (as distinct from a type of law-making) legislation is a collection of written rules and principles that determine in advance and in general terms what is lawful and what is unlawful in a jurisdiction. Legislation, in this sense, is distinct from the decision that are made when these rules and principles are followed or applied by those to whom they apply, including courts in so far as this is how their responsibilities are defined.

These definitions are crafted so as to promote a clear distinction between legislation and adjudication, the making of law and the application of law. Such a distinction is particularly clear when we have the enactment of specific and clear rules that can be applied to particular fact situations without the need for any interpretation beyond the contextual understanding of members of that linguistic community (Naffine *et al.*, 2001, pp. 291-320). It is much less clear when the process of law-making produces not clear rules but general principles that gain applicable meaning more from an evocation of values rather than a prescription of a descriptively clear form of conduct. In these circumstances the application of laws that have been made may itself be a form of law-making because of the degree of creativity that enters into applying a principle to a particular factual circumstance. This adjudicative law-making is not in itself legislation, either in process or outcome, except in so far as the decision overtly or implicitly creates a rule, as is the case when a particular application of a principle sets a descriptively specific precedent for future applications, thereby turning the principle into a rule.

In such cases, we might talk not of judicial law-making but of judicial legislation. However, it is preferable that the practice of making rules in the process of applying principles is referred to as a process of law-making, but not legislation, and that "legislation" be used to identify the creation of rules other than in the process of making decisions about the lawfulness of particular circumstances. Such rules or norms may be denied the label legislation just because they are not the product of a legislature, defined as a law-making body that is not also authorized to apply the rules that it makes. While the concept of legislation could be used so as to cover bodies of rules that emanate from courts in this way, I choose not to go down that conceptual path because it is important to mark the constitutional significance of the separation of powers by declining to regard the law-making practices of courts as legislation and hence with the same normative status as enacted law. This is not to deny that courts do sometimes make laws, but it serves to affirm the democratic principle that legislation (the product of legislatures) trumps any law-making powers that courts may have.

In fact, there is conceptual force as well as practical convenience in excluding judicial law-making from the category of legislation. First, if and when judicial law-making occurs it must be done in the process of adjudication, that is the determination of the lawfulness of a particular circumstance. Second, judicial law-making is done in a quite different manner and form to the law-making of legislators, that is those who make rules in abstraction for determining the lawfulness of particular circumstances.

Thus far, my conceptual apparatus would enable us to speak correctly of legislating bills of rights, as indeed we do when we contrast a legislative with a constitutional bill of rights. By definition, a legislative bill of rights is the outcome of normal legislative process and not special constitution-creating procedures or revolutionary historical events. Such "legislative" bills of rights may be distinguished from ordinary legislation in part by content – the type of law that is made – and in part by function, that is the role that a legislative bill of rights is ascribed within the legal and political system, such as a guide to interpretation.

With respect to content, a bill of rights is characteristically a statement of principles in abstract form, usually with predominantly moral content, in that the key concepts involved are value-laden, asserting the priority of certain interests and institutional mechanisms for their protection. Bills of rights are typically, in their substantive content, brief, forceful and inspirational. They concern liberty, equality, justice, privacy, and life itself. And in their procedural content, they lay down in abstract terms participation rights, such as the right to vote, speak and associate.

With respect to function, the increasing prevalence of the American model of judicial review, raises the presumption that bills of rights function within constitutional judicial review of legislation. This is historically inaccurate. Bills of rights in general have no definitionally essential function (Tushnet, 1999). In fact, in the case of statutory bills of rights, their role is normally limited to an interpretive one, requiring courts to take the requirements of such bills into account when interpreting ordinary legislation, perhaps in such a way as to render that legislation consistent with the legislated bill of rights. The New Zealand legislative bill of rights is a paradigm example. The UK Human Rights Act 1998 represents a more sophisticated version that enacts a wider range of functions to such a bill, including the power of courts to make "declarations of incompatibility" if they consider that ordinary legislation cannot be interpreted in such a way as to render it consistent with the European Convention on Human Rights and Freedoms.

If legislatures can enact bills of rights, it seems natural to assume that, whatever human rights legislation is, it includes legislative bills of rights. Indeed this would seem to be the paradigm example of human rights legislation. However, I do not go along with this assumption, not because bills of rights are not about human rights, but because bills of rights do not conform to my normative model of legislation. Evidently, legislative bills of rights are legislation in the sense that they are the products of legislatures, rather than special constitutional procedures or implied by courts in the process of constitutional interpretation. However, legislative bills of rights are not legislation as a type of law in terms of their content or form because of the predominance of statements of abstract moral principles as contrasted with specific legal rules. If we approach legislation as a type of law-making typically undertaken by legislatures, then undoubtedly legislatures enact bills of rights. Bills of rights can be the product of legislative process. If we approach legislation as a type of law then legislatively processed bills of rights are not appropriately regarded as legislation.

There are at least two reasons to resist the classification of legislative bills of rights as a type of legislation. First, and less controversially, bills of rights differ in function from legislation in general. They are typically used either for courts to render legislation invalid and hence not legislation at all, or as an invitation to courts to make new law on the basis of moral principle. Even where they are ostensibly confined to an interpretive role, they tend to be utilized by courts to bring about de facto legislative review. This means that bills of rights are not only not ordinary legislation, they are, as a type of law, not legislation at all.

Of course, as I have indicated, bills of rights may be given other roles. Thus a bill of rights may not be directly enforceable by courts but serve the function of guiding governments and legislatures. I have suggested, for instance, that a legislated bill of rights could be used as a benchmark for a Human Rights Scrutiny Committee without itself being legislation. Something like this exists with respect to the Joint Human Rights Committee in the UK, which operates with respect to the European Convention on Human Rights, which has been incorporated into the UK by the Human Rights Act 1998 for a limited range of purposes, such as this one. However, this even more clearly does not make it conceptually correct to regard such bills of rights as examples of legislation.

The second and main reason for not regarding legislated bills of rights as legislation is that they are generally so far removed from the ideal of good legislation as to be legitimately denied the description of legislation at all. This is conceptually controversial in so far as it is based on a notion of "good" legislation (here, of course, we mean formally not substantively good legislation) rather than on an evaluatively neutral meaning of "legislation".

Particular evaluative considerations lie behind the conceptual propriety of excluding certain forms of political decision-making from the genre of legislation. Thus a system of governance that gives authority to certain persons to make binding decisions with respect to particular circumstances and particular parties is not appropriately called a legal system because of the absence of rules of general application enabling people to know in advance of their conduct, what is and what is not mandatory within that political system. "Palm tree justice" is not, in this view, legal justice, for the rules that govern it are limited to procedural rules that establish who has the right to make decisions but not limiting what those decisions may be in form or content. By extrapolation from this extreme constitutional circumstance, it may be argued, along lines drawn with delightful clarity by Lon Fuller (Fuller, 1969) that law-making has certain internal norms that require conformity to such standards as clarity, publicity, consistency, practicality, generality and prospectivity. These standards are prescriptive but they are in effect constitutive of what we regard as law, and in particular, as legislation.

This model of legislation is a crucial part of positivist theories of the rule of law and has been become associated with a theory of democracy that ascribes normative significance to the role of democratic decision-making in the process of legislation. Thus, Jeremy Waldron, in his "jurisprudence of legislation" (Waldron, 1999), argues that the dignity and integrity of legislation requires that we respect the compromises embodied in its substance as a result of democratic compromise and accommodation to the views of others through open and public debate addressed directly to the issues (rather than inherited texts). Legislative texts are to be respected as the outcome of reasonable procedures in a situation of deep social disagreement. Legislation is not something to be tidied up by courts even when they are blatantly over and under inclusive. Waldron sees legislation as a text that embodies an "agreed" policy decision arising out of a debate in which all affected parties are participants, the outcome of which is determined by a process that gives equal weight to the choices of all those involved.[11]

Some of the ideals of good legislation that serve to identify its conceptual essence are exemplified in such instruments as the Legislative Standards Act 1992 (Qld) which establishes certain "fundamental legislative principles" to ensure that Queensland legislation is of the "highest standard", principles which are to be promoted through the Office of the Queensland Parliamentary Counsel. These "are the principles relating to legislation that underlie parliamentary democracy based on the rule of law" (...) that "legislation has sufficient regard to (a) rights and liberties of individuals; and (b) the institution of Parliament".[12] Enumerated examples of such principles include avoiding undue dependence on administrative power only, ensuring natural justice, limiting delegation of administrative power, retaining the onus of proof in criminal cases, keeping tight restrictions on search warrants, avoiding self-incrimination, excluding retrospectivity, requiring justification for granting immunities, achieving fair compensation for compulsory acquisition, having sufficient regard for Aboriginal tradition, and, importantly, requiring that legislation "is unambiguous and drafted in a sufficiently clear and precise way."[13] The Act requires that bills must include a brief assessment of the consistency of the Bill with fundamental legislative principles and, if inconsistent with fundamental legislative principles, give reasons for the inconsistency.

Whatever standards of good legislation we adopt, and how far we write these standards into the concept of legislation, it is clear that some of these standards are not met by bills of rights, hence my exclusion of such bills from the category of human rights legislation for they seek to promote human rights objectives in ways that contradict the principles of legislation, including respect for the democratic legislative process. This creates logical space for the development of the concept of human rights legislation as an alternative to (or perhaps for others a supplement to) bills of rights, legislated or not.

The political justifications for this position are the familiar difficulties with bills of rights as a form of law. In form, bills of rights are made up of vague moral assertions in a form that render them unfit for the purpose of guiding conduct, settling disputes and facilitating cooperation. Other problems arise in connection with their anti-democratic role in enabling courts to override the legislation of elected law-making assemblies. The first difficulty is constitutionally neutral but fundamental to the fairness of formal justice and the efficiency of rule-governance, an efficiency that can be used to serve human rights objectives. A vague right is, in practice, no right at all.

The second difficulty is constitutionally committed in that it endorses a notion of democracy whereby individuals have a formally equal say as to what becomes law. On this latter approach, whether or not bills of rights are to count as legislation, it is certainly the case that an elected assembly enacting a bill of rights is thereby abrogating its future democratic responsibilities as well as corrupting the separation of powers. It follows that, considering both types of objection, there are human rights reasons to avoid bills of rights as being potentially formally unjust and actually undemocratic.

Such bills are potentially unjust (and inefficient) because it is possible for a bill of rights to be formally good law. Thus, a right not to be subjected to capital punishment under any circumstances is as clear, unambiguous, practicable, and prospective as can reasonably be hoped for. But bills of rights tend not to be like that. They normally consist of highly abstract affirmations in basically moral language. Indeed, this may be considered essential to their functioning in enabling judges to override legislation to protect vulnerable minorities through a direct appeal to fundamental moral values, thus limiting the power of elite minorities and populist majorities. However, to the extent that bills of rights do conform to Fuller-style criteria of rule-governance, then they do indeed present an exemplar of human rights legislation.

The question that then arises is what the institutional function of human rights legislation might be. The first, and primary, answer must be that there is, or could be, a constitutional requirement that there be human rights legislation so that the human rights objectives are not ignored or relegated to a subordinate place in that jurisdiction. The demand that all states have bills of rights is thus replaced by the demand that all states have comprehensive human rights legislation. This has the potential to secure more effective, because more radical and specific, legislation than is likely to emerge from judicial "interpretation" of fundamental moral values or rare examples of judicial override of legislation.

It is not in fact necessary for human rights legislation to be given any particularly function beyond the realisation of the specific objectives of the legislation in question. If applying such law serves human rights then this is in itself a sufficient justification for its enactment. Human rights legislation is directly applied to the conduct of those who bear the correlative duties contained therein, be it government departments, private organizations or individual citizens.

However, many of the arguments in favour of bills of rights make important points about the need to avoid certain negative human rights outcomes that are a natural consequence of the typical systematic failure of electoral systems of democracy. Even if the solution offered by bills of rights is unacceptable because it is incompatible with the very rights it seeks to protect, or because it is ultimately ineffective in curbing entrenched power, this does not weaken the force of the critiques of electoral democracy, but merely casts doubt on the proposed cure. It is therefore an appropriate human rights objective to see whether this democratic deficit can be corrected through mechanisms that give a measure of entrenched priority to human rights legislation that is not vulnerable to the anti-democratically objections that are directed at bills of rights.

This takes us back to the constitutional devices indicated in the introduction to this essay; namely, the idea that human rights legislation trumps ordinary legislation, that human rights legislation affects the interpretation of ordinary legislation, and, perhaps, that such legislation is enacted or protected in distinctive ways that are designed to give it a measure of entrenchment without blocking its progressive development

Super-Statutes

The proposal to recognize a specific type of legislation, human rights legislation, as a having a special, quasi-constitutional status, to some extent echoes the idea of "super-statutes" put forward in Eskridge and Ferejohn (2001).

According to Eskridge and Ferejohn, "[a] super-statue is a law or series of laws that (1) seeks to establish a new normative or institutional framework for state policy and (2) over time does 'stick' in the public culture such that (3) the super-statute and its institutional normative principles have a broad effect on the law – including an effect beyond the four corners of the statute. Super-statues are typically enacted only after a lengthy normative debate about a vexing social or economic problem, but a lengthy struggle does not assure a law super-statute status. The law must also prove robust as a solution, a standard or a norm over time, such that its earlier critics are discredited and its policy and principles become axiomatic for the public culture" (Eskridge and Ferejohn, 2001, p. 1215).

Examples of super-statutes provided by Eskridge and Ferejohn include The Sherman Antitrust Act of 1890, The Civil Rights Act of 1964 and the Endangered Species Act of 1973. Each in their own way occupies "the legal terrain once called 'fundamental law', foundational principles against which people presume their obligations and rights are set, and through which interpreters apply ordinary law. Today, this kind of law might be considered 'quasi-constitutional' – fundamental and trumping like constitutional law, but more tentative and susceptible to override or alteration by the legislature or determined judges and administrators" (Eskridge and Ferejohn, 2001, pp. 1216-1217).

In some respect the idea of super-statutes provides a model for my concept of human rights legislation. Super-statutes have a higher constitutional status than ordinary, more humdrum, legislation, which makes it difficult to change a super-statute and carries interpretive significance for other legislation. In particular, the idea that such legislation cannot be overridden by subsequent legislation unless this is done explicitly accords with a central aspect of the status I would accord to human rights legislation.[14] Human rights legislation, like super-statutes is not vulnerable to implied repeal.

However, in other respects super-statutes are different from human rights legislation. Super-statutes achieve their status through broad political support garnered over time.[15] Human rights legislation gains its status from being formally identified as such. No doubt human rights legislation aspires to achieve broad and lasting recognition, but legislation which, for instance, is designed to protect minorities, may function legally as human rights legislation without broad and deep political support of the sort that applies by definition to super-statutes.

Nor is there a requirement that the enactment of human rights legislation always represents a major shift in national policy or norms.[16] In fact, much human rights legislation may be designed to consolidate and refine existing human rights protections, as they exist, for instance, in the common law. No paradigmatic shift of emphasis is required of human rights legislation.

Again, for Erskine and Ferejohn, it is a feature of super-statutes that they are liberally interpreted on a progressive understanding of their basic principles and the goals of the legislation in question, such as free trade, racial equality or the protection of endangered species. Thus, we are told, the Civil Rights Acts of 1866 were "narrowly construed by the post-Reconstruction judiciary afraid to disturb the political consensus in favor of segregation" and only became super-statues when "the post-World War II civil rights movement revived interest in those laws and the Warren Court breathed new life into them in the 1960s with liberal interpretations" (Eskridge and Ferejohn, 2001, pp. 1225-1226). So-called "dynamic readings"[17] are in fact a common feature of many judicial approaches to bills of rights, but they are antithetical to the democratic basis of human rights legislation through which legislative assemblies seek to determine the scope and boundaries of rights with some precision.

This does not mean that human rights legislation is to be interpreted "stingily" (Eskridge and Ferejohn, 2001, p. 1226), or that, where judges do have good reason to resort to broad-based judicial reasoning they should not resort to principles drawn from legislation as well as principles drawn from common law. Where gaps in the law require to be filled there is no reason to exclude principles embodied in legislation from the relevant judicial reasoning. It is not the role of human rights legislation, however, to provide the basis for a new source of judicial creativity. That is to go down the bill of rights path.[18] Human rights legislation is not characterized principally by broad statements of principle that invite judicial law-making. The principles involved in human rights legislation are there to provide the context that helps to give meaning to the rules established in the legislation, not to give the courts a basis for delegated law-making. Formally good legislation not only identifies goals but lays down how and to what extent those goals be pursued by establishing clear rules that are designed to capture the parameters of the right that the legislature intended to enact. The high priority given to such legislation is operationalized in terms of the superiority of its rules when they come into conflict with other enactments or common law decisions.

Three issues remain to be resolved in order to render the strategy of protecting human rights by human rights legislation feasible: (1) Can human rights legislation be distinguished from ordinary legislation? (2) Can human rights be reduced to specific rules that can be applied without recourse to moral and other disputable judgments? (3) Can human rights legislation be privileged without engendering new anti-democratic objections?

Can Human Rights Legislation be Distinguished from Ordinary Legislation?

Human rights legislation could be distinguished simply by the constitutional priority that is given to it, but this does not help us determine which legislation ought to be given such priority. That could readily be settled by identifying human rights legislation as legislation that is designed to and explicitly does seek to implement international treaty obligations with respect to international human rights law. This would identify human rights legislation through its origins in international law. A paradigm Australian example would be the Racial Discrimination Act 1975, a type of legislation that has been enacted in many jurisdictions in order to implement the Covenant Against All Forms of Racial Discrimination.

This approach, neat as it is, cannot purport to define human rights legislation exclusively. Not every article of the Universal Declaration on Human Rights (UDHR) or the two covenants (the International Covenant on Civil and Political Rights, and the International Covenant on Economic, Social and Cultural Rights) has given rise to a convention, and many conventions, such as the Convention Against All Forms of Discrimination Against Women, are designed to supplement rather than explicate the UDHR and the Covenants.

However, if we take a broad view and include in human rights legislation any statutes that promote ends identified as human rights in the UDHR, for instance, then this has the potential to include all statutory provisions relating to the protection of life, physical integrity, property and basic welfare. On this approach almost any legislation might count, at least in part, as human rights legislation (Kinley, 1998). Certainly any government seeking to respect the UDHR could treat the basic provisions of its Crimes Act as human rights legislation. The right to life requires at least the prohibition and punishment of murder. And on a broad reading of the UDHR it would be possible to regard criminal law as an extended exercise in rendering certain human rights more specific and better protected. A similar approach to any area of law may be taken, rendering the boundary between human rights and ordinary legislation nugatory, especially if we give equal status to social, economic and rights along with the more traditional and generally prioritized civil and political rights.

However, in addition to identifying whole acts as human rights legislation it would be possible to specify certain sections or clauses of acts as dealing with human rights matters, thereby signalling its special status as human rights legislation. Thus, in relation to criminal law, human rights legislation could be identified as that part dealing with due process safeguards as are identified in the ICCPR, such as the minimum safeguards for accused persons listed in Article 14(3) which are required as part of the right to a fair trial.

Such a process of picking and choosing is dauntingly complex and controversial and would not be worth undertaking unless the benefits were evident and significant. This suggests it would be wise to retreat to a positivist bedrock for which the process of selection could be the international agreements entered into by the government concerned that are uncontroversially identifiable as dealing with human rights. This does not entail accepting as definitive of human rights all rights-oriented international legal sources, such as the case law emanating from the application of bills of rights in different jurisdictions, although such material could be relevant to the moral and political choices involved in identifying human rights legislation that is not treaty based.

On the other hand, it seems inadequate simply to accept the external authority of international human rights treaties or judicial views as to what counts as a human right, as exhaustive of what can be counted as human rights legislation. The content and boundaries of human rights are questions of moral and political substance on which there is reasonable disagreement of a sort that, according to human rights principles, ought to be settled by democratic process. Each jurisdiction must determine for itself what it counts as a human right, and what it means to identify something as a human right. It is an integral part of the idea of having human rights legislation rather than bills of rights that this gives the opportunity to determine the operative content of these categories through the democratic deliberative and decision-making processes of each self-determining jurisdiction. The fact that there can be reasonable disagreement as to what counts as a human right does not disable polities for developing and changing its own views on such matters and making clear legal determinations on what is and what is not to count as human right legislation through explicit textual determinations. Giving human rights responsibility to individual nation states is undermined by external determinations of what counts as a human right.

Can Human Rights be Reduced to Specific Rules that can be Applied without Recourse to Moral Judgments?

If human rights are affirmations of fundamental interests that ought to have priority protection in all jurisdictions then they would appear to be, at base, value affirmations. There are a number of problems this raises for the concept of human rights legislation, principally (1) the moral status of human rights, (2) the abstract formulation of most statements of human rights, (3) the particular lack of specificity of human rights with respect to the correlative duties implied by rights discourse (Campbell, 1996).

The Moral Status of Human Rights

With respect to the moral status of human rights, it may be argued that human rights are moral affirmations that cannot be captured in a body of specific and clear rules, particularly if they are to be applicable without the exercise of moral judgment as to their content. The right to a decent standard of living, for instance, incorporates a moral term ("decent") that is empirically imprecise and depends on judgments as to what are morally acceptable living conditions for any human being in different types of economy. In this view, the whole enterprise of human rights legislation is misguided. Human rights are broad moral principles, not empirically applicable rules.

One response to this line of argument is to point out that some human rights are given precise descriptive content. That there shall be no capital punishment is an example already mentioned. That there shall be two weeks holiday with pay is another precise requirement laid down in the UDHR. However, with respect to human rights, such precision is relatively uncommon, and such provisions as a requirement for two weeks holidays with pay have been strongly criticized as inappropriate precisely because of their specificity, which undermines the universality, and in this case also the importance of human rights (Cranston, 1962, p. 42).

However, the counter-examples given do suggest that there is no intrinsic problem in rendering human rights not only specific but morally neutral with respect to the content of the criteria used to identify the prescribed right. There is little descriptive dispute as to what is and what is not capital punishment. There is a lack of descriptive clarity as to what counts as leisure for the purpose of a right to leisure, but not as to what counts as two weeks holiday per year. Further the development of human rights from the UDHR onwards can be seen as a process of increasing empirical specificity through the adoption of more specialiZed international instruments and a developing case law.

Of course, this move to specification in non-moral categories can itself be criticized as an unwarranted positivizing of human rights. Certainly there are reasons for disquiet if human rights are simply identified with positive law, even positive international human rights law, especially if it is evolving in the direction of codes of rules. There will always be a need to use human rights morally to criticize such positive concretized human rights law as failing to meet proper human rights standards.

We have here a dilemma for human rights discourse. When states accept the broad principles of human rights, such as the right to life or the right to equality before the law, but deny that they are violating such rights by, for instance, having capital punishment or failing to provide legal aid to accused persons, it becomes necessary to spell out in more detail what it is that these rights require of us.

Hence the drive to specificity. But to identify a human right with very particular matters, such as a particular abortion regime, seems to undermine the critical role of human rights discourse.

The way forward here is to combine affirmations of human rights values, such as equal worth, respect for persons, human dignity, and autonomy (and perhaps embody them in a non-justiciable democratic bill of rights for the guidance of legislatures and governments) with specifications of what these values require in terms of empirically identifiable outcomes in the specific conditions of the societies to which they apply, while keeping such formulations open to constant revision and development. This requires the development of human rights rules, rules that have in common their justification by human rights values. This recognizes that human rights include but go beyond calls for certain interests to be protected by law and recognizes that one means for protecting and furthering such rights is through legal mechanisms. It is these mechanisms, rather than human rights as such, that are to be identified as human rights legislation. At the same time the basis of all human rights discourse remains a set of moral and political values.

This approach has many advantages. One is that it retains the discourse of rights as a basis for the critique of all law, including constitutional law. Further, it serves to mitigate one of the perennial problems about the concept of human rights, namely the alleged universality of such rights, which comes up against the evidently relevant differences between cultures and social systems: the human rights values are universal, while the human rights rules are relative to the type of society, be this defined in terms of its economic system or in some broader way.

However, it is clear that the substance of human rights discourse goes beyond universality of values and claims a universality with respect to at least some human rights rules. The right to life does require a general prohibition on killing. Equal worth does require a general prohibition on the use of racial criteria in positive law. Respect for persons is inconsistent with the denial of freedom of expression. Human dignity does require the outlawing of slavery. Autonomy is inseparable from some quite precise democratic rights with respect to freedom of association and the opportunity to vote in elections.

That there is disagreement about human rights rules is undeniable, but it is equally undeniable that the discourse of human rights seeks to go beyond assertions of abstract value to the concretization of these values in specific demands relating to social, economic and political arrangements in all societies. The moral role of human rights is to support morally irresistible demands for securing concrete protections for certain fundamental human interests. Providing specific rules compliance which can be determined in an empirically objective manner is an essential part of a human rights program. Human rights legislation is, therefore, something human beings have a right to expect. But even this stronger position does not require that human rights are constituted by human rights legislation.

The Abstraction of Human Rights

Turning to the second issue, concerning the reduction of human rights to a system of rules, why should it be thought that human rights are essentially abstract?

This assumption, along with the claim that human rights are moral abstractions, derives in part from the natural rights origins of human rights in political manifestos associated with revolutionary movements to curb or overthrow existing political authorities. To the extent that human rights still have this role then there is a reason to focus on abstract moral claims, although these may usefully be combined with more specific demands, such as "no taxation without representation". However, the continuing assumption that human rights are essentially abstract moral claims gives support to the belief that the chief function of human rights is to provide courts with moral principles that they can use to correct legislation which they deem to conflict with these values. That is why it is so often assumed that we need bills of rights that are broad value assertions and hesitate to identify human rights with any set of specific rules.

Once we drop this assumption the way is open for us to seek more precise formulations of human rights as part of what is involved in rendering human rights protectable. Nevertheless, there is danger in identifying human rights with these specific formulations when we use the discourse of rights to critique existing and proposed legislation. This suggests that we need to sustain a constant dialectic between human rights abstractions and more concrete articulations of these values in relation to specific sets of circumstances.

Open-ended Correlative Duties

The third reason given why human rights rules cannot encompass human rights is the openness of rights to the discovery or imposition of new correlative duties. Here we come to a feature of legal norms that cuts across the boundary between legislation and common law. Anglo-American common law is a system that emphasizes remedies and causes of action, so that legal rights depend on identifying a prior legal duty, neglect or violation of which has led to a wrong on the basis of which a legal claim may be made for compensation, or legal punishment be administered as the result of a criminal act.

In contrast, what has come to be called a right-based morality starts with the foundational claim that individuals or persons have certain rights, that is interests that are or ought to be protected, by law in the case of legal rights. This leaves it an open ended-matter as to who has the duties and precisely what these duties might be that are required to protect and further the right in question (MacCormick, 1977).

In the case of human rights it has usually been taken that states are the main bearers of human rights duties, that is the duties that correlate with human rights, although there is an equally strong assumption that such duties apply to all human beings and human collectives. Nevertheless, states are assumed to have the primary obligation of seeing to it that such universal human rights duties as there may be are respected. This now needs to be supplemented by obligations of non-state actors, such as multinational corporations. Even where there is a fair measure of clarity as to the rights-bearers, there is little that can be assumed about the nature and scope of the duties involved. Thus, governments may accept that they have duties in relation to the right to development, but have very different views about whether these duties are negative or positive, and in either case what these duties might be. The logic of a rights approach is that the right is established and then we work out how to go about securing that right.

On this view, human rights legislation could involve the ascription of specific rights, that is rights to quite specific things and conditions, but would leave it open what this involves by way of correlative duties. Since, by norms of "good legislation" such legislation would be deficient through its failure to provide a basis for regulating human interaction in a foreseeable ways, it can be argued that there is an incoherence in the idea of human rights legislation.

It is feasible to rebut this claim by arguing that we have moved beyond this historical stage in the development of human rights and come to realize that their effective protection depends on specifying correlative duties in such a way as to ensure the protection of the relevant interests. If human rights are to be more than pleasing rhetoric they must be concretized in legislation that is up front on the matter of correlative duties, particularly as governments are by no means the sole source of human rights violations. Any resistance to this development could be put down to a desire to reserve for judiciaries decisions as to what these duties are to be.

However, some concession can be made to the idea of a relatively duty-free rights approach to morals and law by accepting that the concept of rights can usefully be deployed to identify core interests that are protected in a variety of duty-specified ways. Moreover, it is to be expected that the content of these duties must be open to constant revision as these interests are threatened in new ways or new sources of remedial action become available. This, however, argues only for constant and on-going revision of human rights legislation, particularly with respect to the locus and other details of the correlative rights and does not involve a rejection of the concept of human rights legislation. Indeed, it strengthens the case for developing human rights legislation to articulate who it is, in the circumstances of the time, that bears the specific correlative obligations.

Can Human Rights Legislation be Privileged without Engendering Anti-democratic Objections?

A third problem that complicates the passage to acceptance of the idea of human rights legislation is that any special status given to such legislation undermines the democracy it is meant to protect and is therefore itself a violation of human rights in much the same way as court-centred bills of rights. The preference for human rights legislation over court-administered bills of rights is based in part on the idea of effective democracy. This in itself is enough to raise questions about the idea of human rights legislation because much human rights discourse is based on a critique of democracy, and this includes a disparagement of legislation in so far as it emanates from the wheelings and dealings of democratic politics.

This is one of the topics explored by Jeremy Waldron in his "jurisprudence of legislation" (Waldron, 2000). Waldron seeks to re-establish what he calls "the dignity of legislation" by showing that elected representative legislatures are entitled to respect simply because they are the product of a process that institutionalizes the belief that each human being's opinion has equal value and ought to be respected. Standard arguments for court-administered bills of rights systematically disparage democracy by arguing that such bills of rights are necessary for the protection of democracy (Ely, 1980), thus exhibiting a double standard in both extolling and diminishing democracy. It is not difficult to show, as Waldron does, that there are models of democracy totally different from the caricatures of majoritarian self-interest that are taken for granted in court-administered bills of rights (Campbell, 1998 and Waldron, 1999).

Nevertheless, I have argued that there is a need to prevent actual democracies tending towards such aberrant models in which people whose interests are not compatible with those of majorities have those interests discounted simply because of the accidental fact that they are in a minority. The problem is how to counter this tendency without privileging a minority, as is the case with a court-administered bill of rights.

One essential ingredient in the strategy for making and keeping democracies more democratic is to foster a culture in which it is accepted that voting ought to be based on opinions as to the common good and impartial social justice and not on calculations of individual or group self-interest. This is not incompatible with using the vote as a source of power to protect certain interests, but these interests must be selected on the basis of their justified importance and not because they just happen to be the interests of the voter. That culture can be fostered in many institutionalized ways. Some of these relate to sustaining such civil and political rights as freedom of speech. Others relate to social and economic rights such as education.

Beyond these broad societal prerequisites of an effective democracy, there are many specific constitutional devices that can be deployed to bring systematic institutional pressure to bear on those who neglect the common good by steering the decision-making agenda and its procedures in the right sort of democratic direction. Some of these devices have presented bills of rights as justified only in so far as it is their function to maintain the conditions of democracy. And in the attempt to deal with anti-democratic objections to bills of rights, mechanisms have been suggested and adopted to make legislatures more responsive to human rights and less responsive to sectional interests. These, as we have seen, include scrutiny of bills committees and delaying powers of second chambers.

In the case of court-centred bills of rights, the cure is in general worse than the curse, but it may well be that the less radical devices for discouraging the tendency of majorities towards illegitimate self-interest are not, on balance, anti-democratic devices, if democracy is seen as a model of government that is designed to instantiate equal political power in a system that is committed to justice and human rights. In that context, a constitution that gives power to vulnerable minorities so that they can play a more effective role in determining agendas and debating and delaying certain matters that threaten their well-being, need not be viewed as a democratic deficiency. Indeed such procedures can be viewed as ways of enhancing the dignity of legislation and respect for the rule of law.

Perhaps the crucial factor here is how far these devices are imposed through a constitution or common law convention that it is beyond the power of a democratic legislature to change, and how far it is the outcome of self-denying ordinances by the legislatures themselves. Clearly, the latter is democratically preferable although it may only be feasible in a jurisdiction imbued with a significant human rights culture. The challenge is to promote that culture without weakening those human rights that are enshrined in the democratic rights of citizens. To this end, it is better to give quasi-constitutional status to human rights legislation than to subordinate human rights to judicial power.

* Professorial Fellow, Centre for Applied Philosophy and Public Ethics (CAPPE), Charles Sturt University, Canberra.

Notes

1 Such as the New Zealand Bill of Rights Act 1990.
2 Such as the UK Human Rights Act 1998.
3 An example would be the Australian Racial Discrimination Act 1975 and its various state equivalents. Interestingly, these have been put forward as a model for an Australian Bill of Rights (Atkinson, 1999).
4 Something like this is achieved through the idea that certain provisions of an act are "dispositive", a term used in ACT legislation to identify a provision that can only be repealed explicitly or from necessity A stronger mechanism is to require a specific "manner and form" in the wording of an Act that is to amend the existing legislation, as is provided for the Australia Act 1986 (Cth) UK (Goldsworthy, 2004).
5 Laws L.J.: "A constitutional statute can only be repealed, or amended in a way that significantly affects its provisions touching fundamental rights or otherwise the relation between citizen and State, by unambiguous words on the face of the later statute" (Laws, 2002).
6 R v Home Secretary Ex p Leech [1994] QB 198 and R v Lord Chancellor Ex p Whitham [1998] QB 575.
7 See also the Queensland Legislative Standards Act 1992.
8 Concerning the Migration Legislation Amendment Bill (No 1) 2002. Alert Digest No 3 of 2002 to the Minister for Immigration and Multicultural and Indigenous Affairs, 63.
9 Senate Standing Committee for the Scrutiny of Bills, Second Report, 2003, p. 64.
10 Op. cit., p. 66
11 See also Wintgens (2002) which deals with "legisprudence", an approach to the study of law-making that concentrates more on exploring standards for "rational legislation" which moves beyond criteria such as consistency, to the duties of legislators with respect to establishing facts, weighing up alternatives, calculation of consequences and their advantages and disadvantages, and preparedness to modify legislation in the light of later experience.

12 Legislative Standards Act 1992 (Qld), Sec 4.
13 Op. cit., Sec (3)(k).
14 Eskridge and Ferejohn (2001, p. 1235): "the Court has repeatedly held that 'repeals of the antitrust laws by implication from a regulatory statute are strongly disfavoured, and have found to only in cases of plain repugnancy between antitrust and regulatory provisions'" quoting *United States v. Philadelphia National Bank*, 374 U.S.321, 350-51 (1962).
15 "The key to super-statutedom is acceptance in public culture. This cannot be mandated, nor is it earned exactly. It is a trial-and-error process which, when successful, creates it own gravitational field" (Eskridge and Ferejohn, 2001, p. 1230).
16 "Our first criterion for super-statutes is that they alter substantially the then-existing regulatory baselines with a new principle or policy" (Eskridge and Ferejohn, 2001, p. 1230).
17 Here this term is used to identify purposive, developmental, progressive and liberal methods of judicial interpretation: "Super-statutes should be construed liberally and in a common law way, but in light of the statutory purpose and principle as well as compromises suggested by statutory texts" (Eskridge and Ferejohn, 2001, p. 1247).
18 The authors cite the UK Human Rights Act 1998 as an example of a super-statute that has quasi-constitutional status, and note that the judiciary assumes that such a statute should be interpreted "liberally and imperially" (Eskridge and Ferejohn, 2001, p. 1265).

References

Atkinson, R. (1999), 'Are Anti-Discrimination Statutes a Model for a Bill of Rights?', Public lecture – University of Queensland, 16 September 1999.

Campbell, T. (1996), *The Legal Theory of Ethical Positivism*, Dartmouth, Aldershot.

Campbell, T. (1998), 'Legal Positivism and Deliberative Democracy', *Current Legal Problems*, Vol. 15, pp. 68-92.

Cranston, M. (1962), *Human Rights Today*, Ampersand, London.

Ely, J.H. (1980), *Democracy and Distrust: A Theory of Judicial Review*, Harvard University Press, Cambridge (Ma).

Eskridge, W.N. and Ferejohn, J. (2001), 'Super-Statutes', *Duke Law Journal*, Vol. 50, pp. 1215-1276.

Goldsworthy, J., (2004) 'Parliamentary Sovereignty and Statutory Interpretation' in Bigwood, R., *The Statute: Making and Meaning*, LexisNexis, Wellington, pp. 187-204.

Fuller, L.L. (1969), *The Morality of Law*, Yale University Press, New Haven.

Kinley, D. (ed.), (1998), *Human Rights in Australian Law*, Federation Press, Sydney.

Laws, J. (2002) in *Thoburn v Sunderland City Council* [2002] 3 WLR 247 at 281.

MacCormick, D.N. (1977), 'Rights in Legislation' in P. Hacker and J. Raz (eds.), *Law, Morality and Society*, Clarendon, Oxford.

Naffine, N., Owens, R. and Williams, J. (eds.) (2001), *Intention in Law and Philosophy*, Dartmouth, Aldershot.

R v. Secretary of State for Transport ex parte Factortame Ltd (No 2) [1991] 1AC 603.

Tushnet, M. (1999), *Taking the Constitution Away from the Courts*, Princeton University Press, Princeton.

Waldron, J. (1999), *Law and Disagreement*, Oxford University Press, Oxford.

Waldron, J. (2000), *The Dignity of Legislation*, Cambridge University Press, Cambridge.

Wintgens, L.J. (ed.), (2002), *Legisprudence: a New Theoretical Approach to Legislation*, Hart, Oxford.

Chapter 11

Legitimacy through Rationality: Parliamentary Argumentation as Rational Justification of Laws

A. Daniel Oliver-Lalana*

Introduction

It has been said that, under certain circumstances, casting dice might be a good method to take judicial decisions (Elster, 1989). Should the judges follow such a suggestion, as Rabelais' Bridoye used to do,[1] jurists would feel indignant about it. Needless to mention, a number of reasons could support this feeling. A judicial judgement is a practical or normative decision entailing a claim to justifiability; yet not any kind of *justification* suffices to fulfil this claim: in our legal culture it requires good reasons, that is, rational *arguments*. The acceptability of any legal justification rests precisely upon their rationality. Therefore it cannot be made at random.

If one shares the view that legitimacy is also a matter of rationality, however this is to be interpreted, the following starting thesis may be put forward: every legal decision must be rationally justified, i.e. rational arguments must underlie it, because otherwise it cannot be legitimate. It is worth noting that legal decisions are not only taken by applying laws but also by enacting them, so that this thesis covers not only judicial but also legislative decisions *and justifications*. Statutes may be actually regarded as normative decisions entailing a claim to (rational) justifiability, where their legitimacy depends thereupon. One may venture to contend that a law cannot be at the same time both irrational and legitimate, or both rational and illegitimate. In this respect, rationality and legitimacy cannot be separated from each other. They are two sides of the same coin. If this is correct, the legitimacy of laws cannot solely derive from certain procedural conditions (*legality*), but it is also bound to the rationality of the argumentation that justifies them, that is, to parliamentary argumentation. In spite of this, the parliamentary argumentation has seldom been analysed as a modality of *legal* argumentation aiming for justification nor addressed as a pattern for legislative rationality and legitimacy. There is a range of works on legislation theory, political communication and legal argumentation which tackle this question in passing. Still, specific studies on this topic, which combine the theory of legal argumentation and the theory of legislation, are few and far between (see Atienza,

1992; 1993; 1997; 2003; D'Auria *et al*., 1997). It would seem that there are not many expectations about any rational argumentation justifying statutes. What is more, the rationality of legislators has been largely rejected among jurists.

It is certain that, at least in statutory law systems, the scholarly or dogmatic community presumes that laws are rationally constructed. This presumption has been strongly challenged because it entails an ideological vision of the judicial application of law. As Wróblewski (1990, p. 113) puts it, the *rational legislator* is "a catchword covering a variety of arguments in any ideology of law-applying in which the separation of law-making and law-applying is presupposed". In the last analysis, the model of a rational lawmaker would have us to belief that judicial decisions apply statutory provisions automatically, in a merely logical-subsumptive manner. The falsehood of such a belief constitutes, however, "one of the few points of agreement in contemporary discussions of legal methodology" (Alexy, 1989, p. 1). As a matter of course, that model, albeit fictitious, renders an important function as methodological postulate guiding statutory interpretation and application. Anyhow, apart from this, few jurists would bet on there being legislative rationality *in fact*.

A likely explanation for this is that legislative rationality, when analyzed from the legal point of view, is usually conceived as an equivalent to coherence and logical consistence of the legal order. In accordance to the Weberian tradition, this would correspond to a formal and systemic notion of rationality. But, in the welfare state, this conception has been dramatically overridden by phenomena such as the law explosion or the regulative law accompanying the ever-increasing complexity of post-industrial societies. As a result, nowadays statutes are rather seen as mere *political* instruments coming out from *political* decision-making processes which are not governed by any criteria of legal rationality. This is accepted as the construction of the legal system does not seem to be legislators' business. After all, they have not been elected because of their legal expertise.[2]

Jurists have contradictory attitudes towards legislative rationality. Whilst they often take it for granted and resort to the rational lawmaker postulate, they also claim that legislation is just a matter of political will. It would seem then that there is no halfway position: either we presume the rationality of the lawmaker for methodological purposes or we simply give up the very idea of rational legislation and bow to political arbitrariness. A due assessment of legislative rationality is waived in both cases.

Legislative Rationality and Legitimacy of Law

When dealing with the rationality of law, one tends to draw a strict barrier between legislation and adjudication. Only the latter would be steered by *rational* decision and argumentation rules, whereas the former remains subordinated to political opportunism. Of course, if statutes do not have to be rational, their *justification* must be found elsewhere. The principle of democracy may be well invoked for this purpose. Whenever the lawmaker is respectful to the citizens' sovereign will and provided that he complies with certain procedural rules, the need for legislative rationality would ultimately fade out. It would be only in the judicial argumentation practices where justification, rationality and legitimacy flow together. As judges' *legitimacy* does not result from democratic votes, it is sought for in the *reasons* they bring forward to *justify* their decisions. The snag about this position is that, in confining legal rationality only to judicial decisions, the connection between rationality and legitimacy of law gets broken. This divorce is linked to five issues, which can be posed, in turn, at the core of a *legisprudential* perspective on legislation.

The first question is whether the concept of legitimacy comprises the rational justification of laws or not.[3] Legitimacy might be detached from the rational justification by arguing, for instance, that it equates to people's belief in (the rationality of) legality, which is a given socio-psychological fact (Weber, 1978); or by saying that laws are legitimated since they result from any procedure that guarantees their factual acceptance (Luhmann, 1975). Understood in this empirical sense, there is no difference between legitimacy and legitimation: the concept of legitimacy is deprived of its ideal character and cannot be used for a critical assessment of legislation. For its part, the normative concept of legitimacy focuses on how should legislative decisions be taken (procedural concept) or what content should they have (substantive concept). In the former case, a normative conception defines those conditions for law-making which should be met to grant a legitimate result, which further includes how this result should be justified. This is to say that even democratic law-making does not exhaust the (normative) legitimacy of statutes (see Habermas, 1989, p. 151). Legitimacy is a gradual magnitude and flows from various sources. The interplay of democratic elections, public opinion and parliamentary law-making grants a minimum of (normative) legitimacy which certainly may determine the citizens' factual acceptance of norms (legitimation). To better satisfy the normative claim to (normative) legitimacy they raise, however, statutes require an underlying rational justification, whereby it still must be determined under which conditions they can be said to be rationally justified.

Secondly, the separation between legislation and adjudication suggests that there is some sort of contradiction between rationality and democracy, as if the principle of democracy would entitle legislators to pass irrational statutes. Such a contradiction does not exist necessarily. Quite on the contrary, the principle of democracy may significantly constrain the irrationality of legislative decisions in various ways, for instance, as it allows public deliberations on them. In this view, the rationality of statutes might be discussed on the grounds that, although they have been duly enacted, legislative deliberations have not been surrounded "by such debates in civil society as the principle of democracy would require" (Tuori, 2002, p. 278). The argument that parliamentarians do not behave and argue rationally as they represent citizens who would not have any interest in it, is highly disputable.[4] Democracy cannot be reduced to the election of a representative body to take fundamental decisions affecting the whole community, but further implies that those who have been appointed are expected to give their electors a rational justification for their decisions. As Alexy (1995, p. 163) concludes, whoever is interested in rational justifiability and legitimacy, must be interested in democracy as well.

The claim that the lawmaker undergoes a duty to justify the norms he produces may be understood in a theoretical-normative sense. The aforesaid conceptions of legitimacy and democracy are examples of this. In addition, one can state that there exists a legal duty to justify legislative decisions. For these are not totally free, but conditioned by the legal order as a whole, in particular by the constitutional provisions and the principles expressed through them. The competence a legislative body possesses "to enact legal rules is never arbitrary, even if at first sight this authority remains within the limits of its competence and follows the required procedures scrupulously" (van Hoecke, 2002, p. 112). It cannot be denied that the constitution only imposes minimal rationality standards for legislative decision-making (see Karpen, 1989, p. 42), but these must be respected anyway. The principle of proportionality or, even more clearly, the ban of arbitrariness laid out in some constitutions show striking instances of this constitutional restriction to legislative irrationality.[5] In those legal systems where judicial review exists, the constitutional court has been entrusted to monitor the rationality (as a form of constitutionality) of laws.[6]

Irrationality has been deemed an inseparable feature of legislators, because of the fact that they, as opposed to judges, do not often behave according to rational criteria, but rather to private interests (lobbying) or even to maximize their own benefit. So to speak, we jurists are used to underrate legislation because of its *facticity* (see Prieto, 1987, pp. 16-22). Inversely, we are inclined to think that judges behave rationally in spite of the fact that many of them, e.g. in lower courts, do not actually fulfil the rationality requirements that have been set forth by the theories of legal argumentation. In one word, we seem to approach adjudication without having (much) regard to its *facticity*. An explanation for this paradox may be found in the lack of legal-theoretical models that can be used for the critical assessment of legislation. Whilst law-applying practices can be guided and evaluated through legal methodology and argumentation theories, law-making practices cannot. Lawyers have at their disposal a number of (normative) rational criteria to which they may resort when it comes to analyse judicial decisions. As these criteria can hardly apply to legislation, they tend to believe that legislation is not a matter of (legal) rationality.

Finally, the denial of legislative rationality could be misleading in the assessment of the rationality of judicial decisions. When judges apply statutes to concrete situations, their argumentation is mainly concerned with valid legal norms whose rationality is presupposed. Yet a norm may be not considered as rationally justified or its rationality may be contested. And what should judges do if a rational justification is lacking? As Atienza (1992, p. 285) observes, "legislative rationality is a necessary presupposition in order to speak of rationality in the application of law". In similar terms, Alexy (1989, p. 289) states that "the rationality of legal argumentation is, to the extent that it is determined by statute, relative to the rationality of legislation". The issue of legislative rationality (and legitimacy) becomes through this way a problem necessarily connected to any theory of legal argumentation, as statutes are an essential part of judicial and dogmatic argumentation practices. Alexy's (1989) theory of legal argumentation may serve as an example of the theoretical difficulties caused by this issue.

It is well-known that one of the conceptual pillars of Alexy's theory is the claim to correctness, which relates to the rational justifiability of utterances within the framework of a valid legal order. This claim is a defining element of any legal argumentation and sustains, in turn, the consideration of legal argumentation as a special case of moral practical discourse. Both the claim to correctness and the special case theses may be called into question whenever the norms applied by the judge (or interpreted by the dogmatist) cannot be considered to be rational (or just) norms. If the applied law is not rationally justifiable, its application cannot raise a claim to correctness. For whatever the judge opts to do, either to respect the valid legal order by applying an unjust or unreasonable law or not, one of the elements, the legal or the moral one, which simultaneously integrate the claim to correctness, shall be sacrificed. In either case, the special case thesis would be damaged.[7] In order to avoid this problem, as Alexy himself has suggested, the theory of legal argumentation must be embedded in the framework of a general theory of law, which comprises those institutionalized law-making procedures which realize as far as possible the ideal of discursive rationality.

Parliamentary Argumentation

The foregoing remarks nearly point to a truism, namely that the questions of (normative) legitimacy of law, democracy, rational legislation and legal argumentation are tightly intertwined and cannot be fruitfully dealt with by relying upon the complete detachment of legislation from legal theory. Thus in recent years an approach is sought that is able to bridge these gaps between legitimacy and rationality of law. The key-point is that legislative decisions are not only the main starting points for legal (judicial or dogmatic) argumentation, but they are also, in themselves, the result of certain argumentative processes. A good way of looking at this issue would be therefore to consider that these processes are a special modality of legal argumentation, which is expected to convey a rational justification for statutes. Rational argumentations can also be found in the field of *de-lege-ferenda* considerations, and "it is an important task of legal theory to study these argumentation structures" (Weinberger, 1984, p. 223). To do this, a theory of parliamentary or legislative argumentation must be developed. By extending the theory of legal argumentation, through the parliamentary argumentation, to the moment of legislation, we may gain insight as to the five problems presented above.

Parliamentary Argumentation

To the expression 'parliamentary argumentation' may be attributed multiple meanings. Etymologically, the word parliament means a place for talking or speaking, whereas this talking is carried out in many different environments and for many different purposes.[8] The legal-theoretical focus must be on those parliamentary debates that are devoted to the discussion (about the justification) of statutes, which are held both in plenary and commission sessions preceding the final enactment. In the following, I will not be concerned with the share these debates have in the totality of the parliamentary communications; neither with their relation to corridor argumentations, not nearly with private or internal party discussions. Due to these restrictions, this concept of legislative or parliamentary argumentation may be objected to be skin-deep. Argumentative guidelines in plenary and commission sessions are tightly bound to those private discussions, so that the real motives and contributions should better be sought there. For there is an abyss between what parliamentarians say and what they mean or think, as well as between what they really do and they pretend to do. Legislators often do "as if they would argue, but they argue and justify very little" (D'Auria *et al.*, 1997, p. 50). In a nutshell, parliamentary debates would seem to be intrinsically deceptive and would not constitute a proper justification for statutes.[9]

It is possible that this is too pessimistic a view of the role of legislative deliberation. Certainly some representatives enter the debate under the influence of predefined solutions or hunches and, before the public, they intend to give some kind of "reasons". Unfortunately, however, we have no access to the *real* decision process carried out in private, secretly or just internally within the party. Furthermore, that kind of retrospective justifying argumentation is usual in practical discourses and especially in legal ones. What is at issue now is the justification that parliamentarians put forward in public debate. We can often presume which hidden factors lay behind it, but we can hardly analyse them on the theoretical level. Neither the honesty nor the sincerity of parliamentarians is easy to measure. This can be done only by comparing their utterances to their behaviour, to put it in terms of speech act theory. Therefore we have to confine ourselves to the public side (or "context") of the justification of statutes. To this concern, publicity is of paramount significance. Even if parliamentarians have no real interest in correctness or rationality, they shall present their position, so that such an interest becomes visible (see Alexy, 1995, p. 152). In a Kantian sense, publicity renders a preventive or *ad cautelam* function which makes it possible to find out in the plenary and commission debates – where accessible or published – on which reasons do parliamentarians justify their decisions, as well as which conception of justification they defend before the public.

The Legal Character of Parliamentary Argumentation

That legislative discussions are a kind of legal argumentation might be disputed by challenging not only that they are argumentations at all, but also that they are of legal character. Beyond the objections faced in the preceding paragraph, I will take the first aspect for granted,[10] and discuss the second one.

Legal argumentations may be characterized by two features: they are, in essence, instances of *justificatory* reasoning *related to valid law*. Depending on how we conceive of this relation and whose argumentation we take into account, we arrive at broader or narrower conceptions of legal argumentation. In any event, one might state that the kernel of legal argumentation lays in the justification of legal-normative decisions or the interpretation of legal norms, which are the main activities carried out by legal officials (e.g. judges) and scholars. In this respect, legislative debates are also a modality of legal argumentation, that is, of justificatory reasoning related to law. For statutes are also legal-normative decisions whose justification involves contributions on the application and interpretation of valid legal norms.

In other words, the parliamentary argumentation holds a twofold relation to valid law which reveals its legal character: firstly, it conveys the justification for the enactment or amendment of a legal norm (a statute); and secondly, it comprises interpretative standpoints on legal norms (e.g. constitutional provisions). As for the *justification* of statutes, the parliamentary argumentation must be concerned with both their content and their formulation or drafting. In the framework of this justificatory argumentation, the parliamentarians often present *interpretative standpoints* on valid legal norms, which may be simple or constitutional norms (this shall depend on the subject under focus). In the latter case, one might even say that, up to a point, parliamentary argumentation aims to apply the constitution, as it occurs when statutes affecting fundamental rights are debated. Here, it is not only the presence of constitutional arguments, i.e. the nature of premises, that may give parliamentary argumentation a legal character, but also the method used for their assessment, that is, weighing or balancing. The resort to this argumentation technique can also be regarded as a typical legal feature.

Special Features

Understood as a part of the law-making process, as public justification of statutes, and as interpretation of legal and constitutional provisions, the parliamentary argumentation is a special modus of legal reasoning. Its special character derives from the environment in which it takes place: the institutional interface between law and politics (see D'Auria *et al.*, 1997, p. 13). We might agree that the overlap between the political and the legal sphere may be identified in many other moments of legal life, even that it belongs to the very concept of law. Yet the political significance and thus the complexity of parliamentary argumentations transcend that of judicial or dogmatic argumentation. Compared with less politicised legal contexts, the parliamentary argumentation shows many particular features as legal argumentation (see Atienza, 2003 and 1993, pp. 241ff.; La Spina, 1989, pp. 240ff.). In this respect, I would like to underline the distinction between *justification of contents and that of wording*, certain *institutional conditions* of the parliamentary argumentation and, finally, what might be termed the *open character of its justification possibilities*.

Content and wording Parliamentarians not only discuss the justification of the content of legislation, but also about the wording to convey the legislative message. Correspondingly, we may distinguish between an argumentation on justification and an argumentation on wording. This difference cannot be made in dogmatic or judicial argumentation. Judges or legal scholars do not normally argue on the way they write down their arguments: there is no specific concern for the wording of the judicial decision or the interpretative standpoint. The justification and its formulation are almost simultaneous.

Legislators, by contrast, debate both the reasons to regulate a given subject and the wording (the textual fashion) which that decision must be given. In the first place, it may come to debate the reasons for passing a legislative proposal. On this level, what must be rationally justified is the policy component of the statute, i.e. its goals or ends, as well as the appropriate (legal) means to attain them. Moral and ethical arguments are prevalent in this justification stage. They may be put forward in a purely moral and ethical, or in a legal fashion. In the latter case parliamentarians normally present constitutional or constitutionally-tinged arguments. Further arguments, such as economical or statistical ones, are not presented as independent, but integrated with moral, ethical or constitutional arguments.

Besides, the legislative argumentation is concerned with the drafting of policy decisions. Parliamentarians, of course, do not draft the text upon discussion – specialized civil servants or draftsmen are responsible for this. Anyhow, they discuss on it, mainly in commission sessions, and may often influence its wording. The successive versions of the drafted legal text become then a focus of political-legislative discussions, where contributions can be found not only for taking and justifying a policy decision (on goals and means), but also as to how to translate this decision into a legal text. This translation raises occasion to further debates on the adequacy of the drafted text to the political intent, as well as on those problems attached to the text as such (internal consistency, integration into the legal order, terminology an so on).[11] Here, the justification of goals and means may remain in the background. Parliamentarians point at the weaknesses of the drafted wording and stress those interpretation and application problems that it may provoke. They carry out a sort of hypothetical interpretation of the projected clauses, discuss the application of these clauses to real cases and criticize the results obtained thereof.

Collective justificatory process The parliamentary argumentation is an institutionalized collective undertaking in which many different participants and opinion-bearers partake by presenting arguments and counter-arguments. Within parliamentary debates, arguments are frequently put forward that are incompatible or even incommensurable with each other.[12] This makes it difficult to attribute the legislative argumentation to the parliament as such. This attribution problem does not exist in judicial or dogmatic argumentation. What should count as legislative argumentation justifying the (enactment of the) statute? This question might be solved by considering parliamentary argumentation as a resemblance of the argumentation taking place in collegiate judicial bodies or in judicial proceedings, where the parties present contradicting arguments. We might think, then, that the argumentation underlying the final decision is the most rational one (as if a hypothetical judge would have settled it). The final voting on the enactment would also decide on the justification of the statute. However, certain institutional constraints prevent us from accepting this idea. In this respect, the textbook examples are the party voting discipline and the responsibility of representatives to their electors.

The voting discipline has been explicated, in parliamentary political systems, because the stability of the government requires a homogeneous support by its parliamentary group. It might be added that the members of the same group must trust in each other to make parliamentary undertakings workable (Patzelt, 1998, p. 434). However, one is still inclined to believe that this discipline causes outstanding effects as to the "rationality" of final decisions. In many cases, the winning argumentation might not be the most rational one – but, there are outstanding exceptions, as this discipline may be suspended in certain cases, e.g. when moral or ethical questions are affected. Finally, let us not forget that the parliamentary argumentation renders a political-representative function. The attachment of the legislators to the citizens' will, i.e. the *representativeness* of parliamentary argumentation shows another form of institutional constraint. Two capital questions emerge at this point: Must parliamentarians argue on behalf of citizens? In that case, how far can this "representativeness" influence the yardsticks we use to assess the rationality of arguments? I return to this point below.

Justification spectrum As mentioned, the parliamentary argumentation pursues the justification and enactment of a (general) *legal norm*. Roughly speaking, this twofold function does not differ much from the overall function of post-legislative, application-oriented legal argumentation pursuing the enactment and justification of a (particular) *legal norm*. It is the nature of premises that makes the difference here. The premises of parliamentary argumentation are not only of legal nature, as may be typical for judges and scholars, *but also* of ethical, moral, political or economical character. It is true that a like-minded openness to extralegal arguments has gained ground in judicial and scholarly legal argumentation throughout recent decades. But, in the end, the legalist approach remains hegemonic, and even if extralegal factors are considered, then they are clearly subordinated to legal premises. What distinguishes parliamentary argumentation is that it is not constrained by existing legal or statutory norms, but rather by the order of constitutional values underlying the whole legal system.[13] As this limitation is not too restrictive, the parliamentary debate is made of arguments of different scope compared with the ones we find in the judicial or dogmatic argumentations. Its justification potential or "spectrum" is a more free and open one (Habermas, 1992, p. 191). To deal with this, some adaptations must be introduced in the theory of legal argumentation.

Rationality Patterns for Parliamentary Argumentation

Thus far, the theory of legal argumentation has set forth by what criteria the rationality of judicial decisions (and dogmatic interpretations) should be assessed. Yet as "legislators inhabit an argumentative system different from that of the judges" (Jackson, 1999, p. 14), the criteria of rationality to be applied to their argumentation may have not exactly the same scope as the ones used for interpretative and applicative discourses (Noll, 1973, p. 29). Put another way, when it comes to pass a statute, additional criteria, which have no room or are presupposed in the judicial argumentation, may play a leading role. In legislative debates, all the relevant questions attached to a drafted statute, such as its ethical and moral value, its implementation costs, its social consequences and effects, its legal-technical features, its consistent and coherent integration into the legal system and so on, may be posed. This range of issues falls beyond the current scope of the theory of legal argumentation. The obvious claim that these aspects amount to the justification of statutes implies the use of yardsticks for assessing the parliamentary argumentation different from those used for assessing the *legal-systemic* rationality. Certainly, any judicial argumentation *may* refer to more than one criterion of rationality (Wróblewski, 1990, p. 108), but legislation *must always* comply with several criteria. In order to analyse the rationality of parliamentary argumentation, a manifold combination of rationality patterns – or criteria of justifiability for statutes – must be defined. The theory of legislation provides guidance for this purpose.

Dimensions of Legislative Rationality

Some models of (rational) legislation have defined a pool of criteria that may serve to assess the strength of arguments and the complex rationality involved in the legislative debate.

According to Karpen (1989, pp. 41-42), for instance, the legitimacy of legislation points to three dimensions of rationality: (1) the formal rationality, based on a procedure which is acknowledged as legitimate (e.g. the procedure laid in democratic constitutions); (2) the material rationality, based on shared goals and values (e.g. human rights); and (3) the scientific knowledge, which would be a necessary requirement for legislation in complex societies and would help avoiding axiological conflicts. In addition, any attempt to rationalize legislation should cover both its political component and its social-integrative function, which demand a strong orientation to compromises.

Tuori (2002, pp. 134-37; 1989a, p. 142; 1989b, p. 221) has proposed a threefold notion of legal (and legislative) rationality, namely (1) a subject or object rationality, which is measured by the ability of legislation to fulfil its social functions, to achieve collective goals and to secure morally mediated social integration; (2) an internal rationality, related to the internal consistency and coherence of the legal order; and (3) a normative rationality or rational acceptability (legitimacy).

La Spina (1989, p. 179ff.) claims that legislative decisions are to combine several forms of rationality, including (1) the formal rationality, which is related to the systematic coherence and the certainty of the legal order; (2) the scope rationality, which concerns the end-means relation, the efficiency and the social consequences of legislative decisions; (3a) the material (utilitarian) rationality; (3b) the value rationality in a Weberian sense; and finally (4) the political rationality, which serves as meta-rationality articulating a reasonable combination of all the rationality levels (reasonableness) and warrants the maintenance of decisional structures within a given political system..

For his part, Atienza (1997, p. 27ff.; 1992, p. 277ff.; 1993, p. 197ff.) singles out five rationality levels in legislation: (1) a linguistic rationality, inasmuch as the law emitter must successfully transmit a message to the addressee; (2) a legal-formal rationality, as the law must fit into the existing legal system; (3) a pragmatic rationality, as the law must be complied with by its addressees; (4) a teleological rationality, because the law must achieve the ends it pursues; and finally (5) an ethical rationality, since legislation presupposes that both the content of the law and the values underlying it are ethically justifiable and thus legitimized.

The choice of one or another model of legislation in order to set forth a manifold criterion of rationality for parliamentary argumentation is a matter of theoretical strategy. Nevertheless, comparing the above models, it follows that the parliamentary law-making is expected to account for, and thus can be assessed by, three mayor criteria. The legal-systemic criterion concerns the procedural aspects of law-making itself, as well as certain features of the final results (statutes). More specifically, systemic rationality refers to the wording and terminology of statutes, their internal and external consistency and, to the highest degree possible, their coherent integration with the relevant legal branch and with the rest of the legal order. Secondly, legislation underlies an axiological dimension. In the justification of statutes, moral, ethical and constitutional principles play the key-role as normative arguments. Whenever these values do not come into consideration, they should be at least respected.[14] Thirdly, legislative rationality is accorded an outstanding political role. This role would defined, on the one side, by the purposive rationality, which is assessed on the basis of goals-means relation, and the considerations on the social efficacy and the economic efficiency of statutes; and, on the other, by a socially integrative element which implies the presence of compromises and political arrangements.

The Representativeness of Parliamentary Argumentation

In the legislative debates, arguments may be brought forward that do not fit into any of the "usual" rationality conceptions. This raises a major issue for the theory of parliamentary argumentation. Take the example of the religious arguments. In principle, the focus on rationality prevents, from content arguments and legitimacy, appeals that we regard as irrational inasmuch as they cannot be rationally justified. Must we consider religious invocations as irrational within law-making procedures? Should we exclude them from the parliamentary debates? To answer these questions we have to return to the representative value of parliamentary argumentation.

Parliamentary argumentation contributes to two major functions of the parliament: the legislation *and the political representation.* Parliamentarians taking part in the argumentation are representatives of citizens that have delegated their autonomy for the purpose of enacting laws. This renders legislative argumentation a representative discourse, which is also expected to reflect social normative conceptions. As mentioned, statutes are not only enacted, but also *justified on behalf of* the people. Therefore, the normative conceptions of citizens, albeit these cannot be always communicatively or rationally justified (e.g. religious invocations), must be given a place in the legislative argumentation. Of course, a law which entails people's ethical convictions (social morality) may be deemed irrational or unjust. Yet it cannot be regarded as wholly rational if it violates people's normative convictions. Such a law would be enacted in vain, as Horace warned. Here, the social morality may be understood in two senses, either as a social fact or as a justificatory motive.

In the first case, it is taken as one of the empirical factors determining people's behaviour and thus the effects of the law. Ross (1963, p. 359) has argued for this interpretation, conceding that the legislator "cannot shape evolution arbitrarily: his possibilities are limited (among others) by the legal consciousness prevailing in the community". In the second case, the content of social morality is resorted to as an argument *for the justification* of statutes. This interpretation matches better the representative character of parliamentary argumentation. Legislative debates must be taken as if the circle of participants would be broader than merely comprising parliamentarians. One must bear in mind that many representatives may have been elected because they incarnate certain values. To this concern, an extreme thesis would be that the legislator should execute his decisions solely according to the wishes and convictions of the society which elected him (see Perelman, 1967, pp. 68-71). In this view, legitimacy and rationality seem to follow, in the end, different paths. However, it is not necessary to defend a complete attachment of legislators to citizens' convictions: for a theory of parliamentary argumentation, it suffices to say that the parliament must be not only conceived as the guardian of practical reason, but also as the meeting-place for social convictions and experiences (see Habermas, 1992, pp. 193-194). If parliamentary argumentation is called to reflect social plurality, the possibility of strong forms of justification must be accepted. Otherwise, how could we justify the ban of religious arguments in a country whose population is deeply catholic?

Balancing

When it comes to assessing the rationality of parliamentary argumentation in the light of the theories of rational legislation, one may be confronted with two further problems: How to decide on mutually opposed argumentations, and how to rank the dimensions of rational justifiability? Since legislative rationality must be taken to comprise a set of rationality levels, one may speak of internal conflicts within one level of rationality and external conflicts between two (or more) levels of rationality.

Within the legislative debate, it is often the case that parliamentarians present contradictory interpretative standpoints on valid law; controversial arguments may be put forward as to the coherent integration of statutes into the legal order; diverging positions can be held as for the adequacy of the (legal) means chosen to attain given ends; finally, incompatible moral or ethical conceptions may be defended to justify the goals of legislation or to interpret constitutional principles. When conflicts arise within one level of rationality, they are to be solved by resorting to the other levels. If an argument is contested, say, on the legal-systemic level, it may be backed by arguments taken from the moral or ethical level. Likewise, if moral arguments are brought forward to justify the legislative goals, they can be responded, as frequently occurs, by political arguments on the scarcity of funding. This shows that, after reconstructing the pool of criteria for legislative rationality, the problem remains of defining their mutual relationships.

When handling a variety of criteria of rationality, different rationalities may easily conflict or collide with each other.[15] It may be quite difficult, even impossible, to fulfil the requirements of all of them at the same time (Atienza, 1992; p. 282; 1997, p. 56). As La Spina (1989, p. 180) remarks, legislative decisions are "medleys" (*amalgami*) of various forms of rationality, whereas the adequate proportions of each of these forms are still disputable. In case of collision, one criterion must be given priority. Yet, does moral rationality outweigh legal-systemic rationality? Are accurate wordings preferable, for the sake of accountability and legal certainty, to enhanced implementation chances offered by ambiguous wordings? To what extent should the citizens' strong convictions be respected against other forms of justification? It may be easily admitted that law "cannot any more be correctly understood within a paradigm of one-dimensional rationality" (van Hoecke, 2002, p. 10), yet one cannot undertake a fixed ranking of rationalities. Herein lies a big theoretical problem, since the "polytheism of partial rationalities" claiming at the same time universal validity as legitimacy sources (Teubner, 1996, p. 200), underlies modern society. This polytheism affects, in turn, the conceptions about the criteria of rationality that should prevail in both adjudication and legislation.

Theoretical models of legislation do emphasize such conflicts, but they do not offer univocal answers to the "problem of proportions". For Tuori (2002, p. 223), the object rationality seems to be the *factually* prevailing criterion for legislation, inasmuch as "the legislator generally adheres to the purposive-rational pattern of reasoning, where legislation is achieved as a means to achieve political ends". He remarks that "in certain stages of the law-making procedure the main concern is the internal rationality of the legal order", but in the end the "internal rationality is subjected to object rationality, to the purposive-rational perspective of the politicians and the bureaucrats" (Tuori, 2002, p. 136). Few will dispute this claim: the prevalence of political criteria is a matter of fact. Yet, could we define any theoretical yardstick to solve the "problem of proportions"? Atienza (1997, p. 93) holds that there would exist a transversal or cross-level dimension of rationality which he terms "efficiency". This dimension, which has no economic connotations, would be part of all the levels of rationality and would guide the consecutiveness of an optimal equilibrium between them. A like-minded search of optimal combinations of criteria lies behind La Spina's criterion of political rationality. These criteria of optimality, however, are often not detailed enough to surmount the fundamental problem, namely when can we consider that a given combination of criteria of rationality can, in itself, be regarded as rational. The rationality of parliamentary argumentation does not only depend on taking several forms of rationality into account, but rather on how these forms have been articulated. This question can be only posed in terms of balancing or weighing among rationalities (or levels of rationality).[16] In this regard, the quality of the balancing would ultimately determine the rationality of the parliamentary argumentation and, by this, the rationality of statutes.

A Discursive Theory of Parliamentary Argumentation?

In order to illustrate the difficulties in extending the theory of legal argumentation to legislation, I would like to refer to the discursive theory of legal argumentation, which applies the so-called communicative rationality as a yardstick for judicial and dogmatic rationality.

In the first place, it seems clear that the communicative rationality does not embrace all the relevant questions arising in the law-making process, for communicative rationality is a moral criterion, whilst legislation is not *only* concerned with moral or morally-laden problems. Nevertheless, the fact that legislative decisions do not only embrace moral questions does not say anything against the relative *priority* of the moral dimension in the justification of legislation, to put it in terms of balancing. Quite the opposite, the ultimate criterion of assessment for legislative rationality can be only a moral one.[17] And this opens the possibility to establish the communicative rationality as the overarching normative criterion governing legislation. To do this, however, it must be possible to combine it with other criteria. Can the normative appeal to consensus be non-exclusive? Can the discursive theory of legal argumentation be extended to comprise a variety of rationality levels?

Actually, the major objection against discourse theories is that they do not allow for non-communicative rationalities, which seem to be the leading drives in the law-making process. Within parliamentary debates, the communicative rationality is supposed to be constantly overridden by rationality approaches that prioritize economic efficiency and political interests over communicative actions. A discursive theory of parliamentary argumentation can be further criticized because its emphasis on consensus does not pay due attention to important features of the democratic world view, such as the right of diversity of ways of life, the right of criticism and dissenting opinions, and the cultural diversity (Weinberger, 1999, p. 351). These objections must be taken seriously. If the parliamentary argumentation is to be analysed in the light of ideal dialogical conditions, the communicative rationality must be so broadly conceived that it can coexist with non-communicative rationalities. Otherwise, as Habermas (1992, p. 196) points out, an immediate application of discursive ethics to the democratic process would lead to nonsense and would raise occasion for sceptics to undermine the very idea of a discursive theory of legislation.

The weight of ideal consensus in law-making must be "relativized" to the extent that it can be taken as an ensemble or frame parameter for legislative rationality integrating further non-communicative criteria. If we want a realistic model, a weakened version of communicative rationality proves unavoidable. This weakened version opens the legislative argumentation to strategic and instrumental arguments. Habermas (1989, p. 151ff.; 1992, p. 197ff.), for instance, has included strategic argumentations and bargaining processes in his theory of legislation. The strategic rationality is based on compromises among particular interests, and that is exactly one of the ancient functions of any legislation: compromises constitute the very core of politics. Furthermore, Habermas has integrated the instrumental rationality into his model, by making the difference between law as medium (system-related) and law as institution (life world-related): while the communicative rationality applies to life world's law, instrumental rationality proves sufficient for systemic law. Legislating often implies arguing and deciding which is the best way to achieve a given goal. Unlike the problem of setting that goal, this one is a matter of instrumental-teleological rationality, which deals with determining the degree of suitability of a means to achieve a given end. It follows that, even if one accepts the priority of the communicative rationality, it cannot be regarded as the only relevant rationality pattern for parliamentary argumentation. As Alexy (1999, p. 377) states, the suitability of means for attaining certain goals, the balancing of interests and compromises and the collective self-understanding of a given community, as is embodied in traditions and strong evaluations, are *legitimate* reasons in democratic decision-making.[18] But, provided that these reasons may hinder the reaching of consensus, should we not consider that the political side of parliamentary argumentation puts the communicative rationality at stake?

The condition under which a discursive theory of parliamentary argumentation can accept the weakening of communicative rationality is that democratic procedures must be supposed to grant an approximate resemblance of the ideal communicative situation and channel socially-born communicative forces into positive law. This prevents unfair compromises and implies the communicative justification of the legislative projects on fundamental constitutional matters. The law-making procedures would assure this way, so to speak, an indirect discursive legitimacy. This presupposes, in turn, two further conditions whose (actual) fulfilment is at least debatable. On the one hand, representative discourses must remain open and sensitive "to those communicative flows of autonomous public spheres where the formation of beliefs, issues and arguments is not yet integrated into the institutionalised decision making-process" (Habermas, 1989, p. 154). In this respect, a genetic analysis of arguments would be needed to find out whether social arguments and contributions are properly *transported into* the parliamentary debate. Law-making practices can ultimately legitimize only "if they include as an integral element debates on legislative projects within civil society, debates that to a sufficient degree match the freedom, equality and rationality of an ideal discourse" (Tuori, 2002, p. 279). But, do such debates take place really? Does every citizen have the equal opportunities to exert influence on the arguments discussed in legislative debates? On the other hand, it should be discussed how, and to which extent, the parliamentary argumentations are *exported to* the public sphere. Do people really know the arguments parliamentarians bring forward to justify forthcoming statutes? Is parliamentary argumentation accessible or understandable from the citizen's standpoint? Is it properly covered by the mass media? One might suppose that a negative answer to these questions could cast doubts on the (communicative) rationality of parliamentary argumentation, if it is conceived in descriptive terms. My concluding remarks are devoted to this point.

Rationality of Parliamentary Argumentation and Publicity of Law

If one accords the parliamentary argumentation a representative function, one must be ready to admit that the attachment of the representatives to their electors plays a role as a justificatory criterion for parliamentary decisions. This thesis will be reproached that the representativeness of parliamentary debates, rather than being a kind of rational criterion, in fact reduces the scope for legislative rationality. However, such an objection leads to a paradox: is the very condition for democratic legitimacy a threat for legislative rationality or a part of it? The rational-communicative theory of legislation may have solved this problem. As we have seen, it accepts the significance of non-communicative rationalities (instrumental rationality and fair compromises based on strategic rationality) and strong ethical values because legislative deliberations are surrounded by deliberations in the public spheres (whereby "surrounded" could be replaced by "influenced"). All this presupposes that citizens deliberate rationally on legislative projects. But, to what extent can citizens deliberate rationally about legislative undertakings if those deliberations held in the parliament are not communicated to the public? As it concerns the rationality of parliamentary argumentation, whether the public constitutes a threatening or an enhancing factor depends, ultimately, on the information released about the parliamentary argumentation itself.

It is often overlooked that there exists a close relation between publicity of law and rational legislation, between public communication and rationality of parliamentary argumentation. The people themselves being the ultimate legislators, both the law-making process and the final content of laws should be accessible, transparent and rationally controllable to everybody (Noll, 1973, p. 15; see Habermas, 1992, pp. 225-226). Yet, how much legislative information do citizens receive? It has been reported that there is in the public sphere much more information on legislative results than on related argumentations (see Kißler, 1984, p. 89ff.). Legal norms are published and advertised as a product taking the form of a legal text, i.e. as the definite result of legislative procedures, but the process of law-making on its own attracts no publicity. As Patzelt (1998, p. 438) puts it, the way in which the parliamentary work progresses is seldom the object of media coverage, which is almost exclusively concerned with plenary discussions. This makes it difficult to enable the citizens to know how and to what extent they are actually represented in the parliament. In a sense, they are kept informed about how the things ought to be, whereas there is not much room left for justification. Furthermore, one can hardly be content with the way in which the reasons for law-making are released to the public (which, by the way, bears the blame of being irrational). Without the benefit of either the text of legislation or that of the legislative debates, the public obtains information on the legislative undertakings only through the mass media, where the parliamentary discussions "are seen in terms of the conflict between political parties" (Jackson, 1999, p. 26). All in all, the publicity of legislation still operates demonstratively (see Habermas, 1990, pp. 337-338). This is insufficient to satisfy the communicative duties of representative (legislative) argumentations. It is not enough to grant access to the normative results, but furthermore it is necessary that people are able to know on which grounds those results are based.

Compared to legal promulgation, which remains a publicity of results, the publicity of parliamentary argumentation is a publicity of reasons. Hence it operates as a means of *participative publicity*. Leaning on the Habermasian category of critical publicity, Kißler (1984, p. 61) termed the participative publicity as the one not only informing about the results of decision processes of legislation and application, but also making public how those results come into existence and which arguments have been considered for the purpose of justification, so that citizens are enabled to subsequently participate in the decision review (see Habermas, 1990, p. 274ff.). Such publicity is the ideal form of parliamentary law-making, as it addresses the public before the end of the legal decision processes, enabling citizens to know and understand the reasons their representatives present to justify statutes.

If participative publicity counts towards the conditions that the parliamentary argumentation is normatively expected to fulfil, it might be set forth as an "external" criterion of communicative rationality. This criterion conjugates the representative function of parliamentary argumentation with the legitimatizing value of publicity. In this concern, my last thesis would be that legitimacy of statutes does not only depend on the democratic process, but also, cumulatively, on both the rationality and the public communication of their justifying arguments. In other words, that parliamentary argumentation, which is able to articulate rationally a complex cluster of rationalities, and which remains open and transparent to the public, provides for a twofold source of legitimacy of law.

* Department of Penal Law, Legal Philosophy and Legal History, University of Zaragoza, Spain. I wish to thank Professors Jan Sieckmann, Laura Clérico and Michael Becker for critical comments on early drafts of this paper.

Notes

1 *Pantagruel*, Chapter XXXIX

2 "Bei den Abgeordneten die Fähigkeit zu vermuten, Rechtsvorschriften zu entwerfen oder juristisch zu verbessern, ist eine wirklichkeitsfremde, aber auch demokratiefremde Vorstellung (…). Die Abgeordneten sind nicht als Sachverständige für irgendein Fachgebiet ausgesucht und gewählt worden, sondern als politische Willensträger" (Schneider, 1991, p. 89).

3 The concept of legitimacy is not easy to grasp, as it is used in both descriptive and normative terms. On the difference between legitimacy and legitimation or between the normative and empirical notions of legitimacy, see Garzón Valdés (1993, pp. 506, 516 and 842) and Tuori (2002, pp. 244-247).

4 "Ein möglichst hoher Grad an Rationalität des Rechts (...) steht nicht nur nicht in einem Gegensatz zur Demokratie, sondern ist wohl sogar Teil der Legitimation von Demokratie: (...) wir wählen nicht ein Parlament, um schlechtere, sondern um bessere Gesetze zu erhalten" (Öhlinger, 1982, p. 1).

5 The Article 9 of the Spanish Constitution provides for a ban on the arbitrariness of the public powers (see also Article 9 of the Constitution of the Swiss Federation). This article may be interpreted to obligate legislators to give reasons capable of justifying their decisions. However, the Spanish constitutional court seems to be extremely cautious as far as it concerns legislative arbitrariness, whereas its attitude changes radically when assessing the arbitrariness of administration (see Fernández, 1998, pp. 28-29 and 160). Such a different treatment of arbitrariness resembles the divorce between irrational politics and legal rationality that the legal community normally experiences.

6 Further forms of control can also be found in constitutional states. For instance, in some countries there exists an internal (parliamentary) control of the rationality (constitutionality) of legislation carried out by the constitutional law committee (see Article 74 of the Finnish Constitution).

7 Alexy (1999, pp. 381-382) replies by making two distinctions. On the one hand, the claim to correctness would comprise two different aspects: the correct application of the law and the assumption that the law on which the judicial decision bases is just and reasonable. "A judicial decision which correctly applies and unjust or unreasonable statute does not fulfil the claim to correctness raised by it in all respects". On the other, he resorts to the distinction between raising a claim and its compliance: "the special case thesis needs only claims and not their compliance".

8 Patzelt (1998, pp. 437-38) distinguishes three types of parliamentary communication: "specialised or working communication" (*Arbeitskommunikation*), "strategic communication" pursuing the imposition of own opinions through persuasion (*Durchsetzungskommunikation*) and "presentational communication", which intends to enhance the attractiveness of own positions and to awake the public's favour (*Darstellungskommunikation*).

9 Jackson (1999, pp. 25-26) wonders "whether the speeches made in parliament are good evidence of the reasons for the legislation, as opposed to the reasons for the act of legislating. In political terms, the latter is often more important than the former. (…) We, the legislators, are responding to public concern; we are doing something; we are passionate in the cause. (…) The reasons for speaking in a parliamentary debate may not be the same as the reasons the draftsman had for proposing specific enactments".

10 According to Atienza (2003), we may speak of legal reasoning "in relation to both a parliament debate over a statute and a motivation of a judicial decision because they share a number of features; in both cases there is an activity (…) which has language as its vehicle; they both result from a problem to which resolution legal reasoning contributes; they have basic units – arguments – which have premises and conclusions (…), and they may be evaluated according to some criteria for classifying arguments (and argumentation) as valid, persuasive, fallacious, etc." This comparison supports that parliamentary debates are *argumentations*, rather than *argumentations of legal kind.*

11 As Jackson (1999, p. 12) remarks, "the bulk of legislative language does not originate from the legislators themselves. In the case of complicated legislation, it is a polite fiction to say that the legislators themselves understand it; indeed, in many cases they may not even have read it. That does not, however, prevent them from talking about it".

12 Due to the organizational constraints (e.g. limited time), arguments must be frequently presented in an incomplete way. Therefore, instead of attributing contributions to single parliamentarians, we have to construct them as argumentative connections, grouping all those arguments which are mutually compatible, that is, "which can be defended simultaneously by a rational actor" (Sieckmann, 2005).

13 Kelsen (1967, paragraph 46) claimed that the difference between legislation and adjudication is not a qualitative, but a quantitative one: the legislator is subject to fewer

limitations than judges are. In the same view, Ross (1963, paragraph 29) argued that, apart from the limits posed by the wordings of statutes to the freedom of judges, there is no fundamental difference between the legal-political argumentation *de lege ferenda* and *de sententia ferenda.*

14 It remains to be clarified which position is assigned to the constitution in the above models (legal, moral or ethical).

15 "In caso di conflitto, I portatori degli argomenti di ciascuna *r* [standing for rationality] tenderanno a violare i valori ispiratori delle altre" (La Spina, 1989, p. 221).

16 This raises some questions which must be left aside here, e.g. whether a balance between different criteria of rationality is possible at all (see Ross, 1963, paragraphs 86-87), or whether the legislative weighing which may be carried out to justify the goals and means of legislation (or even its wording) is comparable to the judicial balancing (see Sieckmann, 2005).

17 As Nino (1994, pp. 79-80) remarks, non-moral discourses can provide justification for decision only in two situations: either in the free room left by moral discourses or whenever a principle applies which may be put forward on the moral level to justify those non-moral discourses. See also Habermas (1990, p. 40).

18 "In der legislativen Politik sind Informationszufuhr und zweckrationale Mittelwahl mit Interessenausgleich und Kompromißbildung, ethischer Selbstverständlichkeiten und Präferenzbildung, moralischer Begründung und rechtlicher Kohärenzprüfung verflochten" (Habermas, 1992, p. 345)

References

Alexy, R. (1989), *A Theory of Legal Argumentation*, Clarendon Press, Oxford.

Alexy, R. (1995), *Recht, Vernunft, Diskurs. Studien zur Rechtsphilosophie,* Suhrkamp, Frankfurt.

Alexy, R. (1999), 'The special Case Thesis', *Ratio Juris*, Vol. 12, pp. 374-384.

Atienza, M. (1992), 'Practical Reason and Legislation', *Ratio Iuris*, Vol. 5 pp. 269-287.

Atienza, M. (1993), *Tras la justicia. Una introducción al Derecho y al razonamiento jurídico*, Ariel, Barcelona.

Atienza, M. (1997), *Contribución a una teoría de la legislación*, Civitas, Madrid.

Atienza, M. (2003), 'Argumentation and Legislation', paper presented at the IVR 21st World Congress, Lund.

D'Auria, A. *et al.* (1997), *Las razones de nuestros representantes*, Eudeba, Buenos Aires.

Elster, J. (1989), *Solomonic Judgements. Studies in the Limitations of Rationality,* Cambridge University Press, Cambridge.

Fernandez, T.R. (1998), *La arbitrariedad del legislador*, Civitas, Madrid.

Garzón Valdés, E. (1993), *Derecho, Ética, Política*, Centro de Estudios Constitucionales, Madrid.

Habermas, J. (1989), 'Towards a Communication-Concept of Rational Collective Will-Formation. A Thought-Experiment', *Ratio Iuris*, Vol. 2, pp. 244-254.

Habermas, J. (1990), *Strukturwandel der Öffentlichkeit*, Suhrkamp, Frankfurt.

Habermas, J. (1992), *Faktizität und Geltung: Beiträge zur Diskurstheorie des Rechts und des demokratischen Rechtsstaats,* Suhrkamp, Frankfurt.

Jackson, B.S. (1999), 'Legislation in the Semiotics of Law' in H. van Schooten (ed.), *Semiotics and Legislation. Jurisprudential, Institutional and Sociological Perspectives*, Deborah Charles, Liverpool.

Karpen, U. (1989), *Gesetzgebungs-, Verwaltungs-, und Rechtsprechungslehre. Beiträge zur Entwicklung einer Regelungstheorie*, Nomos Verlag, Baden-Baden.
Kelsen, H. (1967), *Pure Theory of Law*, University of California Press, Berkeley.
Kißler, L. (1984), *Rechtssoziologie für die Rechtspraxis*, Luchterland, Neuwied.
La Spina, A. (1989), *La decisione legislativa. Lineamenti di una teoria*, Giuffrè Editore, Milan.
Luhmann, N. (1975), *Legitimation durch Verfahren*, Luchterland, Neuwied.
Nino, C.S. (1994), *Derecho, moral y política*, Ariel, Barcelona.
Noll, P. (1973), *Gesetzgebungslehre*, Rowohlt, Reinbeck bei Hamburg.
Öhlinger, Th. (1982), 'Planung der Gesetzgebung und Wissenschaft' in Th. Öhlinger (ed.), *Methodik der Gesetzgebung*, Springer, New York/Vienna.
Patzelt, W. (1998), 'Parlamentskommunikation' in O. Jarren, U. Sarcinelli and U. Saxer (eds.), *Politische Kommunikation in der demokratischen Gesellschaft. Ein Handbuch*, Westdt. Verlag, Opladen.
Perelman, Ch. (1967), *Justice*, Random House, New York.
Prieto Sanchís, L. (1987), *Ideología e interpretación jurídica*, Tecnos, Madrid.
Ross, A. (1963), *Sobre el derecho y la justicia*, Buenos Aires, Eudeba.
Schneider, H. (1991), *Gesetzgebung*, 2nd ed., C.F. Müller, Heidelberg.
Sieckmann, J.R. (2005), 'Argumentation im Parlament: Die Debatten über das Stammzellgesetz', in J.R. Sieckmann (ed.), *Verfassung und Argumentation*, Nomos Verlag, Baden-Baden (in press).
Teubner, G. (1996), '*Altera pars audiatur*: Das Recht in der Kollision anderer Universalitätsansprüche', *ARSP*-Beiheft 65, pp. 199-220.
Tuori, K. (1989a), 'Discourse Ethics and the Legitimacy of Law', *Ratio Juris*, Vol. 2, pp. 125-144.
Tuori, K. (1989b), 'Legitimität des modernen Rechts', *Rechtstheorie*, Vol. 20, pp. 221-243.
Tuori, K. (2002), *Critical Legal Positivism*, Ashgate, Aldershot.
Van Hoecke, M. (2002), *Law as Communication*, Hart Publishing, Oxford.
Weber, M. (1978), *Economy and Society*, University of California Press, Berkeley.
Weinberger, O. (1984), 'Gesetzgebung und Demokratie' in H. Schäffer and O. Triffterer (eds.), *Rationalisierung der Gesetzgebung. Jurgen Rödig Gedächtnissymposion*, Nomos/Manz, Baden-Baden/Vienna.
Weinberger, O. (1999), 'Legal Validity, Acceptance of Law, Legitimacy. Some Critical Remarks and Constructive Proposals', *Ratio Iuris*, Vol. 12, pp. 329-335.
Wróblewski, J. (1990), 'Principles, Values, and Rules in Legal Decision-Making and the Dimensions of Legal Rationality', *Ratio Juris*, Vol. 3, pp. 100-117.

Chapter 12

The Sources of Legitimacy of Political Decisions: Between Procedure and Substance

José Luis Martí Mármol*

One of the most important and oldest controversies in political philosophy has to do with defining and determining the sources of political legitimacy, a problem which has important implications for jurisprudence, our understanding of the law, and the actual design of political institutions. An adequate account of political legitimacy should be concerned with a theory of justification of political decisions. That is, we state that a political decision is legitimate, I assume, when we regard it as justified. Accordingly, such controversy is also concerned with the theory of legislation to the extent that legislation is one of the results of such political decisions and that the theory of legislation should be committed to some view of the justification of law.[1] The issue of political legitimacy has traditionally been associated with other highly contested problems in the realm of political philosophy, such as the concept of political authority, the role of morality in political decisions, the practicality of such decisions, the place for (and the role of) reason in political judgements, the limits and the very conception of democracy, the status of human or basic rights, and so on. All this complexity makes it very difficult to deal with and it is not my intention to address all these issues in this paper. Instead, my aim is rather to focus on the legitimacy of political decisions in the light of the tensions between the ideals of democracy (i.e. popular sovereignty or self-government) and basic rights (i.e. constitutionalism or human rights). This is only one of the perspectives implied by this multidimensional problem,[2] but it is, from my point of view, very fertile to apprehend the whole discussion and, at least, the most disputed matter in the last few years.[3]

Even such a concrete perspective of the problem calls for various nuances, and I do not seek to analyse all of them here. My particular aim is to connect this perspective of the problem with the pervasive tension between two patterns of justification of collective decisions: the so-called proceduralism and substantivism. I will start by presenting the principal face of the problem of political legitimacy as a tension between democratic and liberal ideals. I will relate them to proceduralism and substantivism and try to show why a combination of both is required. I will briefly examine some arguments for and against each of the two patterns of justification, and argue for the superiority of the procedural view, further proposing a conciliatory argument based on the distinction between moral and political legitimacy. And I will conclude by defending the idea that a democratic deliberative process is the most adequate source of legitimacy of political decisions, particularly in dealing with procedure and substance.

The Problem

Before presenting the theoretical face of the problem, let me present a hypothetical case that can enlighten our analysis: the five-shipwrecked-people-society. Suppose that five people have landed on a little, desert island after a shipwreck. They soon realize a couple of things: 1) the island has scarce resources; and 2) they must coordinate their actions if they want to survive – that is, they need some degree of social cooperation. This fact does not exclude the possibility of free-riding for some of them, but society cannot work without a minimal degree of cooperation. Furthermore, because of the island's size, their behaviour is necessarily interdependent. This means that most of the individual acts affect the choices, aspirations and prospects of the others. Now, they have to organize their life together: to establish the basic rules of their mini-society. They have to distribute some rights and duties (the division of labour, build a shelter, get food, protect themselves against wild animals, and so on, the distribution of resources, and the distribution of free time). All these issues are collective struggles and have to be collectively decided. And, despite the small number of members of this society, there is unlikely to be unanimity on all these issues. Of course, the first thing to do is to agree on a decision-making procedure, in order to make the other decisions.

We can identify several essential features of our societies in this hypothetical case, all of them being relevant for politics: (a) the scarcity of resources and the emergence of social conflict – to the extent that all of the five shipwrecked have partially different interests at stake; (b) a shared interest in survival; (c) the fact of political pluralism: that is, the fact that they also support different views about the best collective decision to be made;[4] (d) the interdependence of acts; and (e) the impossibility of leaving: that is, the fact that they have to live together by necessity, since they cannot abandon the island. Attending to these five essential features, we realize that they need collective (political) decisions to coordinate their actions, precisely because of all these essential features. These are necessary, and conjunctively sufficient, conditions of political decision-making. Even social disagreement (or the fact of political pluralism) is not incompatible with politics, but its primary necessary condition.[5] On the other hand, implicit in the combination of (a), (b), and (c), is the assumption that political decisions must favour the public good (or public interest). Since a political decision is a collective response to a social conflict or struggle, this response should be made from a "public good" point of view to be legitimate.[6] "What counts as public good" and "how can we know the content of such public good" are respectively the ontological and epistemic questions at stake in the legitimacy problem, to which I will return later.

Three different questions related to the legitimacy of political decisions have been distinguished. Thus, we could say that we have to answer at least these three fundamental (and different, though interrelated) questions: 1) Who has to decide? (*the authority question*); 2) How has this authority to decide? (*the procedural question*); and 3) What has this authority to decide? (*the substantive question*). The substantive question is indeed ambiguous. It could be asking about which matters the authority can decide (and, then, which matters should be excluded from authoritative decision) or about what the concrete contents of decisions should be. All three questions are certainly relevant in developing a complete theory of political legitimacy, but this does not mean that we need a full theory of authority, a full theory of political procedures and a full theory of substantive correctness, to deal successfully with the legitimacy problem. Many theories of political legitimacy offer a complete answer for one of these questions and presume the answer to the other. Furthermore, giving a particular answer to one of these questions often implies an answer to the other two.

Anyway, for the sake of the argument, we can leave aside the "authority question". I will assume the popular sovereignty principle and, hence, a democratic conception of authority, since both constitutional liberalism and democracy share roughly this same line of argument. The only political authority is, then, the people itself. To quote the words of Joshua Cohen, "the fundamental idea of democratic legitimacy is that the authorization to exercise state power must arise from the collective decisions of the members of a society who are governed by that power" (Cohen, 1997, p. 407). This does not preclude the possibility of defending a theory that limits the popular sovereignty principle. Indeed, I will refer later to such theories as the substantive ones. But if we enter into such a discussion we are moving from the "authority" question to the other two. To assume a democratic conception of authority only implies believing that there is no other authority than the people itself. And it says nothing about whether this authority should be restricted for substantive reasons or not. I stress that this is another question. On the other hand, I am not assuming a particular conception of authority committed to a particular conception of the practicality of rules or political decisions.[7]

Let me turn to the hypothetical case to explain the core of the legitimacy problem. Our five shipwrecked are aware that they have to live together and that they have different interests (conditions (a), (b) and (e)). Suppose they meet on the first day in order to take some basic decisions about their coexistence. When they begin to talk about the distribution of costs and benefits, they verify their disagreement about basic criteria for such distribution. It is not only that they have individual interests at stake (for instance, that each one of them wants to take all the benefits and be free of costs), but also that they support different basic criteria for such a distribution from a common-interest perspective (condition (c)). Now, suppose first that all five of the shipwrecked agree that they need a particular procedure to take decisions and consider they are the only relevant authority to decide within the household. They also think that the more impartial procedure is the democratic one, including majority vote.[8] They have more or less answered the *procedural question*, and this answer sounds very sensible at first sight.

They are now ready to vote about all the distribution issues that should be decided. Suppose, now, that three of the shipwrecked form an alliance against the other two, and they systematically vote to take all the benefits and leave the costs to the minority. So, imagine that the two shipwrecked in the minority are (democratically) obliged to carry out all the duties and burdens; they are even obliged, for instance, to think and express themselves in a particular way, and to believe in God. How could they react? The minority could claim two things. First, "there are things that should not be collectively decided, since they belong to the private sphere. Ideas, expressions and religious beliefs must be freely chosen by everyone, not by the majority". And second, "even with respect to those things that can be collectively decided, the majority cannot tyrannically impose its will over the minority. Thus, it is unfair (it is not legitimate) to oblige us to do all the work." They are arguing in response to the *substantive question* of legitimacy, in its two senses mentioned above, and to do so, they can argue that they have rights that have been violated by the decisions taken before.[9] And, again, this response sounds very sensible at first sight.

The problem, of course, is that these sensible responses to the procedural and substantive questions lead us to contradictory results. The example stresses, then, the core of the legitimacy problem of collective decisions: the dilemma between democratic proceduralism and substantivism. In contemporary liberal democracies, this general problem of legitimacy is instantiated by the tensions between popular sovereignty and liberal rights. Habermas remarks:

> [t]he two sources of legitimation also compete with each other in the history of political philosophy. Liberalism and civic republicanism disagree on whether the "liberty of the moderns" or the "liberty of the ancients" should enjoy priority in the order of justification... If the normative justification of constitutional democracy is to be consistent, then it seems one must rank the two principles, human rights and popular sovereignty. To be legitimate, laws, including basic rights, must either agree with human rights (however this in turn are legitimated) or issue from democratic will-formation. On the first alternative, the democratic lawgiver may decide in a sovereign manner only within the boundaries of human rights; on the second alternative, the democratic lawgiver can set up any constitution it wants, and, as the case may be, violate its own basic law, thus impairing the idea of the constitutional state. (Habermas, 2001, pp. 766 and 767)[10]

From my point of view, the conflict between popular sovereignty and liberal rights is a particular case of a more generic dilemma between proceduralism and substantivism. We have two ideals in conflict, both of them sensible and right at first sight. And, therefore, in facing the problem, three possibilities are open:

1. We can be aware of the dilemma, and favour proceduralism rather than substantivism.
2. We can be aware of the dilemma, and favour substantivism rather than proceduralism.
3. We can deny the existence of the dilemma, reinterpreting both ideals to make them equally compatible.[11]

Proceduralism versus Substantivism

As mentioned above, while proceduralism can be seen as addressing the question of "how the authority has to decide", substantivism can be seen as addressing the question of "what has the authority to decide", in its two-folded way. But they are not logically independent questions. If they were, there would be no dilemma at all: we would have a response to the procedural question (for instance, popular sovereignty) and another to the substantive question (based on liberal rights, or on a thicker theory of justice). But as the "shipwreck people's case" shows, if we implement both ideals into practice, it could raise conflicts between them. That is the reason why we need a second-order approach (a second-order question) to integrate both questions and to find one non-conflictive theory capable of answering it. From my point of view, this second-order question is the core of the legitimacy problem.

Indeed, the relationship between procedure and substance can be seen as one of the most striking issues in political philosophy. And, although this issue is underlying most contemporary political theories, the latter has not paid enough attention to it in order to clarify at least its problematic faces. Some authors have identified the relevance of such a relationship between procedure and substance for the legitimacy question, particularly in the light of political pluralism (Rawls, 1971, pp. 3-117, and Rawls, 1993, pp. 11-22; Gutmann and Thompson, 1996, pp. 26-39; Manin, 1987; Cohen, 1989; Cohen, 1997). But they often fail to be aware of the dilemmatic structure or their arguments miss the practical point, hiding it under very complex considerations on the interrelated issues mentioned above. My analysis pretends to cast some light onto what I consider to be the core of the problem, simplifying the scope, and ignoring some of the important matters involved, in order to make available some clear standpoint.

In facing this second-order question, we can distinguish between two radical conceptions placed in the extreme positions of an ideal line. On the one hand (suppose the right side), we have "radical proceduralism", holding that the legitimacy of political decisions depends purely on the procedure by which they have been made, since we have no independent substantive standards of rightness to be applied. "Radical substantivism", on the other (suppose the left side), claims precisely the opposite. That is, as we have independent substantive standards of rightness (and we know them), a political decision is legitimate if and only if it meets such standards, the procedure of decision-making being irrelevant. Both extreme positions face difficulties, as I will try to argue. But, of course, there are a lot of intermediate positions. All the intermediate positions placed short of the right extreme are occupied by conceptions that favour proceduralism rather than substantivism (I will call them "soft proceduralism"). All the intermediate positions placed short of the left extreme are occupied by conceptions that favour substantivism rather than proceduralism (I will call them "soft substantivism"). Favouring substance or procedure rather than the other, means that we privilege one of these ideals in legitimating political decisions, accepting the necessary (and/or desirable) presence of the other ideal too. Finally, the position exactly in the middle is occupied by the conception that believes in the co-originality of basic rights and democracy. This position denies the existence of the dilemma and corresponds to position 3 mentioned above (I will call this position "the co-originality conception").[12]

The co-originality conception is often defended through the idea of constitutional democracy. As Habermas has put it:

> [T]hese alternatives [to give priority to human rights or to give it to popular sovereignty] contradict a strong intuition. The idea of human rights that is spelled out on in basic rights may neither be imposed on the sovereign lawgiver as a limitation nor be merely instrumentalized as a functional requisite for legislative purposes. In a certain way, we consider both principles as equally original. One is not possible without the other, but neither sets limits sets limits on the other. The intuition of "co-originality" can also be expressed thus: private and public autonomy require each other. The two concepts are interdependent; they are related to each other by material implication. (Habermas, 2001, p. 767)[13]

The core idea in Habermas' position is that both basic (or human) rights and popular sovereignty, both private and public autonomy, are mutually dependent. The protection of basic rights is a necessary condition for achieving the goal of popular sovereignty, and the exercising of political rights in a democratic system is a necessary condition for the exercising of basic rights:

> Practical reason is realized in the form of private autonomy no less than it is in that of political autonomy. That is, both are as much means for the other as they are ends in themselves. The demand to orient oneself to the common good, which is connected with political autonomy, is also a rational expectation insofar as only the democratic process guarantees that private individuals will achieve an equal enjoyment of their equal individual liberties. Conversely, only when the private autonomy of individuals is secure are citizens in a position to make correct use of their political autonomy. The interdependence of constitutionalism and democracy comes to light in this complementary relationship between private and civic autonomy: each side is fed by resources it has from the other. (Habermas, 2001, pp. 779 and 780)

Ronald Dworkin shares a similar point of view, though in my opinion his view is closely anchored to the left side of the legitimacy line mentioned above.[14] Dworkin's account of constitutional democracy stresses the point that rights, by definition, constrain democracy. Thus, constitutional democracy rejects what he calls the "majoritarian premise" (that is, a radical proceduralist defence of popular sovereignty that rests on majority rule):

> [Constitutional democracy] denies that it is a defining goal of democracy that collective decisions always or normally be those that a majority or plurality of citizens would favor it fully informed and rational. It takes the defining aim of democracy to be a different one: that collective decisions be made by political institutions whose structure, composition, and practices treat all members of the community, as individuals, with equal concern and respect... Democracy means government subject to conditions – we might call these "democratic" conditions - of equal status for all citizens. When majoritarian institutions provide and respect the democratic conditions, then the verdicts

of these institutions should be accepted by everyone for that reason. (Dworkin, 1997, p. 17)

Both Habermas and Dworkin affirm that, if properly understood, constitutional democracy avoids the tensions between rights and popular sovereignty (between constitutionalism and democracy), because they are co-original or conceptually interrelated. From my point of view, however, this is a misguided solution. If we define democracy to contain rights, and we include political participation and public autonomy within the bill of rights, then it is a truism that there are no tensions between democracy and rights. Any democratic decision that does not respect basic rights will not be considered to be a real exercise of popular sovereignty, but an abuse of it. And if the constitution that enacts basic rights does not include democratic procedures to make political decisions, then it should be considered an illegitimate one. But the tensions, as I will try to show later, remain.

However, there is a good argument for rejecting radical proceduralism implicit in the accounts of Habermas and Dworkin. Suppose, under this extreme position, that we adopt a particular procedure to make collective decisions: majority rule. We are not adopting such a procedure for arbitrary reasons or motivations. Our five shipwrecked do not decide to adopt such a democratic procedure accidentally. They have reasons (probably good reasons) for adopting it. We favour democracy, rather than any other procedure (like tossing a coin, or dictatorial decision-making), because we believe that democracy is the best procedure in the light of other values we previously hold (like individual autonomy, human dignity, equality of concern and respect, impartiality, and so on). We cannot be completely sure about its worthiness. We could differ on its concrete instantiation. But these values are the basis for our support for a democratic procedure (Gutmann and Thompson, 1996, pp. 26 and 27; Cohen, 1997, pp. 417ff; Dworkin, 1997, pp. 16 and 17; Habermas, 2001). Furthermore, majority rule, or any other procedure, must be implemented through rights and duties. For instance, the right to political participation, the right to free speech, the equal treatment and consideration of preferences and votes, and so on. All these rights stress constitutive rules of the procedure itself (for more on constitutive rules see Rawls, 1955 and Searle, 1995, pp. 46-47). And, therefore, a radical proceduralist fails to avoid any consideration about rights, since some degree of such considerations is unavoidable.

On the other hand, a radical substantivist affirms that procedure in decision-making is irrelevant in judging the legitimacy of political decisions. He must be strongly committed to a particular conception of justice for doing so; for instance, a human rights approach. Thus, only those collective decisions that respect and encourage the protection of human rights are legitimate from his point of view. Which procedure to take and enact such collective decisions is not important. From my point of view, there are four problems in such a radical position. First of all, there are political issues that are not concerned, directly or indirectly, with human rights, for instance the pure coordination matters (e.g. most traffic rules). Since they are not related to substantive moral questions, they should not be considered capable of being legitimate or illegitimate. And it is quite strange to hold that there are some political decisions for which we do not have any pattern of legitimacy.

Secondly, the fact of reasonable pluralism and the epistemic difficulties in identifying the content of the just substantive principles force us to adopt some decision-making procedure.[15] Even if the legitimacy of political decisions depends more on its substantive adequacy, it is not true that the procedure to make decisions is irrelevant. A dictatorial decision-making procedure, even if it produces very just outcomes, actually violates some of the very substantive principles defended by a radical substantivist. In other words, the choice of a particular decision-making procedure is not neutral from substantive principles. There is a third problem related to the second one. A radical substantivist typically uses independent standards of legitimacy for judging political decisions. Such standards are expressed in principles. But these principles do not possess stable and complete meanings independent of their interpretation and application to concrete cases. Even if we knew the content of the general, substantive principles, we would need to make a decision to interpret and apply them (that is, to complete its meaning). The crucial point will be, then, who has to make it and how should such a decision be made. And, therefore, the procedure becomes relevant again (Michelman, 1999, p. 1023; Waldron, 1999, pp. 211-312). Finally, the fourth problem does not affect radical substantivism in general, but those who adopt such a position in relation to human or fundamental rights. All the defenders of basic rights unanimously accept the value of political participation and the popular sovereignty principle. And, as Waldron has shown, even if we only committed to rights-based theories, we should recognize that the right to participate is not only one of the basic rights to be protected, but "the right of rights" (Waldron, 1999, pp. 232-254). Consequently, we cannot adhere to radical substantivism if we want to be consistent.

Although the three possibilities in facing the problem of procedure and substance mentioned above remain open, we have good reasons to abandon the two extreme positions, radical substantivism and radical proceduralism, and to try developing an intermediate one, that balances both proceduralism and substantivism (popular sovereignty and basic rights).

The Prevalence of Proceduralism

Having rejected both extreme positions and convinced that we need a theory of legitimacy that combines both procedural and substantive elements, and putting provisionally to one side the co-originality conception, the following alternatives must be analysed: 1) to give priority to substance (*soft substantivism*); or 2) to give priority to the procedure (*soft proceduralism*).

One of the arguments for giving priority to substantivism is the absence of mechanisms of pure procedural justice and perfect procedural justice in political decision-making, using the Rawlsian terminology (Rawls, 1971, pp. 84-89).[16] That is, the belief that we have (or presuppose the existence of) independent standards of legitimacy, and we do not count on any procedure that could grant that their outcomes could ever meet such standards. Thus, political decision-making is fallible, and not all the political decisions seem to be legitimate.

A soft proceduralist can threaten the very idea of the existence of an independent standard (as pluralist democracy does), but soft proceduralism in general is not committed to this kind of scepticism. Instead, soft proceduralism can believe in such independent standards and choose the best procedure to meet them. Hence, soft proceduralism could alternatively propose a means of pure procedural justice or imperfect procedural justice. The question about the existence and nature of an independent standard of legitimacy is a meta-ethical one. This question is certainly not easy to manage – but fortunately, I think I can offer good reasons to be soft proceduralist even without responding this challenge.

The Relative Irrelevance of the Meta-ethical Question

I assume, in this paper, that those who claim the existence of an independent standard of legitimacy regard such a standard as moral.[17] If so, the question about its existence and nature is a meta-ethical question. At this point, meta-ethics seems to be relevant for my proposal. But I want to show that such relevance is not absolute.

As we have seen, radical proceduralism fails to reject all substantive considerations. Any procedure we choose is preferable to others on the basis of some substantive value; and, for conceptual reasons, such a value must be process-independent. This means that we need to start with some substantive and independent standard. To be more precise, we need to presuppose such a standard. It still says nothing about the real existence of substantive independent values and their nature. But it commands us to behave *as if* they existed. In other words, when we are engaged in a political dispute, even when following a particular decision-making procedure, we must presuppose that an independent standard of legitimacy exists. Indeed, we often appeal to such a standard when arguing for or against a particular political decision. If we disagree about the substantive independent standards, we need a procedure. But the reasons for or against a particular procedure are dependent on another substantive independent standard. And even when we disagree about these second-order substantive standards, we must presuppose their existence. If we do not presuppose them, we have to deny the possibility of rightness in political decisions, and therefore, the very notion of legitimacy.[18]

In any case, we do not need to prove the real existence of substantive values. We do not need to believe in strong objectivism. As Jeremy Waldron accurately shows, there is no practical difference between moral realists and anti-realists when confronted with the fact of moral disagreement (Waldron, 1999, pp. 164-187). A shared commitment to an intersubjective value as impartiality will be enough to act as a foundation for the rest.[19] It implies only that extreme scepticism in meta-ethics must be rejected to make political legitimacy possible.[20] This is the relevant point of the meta-ethical question. In other respects, meta-ethical disputes (at least in the ontological sense) become irrelevant. And this is so, even when most of the political disputes have a moral basis, and such disputes are widespread, as the fact of pluralism shows.

The Fact of Political Pluralism

As I stated before, our contemporary societies are strongly characterized by disagreement. This is one of the most striking features of contemporary social relations and one of the most important challenges for political philosophy (Rawls, 1993, pp. 48-66 and 133-172; Gutmann and Thompson, 1996, pp. 11-51; Waldron, 1999). People disagree about moral values. People disagree about the right method to find out such moral values or even about the mere existence of such values. And, of course, people disagree about concrete political decisions and about the adequate means to cast correct political decisions. This means that disagreement is relevant for our purposes at least at three levels:

1. Disagreement about the existence and, in this case, about the content, of independent standards of legitimacy.
2. Disagreement about the best epistemic procedure to find out the content of the independent standards of legitimacy, and thus to solve the first level's disagreements.
3. Disagreement about the best procedure to make political decisions in the light of the disagreements at the other two levels.

If we put this case in the shipwrecked people's example, the outcome is that the five shipwrecked disagree about the content of the concrete decisions to be made; they disagree about the reasonable ways to take those decisions; and about the independent patterns to be applied in the decision-making process.

The three levels of disagreement mentioned above are the outcome of political pluralism. Political pluralism is not considered here as the theory that holds the ontological plurality and incommensurability of moral values, but as a mere fact of our social reality. As I said, pluralism implies social conflict, and social conflict is a necessary condition for political decisions. In this way, pluralism is not morally harmful nor an obstacle for political decision-making, but its *raison d'être*. Taking it as a mere fact, pluralism says nothing about the existence of objective moral values (or independent standards of political legitimacy). It is not evidence for sceptical ontological arguments in morals. Notwithstanding, it says something about moral epistemology.

The Epistemic Problem

If we have to deal to some extent with substantive patterns of legitimacy, we need a good epistemological account of such patterns. In other words, for an ideal substantive judgment of legitimacy we should be able to obtain widely shared ways to find out the content of such substantive patterns. If we count on such shared epistemic roots for judgment, substantivist arguments would be stronger. But if we instead lack such secure and well-established epistemology, substantivism misses the point.

Substantivist positions have two possible responses to the epistemic questions. They could demonstrate at a theoretical level that there is indeed a secure, infallible means of knowing the content of substantive values, and that the fact of pluralism only shows a general failure in the epistemic frameworks of people who disagree with them. If this is the case, the solution for the legitimacy problem consists of only convincing people of the goodness of such a secure means of knowledge. Then, when people adopt this infallible epistemology, moral disagreement will disappear. The problem with this first solution is that contemporary epistemology has not granted the existence of that means. But a substantivist could say that, lacking a theoretical well-established epistemic means of knowing the content of substantive values, people actually share a similar epistemic mechanism in practice. If so, people could behave *as if* such a shared epistemic mechanism was the right one. The problem here is that the fact of pluralism indicates exactly the contrary (Waldron, 1999, pp. 221-231).

There is no such infallible epistemology. We have to deal with disagreement about both values and epistemology. Even if we accept the existence of substantive patterns of legitimacy, the fact is that we cannot agree on them. And so they are useless. Turn to the shipwrecked people's example. Suppose that they disagree about the substantive patterns of legitimacy. If the majority of them take a decision to exploit the minority, we could reject such a decision from an external point of view. Some of them, the minority, believe that such a decision infringes basic rights.[21] But the majority rejects this claim, and thinks that no basic right is affected. How can they solve the dispute? If we appeal only to substantive values, we will have no social pattern of legitimacy at all.[22] My point here is that if we have identified a pattern of legitimacy of political decisions that is not widely shared (or that cannot be reasonably shared by anyone) in our society, such a pattern becomes useless. What we need, then, is a pattern of legitimacy that could be acknowledged by reasonable people. That is, reasonable people have to agree in saying that a particular political decision is legitimate or not. Otherwise, we lack a useful pattern of legitimacy.

Political Legitimacy, Moral Rightness and the Prevalence of the Procedure

An important distinction can help us at this point. We have admitted that we need to presuppose the existence of substantive patterns in some way. At the same time, we have accounted for the epistemic problems in determining the precise content of these patterns. We need to conciliate three elements: 1) the assumption that there is something like (objective or intersubjective) moral rightness, to have a meaningful conception of political legitimacy; 2) the epistemic problem, which casts doubts on any unilateral intent to determine the content of moral rightness; and 3) the necessity to have a widespread and common pattern of political legitimacy.

From my point of view, we can conciliate these three elements by distinguishing between political legitimacy and moral rightness (for a similar distinction, although for different reasons, see Lafont, 2003). As I said, I think that political legitimacy must be conceptually related with moral values in order to save its practicality and the intuition that a legitimate decision should tend to be morally right. In ideal conditions, say, a political decision is legitimate if, and only if, it is morally right.[23] This seems to be a concession to the substantivist approach. But, as we have seen, we lack of a secure pattern of moral rightness in practice (since we are not in ideal conditions). In the absence of such a pattern, it would be desirable to partially separate political legitimacy from moral rightness. We could establish a clear and acceptable conception of political legitimacy, a procedural one, still holding that the reasons for supporting it are based on its epistemic value. That is, arguing that this particular procedure is more likely to meet moral rightness than any other. This is a curious, but from my point of view very fertile, way to adopt a soft procedural account of legitimacy. For many authors, talking about the epistemic value implies moving from proceduralism to substantivism (Gutmann and Thompson, 1996, pp. 26-39, 2000, 2002; Cohen, 1997). In my view, however, if we properly distinguish between political legitimacy and moral rightness, we actually concede a point to substantivism when recognizing that we choose the best decision-making procedure for epistemic reasons – and, thus, we keep the link between the two notions, but we remain strictly in the soft proceduralist domain, since the only pattern of political legitimacy we use is a procedural one. As we saw, persisting in substantivist positions leads us to the collapse of the political legitimacy criteria. We can state, then, the prevalence of proceduralism. Even accepting the substantivist concerns as a starting point, we have to accommodate reasonable disagreement not only on substantive values but also on the epistemic means to identify substantive values. And to deal with that, we inevitably need a procedure.

Finally, since there are no completely reliable procedures (there are no perfect procedural justice devices), we must admit the fallibility of any political decision-making procedure. Being aware of this, if we maintain our belief in independent standards and we want to keep political legitimacy and moral rightness related, we should choose that political procedure which offers us a higher probability to meet moral rightness. That is, the procedure with a greater epistemic value. To defend the epistemic value in terms of probability allows us to say that political legitimacy is still "moral rightness-oriented" and at the same time to count on a clear, procedural pattern of political legitimacy; and allows us to say that political decisions can be morally wrong in particular cases, even when they are legitimate. The key is in separating the conception of political legitimacy from moral rightness. It may sound quite strange to affirm that a political decision is legitimate and morally wrong at the same time. And this would show the absurdity of my proposal, if we counted on secure epistemic patterns of moral rightness. But it is not the case.

Hence, we should turn to proceduralism to find the best epistemic procedure to take legitimate political decisions (in a similar vein, Cohen, 1986; Estlund, 1993a, 1993b, 1997; Nino, 1996). As Waldron points out, since no one is privileged in moral knowledge, all of us should have the opportunity to participate in political decision-making (Waldron, 1999, pp. 211-231 and 282-312). The epistemic problem leads us to democratic procedures. More concretely, it leads us to majority rule. Following the famous Condorcet's argument (see Condorcet, 1976; Grofman and Feld, 1988), the will of the majority is more likely to meet moral rightness, than the will of a minority.[24] Note that the argument for majority rule is an epistemic one. This is not incompatible, of course, with also justifying it in terms of equality, impartiality or individual autonomy, as mentioned above.

Since our five shipwrecked cannot agree on the substantive rightness of some possible collective decisions, they need a procedure to solve controversies, to overcome social conflict. Suppose they agree on the existence of moral rightness, but disagree on the concrete face of it, and lack an infallible means to identify it. Thereafter, they decide to adopt majority rule as the most impartial and the most epistemic-worthy procedure. If they all agree on the procedure and on the reasons that support it, they have solved the problem of the legitimacy of collective decisions. Their "political" legitimacy will be based on the democratic procedure. A collective decision will be considered legitimate in practice if, and only if, it is the result of a majoritarian vote. Of course, one of them can disagree on a particular decision (considering that it is, for instance, morally wrong). But, since he is committed with democratic procedure as the source of legitimacy, he will have to admit the legitimacy of the decision.[25]

A Chicken-and-Egg Situation and the Prevalence of Deliberation

But can we be sure about the superiority of democratic procedure? What happens if one of the shipwrecked people disagrees on the value of majority rule? Should we privilege it over human rights considerations? As we said, we favour a particular procedure on the basis of particular substantive values. This could imply the conceptual prevalence of substance to procedure. But, is there general agreement on such second-order values? The answer is obviously no. And, then, we need a "second-order" procedure to establish the second-order values. And, again, such second-order procedure must be based on substantive values to be legitimate. It leads us to an infinite regress or a chicken-and-egg situation. What is first, procedure or substance?

In my view, if the chicken-and-egg situation is true, as the shipwrecked people's case shows, the conception of co-originality is wrong. Habermas could responsd that it is precisely this infinite regress relationship between basic rights and democracy that proves that both ideals are co-original. In other words, they imply each other. But co-originality could be interpreted in two different ways on this point. If mutual implication between both ideals means that we are engaged in an infinite regress of mutual justification between procedure and substance, then this claim is tautologically true. We would be excluding radical substantivism and radical proceduralism, as I did, and claiming an intermediate position. But if co-originality means, as I think it does, that there is no tension between basic rights and democracy, between constitutionalism and popular sovereignty, and finally, between procedure and substance, then I think that such a conception is clearly wrong, because the tensions, as the shipwrecked people's case shows, are, at least, hypothetically, present in practice. And, then, we need some criteria to solve the dilemma.

That is, what we need is an end point of such an infinite regress. Imagine now that two of our five shipwrecked disagree on majority rule; on the procedure itself.

They have what I called a second-order disagreement about the values that support the first-order procedure. And they now need a second-order procedure to overcome (or to deal with) their disagreements. What can they do? As far as I can see, five possibilities are open:

1. They can delegate the decision to one of them: *dictatorial decision-making.* However this solution is probably unsatisfactory for everyone, since as we saw there should be no privileged people in settling collective issues. Even if such a single person who has to settle the second-order disagreement has been democratically elected, it seems paradoxical that someone who rejects majority rule would want to accept dictatorial decision-making.
2. They can vote again to settle the second-order disagreement. But this possibility is absurd, since the second-order disagreement is just about the very majority rule. One could reject that this second-order voting should require unanimity, and not majority rule. But, if so, no decision could be made, to the extent that they indeed disagree. If there is disagreement, the requirement of unanimity leads us to nowhere. If there is no disagreement, neither unanimity nor any other procedure are required.
3. They can also adopt an irrational means to solve the problem – like using force, or tossing a coin: *irrational decision-making.*[26] But this also seems unsatisfactory, since we are trying to find a procedure that grounds legitimacy. If we disagreed about the values that justify a first-order, legitimate procedure of decision-making, and if we adopted an irrational means of overcoming such a disagreement, irrationality would extend to the first-order procedure. The outcome would be an irrational conception of legitimacy, something that we are rejecting here from the beginning.
4. The majority can negotiate with the discordant minority in order to reach unanimity on the procedure, bargaining and haggling with them: *negotiate decision-making.* Negotiation conceptually includes mutual concessions, threats, tricks, promises and deceptions (Elster, 1995 and 1998, pp. 5 and 6).
5. Or, finally, they enter into a deliberative procedure: *deliberative decision-making.* Deliberation implies the exchanging of arguments, the participation of all who will be affected by the decision, by means of arguments offered by and to participants who are committed to the values of rationality and impartiality (on deliberative democracy, see for all Manin, 1987; Cohen, 1989; Gutmann and Thompson, 1996; Bohman, 1996; Bohman and Rehg, 1997; Elster, 1998; Macedo, 1999; Dryzek, 2000; Goodin, 2003; and Fishkin and Laslett, 2003).

From these five possibilities, only negotiation and deliberation seem capable of giving a justified response to the second-order disagreement (on the conceptual distinction among voting, bargaining and arguing as the three logics of democratic decision-making, see Elster, 1998, pp. 5 and 6). There are a lot of arguments for preferring deliberation to negotiation as a basic collective decision-making procedure (see for all Manin, 1987; Sunstein, 1988; Cohen, 1989; Elster, 1995; Gutmann and Thompson, 1996; and Elster 1998), but I will point out here only one of them. As it has been traditionally understood, we negotiate on private interests, but deliberate on beliefs about values. To the extent that we are committed to the ideas of independent substantive standards, moral rightness, political legitimacy, and the requirement of epistemic value, negotiation is not a good means of justifying or legitimating political decisions, even second-order ones. The deliberative process itself, according to a common interpretation of it (Cohen, 1986; Estlund, 1993a, 1993b, 1997; Nino, 1996), is committed to the exchange of arguments in order to improve the epistemic quality of our collective judgments. That is the reason why democratic deliberation can be seen as the ultimate source of political legitimacy (see for all Manin, 1987; and Cohen, 1989).[27] A collective (political) decision about the best procedure to make other political decisions is not a matter of bargaining, but of offering better reasons to adopt it. In short, a political decision is legitimate when we have given the best reasons to support it. Independent from our notion of moral rightness, the best account of political legitimacy is a soft procedural one, and, for epistemic reasons, the best procedure is a deliberative process: deliberation is prevalent.

But the infinite regress problem remains. Collective deliberation, as with any other procedure, is based on particular values (in this case, at least rationality and impartiality). Furthermore, deliberative democracy is more demanding than simple democracy (only majority rule, without previous deliberation) in terms of substantive rights – which can be seen as strong preconditions or as constitutive rules of the process itself (Manin, 1987; Cohen, 1989; Gutmann and Thompson, 1996; Bohman, 1996; Nino, 1996). Basically, both preconditions and rights and duties lead us to the protection of certain basic liberties (such as freedom of expression, the right to participate in equal conditions, and so on). And, then, it falls into the same infinite regress we want to avoid, since people can disagree about such preconditions and constitutive rules, and since there can be tensions between the outcomes of the deliberative process (the decisions made) and the basic rights involved by the process itself. Are we condemned to find ourselves in a third-order disagreement? The problem is probably harder in this case than in the majority rule's justification, since it seems more likely to get agreement about a less demanding procedure such as majority rule than to get it about a thicker procedure such as deliberative process.[28] Therefore, to the extent that we are committed to find a solution to the actual problem of disagreement, to the extent that what matters is practice, then it seems better to turn to simple majority rule.

Open Deliberation, Practice and Social Legitimacy

What matters after all in practice? What we have to find is a coordination point on which people could agree about a particular procedure of political decision-making? Yes and no. We need a solution to the infinite regress because we need to give a response to actual disagreement about it. If there were no disagreement, if all of us were committed to majority rule or to deliberation, we would have overcome the chicken-and-egg situation, at least in practice. But, on the one hand, there is no such social consensus. And, on the other, an uncritical agreement on the procedure is not the solution, when normative issues – such as legitimacy - are involved. I will try to argue that deliberation, despite being a more demanding process, is conceptually prevalent to majority rule and it generates the solution for the infinite regress problem. In short, a democratic deliberative process is to be the only source of political legitimacy.

First, why is deliberation the conceptually prevalent procedure? Turn to the point of disagreement about majority rule in our shipwrecked-people's case. When we disagree about basic, social rules (like procedural ones), we are claiming for a justification of such basic rules. It is not a matter of whim or irrational desires. It is not that I do not like majority rule, as I do not like football. It is not that I prefer expert-elitist decision-making, as I prefer to read Nabokov's novels. If I claim for majority rule or for deliberation, in such contexts, it is because I believe I have good reasons for doing it. If others claim for other procedures, or simply reject these ones, it is because they think they have good reasons for doing it. In the end, it is a matter of offering and balancing reasons – a matter of justification. What matters, then, is not only finding an actual coordination point, whatever that is. What matters is finding a decision-making procedure, supported by good reasons and on which people could agree. When we disagree about what this procedure is, we have to exchange our respective reasons and try to find a rational agreement.[29] And this is what public deliberation is looking for. The conceptual prevalence of deliberative process derives, then, from the very notion of rational justification in contexts of disagreement. Of course, social disagreement is contingent, and not a necessary feature of human societies. But this is so only from a logical point of view. In practice, this is a pervasive and constant element that we have to manage.

Democratic deliberation is certainly a very demanding procedure. We should ideally grant a lot of preconditions and implement a lot of constitutive rules, in order to make actual deliberation as close as possible to ideal conditions of collective deliberation. One could question whether the protection of such preconditions is equivalent to the protection of human rights, and if so, why considering a deliberative and democratic process as the only source of legitimacy overcomes the problem of the tensions between popular sovereignty and basic rights. But in response to this we have to emphasize three central features of deliberative processes:

1. The basic rights and duties protected for permitting and promoting deliberation are preconditions of the procedure itself. They are not protected to honour some substantive, objective and universal values (as from human rights conception). They are not supposed to be the pattern of the validity or legitimacy of political decisions. And, then, they are not external constraints on popular sovereignty, but internal conditions of the good functioning of the process itself. Such a difference could seem irrelevant, but it is not. The protection of such basic rights (understood as preconditions) can never be an excuse for avoiding deliberation on a specific matter or for considering a democratic and deliberate decision as illegitimate. They are worthy only by its instrumental value, and not by its intrinsic value. In other words, they are second-order rights.

2. Public deliberation is an open and self-critical process. That is, people can challenge the very preconditions of the deliberative process. If people disagree about such preconditions, they should deliberate about them. People can deliberate, and often they should do it, about the deliberation process itself. As Habermas has pointed out, participants in deliberation can challenge one by one whatever condition of communicative action – whatever precondition or constitutive rule of the deliberative process, from within the process itself. The only constraint is that they cannot challenge all of them at the same time (Habermas, 1984, vol. 1, pp. 8-42; see also Benhabib, 1990; Gutmann and Thompson, 1996, p. 4 and pp. 11-51; Bohman, 1996).[30] One could reject some particular preconditions of the deliberative procedure, and could offer reasons for this, but being ever engaged in some kind of deliberative process. What anyone could reject is that for justifying the adoption of a particular decision-making procedure, we need to offer good reasons in favour. And this self-reflective feature of deliberation makes the difference in respect to the infinite regress. We do not need third-order considerations to evaluate the second-order's democratic deliberation, because deliberation itself opens the floor to criticisms.
3. Finally, democratic deliberation is an ongoing process (Cohen, 1989, p. 21; Gutmann and Thompson, 1996, pp. 52-94; 2000, p. 161). It means that, even when it produces provisionally justified outcomes, as political legitimacy requires, we can always turn to revise some of the decisions made in the light of new arguments. Thus, we can give a good account of the relationship between political legitimacy and moral rightness. In ideal conditions, deliberative process would be a means of perfect procedural justice. And then political legitimacy would collapse into moral rightness. Instead, in real conditions it is only a means of imperfect procedural justice, and therefore it is an adequate source for political legitimacy, while it cannot ensure moral rightness. That is the reason why it fits well into the fallible condition of political legitimacy.

What happens then in practice? People should agree at least to accept a democratic deliberative process as the procedural source of political legitimacy. But what if it is not the case? People have then to discuss in order to reach agreement. There is no other satisfactory solution. Obviously, this discussion cannot be properly considered deliberation – in the same formal sense - unless it met some preconditions and constitutive rules. And it shows that behind every adoption of a deliberative process as a decision-making procedure there is another kind of discussion. I purpose to call it informal deliberation. But which is, then, the ultimate source of political legitimacy, formal or informal deliberation? If we state "the latter", we will be dangerously close to the Humean fallacy, since informal deliberation and "informal" agreement are matters of fact, and not matters of principle.

The response to this is that, in the end, human beings are as they are. We look for rational and just political decisions. We disagree. We look for just decision-making procedures in order to solve disagreements. We disagree too. We exchange arguments and reasons for and against several procedures, or about the concrete configuration of such procedures. And we persistently disagree. But at the same time, we persistently trust in our capacity to generate a better argument. And this is for us the best way to find out a satisfactory source of legitimacy of political decisions. Is that way legitimate itself? At least, we could say, informal deliberation counts as the ultimate source of legitimacy in our societies. This is an institutional fact, to use Searle's term, and belongs to our social reality (Searle, 1995). Of course, an institutional fact is nothing other than a fact, not a principle. But the patterns of political legitimacy are probably, in the end, institutional rules reducible to institutional facts. Those decisions made according to a particular procedure, democratic deliberation, in this case, count as politically legitimate in our society. This does not mean that they are morally right. I have emphasized this point. But to the extent that we have more or less agreed on the procedure, we accept their outcomes as legitimate, even if we think they are morally wrong. All these institutional rules and facts are logically contingent, but they are as pervasive as disagreement. This is only a reconstruction of how human beings place rationality in politics. But such reconstruction, as Habermas emphasizes, counts as universal pragmatics (Habermas, 1984).

In conclusion, I have tried to show that there are unavoidable tensions between the popular sovereignty and human rights ideals (and, more generally, between proceduralism and substantivism), considered as sources of legitimacy of political decisions. We must try to conciliate them, but we are then exposed to an infinite regress. In my proposal, soft proceduralism, although it cannot be completely separated from substantivism, is conceptually prevalent. It means that we have to pay more attention to procedural issues than to substantive ones in defining a mutually acceptable pattern of legitimacy. I defended democracy as the more justified procedure. And I argued for deliberative democracy as the best democratic model. This proposal has implications in the way we understand basic rights. Among others, it rejects substantive rights as a source of legitimacy of political decisions, and assumes the existence of second-order rights, being only instrumental to the validity of the deliberative and democratic process.

Finally, the only source of legitimacy of political decisions should be, in my view, deliberative democracy procedures. To the extent that legislation is the result of political decisions, it has to be democratically deliberated and voted to be politically legitimate. It still says nothing about its moral rightness. And I think this is a good thing. My proposal involves procedural as well as substantial concerns. The difficult relationship between these ingredients – procedure and substance, affects most domains in political thought. I am aware that my proposal could be rejected. Many of you will surely disagree with me. Do you want to deliberate about it?

* Lecturer on Legal and Political Philosophy at the Law School of the Pompeu Fabra University in Barcelona (Spain). An earlier version of this paper was presented at the "Theories of Legitimacy Workshop" at the 21st World Congress of the *Internationale Vereinigung für Rechts und Sozialphilosophie* (IVR), which took place in Lund

(Sweden) in August 2003, and in a seminar at Pompeu Fabra University in Barcelona (Spain), in November 2003. I am very grateful to all the participants in both colloquia, and especially to Juan Carlos Bayón, Samantha Besson, Roberto Gargarella, Cristina Lafont, José Juan Moreso, Félix Ovejero, and Águeda Quiroga, for their very helpful comments. I am also grateful to Sarah Turner for her linguistic advice.

Notes

1 For the sake of simplicity, I will assume in this paper that political decisions are those made by officials, expressed through legal norms, individual or general, in exercising their competencies, with a certain degree of discretion. Accordingly, only those public decisions that we might call "of mere application", when an official limits himself to apply another legal norm to a case, are excluded from my analysis. Discretion in these cases depends, then, on the existence of a higher and uncontested legal norm being applied. By contrast, a judicial decision made by a Supreme Court, for instance, in which the court discretionally interprets a written constitution, would be considered a political decision in my scope. Discretion is not arbitrariness. But, of course, it is a matter of degree. An official can make a decision with more or less discretion. Hence, my definition of political decision has to deal with some degree of vagueness. The more discretion the official has in decision-making, the more political the decision is.

2 Indeed, to provide a complete account of the legitimacy of political decisions one has to address the other issues involved – a task that I could not do here.

3 I will deal basically with an ongoing controversy among philosophers such as Ronald Dworkin, John Rawls, Frank Michelman, Jürgen Habermas and Jeremy Waldron. In their work, they often refer to another related dispute about the role of judicial review and its implications for democracy. I think that this problem reflects the more general question about legitimacy. And hence, the answer we offer for the more general one is crucial in taking a position with respect to the more concrete one. Besides, the former has conceptual priority over the second.

4 I am using the term "political pluralism" to refer to the *actual* social divergence about the best conception of the public good. But I am referring here to a thin conception of "public good" that could be accepted by anyone; a conception according to which collective decisions can be right or wrong, keeping the particular criteria that make them right or wrong open. This is what I call social disagreement about the public good.

5 The most interesting combination of the presence or absence of these five conditions is the case when, having to live together, and having different interests at stake, we unanimously agree that individual behaviour must respect the public good and share exactly the same conception of the public good. If this is the case, political decisions would not be necessary (they would be redundant). Indeed, even in the unlikely case of full, social agreement about the distribution of rights and duties and the distribution of resources, political decisions would be necessary at least for ruling out the "mere coordination" situations. This is the case, for instance, for some of the traffic regulations. But I will leave out this sort of rule in my argument, because most of our regulations, and surely all of the important ones, are not rules for "mere coordination" situations.

6 This only excludes "private good" responses to collective problems (this is probably only a conceptual implication). Note that I am adopting a thin conception of the public good. To the extent that we are committed to the idea of rightness in political decisions,

since we are concerned with their legitimacy, this rightness must be objective, or at least intersubjective. I will return to this point later.

7 I think that the question about the role of political (and legal) decisions in the light of the "reasons for action" debate can also be, at least partially, dismissed. Of course, there seems to be some close connection between a theory of legitimacy and the "reasons for action" issue: in my account, *to* consider some decision legitimate means that a) we are bound by it, b) we are obliged to comply with it, and c) we recognize in it some reasons for action. But accepting c does not commit us to a particular conception of the "reasons for action". In other words, c can mean that we have only a *prima facie* reason for action (even a distinguished one) or can mean that we have an exclusionary reason for action, as in Joseph Raz's account; see Raz (1975). The only possibility excluded is that of denying that law offers reasons for action at all. But I do not need to deal with such an issue here.

8 I am not arguing yet that we should favour majority rule in general in order to protect impartiality. This is only a part of the example.

9 Obviously I am not referring to legal rights, since there is still no law on the island. They are instead claiming moral rights, rights that should be recognized by the majority itself.

10 There is a slightly different (and apparent) paradox between democracy and the rule of law. Habermas again: "The idea that the addressees of the law must also be able to understand themselves as its authors does not give the united citizens of a democratic polity a voluntaristic, carte blanche permission to make whatever decisions they like... Correctly understood, the idea of self-legislation engenders an internal relation between will and reason in such a way that the freedom of everyone – that is, *self-legislation* - depends on the *equal* consideration of the individual freedom of each individual to take a yes/no position – that is, *self-legislation*... [T]he allegedly paradoxical relation between democracy and the rule of law resolves itself in the dimension of historical time, provided one conceives the constitution as a project that makes the founding act into an ongoing process of constitution-making that continues across generations." (Habermas, 2001, pp. 767 and 768).

11 This is clearly Habermas' strategy. See Habermas (2001 and 2003). In a similar, but not identical, way, see Dworkin (1997). Other authors deny implicitly the existence of such a dilemma, but mainly because they do not think that the relations between procedure and substance could be dilemmatic.

12 It is conceptually impossible to accept the dilemma between proceduralism and substantivism, while also claiming the compatibility in equal proportion between both ideals. If the dilemma is accepted, one of the ideals must be favoured.

13 Also Habermas (1998 and 2003).

14 Dworkin admits two possible interpretations. According to the passages quoted, he seems to adhere to the co-originality conception. According to his complete political and legal theory, he instead seems to be adhere to the soft substantivist conception.

15 The term "procedure" is ambiguous in this context. It could mean the procedure to make collective or political decisions, or it could refer to the epistemic procedure - of knowing the content of substantive principles. I am using the first meaning to characterize proceduralism, but we will return to the latter below. This ambiguity has not really been referred to in the recent literature, but it seems to me very important to keep it in mind.

16 Although Rawls explicitly declares that he is propounding a pure procedural justice, what is a pure procedure in his account is the "original position" device. But the political decision makers have to make decisions according to the two principles of justice, and such principles count as independent standards of legitimacy, at least in the sense in which I am using this term.

17 Obviously, it is conceptually possible to think that an independent and non-moral standard exists. But if we are committed to an idea of a substantive and normative standard of legitimacy, it seems reasonable to presuppose that such a standard is moral, at least if we believe (at this level) in the unity of practical discourse.

18 From a sceptical or subjective view of meta-ethics we could only reach subjective patterns of legitimacy. But this is equivalent to saying that there is no pattern of legitimacy.

19 From my point of view, the difference between an objective value and an intersubjective one is that the former is absolutely independent of individuals' wills or attitudes, while the second is ultimately founded on them. However, the difference between a subjective value and an intersubjective one is that the former is absolutely dependent on individuals' wills or attitudes, while the latter is not.

20 When Waldron says that even an extreme anti-realist position, such as emotivism, is irrelevant for jurisprudence and political theory (see Waldron, 1999, pp. 164-176), and, in the end, is compatible with the rational arguments for majority rule, he is taking into account soft conceptions of emotivism, such as for instance, Simon Blackburn's "quasi-realism". But to the extent that emotivism is close to scepticism, as in the case of Alfred Ayer's emotivism, we certainly should reject it in order to make rational arguments in normative political theory possible.

21 I am not referring to legal external rights, to the extent that no legal system exists on the island. The claim here is that such a decision infringes basic moral rights.

22 The majority of people in contemporary Western democracies presuppose the existence of human rights. They agree on the value of liberty in broad terms. They also agree on the value of equality in broad terms. But they strongly disagree over the concretization of such values. Anyway, widespread agreement on values in abstract terms is contingent. As the shipwrecked people's example shows, widespread agreement in opposite values is possible.

23 I am leaving aside for now those political decisions that only attain social coordination - and morally irrelevant - issues.

24 Note that it is established in probabilistic terms. The majority view can be wrong. The minority view can be wrong too. The point here is that the majority is more likely to be right than the minority.

25 It has only weak implications for the theory of reasons for action. I am not affirming that every legitimate political decision must be obeyed, but that if an agent thinks that it is legitimate, then such a decision can count as a *prima facie* reason for action, a reason that can be overridden by other considerations.

26 I am aware that there are contexts in which tossing a coin, or any other equivalent procedure, can be rational, or even just. But this is not the case when dealing with fundamental disagreements with moral relevance.

27 Other justifications of deliberative democracy have to do with the fact that deliberative process is more respectful of the equality principle or of the citizens' liberty.

28 I thank Samantha Besson (who argues for a "deliberative voting ethics", i.e. for majority rule preceded by deliberation in Besson, 2003), for this point.

29 Obviously, this argument is appealing only to the extent that we think that there is a place for practical reason in politics. As I said, this would not be the case for a radical emotivist.

30 It is important to note there is no necessary relationship between the Habermasian ideas contained in *The Theory of Communicative Action*, and those mentioned when examining the co-original conception.

References

Ackerman, B. (1989), 'Why Dialogue?', *Journal of Philosophy*, Vol. 86, pp. 5-22.

Benhabib, S. (1990), 'Communicative Ethics and Contemporary Controversies in Practical Philosophy' in S. Benhabib and F. Dallmayr (eds.), *The Communicative Ethics Controversy*, MIT Press, Cambridge (Ma.).

Benhabib, S. (1996), 'Toward a Deliberative Model of Democratic Legitimacy' in S. Benhabib (ed.), *Democracy and Difference*, Princeton University Press, Princeton (N.J.).

Besson, S. (2003), 'Disagreement and Democracy: From Vote to Deliberation and Back Again? The Move Toward Deliverative "Voting Ethics"' in J. Ferrer and M. Iglesias (eds.), *Globalisation, Democracy, and Citizenship – Prospects for the European Union*, Duncker und Humblot, Berlin.

Bohman, J. (1996), *Public Deliberation. Pluralism, Complexity and Democracy*, MIT Press, Cambridge (Ma).

Bohman, J. and Rehg, W. (1997) (eds.), *Deliberative Democracy. Essays on Reason and Politics*, MIT Press, Cambridge (Ma).

Cohen, J. (1986), 'An Epistemic Conception of Democracy', *Ethics*, Vol. 97, pp. 26-38.

Cohen, J. (1989), 'Deliberation and Democratic Legitimacy' in A. Hamlin and P. Pettit (eds.), *The Good Polity: Normative Analysis of the State*, Blackwell, Oxford.

Cohen, J. (1997), 'Procedure and Substance in Deliberative Democracy' in J. Bohman and W. Rehg (eds.), *Deliberative Democracy*, MIT Press, Cambridge (Ma).

Cohen, J. (1999), 'Reflections on Habermas on Democracy', *Ratio Juris*, Vol. 12, pp. 385-416.

Condorcet, J.A.N. de Caritat (1976) [1785], 'Essay on the Application of Mathematics to the Probability of Decisions Reached by Majority Vote' in *Selected Writings*, Bobbs-Merrill, Indianapolis.

Dryzek, J. (2000), *Deliberative Democracy and Beyond: Liberals, Critics, and Contestations*, Oxford University Press, Oxford.

Dworkin, R. (1997), *Freedom's Law. The Moral Reading of the American Constitution*, Harvard University Press, Cambridge (Ma.).

Elster, J. (1995), 'Strategic Uses of Argument' in K. Arrow *et al.* (eds.), *Barriers to the Negotiated Resolution of Conflict*, Norton, New York.

Elster, J. (ed.) (1998), *Deliberative Democracy*, Cambridge University Press, Cambridge.

Estlund, D. (1993a), 'Who's Afraid of Deliberative Democracy? On the Strategic/Deliberative Dichotomy in Recent Constitutional Jurisprudence', *Texas Law Review*, Vol. 71, pp. 1437-1477.

Estlund, D. (1993b), 'Making truth safe for democracy' in D. Copp, J. Hampton and J. Roemer (eds.), *The Idea of Democracy*, Cambridge University Press, Cambridge.

Estlund, D. (1997), 'Beyond Fairness and Deliberation: The Epistemic Dimension of Democratic Authority' in J. Bohman and W. Rehg (eds.), *Deliberative Democracy*, MIT Press, Cambridge (Mass.).

Fishkin, J. and Laslett, P. (eds.) (2003), *Debating Deliberative Democracy*, Blackwell, Oxford.

Goodin, R. (2003), *Reflective Democracy*, Oxford University Press, Oxford.

Grofman, B. and Feld, S. (1988), 'Rousseau's General Will: A Condorcetian Perspective', *American Political Science Review*, Vol. 82, pp. 567-576.

Gutmann, A. and Thompson, D. (1996), *Democracy and Disagreement*, Harvard University Press, Cambridge (Ma).

Gutmann, A. and Thompson, D. (1999), 'Democratic Disagreement' in S. Macedo (ed.), *Deliberative Politics. Essays on Democracy and Disagreement*, Oxford University Press, Oxford.
Gutmann, A. and Thompson, D. (2000), 'Why Deliberative Democracy is Different?', *Social Philosophy and Policy*, Vol.17, pp. 161-180.
Gutmann, A. and Thompson, D. (2002), 'Deliberative Democracy Beyond Process', *Journal of Political Philosophy*, Vol. 10, pp. 153-174.
Habermas, J. (1984), *The Theory of Communicative Action*, Two Volumes, T. McCarthy (tr.), Beacon Press, Boston.
Habermas, J. (1997), 'Popular Sovereignty as Procedure' in J. Bohman and W. Rehg (eds.), *Deliberative Democracy. Essays on Reason and Politics*, MIT Press, Cambridge (Ma).
Habermas, J. (1998), 'On the Internal Relation Between the Rule of Law and Democracy' in C. Cronin and P. DeGreiff (eds.), *Inclusion of the Other*, MIT Press, Cambridge (Ma.).
Habermas, J. (2001), 'Constitutional Democracy. A Paradoxical Union of Contradictory Principles?', *Political Theory*, Vol. 29, pp. 766-781.
Habermas, J. (2003), 'On Law and Disagreement. Some Comments on "Interpretative Pluralism"', *Ratio Juris*, Vol. 16, pp. 187-194.
Lafont, C. (2003), 'Moral Objectivity and Reasonable Agreement: Can Realism be Reconciled with Kantian Constructivism?', paper presented at the 21st IVR World Congress, in Lund (Sweden).
Macedo, S. (1999) (ed.), *Deliberative Politics: Essays on Democracy and Disagreement*, Oxford University Press, Oxford.
Manin, B. (1987), 'On Legitimacy and Political Deliberation', *Political Theory*, Vol. 15, pp. 338-368.
Michelman, F. (1998), 'Constitutional Authorship' in L. Alexander (ed.), *Constitutionalism: Philosophical Foundations*, Cambridge University Press, Cambridge.
Michelman, F. (1999), 'Morality, Identity and "Constitutional Patriotism"', *Denver University Law Review*, Vol. 4, pp. 1009-1028.
Michelman, F. (2000), 'Human Rights and the Limits of Constitutional Theory', *Ratio Juris*, Vol. 13, pp. 63-76.
Nino, C. S. (1996), *The Constitution of Deliberative Democracy,* Yale University Press, New Haven.
Rawls, J. (1955), 'Two Concepts of Rules', *Philosophical Review*, Vol. 64, pp. 3-32.
Rawls, J. (1971), *A Theory of Justice*, Harvard University Press, Cambridge (Ma).
Rawls, J. (1993), *Political Liberalism*, Columbia University Press, New York.
Raz, J. (1975), *Practical Reason and Norms*, Hutchinson, London.
Searle, J. R. (1995), *The Construction of Social Reality*, Free Press, New York.
Sunstein, C. (1988), 'Beyond the Republican Revival', *Yale Law Journal*, Vol. 97, pp. 1539-1591.
Sunstein, C. (1996), *Legal Reasoning and Political Conflict*, Oxford University Press, Oxford.
Waldron, J. (1999), *Law and Disagreement*, Clarendon Press, Oxford.

PART IV

PRACTICAL REASON, ARGUMENTATION AND INTERPRETATION

Chapter 13

Legislative Deliberation: Notes from the European Parliament

Neil MacCormick*

Introduction

It is a pleasure to participate in a legal theoretical discussion on the theme of "legisprudence". Many of us have perhaps been too inclined to concentrate on issues of law and interpretation downstream from the law-making process. Yet even in so-called common law systems, the great volume of law currently in force is statute law, the product of the legislative process. For legal systems to be rational practical systems of conduct and of thought, it must be the case that the legislative process has something of the rational in it. The late Jerzy Wróblewski indeed advanced the thesis that any dynamic approach to the interpretation of the enacted text had to be grounded in the presupposition of the legislature as an ideally rational law-maker. This ideal entity intends to introduce into the existing body of law new provisions so designed as to cohere well with the pre-existing norms of the legal order even at the same time as these are being changed or partly replaced with new norms based on at least partly novel purposes and values.

I am in the unusual position of being able to approach these questions from the standpoint of a legislator as well as that of a legal theorist, since I was elected a Member of the European Parliament in June 1999 and for the past four years have been heavily engaged in that role. I have recently had further reason to reflect on the character of the legislative process and on what is an appropriate constitutional framework for law-making activity. For early in 2002 I was elected to serve on the Convention on the Future of Europe. The President of the Convention, Valéry Giscard d'Estaing, recently delivered our final recommendations for a Draft Treaty establishing a Constitution of the European Union to the Prime Minister of Italy as current President of the European Council. In due course, the Member States of the Union will convene an Intergovernmental Conference to decide whether or not to adopt this proposal (with or without modification) and submit it for ratification by appropriate processes in each of the states.

In both capacities, as legislator and as participant in constitution-making, it now occurs to me that Wróblewski's idea needs some supplementation, at least for the context in which I am considering it. It is not enough simply to pose a rational legislator in the sense of Weberian purpose-rationality. At issue is, I think, the question of the rational and democratic legislator, where some value presuppositions flow from the idea of democracy. Moreover, it seems worthwhile to confront the issue of the gap between any real-life law-making process and an ideal-rational or ideal-democratic one.

Questioning Sovereignty and European Democracy

In 1999, I published a book called *Questioning Sovereignty*,[1] with the subtitle *Law State and Nation in the European Commonwealth.* In it, I applied the institutional theory of law to discussing how the states of Europe appeared to have transcended sovereignty as that was traditionally conceived in legal theory and political theory. I suggested they had done so in a way that did not involve any outright or complete transference of sovereignty to the Union, making it into what I suppose you would have to call a superstate. On the basis of that conclusion, I then raised the question of the democratic deficit.

Can there be democracy without sovereignty? If democracy is the exercise of power by a sovereign people, what happens to it if sovereignty is diffused? Anyway, can there be space for real democracy in an entity as complex as the European Union with its curious division of powers between states and Union, and between Commission Council (in its two distinct manifestations)[2] and Parliament, all supervised by the Court of Justice? Is this a setting in which we as Europeans can feel securely in charge of our own destiny? Or is it really a bureaucratic nightmare with façade legitimation papered over it in the form of a Parliament for whose members few citizen-electors trouble to vote, and of whose proceedings they are almost completely ignorant?

The answer I proposed in *Questioning Sovereignty* was an optimistic one, even perhaps a naively complacent one. In the light of an analysis of the complex values implicit in democracy as an ideal form of government, I suggested that the European Union did provide a setting in which these values could flourish through a distribution of powers guided by the principle of subsidiarity. The sense of individual empowerment and engagement in self-government is most powerfully available to us at comparatively local levels, but the necessity for large-scale decisions in managing a single market and a sustainable economy in contemporary conditions is undeniable.

This cannot involve close engagement of all citizens moment-by-moment, but answerability of those who exercise powers of government through representative institutions is a real possibility. If it does succeed in maintaining an effective market, then, on account of the way in which markets decentralise decision making and function as information systems dependent on aggregates of independent individual decisions, subsidiarity in one of its most important senses is promoted and persons are empowered in their economic activities.

Anyway, returning to the issue of answerability, the Parliament is elected by universal franchise and the Council comprises ministers (or, in its guise as "European Council", heads of state or of government) all of whom have a solid democratic title in their own country. In the areas where co-decision prevails, the Council and the Parliament function effectively as a two-chamber legislature, one chamber of which represents the states as such, the other, the citizens directly. The biggest deficiency of the system has lain in the fact that the Council deliberates in secret even when it is engaged in the enactment of laws. Since the Seville Council meeting of 2002, this practice has been abandoned, and legislative deliberation and decision-making are conducted in public. (Moreover, the draft Constitution, if adopted, will give constitutional force to the requirement of openness in law-making, and it establishes bicameral Council-and-Parliament lawmaking as the general rule over the great majority of topics in which the Union has legislative competence.)

Law-making *in camera* has had two related defects. The first is that too much of the work is in effect done by the Committee of Permanent Representatives, and delegated bodies subordinate to it. National civil servants meeting in private hammer out mutually acceptable proposals in the light of governmental instructions. Ministers in Council then effectively confirm what is already mainly a done deal. This protected Ministers-as-European-legislators from being made effectively answerable to their home parliament and electorate. The proper role of the Member State parliaments as part of the process of democratic checks on the governance of Europe was thereby substantially undermined.

The Commission is an extra-parliamentary executive on which the Treaties confer and the Draft Constitution concurs in conferring the principal power of legislative initiative. Its proposals cannot however prevail unless the two legislative institutions adopt its proposals, in whatever amended form seems to them good. This executive Commission, though not the product of popular election, is at least indirectly elected, through a process of Council nomination and parliamentary confirmation. The Commission can, moreover, be dismissed by vote of the Parliament, and the fate of the Santer Commission demonstrated that this is not a theoretical and never-to-be-seriously-contemplated Doomsday Weapon. It is a real control that can be used, without bringing the heavens down or creating a crippling institutional paralysis. In a private conversation, Commission Vice-president Neil Kinnock recently remarked to Mr John Swinney and myself that this had definitely altered the mindset of Commissioners and their civil servants in the directorates general.

My own impressions would confirm that view. Moreover, the democratic legitimacy of the commission will be enhanced if the election of its President, as now proposed, follows immediately after the quinquennial election to the European Parliament, and thus reflects its result in terms of party political balance. That there will be a process of Council nomination and Parliamentary election does not seem likely to impede a real sense of linkage between voting to elect a Parliament and the naming of a political leader to head up, and take the lead in proposing, the Commission for the following five years.

The Court of Justice and the Court of First Instance do effectively secure the rule of law at European level. Competencies exercised by the institutions are subject to quite rigorous scrutiny to check they have an adequate legal base in the law of the Union. This is no mere travesty of democracy. The European Union, including the European Community as one of its "Pillars", is in fact a kind of commonwealth unique in kind. Its uniqueness lies not in its possessing a mixed constitution, but in the particular mix of elements in its constitution, namely a mix of democratic and bureaucratic elements. Among the standard elements of the traditional mixed constitution, what it most signally lacks is the monarchical element – there is neither an elected nor an hereditary head of this union, no king, no emperor, no president, no first minister. Whenever a President of the Commission appears to be setting himself (no "herself" hitherto) for this role, jealous heads of government speedily trash such pretensions as mere *folie de grandeur*.

This may change somewhat under current proposals, but there is also a proposal on the table for a kind of curious dual presidency. The European Council, it is suggested, should elect its own President for a once-renewable two and a half year term, choosing a person who currently holds no national mandate. This President will have a key role in co-ordinating and following through the deliberations of the Council and their conclusions, and will have a certain role in the external representation of the Union. The Roman Republic managed for several centuries on a system of government through two consuls, but it remains to be seen how durable a dual EU presidency will prove to be. I am one of those inclined to predict that a convention may emerge at a quite early date whereby the President of the Commission is also invited to accept election to preside at the Council.

Thus, in quick outline, my conclusions in *Questioning Sovereignty* were reasonably sanguine about the real extent of the democratic deficit, and recent developments do seem to point towards the deficiencies being progressively ameliorated. Being, as I said earlier, in the unusual position of a theorist whose theories are tested by personal practical experiences in a new job, I find that, on the whole, my experiences have reinforced the ideas with which I started rather than leading me to abandon them. This, of course, may as much suggest that I am obstinate in error as that I have been right all along.

Testing the Theory: Experiencing the European Parliament

Parties and Commission

This section commences with an extended sketch of how I have found the life of a European legislator, coming to this role as I did after 36 years spent in the study of law and legal theory.

It is extraordinarily busy and demanding. Life is full of interruptions. Fascinating and deep questions are laid before you with far too little time to think them through in depth. You are called upon to cast vote after vote without always being comfortable that you have grasped what is at issue and are voting with proper reflection. To understand the meaning and probable impact of the proposals on which you are about to vote, you depend on the advice of party colleagues and on other proposals they depend on yours, for no one can follow closely or with expertise every issue that is before the Parliament.

Procedures take time to learn and understand. The facilities and the buildings are vast and labyrinthine. Even to get your telephone working properly, or to find your way round the intranet information system is a struggle. And while you are trying to get on top of all this, requests pour in from constituents and lobbyists, and connections have to be maintained with MPs and MSPs and your own party back home. All very hectic, but you survive it somehow.

You might ask if it does not seem very pointless to arrive as one of two Scottish National Party MEPs in a Parliament of 626 members. Surely this is a minute minority with nothing much to expect in the way of opportunities to influence great affairs? To my agreeable surprise, I have found this is far from being the case. In Europe, the SNP is part of the European Free Alliance, a federation of like-minded national parties from what are sometimes called "stateless nations". From the start, we were ten MEPs (two from Scotland, two from Wales, two from Flanders, two from the Basque Country, one from Galicia and one from Andalucia). On the basis of political affinity and tactical advantage we and the larger Green group decided, after quite drawn-out and tense negotiations, to form a composite Parliamentary Group of the Greens and European Free Alliance. We agreed on a set of political principles, with an overriding right of individual conscience and a clause preserving each party's right to uphold manifesto commitments notwithstanding majority votes within the Group. Apart from a tendency to discuss and debate everything at inordinate length, ensuring that everyone has a say, and sometimes more than one say, on every issue, we have worked in a tolerably cohesive way as a group, with genuine tolerance of internal diversity. We, the "Greens/EFA Group" with 46 members were initially the fourth largest political Group in a Parliament with no overall majority, but in which the conservative PPE/ED Group was, and remains, the largest single faction (232 members), followed by the Party of European Socialists (180 members) and then the European Liberal Democrat and Reform Party (52 members). There were four smaller groups (GUE/NGL 42; UEN 21; TDI 19: EDD, 19) and fourteen independent members. Subsequent shifts of individual allegiance have resulted in a marginal growth of the Liberal and GUE/NGL Groups, while my Group has declined and is now, by a narrow margin, the fifth largest of the groups in Parliament.

Most party Groups are subject to internal difference on particular issues having special national or regional impact, or where ideological persuasions differ on particular points. So voting in the Parliament is quite fluid, and no single group can expect to get its way by a mere act of its own collective will. Members as individuals and as sub-sets have real voting discretion, and votes make a difference. Subject to variations in different parties, whipping is relatively weak, and certainly in my Group our "voting lists", indicating a recommended vote on each issue on which a vote has to be taken, are essentially advisory – usually rather helpful in their advice, I have found.

The critically important fact about work in Parliament follows from the unusual position of the Commission as an Executive Branch only indirectly elected, and answerable to, but not directly controlled by, Parliament. No individual member or political group sits in Parliament with the task of assisting this executive, this "government", to get its programme carried through. The success or failure of the Commission is not success or failure of a single party of government, for there is no such party. Nor does any party measure its success by reference to the degree to which the Commission's programme goes forward unscathed and unchanged. Quite the reverse. Here, the contrast with Westminster is total, and even with Edinburgh it is considerable.

Independence of Judgment

From an MEP's viewpoint, this is not a defect in the European Parliament, but rather the reverse. On each issue, one is entitled, able, and perhaps even obligated, to form one's own judgment based on a balance of considerations, prominent among them are the following:

- one's sense of the rightness, justice or wisdom of a given measure;
- one's sense of the common good of the Union taken as a whole;
- one's opinion as to its impact on the true and legitimate interest of one's constituency or of a particularly affected group or locality or industry within it;
- one's responsibility as a national party representative, with a duty to colleagues to uphold a consistency of line in pursuit of the agreed principles and policies of the party;
- one's obligations as a member of a parliamentary political group, with a fair opportunity to participate in determining the Group's line on a given issue.

The relative weight of these factors is to a degree variable from issue to issue. Some things are almost self-defining as vital constituency interests – the fate of post offices in rural Scotland, or of the island ferry system, or of the fishing industry, to name but a few. Some are critical issues in party terms, as in the case of the high-profile stance on fuel taxes adopted by the SNP in the Scottish Parliament. This is also highly relevant in the European Parliament, but indicates a likely divergence of views with Green colleagues. Issues concerning constitutional principles are also at the heart of my party's *raison d'être*. Some issues, on the other hand, are of special sensitivity inside a Parliamentary Group, particularly those relating to the internal affairs and procedures and immunities of parliament. All engage one's conscience to some extent, sometimes to a very great extent, around questions concerning what is just, right, or wise, or what will serve the European common good.

The situation of a Member of the European Parliament rather closely resembles that of the ideal member of a representative legislature as depicted by, for example, Edmund Burke. One is a representative, not a delegate. Judgment has to be exercised, and for that exercise of judgment one can be called to account. Lobbyists and interest groups, especially those with a significant foothold in one's constituency, have a right to a hearing, or at least a reading of their often all too voluminous literature. But you must make your own judgment in the end.

Democracy makes a real difference however, though Burke was by no means a fan of democracy. Where a legislature is democratic as well as representative, the realities of mass democracy entail the articulation of political processes through parties, and nobody can or should ignore or dodge the obligations inherent in his or her position as also a party representative. Outside of exceptional circumstances, no one gets elected to a Parliament save as a party member and through the efforts of those who plod round the streets canvassing or spend weary hours on the phone in committee rooms or writing or addressing or folding political literature there. Elected representatives have no business to belittle the obligation of loyalty to their own party, though in the end it is for each representative to judge how to interpret that duty, and be ready to answer for that judgment back home. Especially in a list system of proportional representation such as we now have for UK MEPs, there is some risk that the sanction of dismissal is more truly exercised through party than by the citizen electorate as a whole. If that leads to overvaluation of the party duty at the expense of the constituency duty, this is indeed a defect in the electoral system. It could be remedied quite easily, by switching from a system of closed lists to a system of open lists, in which the electorate's preferences between a party's candidates can override the party's, as it should be able to. I would strongly favour such a change.

The Committee System and Co-Decision

What I am saying may look all very fine in the light of a certain conception of representative democracy, but you could still ask me "Where's the beef?" It's all very well to say that MEPs can use their best judgment, but to what end? What real influence can they have? The answer to that question lies in considering the Committee system in Parliament as well as the system of organisation through party groups. There are seventeen permanent committees among which the work of Parliament is apportioned on the basis of subject matter, and in addition there can be a variable number of special committees or committees of inquiry working for a fixed period and dealing with a particular issue of concern to parliament. Each MEP has the opportunity to be a full member of one ordinary committee and a substitute member of another. Membership of the Committees dealing with Fisheries and with Women's Rights for some reason does not count against one's quota of committee memberships, so those who are members of these can also be full members and substitute members respectively of two further committees.

The Committees sit in Brussels during two or sometimes three weeks of every month, and they may have special sittings when Parliament sits in Plenary Session in Strasbourg, as it is obliged by Treaty to do on twelve occasions in the year. Practically no business except for motions on topical matters of urgency and questions by members can come to Plenary Session without prior debate in Committee. What comes to the Plenary takes the form of a report by a committee prepared on its behalf by a Reporter – always in fact referred to in French as *"rapporteur"*. That report emerges by a process of, first, introductory debate in Committee on the issue, then discussion of a draft report put forward by the rapporteur, then amendments and discussion of these, and finally a vote of the Committee. The report as put to Plenary may again be amended, and the votes on these amendments are, of course, votes of the whole house.

Apart from reports, Committees sometimes adopt and put forward what are called "Opinions" by a similar process, for reference to another Committee which is in charge of the main report on the given subject matter, or by way of advice to Plenary about the line Parliament should take on, for example, a Commission Green Paper or the like. When the Commission puts forward a proposal for legislation under the co-decision procedure, the draft legislative text – "Bill" as we would say – is considered in Committee and sent to the Plenary with recommended amendments to the original text by the Commission. Parliament in plenary session may further amend it, and then vote to accept or reject the amended text. If accepted, it then goes to the Council, which can either accept it as it now stands or review the amended text and in consultation with the Commission adopt a new "Common Position" on the matter, that is, a further amended version of the legislative text. This version then returns to Parliament for a Second Reading, at which after debate in and report from Committee it is either adopted as it stands and becomes law forthwith, or Parliament may re-present some or all of its previous amendments, but not amendments that are new in substance. If the Council accepts Parliament's text after second reading, it is forthwith adopted as law. If not, a Conciliation Committee of the two institutions is set up, and deliberates with a view to finding a mutually acceptable text. If that can be done Parliament gives a normally formal third reading, in which the only question is to accept or reject the Conciliation Committee's final text. If it rejects it, or if the conciliation procedure has failed to reach an agreed result, the proposal lapses and has no legislative effect whatever. Conciliation can be a tense business. In 2001, I was involved in conciliation concerning the hotly contested draft Directive on Take-Over Bids. A majority of eight to seven in the parliament delegation eventually found it possible to agree a text acceptable to the Council participants. The following week, the Parliament divided 273 votes to 273 on Third Reading, and the whole proposal thereupon lapsed; a new version is currently moving through the legislative process with prospects of completion before the Election of June 2004.

I serve on the Committee on Legal Affairs and the Single Market and, as a substitute member, on the Committee on Constitutional Affairs. There was in 2000-2001 a Temporary Committee on the Echelon Interception System, of which I was a Vice-President. On the Legal Affairs Committee, I serve as "co-ordinator" on behalf of the Greens/EFA Group. Together with the president and vice presidents of the Committee, the Group co-ordinators are responsible for agreeing the management of committee business including distribution of rapporteurships and the like. In turn, the Presidents of all the Committees perform a vital coordinating role among the committees, while the Committee of Presidents (of Political Groups) has a coordinating and managing role especially in respect of business for plenary sessions. The Parliament's Bureau, comprising President and fourteen Vice-Presidents advised by the Secretary General and other secretariat members has overall responsibility for the running of parliament and successful carrying on of its business.

Discussions in the Committees on which I serve are usually notable for being constructive and interesting. Even through the barrier of linguistic difference, one comes to appreciate the quality of contribution and the quality of mind of fellow committee members. Where clear ideological differences are in issue, they are stated plainly and votes reflect them. But often there is the appearance, and I think the reality, of mutual persuasion and development of ideas through the dialectics of debate. When it comes to drafting reports or opinions, these do reveal the influence of prior discussion, and likewise the amendments that go forward, and the compromise amendments that sometimes reconcile differences point to a similar reality. The Commission is present when required and speaks to us through representatives from the appropriate Directorate General. And the Commissioner with responsibility for the Committee's domain regularly visits and reports, and enters into dialogue with the Committee (Frits Bolkestein, the Internal Market Commissioner at Legal Affairs; Michel Barnier, the Commissioner for Constitutional Reform, at Constitutional Affairs).

At the Echelon Committee, we took evidence from a considerable range of experts both in government and outside it, both from inside the European Institutions, and from outside them. We put forward a report on the lessons to be learned and policies to be adopted in respect of the Echelon System of signal interception that is run jointly by the USA, the UK, Canada, Australia and New Zealand. Our concern was whether this creates a risk of unfair American use of secret information involving effectively industrial espionage on European firms, or is objectionable as leading to blanket invasions of the rights to privacy that are protected by international and European law on Human rights. The Report was naturally overshadowed by responses to the shocking events of 11 September 2001. But in the long run I believe we will all have to review the question how much derogation from our own values and basic rights a war on terrorism can justify without becoming the mirror of that which it opposes.

Other areas on which I have had the opportunity to play a greater or lesser part at committee with eventual influence on Parliament's output include: product liability, e-commerce, the Directive on copyright in the digital age, the debate on subsidiarity, that on the European research area, and the various debates concerning the Charter of Rights. Now, I am in the process of producing a report on a difficult and controversial aspect of parliamentary immunity, an opinion on the future of relationships between the European Parliament and National Parliaments, a report on the possibility of more effective co-ordination between central European institutions and authorities at the regional or internal-national level within member States.

The power of questioning the Commission and the Council can also be used to some effect, and I would claim to have had some useful influence on issues concerning our West Coast Ferries, concerning diabetic drivers, concerning additionality in relation to structural funds, and certain other problems about delays in programmes concerning structural funds. Above all, through the Committee on Legal Affairs I raised a question on behalf of my Scottish constituent David Petrie and the Association of Foreign Language Lecturers in Italy, and this led to the carrying of a motion highly critical of Italy's conduct in relation to these academic colleagues in October 2000, followed by subsequent further interventions in a long-running and rather scandalous case of refusal to conform to basic standards of the Union.

By this point, I have taken a long way round to producing an answer to a short question: Can members of parties with small numbers of MEPs exercise any useful influence at all in this huge assembly? My answer is "yes", and the conclusion I derive from being able to give the affirmative answer is that the democratic deficit may be somewhat exaggerated.

But perhaps I am too quick with this. Is it too easy for small parties to have a disproportionately large influence, and is that undemocratic? I think not, for the point I am essentially making is that the structure and procedures of the parliament give space to individual members as such to play a considerable and active role, exercising responsible but independent judgment. This happens within a political system in which parties rightly play a considerable part, but not one that overwhelms individual judgment to the extent we are familiar with under the Westminster model, where powerful whipping secures Government majorities, and opposition parties languish in relative impotence.

What Idea of Democracy: What should Elections be About?

But now you may be beginning to nurture a suspicion that I am somehow failing to address the real question about democracy. Some of you may be beginning to think the essential question is about whom or what you have the power to elect. Up till now, I have worked on the assumption of a perhaps old-fashioned (indeed, Burkean) idea of the legislator as citizens' representative, exercising an independent judgment. The legislature is then conceptualised as an aggregate of such members all owing party and constituency loyalties, but none behaving as a mere delegate either of party or of constituency. By that ideal of democratic government, the European Parliament is a good example of democracy at work. Westminster (for example) would be a markedly less good one

Some of you could easily say, however, that that is an outdated and false view of democracy. For real people of the present day, democracy is about electing a government. The United Kingdom general election of 7 June 2001 decided to maintain the Blair government in office rather than replace it with a Hague one. Those who vote for parties other than the two alternative parties of government are to a greater or lesser extent missing the point and possibly in the end confusing the issue. For what comes out of it all may then be some kind of a hung parliament. (Notice, the European Parliament works well because it is a "hung parliament", for the Commission does not depend on an all-purpose parliamentary majority to stay in office, as does a UK Government. The Westminster Parliament works badly when it is "hung", because its principal purpose is to provide the basis for strong single-party government, and its role in lawmaking is ancillary to that. I note without present comment that the Scottish Parliament is designed to be a hung Parliament, yet supposed to produce a stable and coherent government.)

Lord Hailsham used to remark that the American Founding Fathers drafted their constitution on the basis of a misapprehension about the true character of the British Constitution. The result was that the United States became a monarchy with an elected King, while the UK continued to develop into a republic with a hereditary President. This is a neatly pointed paradox. It takes me back to my earlier remark that what the European Union appears most to manifest is a monarchy deficit. That is: in Europe we do not at the moment elect a single head of government who marshals the affairs of the Union and maps out the programme of government.

What we have is an elaborate system of checks and balances among institutions that interact differently in respect of the different "Pillars" of the Union, and exhibit variation even in respect of the Community pillar so far as concerns the topics that fall within co-decision by parliament and Council and those – including indeed Agriculture and Fisheries that lie outside it and are subject to consultation, assent, or co-operation procedures rather than to co-decision. But the Draft Constitution, I should interpose, would change most of that. The "Pillars" would give way to a single constitutional structure dealing somewhat differently with certain areas of competence, but centred upon a bicameral legislative process that keeps in balance the Parliament and the Council of Ministers.

Up till now, what has prevailed has been a mixture of transnational and intergovernmental procedures with far too little clarity or transparency from the citizen's point of view about how the whole hangs together or makes sense. The Treaty of Nice fell rather far short of clarifying obscurities. On that account, the Council at Laeken decided to refer the process of constitutional reform to a "Convention" process. This brought together representatives of the governments of all the Member states and of all of what were then "candidate countries" (ten of them now members-elect), together with two representatives of every parliament, and sixteen of the European parliament. For each full member there was also an alternate member, and alternate members were given the opportunity (I am glad to say) for quite substantial involvement in the work of the Convention. For the first time, the basic Treaties defining European Community and European Union, and the constitutional order implicit in these, were subjected to an open, public, and predominantly parliamentary rather than diplomatic process of critique and reconstruction. Quite dramatic improvements have resulted from this.

However that may be, my own experience has been that in the European Parliament, legislative processes do have a rational and discursive quality, though falling well short of perfect rationality. Decision-making is properly multi-factorial for every decision-maker, and final collective conclusions reflect many partial and partisan inputs. Nevertheless, there could be value in constructing something like Wróblewski's ideal rational legislator, in a reconstructed democratic variant. This would be an ideal construct whereby Parliament itself is contemplated as an intelligently purposive actor, aware of the systemic background into which each new piece of legislation has to be accommodated, and conscious of the legal basis on which it is competent to act for the purposes at which particular legislation is directed. Not merely is such a construct of potential help from the point of view of the subsequent applier and interpreter of law, whether in a judicial or in an extra judicial process. Some such idea is also, I think, implicit in the ongoing discourse of the legislature, in which, after all one works towards trying to reach a conclusion that is imputed to Parliament as its conclusion.

* Leverhulme Personal Research Professor and Regius Professor of Public Law, University of Edinburgh, Scotland

Notes

1 Oxford, Clarendon Press, 1999

2 One has to distinguish the "European Council", a deliberative body comprising the Heads of Government and Executive Heads of State of the European Union, which oversees the strategic direction of the Union, and the Council of Ministers, which exercises treaty-defined powers of a legislative and (to a limited extent) executive kind. The Council in this latter sense comprises relevant ministers of the Member States, as in the case of the General Affairs Council, the Agriculture Council, the Economic and finance Council, the Environment Council, or the like. The Draft Constitution gives a distinct constitutional recognition to the European Council and the Council, re-naming the General Affairs Council as the "General Affairs and Legislative Council". See Articles I-20 – I-23.

Chapter 14

Reasoning and Legislation

Manuel Atienza*

Theories on Legal Reasoning and Legislation

The study of the aspects of reasoning in Law has been increasingly gaining importance since the end of the Second World War. At first, in the 1950s, what could be called "pioneering" theories of legal reasoning emerged, the most important examples of which are found in the works of Viehweg, Perelman and Toulmin. Later, since the end of the 1970s, the theory that could be considered as the standard theory of legal reasoning has been developed. This theory is represented, above all, by the works of Robert Alexy and Neil MacCormick (Atienza, 1991), and the article published together by Aarnio, Alexy and Peczenik, in 1981 (in which substantially similar theses to those of MacCormick are defended), works, that could perhaps be considered as a kind of "manifesto" of this conception.

One of its features is that the subject of study concentrates essentially on the justificatory reasoning carried out by judges in the higher courts. In other words, what is of interest are the reasons adduced by judges in favour of the correct or acceptable nature of their decisions (this is what reasoning consists of), and not the reasons that would enable the *explanation* (through a psychological, sociological, ideological or other kind of study) of those decisions. Moreover, when concentrating on the reasoning of judges in the higher courts, what is studied are, essentially, problems of interpretative nature, and not those questions concerning the facts (let us say, the problems of evidence and qualification).

In recent years, a growing interest in reasoning about facts has been noted, this being the case also in Spain (González Lagier, 2003). However this is not true (or, at least, not to the same extent) with regard to (legal) reasoning, which is carried out in spheres beyond the judicial; it is perhaps the reasoning of lawyers, legislators and dogmatists which represents the most important cases. In brief, legislative reasoning, linked to the making of legal norms by political bodies of a legislative nature, generally lies beyond the reach of the expression "theory of legal reasoning".

There are various reasons, which could be adduced to explain this situation. Some are of, let us say, theoretical nature, and others could be considered of practical nature.

The ones of theoretical nature are linked to the fact that the theory of Law in the nineteenth and twentieth centuries focused essentially on description, conceptual analysis, systematization, and (though in a veiled way) development of Law on the basis of its legislative production (or, to a greater or lesser extent, depending on the kind of legal system involved: judicial). Until very recently (more or less in the 1970s), a theory of legislation has not strictly existed (Zapatero, 1994; Marcilla, 2003), although, there have been some important precedents.

Undoubtedly, one of these precedents is the work of Bentham, which is found in the legislative (reformist) project of the Enlightenment. Bentham´s influence and the particular nature of systems of common law (a more limited role is given to statutory law as opposed to case law) probably explain the reason why, in Anglo-Saxon countries, the figure of the professional who is in charge of drafting legal norms (the draftsman) was known much earlier than in continental law systems. However, the positivist theory of Law, prevailing in England since the beginning of the nineteenth century (the *Analytical Jurisprudence*) and greatly influenced by Bentham, took as a starting point a striking distinction between what Law is and what Law should be, which left legislation outside its field of study. As is well known, Austin made a distinction between *Jurisprudence*, or the study of positive law understood as a set of orders given by a sovereign to his subjects; and *science of legislation*, or the proposals about what Law should be, the latter belonging to the moral and political theory. In general terms, it could be said that at least until recently, in the Anglo-Saxon world, prevailed a tendency for considering Law essentially from a judicial point of view (regarding its interpretation and adjudication), and a tendency to place the legislator outside the legal framework (more like a political figure than a legal one). For example, this perspective is adopted by contemporary positivism, developed by authors such as Hart or Raz.

Another precedent, which needs to be underlined, is the legal realism, typical for the United States and the Scandinavian countries. Roscoe Pound, for example, defended in some of his works the need to envisage Law from both a judicial perspective, and that of the legislator. In the same context, the work of Llewellyn adds an important contribution to the drawing up of the "Uniform Commercial Code". With respect to Scandinavian realism, Alf Ross dedicated various chapters of his great work "On law and Justice" to the legislative drawing up of Law, to what he called "Legal politics". I think, however, that both in the case of the United States' and Scandinavian realists, the drawing of Law was considered a political task lying outside the field of legal science. Thus, for example, in Ross's opinion, "legal method" was simply a synonym of the interpretation of Law (in the context of its adjudication); and the great American Law schools (Harvard, Yale, etc.) were organized to train judges and lawyers professionally.

Finally, another important precedent for the current theory of legislation can be found in the European codification movement which has been in existence since the eighteenth century and which, as is well known, has contributed to shape one of the characteristic features, the most characteristic, of the continental type of legal system. The classic concept of codification presupposes, then, a concept of law, of legislation, which differs significantly from the legislative production that takes place in contemporary societies. If we were to use Laporta´s terminology (Laporta, 2003), we would be speaking about the law that characterizes the State that guarantees, but not the State that promotes and protects or the new State that regulates. As a result, the legislative technique of codification cannot be, simply, an appropriate technique for our legislative bodies, at least for the following two reasons. The first is that codification is based on the idea of the immutability of laws, that is to say, a law is seen as a necessary data, not as something that could take one form or another, or have one content or another. As Irti points: "Property rights, freedom to make a contract, hereditary succession are constant institutions, to which the codes add the protection of the State's power, but which they can neither suppress nor modify" (Irti, 1978, p. 7). The second reason (in reality linked to the first) is that laws, the Law, are seen as necessary instruments in order that each individual, can achieve his own ends, but not (this would be the contemporary notion of a law, that of "the age of decodification") as norms which prescribe, suggest or advise certain ends (Atienza and Ruiz Manero, 1996). Expressed in other terms, legal norms from the time of codification are action norms, excluding end norms. In addition, it is important to bear in mind that, as Tarello (1976) pointed out, the codification and the constitutionalization of Law (by constitutionalization he understands the configuration of the relationship between those who hold political power and those who are under that power as a legal relationship) determine a situation, a kind of legal culture, in which the jurist's activity is seen as technical-cognitive and not pragmatic-evaluative. From this perspective, the jurists considered themselves and are considered by others as technicians and not as politicians.

As a result of this, it could be said that the legal thinking of the last two centuries tended to consider laws as fixed data, which had to be used as a starting point, rather than as a product to which draft one had to contribute. Thus, the general theory and the various legal dogmatists have approached the phenomenon of legislation almost exclusively from the field of the sources of law. One could say that the main objective was to study law as a particular and fundamental type of legal norm, but not as a legislative activity as such. The problems arising from the "legal method" refer to the operations linked to the interpretation and adjudication of Law. The legislative method (leaving aside questions of a formal or procedural nature: the regulation of the "legislative iter") and the contents of the legislation are questions belonging to the field of politics or ethics. Here, it is very important to underline again that the modern science of Law (as opposed to the natural Law theory) is a science that does not construct its object, rather, it finds it already given. This is, precisely, the reason why positivism can seek to construct an exclusively descriptive theory of Law. That is also why the fact that the positivist theory of Law has not elaborated a theory of legislation cannot be seen exactly as a deficiency of positivism, but rather as an inevitable consequence of accepting its premises: the comparison between the political sphere (governed, in any case, by the moral theory) which produces the subject of study, positive Law; and the sphere of legal reflection itself, which presupposes the above. As a consequence of this, legislative reasoning could not be considered as a type of legal reasoning, because it is not carried out by Law professionals.

However, there are also, as I said before, other reasons of a practical nature which explain why legal theoreticians (and, in general, jurists) have had no interest in legislative reasoning. To put it briefly, the justificatory discourse linked to the production of legal norms through political assemblies is much more complex than that one carried out by judicial bodies. In order to analyze the justification made by a judge, one can focus on - and limit oneself to - the text of his decision, but the legislative discussion is normally much more open and less structured. In other words, judicial reasoning takes place within relatively strict limits, which makes its analysis and evaluation easier, but this does usually not occur with the legislative reasoning. That is also why conceptual instruments produced in the last decades by the theory of legal reasoning cannot be used as a single mean to justify legislative reasoning.

Judges and Legislators: The Institutional Context

The differences between the context of legislative production and the judicial application of Law, and therefore between the legislator and the judge, constitute precisely a good starting point for the study of legislative reasoning. I will now show, in simple terms, some of these differences, with the aim of constructing ideal types (in the Weberian sense) of the figures of the judge and the modern legislator that, therefore, differ, to a certain extent, from the judicial and legislative institutions as they really exist. In some spheres, one could even speak, about a certain tendency to not differentiate between judicial and legislative functions or to create bodies, which are in some way hybrid. However, I think that this does not cancel out the usefulness of our model. The differences can be considered from various points of view.

To begin with, from the point of view of those who reason, from their normative status, judges are independent civil servants; without political responsibility; carrying out their function in a stable way; being experts on the subject upon which they must decide, experts on Law. Legislators, in contrast, represent the interests of a certain social class or, if preferred, the general interests as they are envisaged from the perspective of a certain ideology. They are further on, not independent from the institution, the political party, to which they belong and their "professional career" depends on the influence they may have within that organization and, in general, on public opinion; and they carry out their function on an occasional basis, without having specific training required. By pointing out this difference, one could see that there are specific, significantly distinct, obligations related to the exercising of the one or the other function. From the politician, the legislator, one expects ideological coherence, and nearly always discipline as well (in relation to the institution, the political party, to which he belongs) and the skill to successfully achieve the aims not essentially set up by himself (although he might have taken part in outlining them). The legislator's "deontological code" cannot be constituted (as is the case with judges) by the principles of impartiality, independence and obligation to reason decisions. Indeed, legislators are not asked to place themselves above the parties, rather, they are asked to efficiently carry out "a party's work" (they are, in this sense, closer to lawyers than to judges). Neither are they asked to be independent, as is the judge who must make decisions based only on established Law (and independently from the other State powers). The legislator must rather consider Law – within the limits established by Constitution, morality, etc., as an instrument to achieve ends, which are social and external or relatively external to Law. Neither does he have the obligation to justify his decisions or, at least, there does not appear to be an obligation similar to the one judges have. The reason usually given for this is that, in a democratic system, those who establish the norms, the legislators, have a legitimate origin (they are elected via a democratic process) which judges lack. The "popular representation" which juries embody is also the reason why, in general, judges are not required to justify their decisions (the case of the Spanish jury is an exception).

Secondly, from the point of view of the composition and organization of the respective institutions, the judiciary and the law-making bodies, the situation is also very different. Judges act as individual bodies or in the context of collective bodies, courts, made up of few members. The organization of the judiciary is designed in such a way that, at least in most occasions, a consensus can be reached through deliberation: the homogeneity of its members, the hierarchy existing in the judiciary, the existence of an appeal system or the drawing up of doctrines which (despite cracks, dissenting votes and sporadic changes) standardize opinions, contribute to this. In general, judges lack initiative with respect to what questions they must pronounce upon. In contrast, modern legislator bodies are made up of many members and one cannot expect its members to be able to maintain the close contacts with each other existing within a judicial body. The size also means (Waldron, 1999) that legislative deliberation, reasoning, has a certain degree of rigidity and formality, which are unnecessary in other contexts: the subject of discussion is strictly defined (whether or not to pass a certain text), interventions are limited, etc. As Waldron (1999) has written, law-making bodies are designed to manage dissent. In other words no "institutional pressure" exists to lead them necessarily to reach a, let us say, a "genuine" agreement, rather, what is asked from them is to try to reach "reasonable" agreements, since those agreements refer to questions with respect to those who deliberately have, or represent, conflicting interests. Therefore, what is sought cannot simply be consensus based upon a "rational" discourse, but rather, a compromise through negotiation (although, naturally, the negotiation must take place within certain limits: in other words, the rational discourse, in the Habermasian sense, or some of its rules, set limits on the negotiation so that it can be considered legitimate). In any case, uniform opinions are not expected to arise from a law-making body, except in relatively exceptional situations. To give a significant example, the unanimity reached by the US Congress and Senate in response to President Bush's legislative proposals after the events of 11 September has been considered (and undoubtedly quite rightly), as a sign of the malfunctioning of the parliamentary institutions. Finally, law-making bodies, as opposed to judicial bodies, enjoy a very great initiative when choosing the topics to be deliberated and decided.

Naturally, the above does not lead one to think that legislative "rationality" is of an inferior rank to the judicial. What is meant is that we are dealing with a different (more complex) rationality for reasons of institutional nature. In other words, the ends typical for each institution determine a certain type of internal organization and means, which are appropriate in order to achieve those ends. The problem that arises as a result is how to articulate this idea of the diversity of rationalities with that of the "unity of practical reason". One possible solution, the one that is adopted with some ambiguity, for example, by Alexy, with Habermas as his inspiration (Atienza, 1991) is this: there are rules of *general* practical reasoning and then there are rules of legal reasoning (let us say, judicial or legislative) which are developments, *specifications*, of the latter: hence the thesis of the *special case*. The rules of each of these instances (legislation or adjudication of Law) cannot contradict those of *general* practical discourse: if they do so, and depending on the extent to which they do so, means a decrease in rationality. I think, however, that the various contexts of action, rational undertakings or whatever you would prefer to call them (Law, science, morality, art, business, etc.) determine that diverse "rules of play" govern each of them (one of these is the game of critical and rational discourse) and that such diversity can mean a certain degree of contradiction between the respective rules. Unity arises if it is possible or were it possible to rationally justify (in accordance with the rules of rational critical discourse) the existence of those other games. The rules of rational critical discourse are not some kind of "supergame" containing, in a very abstract form, all the rules existing in the other games: they are rules which are applied to that sphere of human activity and, moreover, justify whether or not other spheres of activity exist (hence, their particular importance). Nevertheless, let us say in conclusion that it is one thing to say that parliamentary discussion is justified in accordance with these rules, and another thing to say that each of the rules of the "parliamentary game" must be seen as a specification of those of the Habermasian rational discourse.

A consequence of these institutional differences is that a well-founded distinction can be made, between the problems for whose solution a legislative treatment is necessary (or advisable), and those which would be better left in the hands of judicial action (Hart and Sacks, 1994). The field of bioethics offers many examples in which the existence of an accelerated change in scientific and technical questions, the need to have access to criteria of opportunity and to take into consideration circumstances that are impossible to foresee in advance, etc, can make it advisable to use judicial rather than legislative means to solve those problems. In reality, a response to this need is the increased importance of committees of ethics.[1]

Thirdly, from the point of view of the types of reasoning typical for one or another instance, the following could be said. In the case of judges, the basic model is that of subsumption, reasoning of a classificatory type: what is sought is the establishment of whether or not certain facts can be included in the description, condition of application, of a norm and, therefore, whether or not certain legal consequences should be attributed to them. This, of course, requires the carrying out of various operations (it is necessary to determine whether such events took place, to decide how certain expressions present in the norms should be interpreted, etc.) which can, occasionally, become very complex. Nevertheless, it could be said, that this last only happens in exceptional situations: the model of taking judicial decisions (and the reasoning, justification, for the decision) is based upon a dramatic reduction in the complexity (Luhmann, 1974), which is contributed to the orientation towards the past and towards the norms in force.

In contrast, in the case of legislation, the typical model of reasoning responds more to what, since Aristotle, has been called "practical syllogism" or "practical reasoning": given that there is an objective to be achieved it must be shown if the said objective prevails, or to what extent, over others and what the means are (legal norms) that best satisfy it. The decision (and the reasoning) is, therefore, more complex and open here: it is directed towards the future and the obtaining of certain states of affairs, which makes it dependent on causal factors that cannot be fixed in a normative way: that is to say, it is not a question of simply doing what is established as being compulsory or of not doing what is established as being prohibited; the achievement of certain objectives (certain states of affairs) respecting certain limitations also implies a degree of discretion (when selecting the means and when shaping the ends) which does not exist in reasoning of a classificatory nature.

The third basic model of legal reasoning is weighing and balancing. By "weighing and balancing" we understand the process (and the reasoning involved in it) which consists in passing from principles to rules. Various phases can be distinguished within this type of reasoning. The first consists of establishing that in a certain situation there are principles, values, which push in opposite directions and which need some kind of adjustment: that is to say, not all of them can be satisfied at the same time, or not completely. In the second phase, given certain circumstances, the priority of a certain principle or value over another is established, and the reasons for this are adduced. Finally, a rule is constructed that implies the translation of this priority in deontic terms. However, there are also two basic kinds of weighing and balancing. In one of them, the act of establishing priorities consists essentially of constructing a taxonomy, or in identifying properties that are relevant when constructing generic cases and determining under which combination of properties (in which case) what is required by one principle (one value) or by another must prevail. For example, in the case of a clash between the value of intimacy and that of freedom of speech, weighing and balancing could conclude that the value of intimacy prevails by establishing the rule saying that the question of information is not of public relevance. Nevertheless, there is another type of weighing and balancing in which the central activity is that of *defining* an end, taking into account the limits fixed by other ends and values and choosing the appropriate means in order to achieve the end in question. For example, in order to achieve the end consisting of access to housing, the measure, the rule consisting in granting loans under particularly favourable conditions, for example to young people, can be established, as long as they do not enjoy income above a certain amount, and that they use the housing as their usual residence, etc.

Well, this last type of weighing and balancing always requires large doses of discretion (one could, for example, consider favouring immigrants instead of young people) and that is why it should be left outside judicial action. Reasoning, which is characteristically judicial, is a kind of reasoning based upon rules that, therefore, excludes weighing and balancing, at least in principle. This last way of reasoning (which is limited to the first type of weighing and balancing) can only play an important role in the case of high courts.

Finally, from the point of view of the criteria for the evaluation of reasoning (and, in reality, as a consequence of the above), judicial reasoning seems to be directed, at least as a regulative idea, towards the obtaining of a correct answer to the case, and coherence (not in the sense of mere logical consistency) seems to be an essential criterion to achieve this.

However, with regard to legislation, it makes no sense to speak about one correct answer, since it can hardly ever be said that a certain law (with a particular content, structure, etc.) was the only one possible, the correct law. Legislating always implies exercising discretion. This is precisely why the Constitutional Court (because it acts as a legislator) is often criticised when pronouncing an "interpretative" decision, or requiring that a law be interpreted in a certain way when there could be other interpretations that would also be constitutional, as in this way it would be exercising a typically legislative type of discretion.

And coherence is not an important criterion, or it is much less important than it is in relation to judicial decisions. Of course, if coherence is defined (Wintgens, 2005) in a very wide sense and is simply equivalent to rationality, in other words, as "giving sense" or "making sense", then, judicial decisions (judgments) as well as legislative ones (laws) must be coherent, must make sense. In this way, however, very important aspects of the legislator's and judge's justificatory discourse are blurred. Let us look at this in detail.

a) It can be held, in favour of the zero qualitative difference between the justification carried out by the legislator and the judge that the first must also "follow norms": constitutional norms (Wintgens, 2005). Nevertheless, I believe that, in doing so, they forget two important things. The first is that the Constitution consists essentially of principles, not rules. It is not the same to follow reasons, which are not peremptory (principles) as to follow peremptory (rules). The essential difference is that in the first case "to follow" means in reality to deliberate, while in the second "to follow" has quite a different meaning, if not the opposite: to follow a line of action without need to deliberate (although there are exceptions or cases in which the distinction can be less clear). The second thing, which is forgotten, is that the objectives sought by the legislator and the judge are two very different things, and hence so are their attitudes before the Law: the judge's is certainly the internal, "moral" point of view: the judge's end is compliance, the enforcement of Law; the legislator's attitude, however, is not that of *complying* with the Law, but that of *using* the Law to obtain social ends (external ends).
b) This difference in attitude (of the type of justification) can be seen precisely when legislators and judges have to decide on the same problem. The recent case of the Spanish Act governing political parties provides us with a good example.

   The legislative discussion took as a condition (let us say, as a condition of being possible) the constitutional nature of the measure it sought to establish. However, the centre of the discussion (at least, after a certain moment: when an agreement between the two leading parties was being sought) was not if the measure was constitutional or not, rather it was centred on reasoning about whether or not the ends sought would be achieved with the Act; whether other unforeseen and unwanted (or not stated) effects would arise; whether the objectives would be achieved at acceptable cost; whether or not problems would appear regarding its enforcement; etc. We are dealing, then, with questions of opportunity, which are essentially adjustable, and which appear to exclude the expectation of a single correct answer. However, when the question reaches the Constitutional Court things become simpler. The only thing left to discuss by now is whether or not certain contents of this Act contradict certain sections of the Constitution. Questions of opportunity either play no role at all or play only a marginal one. The same or more must be said in relation to the Supreme Court decision to apply the Act (once it had been declared constitutional): here the important thing is only to determine whether a given political party or political group meets the requirements established by the Act in order to be declared illegal.

It is precisely denunciations over confusion in the roles played which has largely constituted the criticism (we do not consider here whether this last is justified) which has been directed at the Act and at the Courts. The law-making body is accused of having acted as a judge: on establishing a "single case Act" it is, in a way, applying the "only correct answer" that the legal system – as the legislator understands it – lays down in the case of a political party, Herri Batasuna and its successors, which supports terrorism. In other words, it is not legislating, but adjudicating. And judges are accused of having acted as legislators: in the case of the Constitutional Court, because it determines whether a certain paragraph in the Act is constitutional, but as long as it is interpreted in a certain way (which means that it is this Court which establishes the norm); and the Supreme Court, because it has to establish the criteria upon which the decision must be based of whether or not an electoral group is the "successor" of such a political party, and therefore is also acting with the discretion characteristic of a legislator.

c) The difference is also very obvious on examining the various types of questions which judicial and legislative justifications must answer. As Wintgens (2005) points out, the legislator's justificatory "obligations" consist of answering questions like, why this law and not another or none at all? Why now? What content must a law have to achieve such an end?, etc. Well, it seems clear that judicial questions are of a different kind: why is such a fact considered proved? Why is this meaning attributed to that norm or statement?, etc.

d) Naturally, the abovementioned points do not mean that there are no criteria for correctness within legislative reasoning, rather that these do not exactly correlate to those of judicial justification. And, in particular, that coherence plays a much weaker role in relation to legislative reasoning, as will be seen later. The reason for this, no doubt, derives from the fact that coherence is, basically, a "conservative" criterion, a criterion of integration, which is orientated towards the system itself (towards the legal system), whereas legislation is essentially innovative, in the sense that it presupposes – as it has been mentioned before, the utilization of Law to achieve certain social ends. The accordance with the legal system (with the Constitution) is a premise, but not legislation's *raison d'etre*. Coherence sets certain limits but the correctness of a legislative decision does not depend on that alone, rather, it depends on certain requirements, which the content and the form of the law must meet.

Elsewhere (Atienza, 1997a), I defended the thesis that legislative rationality could be seen as a structure organized in five levels, to which a kind of meta-rationality level is added: the level of reasonableness. We would have then the level of linguistic rationality, in the sense that the issuer (the edictor) must be capable of transmitting a message (the law) fluently to the recipient (the addressee); that of formal-legal rationality, for the law must fall within a specific legal system in a harmonious way; the pragmatic, since the addressees′ behaviour would have to fit in with that which is envisaged in the law; the teleological, as the law would have to achieve the social ends being sought; the ethical, since the prescribed conduct and the aims of the laws imply values that could be ethically justified; and that of reasonableness, understood in the sense that a balance, a weighing, is required to exist, when achieving the above ends: the sacrifice of some of these ends (if not completely, to some extent) must be made at a reasonable cost). So, as a result, the correctness of a legislative decision depends on the content and the form of the law being clear, systematic (coherent, but in the sense of consistent), effective, axiologically adequate and efficient.

Conceptions of Reasoning

The previous section shows that certain differences must exist between the legislative reasoning and the judicial reasoning, but these differences do not constitute a total separation. Both legislative production and adjudication of Law are instances, scopes of legal reasoning, and the last is a type of practical reasoning, orientated towards the justification of a course of action (which can include – as fragments of itself, elements, reasoning, of a theoretical type). In this sense, if we speak about reasoning, when referring to the discussion on a law (in the parliament, or in the media) as well as to the reasoning of a judicial decision, it is because, in both cases: we are dealing with an activity – or the result of an activity, which uses language as a medium; which arises as a consequence of a problem to whose solution reasoning contributes; which consists of certain basic units, reasoning, in which premises and conclusions (statements which represent a starting point and statements which we arrive at) can be distinguished; units which can be assessed using certain criteria which make it possible to qualify the reasoning as valid, solid, persuasive, fallacious, etc.

Apart from this, in Law and, perhaps in general, no single way of understanding reasoning exists. The above elements can be interpreted in, at least, three different ways, and hence, in my opinion (Atienza, 1997b, p. 2000), one can speak about a formal conception, a material conception and a pragmatic conception of reasoning.

The formal conception (a paradigmatic example, but not the only one: that of standard deductive logic) views reasoning as a series of statements that have not been interpreted (in the sense that an abstraction is made of the content of truth or correctness presented in the premises and the conclusion); and it responds to the problem of whether from statements – premises, of a particular form, one can pass to another – conclusion, of another particular form. The criteria of correctness are provided by rules of inference; and what it supplies are schemes, forms, of reasoning. There is no reason to believe that such schemes are only of a deductive type: reasoning can have an inductive, probabilistic, abductive, etc. form. However, deduction plays, let us say, the role of a "model", because: 1) in reasoning of a deductive form, if the premises are true, then, necessarily the conclusion will be also true. In this case therefore the logical form is the only criterion for control (whereas, in the other types of reasoning, the correctness or solidity of the reasoning also depends on other criteria); 2) non-deductive reasoning can always become deductive if other certain premises are also added, so that deductive schemes can be used, at least to a certain extent, as mechanisms of control: how plausible is the premise which has to be added in order to make a reasoning, for example, an analogical reasoning, deductively valid?

For the material conception, what is essential is not the form of the statements, but what makes the statements true or correct (the natural, social, or institutional facts to which they refer). It responds to the problem of what we must believe in or what we must do, and as a result it consists essentially of a theory of premises: of the reasons for believing in something or for carrying out or having the intention to carry out an action. Its criteria of correctness cannot, therefore, be of a purely formal nature: what is essential is to determine, for example, under what conditions one type of reason prevails over another type; and these criteria do not constitute rules of inference in the sense of formal logic, but – as occurs with rules of the scientific method – they depend on what the world is like (or should be like). The work of Dworkin, Raz, Nino or Summers is an example of this type of conception.

Finally, the pragmatic conception considers reasoning as a type of activity (a series of speech acts) which seeks to persuade a given audience, or seeks to interact with other/s in order to reach an agreement about certain theoretical or practical problem. The success of the reasoning depends on whether the persuasion or the agreement of the other is effectively achieved, respecting particular rules. While in the material conception (and in the formal one) reasoning can be seen in individual terms (reasoning is something an individual can carry out alone), in the pragmatic conception reasoning is by necessity a social activity. Within the pragmatic conception, two approaches could be distinguished. The rhetoric approach on the one hand, focuses on the idea of persuading an audience, which, in reasoning, plays a static role. The dialectical approach on the other hand, perceives reasoning as taking place between participants (the proponent and the opponent) who assume a dynamic role by the constant interaction they are involved in. In a way, it is the distinction that exists between parametric rationality and strategic rationality.

Perelman's and Toulmin's conceptions of reasoning represent, respectively, the rhetoric and the dialectical points of view.

Legislative Reasoning

The question is, then, to connect these three conceptions of reasoning to the characteristics of legislation, in order to find an answer to the three great questions raised by the study of legislative reasoning. How is a legislative reasoning analyzed? How is it evaluated? How does one reason in the context of legislation? The first two operations take place *ex post* and can refer to the product as well as the activity of reasoning. The third is *ex ante*.

How to Analyze a Legislative Reasoning

As I said before, the analysis of legislative activity, which consists of reasoning, seems to require a scheme that has to be more complex than that of judicial reasoning. The reason for this is simple. When it is a question of analyzing judicial reasoning, one does not focus on the discussion that could have taken place among the various members of the court (or in the judge's mind), but rather, in general, the result of this process of reasoning is taken as the subject of analysis: a text which is structured in a certain way; this is the important thing: this is what counts when filing appeals, etc. At this point it is frequent to use the distinction between internal justification and external justification as a scheme for analysis, i.e. internal justification as the logical deductive type. It is, nevertheless, also possible to use other schemes like, for example, arrow diagrams (Atienza, 1997b) which, in reality, do not put into doubt the previous distinction, instead, they seek to present it in a model, which proves to be analytically richer. The basic idea consists of using an arrow to represent the relationship "to be a reason – reasoning, in favour of", and with a double lined arrow in the case of deductive reasoning. The use of capital letters makes it possible to differentiate between the diverse language acts, which can take place in a process of reasoning: affirming, denying, supposing, questioning. The lower case letters combined with numbers represent further on propositional contents. A judicial justification will always have a phase, the last one which is of deductive nature: this is internal justification. However, in order to reach this point, there are usually many more phases, external justification, which may not be of a deductive nature: that is to say, what enables the passing from certain statements to others are reasons (in favour, or against a particular thesis) of a weaker nature, which offer a non-conclusive support.

However, in the case of legislation, the weight of the reasoning is found less in the resulting document (the stated purpose of the law is the equivalent of the reasoning of the sentence) than in the activity, in the process carried out in order to reach that point. The analysis of the legislative activity consisting of reasoning requires, then, some kind of dynamic (interactive) scheme, which gives account of the existence of diverse actors who carry out diverse moves (language acts of a reasoning nature) at different moments. Since, in addition, legislation can be seen as a complex process in which different phases, prelegislative, legislative and postlegislative, can be distinguished, the analysis can refer to all the phases or only to one of them.

If we focus on reasoning in the legislative phase (the one that takes place within the assembly: for example, once the Cabinet has passed a particular draft bill), the first question that needs to be raised is: what kind of discussion are we dealing with? (We are within the pragmatic conception of reasoning.) And the answer, in my opinion, is that this reasoning, in practice, is quite far from the model of critical discussion or from the "theory of discourse", in the sense in which authors like Habermas or Alexy use the term. It cannot, as a result, be analyzed as if we were dealing with a discussion in which the parties were following the rules of rational discussion, simply because that is not the case. It is not true, for example, that each party feels committed to replying to the objections raised by the other party to their thesis (instead, the questions that may appear awkward are avoided); neither is it presupposed that the principle of sincerity, that of universality or that of avoiding ambiguity in the use of language, govern. This being so can perhaps be adduced by the incidence when the public opinion or the audience observing the reasoning applies pressure, which encourages the debate to have aspects of a discussion in accordance with the model of rational discourse. Yet, it seems to me that this is not a convincing reasoning. On the one hand, because this pressure is often insufficient or, simply, non-existent, and, on the other hand, above all because, as I pointed out before, it seems to me to be wrong to expect that, in every context of action, reasoning should follow the same patterns. Apart from that, this last does not mean that the theory of discourse does not play an important role in legislative reasoning. It does not contribute much to the aspect of analysis to which I am now referring, but it has certain explanatory and justificatory power. García Amado has pointed out that the theory of discourse (the model of rationality that he calls procedural or pragmatic) makes demands: 1) with respect to the legislators' conditions (the importance of electoral legislation meeting certain requirements, for example, in relation to the financing of political parties); 2) with respect to the exercise of legislation (parliamentary rules should assure, for example, that those who decide have adequate information, to remove amendments or to discuss upon them, etc.); 3) and with respect to the result, to the law, (the guidelines about the legislative technique should avoid, for example, the proliferation of norms left blank, completely open articles, etc.).

In my opinion, the analysis of legislative reasoning (in the legislative phase, but this can certainly be extended to include the other two phases) can be carried out on two levels or from two different perspectives. On the first level, it is a question of explaining the process of discussion and, so, we will have to take, as a starting point, a scheme that makes a distinction between the different phases of the discussion, the different questions to be discussed in each phase and the attitude (of acceptance, of rejection, etc.) of each party, together with the reasons adduced for this. I stress that it cannot be a scheme of a logical dialogical type formalized by Lorenzen or Rescher, because here the type of continuity which characterizes a dialogue and which is guaranteed through the assumption of certain charges on the part of the participants, is missing. A possible scheme could be:

PHASES	QUESTIONS	ATTITUDES X	ATTITUDES Y	REASONS X	REASONS Y
1	....				
2	....				
3	a	a,P	a,C	R	R'
	b	b,P	b,C	R	R'
	c	c,P	c,P	R	-
4	....				

In other words, various phases can, be distinguished: one of opening, another of confrontation, a third one of development of reasoning and a fourth of closure. In the development phase, three questions have been identified (in which the scheme of legislative rationality mentioned before should play a role: thus, we could be dealing with a question of a linguistic, systematic, etc. kind). If we suppose that the debate is limited to two participants (*X and Y*), it is possible, as is pointed out in the scheme, that they may have different attitudes with respect to *a* and to *b*, but that they coincide (both of them in favour on what *c* represents). Finally, each of them has specified what his reasons are for taking an attitude in favour (*P*) or against (*C*) such a thesis (*Y* does not adduce any reason in favour of *c*, because in this aspect it does not differ from *X*).

The second level of analysis means that instead of the complex activity of reasoning, a piece of the latter is selected: that which a participant carries out in a specific moment during the debate. In order to carry out this analysis we can use an arrow diagram like the one mentioned before, in which the following is represented: the flow of reasoning; the diverse acts of language (questioning, supposing, affirming, etc.); the propositional contents in each of them; and the reasons themselves: the reasons for supporting, for denying, etc. a certain propositional content.

As happens with any other type of reasoning (a judicial reasoning, for example) the beginning and the end are marked by a problem (for example, should a new law be introduced with a given content?) and the corresponding answer (Yes; No). What sets it apart is the type of question, which the reasoning is essentially seeking to answer. In the case of judicial reasoning, it can be a procedural issue (has the appropriate procedure been followed?), a jurisdiction issue (does the judicial body, before which the issue is being raised, have jurisdiction?), an evidence issue (can it be accepted that fact F has been proved?), an interpretation issue (should statement S be understood in the sense of S*?). In the case of legislative reasoning, these issues are determined by the ends and values that characterize legislation as a rational activity. Again, we can here resort to the distinction between five levels of rationality and a sixth level, which runs transversally through the other five. Legislative reasoning can be considered as an activity, which seeks to answer the doubts arising in relation to these different levels of rationality, and hence, all things considered, a typology of legislative reasoning can be devised, taking the following issues as a starting point: 1) does the law in question have a linguistically appropriate form, meaning is it communicability assured?; 2) is it systematic, in other words, it creates neither legal gaps nor contradictions?; 3) is it efficient, in the sense that its addressees' compliance can be foreseen?; 4) is it effective, that is, will the objectives that are sought be achieved?; 5) is it axiologically appropriate (in accordance with constitutional principles and other connected moral criteria)?, 6) is it efficient, or does it achieve the objectives mentioned earlier at a satisfactory cost? it seems to me that, at least, a large volume of the reasoning taking place in the context of a legislative discussion can be led back to these six issues; that is, they are reasonings on linguistic adaptation, on systematization, on efficacy, on social effectiveness, on justice or on the efficiency of the law (or of an aspect of the law).

How to Evaluate a Legislative Reasoning

The evaluation of a reasoning involves judging it using certain criteria of correctness, which makes it possible to distinguish between good, bad and fallacious reasoning, and to attribute to it a greater or smaller justificatory weight or persuasive effect. The evaluation of the reasoning (in the same way as its analysis) has slightly different characteristics, depending on whether it is a reasoning in the prelegislative phase (before the matter goes to a formal legal body: the parliament, for example), in the legislative or the postlegislative phase (Atienza, 1997a), and depending on whether the reasoning is carried out by the legislative bodies themselves, by the citizens through the media, by dogmatists, etc. However, leaving aside this complexity and therefore speaking in general terms, it seems clear, as we saw before, that, for various reasons, the criteria could not be the same as those used in judicial reasoning. To sum up what we saw before:

a) Judicial decisions are closed, in the sense that the judge is, normally, only asked to choose between two options, hence their bivalent nature (conviction/acquittal; declaration of ownership in favour of X or Y, etc.); and they are orientated towards obtaining a single correct answer. Legislative decisions are open, in the sense that it can hardly be said that a law with a certain structure and content is the only one possible: the field of justifiable decisions is, then, much more open.
b) The criteria of correctness in judicial decisions are essentially inherent in Law: judicial decisions are directed towards the legal system, and this is why coherence plays such an important role. In the case of legislation, decisions are directed towards the social system and, so, coherence plays a secondary role: it is a criterion of correctness, which one could say operates, in a negative sense, as a limit.
c) Judicial reasoning responds essentially to a classificatory scheme, in which the problems are: if a fact "f" happened; if it belongs to the F class; How is the F class defined?; What are the consequences of "f" belonging to F?. Correctness is something that is said about the answers given to questions of this type.

However, in legislative reasoning, where means aim schemes and those of weighing and balancing predominate, the questions (and their correct answers) are among others: How does one describe a situation considered as problematic? (For example, the road traffic accident rate.); How can the situation be explained? (Why do accidents take place?); What measures should be taken? (To keep the number of accidents and victims down to a minimum.); What aims are being sought? (Are there any other aims apart from safety?); What reasonable adjustment can be made between these diverse aims?

However, it could be said that, despite everything, schemes of reasoning (those, which have a deductive validity, for example) are always the same, so that, from the perspective of the formal conception of reasoning, there would be no difference at all with respect to judicial reasoning. Nevertheless, this is not so. The peculiarities pointed out before cause judicial reasoning to have certain typical forms (subsumtive syllogism, *a pari*, *a contrario*, *ad absurdum* reasoning) which could not be the same as in legislative reasoning. Thus, a usual classification of reasoning consists of differentiating the deductive reasoning from other types of reasoning like those based, for example, on connections of causality: these last (perhaps the most usual in legislative contexts) respond to schemes of inductive type. And in Perelman and Olbrecht-Tyteca's (1958) famous treatise, *La nouvelle rhétorique* what they called "quasi-logical reasoning" (in which much of judicial reasoning techniques can be included) was opposed to, among others, "reasoning based on the structure of the real" where, among others, the following appear: those which are based on causal links, pragmatic reasoning, means aim reasoning, etc, which are the most characteristically legislative.

From the material perspective, the differences regarding the criteria for assessing judicial and legislative reasoning consist essentially of the following. Judicial reasoning seeks justification for a decision taken (in general) with regard to a specific case and in relation to previously established norms (if not completely, at least for the most part), and therefore the assessment (respecting formal criteria) refers to criteria devised in the theory of procedure, of evidence (when is it justified to consider that an event has taken place?), of validity (which norms, based on sources, are – or are not – acceptable as normative material?), of interpretation, etc. In contrast, legislative reasoning seeks to justify (or reject) general norms that will be applied in the future (judicial reasoning is directed more towards the past) and which (normally) envisage generic cases. As I said before, in order to achieve this justification, it is necessary to show that the content and the structure of the law requires the following characteristics: communicability, systematization, efficacy, effectiveness, axiological adaptation and efficiency. These criteria (these ways of reasoning) possess an importance and strength that vary depending on the phase in question (pre-legislative, legislative or post-legislative) and are structured in relation to each other (for example, those of axiological type predominate over the others, in the sense that they essentially set limits on the others; reasons of efficiency possess a transversal nature; etc.). However, in any case, they refer to theories that, unlike the aforementioned, possess a closer connection with the social sciences (sociology, social psychology, economic analysis of Law, etc.) and a greater complexity.

Finally, the differences are also notable from a pragmatic perspective. On the one hand, in the case of judicial reasoning, the dialectical aspect normally remains hidden (the judge acts as an arbitrator with respect to the dialectics, which takes place between lawyers or between a lawyer and a public prosecutor, but he does not participate in the dialectics "from within"); although, if there are dissenting votes, some traces of these internal dialectics can remain. The rhetorical aspects are of a greater importance: judicial reasoning seeks to persuade the different audiences to which it is addressed: the parties, their lawyers, judges in the higher courts, the legal community, public opinion; and it is assessed depending on its ability to persuade. But, in any case (at least, from the point of view of the judge's professional obligations), what carries the greatest weight is that his decision is justified (from the formal and, above all, the material point of view) even though it is not persuasive.

In the case of legislative reasoning, the approach is, in some ways, reversed. The dialectical aspect (in the legislative phase) is, at least apparently, very pronounced, despite the fact that the contenders are not on an entirely equal footing: in the parliamentary debate there is a president who is in charge of making sure that certain formal rules are observed, but the fact that he belongs to one of the contending groups means that his/her role cannot be wholly identified with that of the judge who is in charge of directing a debate between the parties; and further on, the arbitrators of the debate (who not only participate by voting in favour or against, but also by "pressurising" in different ways throughout the debate) are partial, almost by definition: their attitude is not now, in any way, like that of judges who must decide a dispute. In the same way as in courts, the clash of the contenders' positions is settled by means of voting, but those who vote do not have to justify how they voted and not only can they adopt an attitude of active "partiality", but also quite frequently (in the real functioning of parliamentary assemblies) the possibility that someone can be persuaded by a reasoning put forward by a representative of an opposing political force is ruled out beforehand. Apart from this (and although here the distinction between discussion in committees and discussion in assembly is relevant), what is normal is that the arbitrators of the debate, who settle it by means of voting, are not experts in this field; in some occasions, it cannot even be said that they have a reasonably well founded idea about what they are voting on (and, therefore which reasoning they are supporting and which they are opposing).

As for the rhetorical aspects of legislative reasoning, an interesting element, which should be underlined is that the strength of persuasion is not only exercised (and often not even principally exercised) inwards, towards the assembly, but also outwards, towards public opinion: the ones who are sought to be persuaded are, above all, the voters, and to do so, not infrequently, propaganda slogans, in which the element of rational critical reasoning is minimal, are resorted to. These elements of "irrationality" are at least in principle more contained in the case of judicial reasoning, because here, institutional pressure exists in favour of the material justification of decisions (justification in accordance with Law), although they can be considered not to be persuasive by public opinion.

To sum up, the functioning of politics pushes legislative reasoning in a direction that sometimes has little in common with the reasoning that characterizes critical rational discourse: in order to reach an agreement with other political forces, lobbies, etc. it is negotiation that is, above all, resorted to; and the voters' acceptance can be the result of the use of advertising techniques, rather than reasoning of "rational" nature. In some ways, a consequence of this situation is the tendency to place the main theatre for the exercise of practical reason in our societies, not in the parliament, but rather in the supreme courts, in constitutional courts (Rawls, 1993). It is, of course, naive to think that, in higher or constitutional courts, factors do not exist which distance them conclusively in their composition, real functioning, etc. from what would be an embodiment of "ideal community of dialogue" or Rawls' less idealized "public reason"; and as I underlined earlier, legislative rationality is not only different from the judicial, but it is also more complex and impossible to shape in accordance with excessively idealized models, like that of Habermasian rational discourse. However, the aforementioned tendency shows perhaps that contemporary democracies have been more successful when designing judicial bodies than when designing legislative ones. This is a situation that appears to be in contrast with the one to which Aristotle referred when, at the beginning of *Rhetoric* he maintained that out of the three oratorical genres (the deliberative, the judicial and the epidictical) it is the first which should be considered superior, because "it is more noble and more fitting to the citizens' part". And also with the position taken by Cicero who did not pay great attention to the deliberative genre, apparently because there were speeches of a kind that took place before the Senate, where there was little room for irrational persuasion. The point is, then, how to design, representative (democratic) institutions in which deliberation reaches satisfactory levels, within the context of our complex societies.

How to Reason in the Context of Legislation

Finally, the question of how to reason in order to justify the enactment, amendment or repeal of a certain law (or of a certain aspect of a law) cannot be answered in a general way, without taking into account, which phase of the legislative production one is referring to, who is reasoning it, and in what context it is being reasoned: a publicist in the media, a social scientist, a jurist (a dogmatist of Law), a politician in parliament, etc.

With respect to parliamentary reasoning, before the assembly, the traditional scheme for rhetoric (adapted to the circumstances of a modern legislative body) is, in my opinion, still the best starting point. This scheme is organized around two axes (Albaladejo, 1991). One is that of the distinction between various phases or operations in the production of discourse (oral or written): *intellectio*, *inventio*, *dispositio*, *elocutio*, *memoria* and *actio*. The other consists of the distinction between the diverse parts of discourse: *exordio*, *narratio*, *argumentatio* and *peroratio*. The scheme responds more to the judicial genre of rhetoric but, with certain adaptations, it is also valid for deliberative rhetoric; for example, in relation to *inventio*, the "central" operation consisting of finding and deciding what has to be said, it seems clear that one has to take into account the peculiarities inherent in the type of question or problem, which generates the necessity to reason: as was seen before, "legislative questions" are of different nature compared with judicial ones. On the other hand, the scheme, the art of rhetoric, seeks the persuasion of an audience, but this does not take away the fact that it is also useful in dialectical contexts, that is, when somebody reasons before one or more people who are not simply recipients of a message, but who play an active role in the reasoning. And elements of a formal nature (schemes that are characteristic of legislative reasoning) and of a material nature (reasons in favour of communicability, systematization, etc.) which were referred to before can, of course, become part of the scheme.

The legislative reasoning carried out by a legal dogmatist has different characteristics to the aforementioned, which derive from the particular situation in which the jurist finds himself: he is an expert in the field and he is not bound by "the laws of politics" which affect a member of a parliament. Nevertheless, this advantage is, in a way, counteracted by the orientation towards the interpretation and the application of Law, which characterizes the traditional legal dogmatist (the tendency to separate the "dogmatic" study of a problem), from a sociological study of the same (the ideology according to which the proposal of what laws should be like is a political, and not a legal question, etc). For example, as Díez Ripollés (2003) has pointed out, it seems clear that the theory of crime, in criminal law, is a scheme that facilitates reasoning in judicial contexts, but nothing similar exists in relation to legislative reasoning. Of course, the reasoning of a legislative type, carried out by a legal dogmatist cannot ignore aspects of pragmatic and formal nature, but it is the material reasoning that should constitute the centre, the reasoning directed at the justification of the linguistic, the systematic aspects, etc. that a law should have. This theory of legislation (of legislative rationality) can be considered the pendant to the theory of application and interpretation, but it is important not to forget also that there is only one legal rationality: that there has to be a certain connection between the rationality which comes into play in the drawing up of norms and in their application, which is not difficult to show: for example, there is a clear parallelism between the criteria of rationality, which have been mentioned repeatedly and the traditional canons of interpretation (for the application of norms): the linguistic, the systematic, the historical, the teleological and the axiological. Otherwise, in the scheme I mentioned before, the organization of the levels of rationality is done *in abstracto*, following an order of increasing complexity. Yet, it is reasonable to think (Diez Ripollés, 2003) that in the preparation of a piece of work on legislative dogmatics (in the sense that it is not basically a question of analyzing or of evaluating, but rather of proposing a law with a certain content) this order must be reversed (or changed): to begin with, the ends that must be sought with the law and whether or not these are justified, are discussed; then, which objective and subjective means (implementation and sanctions) should be used in order to achieve them; what methodology a law must have in order to be complete and consistent; and, finally, how its sections should be worded.

* University of Alicante

Note

1 Charles H. Baron (2002) observes the following advantages in the judicial making of Law in contrast to the legislative type (he is thinking within the context of *common law* and, in particular, that of US Law): 1) judges have to reason their decisions; 2) they have a greater "charge" to show the correctness of the decision, since the rules which they make are applied retroactively; 3) they are free of the pressure put on legislators by the fact that the latter have to try to be re-elected; 4) they cannot refuse to settle the cases over which they have jurisdiction; 5) they make Law case by case, not in abstract; 6) the norms respond to the characteristics of the problem which caused them to arise; 7) judges have to take responsibility for the consequences that their decision might evoke; 8) the making of Law takes place within a dialectical context (accusatorial procedure) in which, as well as the judges, legal experts, lawyers, Law students, etc. participate.

References

Aarnio, A., Alexy, R. and Peczenik, A. (1981), 'The Foundation of Legal Reasoning', *Rechtstheorie*, Vol.12, Berlin, pp. 257-279.

Albaladejo, T. (1991), *Retórica*, Ed. Síntesis, Madrid.

Aristóteles (1994), *Retórica*, Q. Racionero (ed.), Gredos, Madrid.

Atienza, M. (1991), *Las razones del Derecho. Teorías de la argumentación jurídica*, C.E.C., Madrid.

Atienza, M. (1997a), *Contribución a una teoría de la legislación*, Civitas, Madrid.

Atienza, M. (1997b), *Derecho y argumentación*, Universidad Externado de Colombia, Bogotà.

Atienza, M. (2000), *El sentido del Derecho*, Ariel, Barcelona.

Atienza , M. and Ruiz Manero, J. (1996), *Las piezas del Derecho*, Ariel, Barcelona.

Ciceron, *Sobre el orador*, J.J. Iso (ed.), Gredos, Madrid.

Díez Ripollés, J.L. (2003), *La racionalidad de las leyes penales*, Trotta, Madrid.

Eemeren, F.H. v. and Grootendorst, R. (1984), *Speech Acts in Argumentative Discussions. A Theoretical Model for the Analysis of Discussions Directed Toward Solving Conflicts of Opinion*, Foris, Dordrecht.

García Amado, J.A. (2000), 'Razón práctica y legislación', *Derechos y libertades*, Revista del Instituto Bartolomé de las casas, No. 9. pp. 299-368.

González Lagier, D. (2003), 'Hechos y argumentos', *Jueces para la democracia*, Madrid, No. 46, pp. 17-27, and No. 47, pp. 45-46.

Hart, H.M. and Sacks, A.M. (1994), *The Legal Process. Basic Problems in the Making and Application of Law*, in W. N. Eskridge and Ph.P. Frickey (eds.), Foundation Press, Westbury, New York.

Irti, N. (1978), *L'età della decodificazione*, Giuffrè, Milan (2nd ed. 1999).

Laporta, F. (2003), *Teoría y realidad de la legislación,* Colegio de eméritos, Madrid, (forthcoming).

Luhmann, N. (1974) *Rechtssystem und Rechtsdogmatik* , Kohlhammer, Berlin.

Marcilla, G. (2003), *Crisis de la ley y ciencia de la legislación*, doctoral thesis, Universidad de Castilla-La Mancha.

Perelman, Ch. and Olbrecht-Tyteca, L. (1958), *Traité de l'argumentation. La nouvelle rhétorique*, P.U.F., Paris.

Rawls, J. (1993), *Political Liberalism*, Columbia University Press, New York.

Tarello, G. (1976), *Storia della cultura giuridica moderna*, Il Mulino, Bologna.

Waldron, J. (1999), *Law and Disagreement*, Oxford University Press, Oxford.
Wintgens, L.J. (2005), *The Justification of Legislation. An Introduction to Legisprudence, a New Theory of Legislation* (forthcoming).
Zapatero, V. (1994), 'De la jurisprudencia a la legislación', Doxa, Vol. 15-16, Alicante, 1994, pp. 769-789.

Chapter 15

Evaluating References to the Intention of the Legislator

H. José Plug*

Introduction

One of the places where arguments from law may meet arguments from politics, is in interpretative judicial decisions. When a judge has to apply a legal rule, there may be differences of opinion as to its precise interpretation. In order to establish the meaning of a rule, it is not uncommon for the judge to refer to historical arguments. This could mean that the judge falls back on the intention of the legislator as expressed in a preamble, in explanatory memoranda or in arguments that were exchanged during parliamentary debates. In this way, standpoints or arguments put forward in a political debate on social and political topics that resulted in legislation, could play a role in a legal discussion as well.

The following example illustrates the way in which a reference to the parliamentary record was used in the Brongersma case. The question in this much-discussed case was whether tiredness of life (*taedium vitae*) was acceptable as one of the main grounds for assisted euthanasia. According to Dutch law, a doctor is allowed to assist a patient desiring euthanasia without being prosecuted, on the condition that the patient's suffering is considered to be unbearable and without hope of improvement. The Dutch Supreme Court decided that the doctor, Mr Sutorius, who assisted his 86-year-old patient, Mr Brongersma, with euthanasia because his patient was tired of life, had acted against the law. In the motivation of this decision the Supreme Court referred to the parliamentary record and quoted the Dutch Minister of Justice as follows:

> Several speakers asked (…) for a clear standpoint of the government on the question whether persons who are "weary or tired of life" qualify for assisted euthanasia on the grounds of this enactment concerning euthanasia or assistance with termination of life. The answer to this is unmistakably negative. (Supreme Court, 24 December 2002, *NJ* 2003, p. 167)

The Supreme Court used this quotation of the parliamentary debates as one of the arguments to interpret "unbearable suffering" and to conclude that the euthanasia law "does not state that euthanasia is permitted in case of absence of medically classified physical or mental diseases and afflictions, such as tiredness of life".

In a quantitative survey of the practice of the application of legal rules by Snijders (1978) it appears that the history of the law is one of the most widely used arguments in the jurisprudence of the Supreme Court of the Netherlands. A comparative study on jurisprudence by MacCormick and Summers (1991) shows that, apart from the Netherlands, the historical argument is widely used in a great number of other legal systems as well. The study also shows, however, that different countries may take different views of historical arguments. Moreover, as to when this type of argumentation is acceptable and how it could be effective, opinions may differ considerably.[1]

Discussions about the acceptability of legislative history as an interpretative argument are related to discussions about the role of the judge and the requirements for justification in legal practice. At the same time this interpretative argument gives cause to look into the justification requirements in political practice, because it introduces arguments from a political discussion into a legal discussion.[2] From a descriptive perspective, these requirements may provide an explanation of the way in which historical arguments are used in interpretative judicial decisions. From a normative perspective, it may be useful to see how these requirements could be supplemented and modified in order to let them best fulfill their function for interpretative judicial decisions.

In the pragma-dialectical approach to argumentation, as developed by van Eemeren and Grootendorst (1984, 1992), both legal and political argumentative practices may be considered as a critical discussion that has to meet certain standards of rationality. Participants in these discussions are looked upon as rational decision-makers. In the justification of their judicial or legislative decision they have to overcome rational criticism on their points of view. The pragma-dialectical argumentation theory offers a general theoretical instrument for the analysis and evaluation of argumentative discussions. In combination with theoretical and practical insights into political and legal institutions, the instrument may be of use to specify the elements that should be submitted to rational criticism and to establish whether the argumentation is acceptable. A pragma-dialectical framework may serve as a starting point to compare the argumentation for (interpretative) legal decisions and legislative decisions and to establish similarities and differences between argumentation in the legal and political arena.

In this contribution I will restrict myself to demonstrating how a pragma-dialectical approach may be of use when analyzing historical arguments containing references to the intention of the legislator and to examine the pros and cons of applying these arguments. A clear view on what these historical arguments amount to and on how they may function in the justification of interpretative decisions is necessary to evaluate their acceptability. Problems concerning the effectiveness of historical arguments in judicial decisions will be discussed by making use of the insights from van Eemeren and Houtlosser (2002) on strategic manoeuvring in argumentative texts.

Historical and Genetic Arguments

If the meaning of a rule is unclear and a judge has to make a decision on the interpretation of the rule, he may justify his interpretative decision by making use of various interpretative techniques, also known as argumentation sources or interpretative arguments. In order to defend his interpretation of the rule, the judge may for example refer to the everyday meaning of a term (grammatical argument) or to the goal or the purpose of the rule (teleological argument).

If a judge justifies his interpretation of a legal rule by a historical argument, he may refer to assertions that were made by politicians in public debates or to statements from other persons or institutions that were involved in the legislative process. In different legal systems the historic argument is, however, conceptualized in a number of different ways. In the Netherlands, for instance, arguments in which the judge only uses the words "the legislative history" or "the history of the realization of the law" are considered to be historical arguments. Arguments in which the judge refers to the intention or the will of the legislator too are regarded as historical arguments.

As becomes clear from the study of MacCormick and Summers (1991), in other legal systems, this last category may also be referred to as the genetic argument. Both the historical argument and the genetic argument are aimed at determining the meaning of the statute through the will or the intention of the legislator. The historical argument, however, often seems to refer to an interpretation taking into account all the relevant historical developments that have taken place *since* the enactment. The genetic argument seems to refer to historical conditions *prior* to the enactment or at the time of the enactment. In this argument, texts that constitute legislative preparatory materials are considered to be an important help to determine the interpretation of the rule.

Within the genetic argument, Alexy (1989, p. 236) distinguishes two basic forms of this type of argument. To clarify how exactly the intention of the legislator can play a role in the genetic argument, these two forms may serve as a starting point. The first form has the following structure:

I=R' was what the legislator directly intended

The structure of the second form is as follows:

R is, for the legislator, a means to end Z
$\neg R' \rightarrow \neg Z$
R'

In the first form, there is a direct reference to the intention of the legislator. In the second form it is claimed that the legislator adopted R as a means for advancing a certain goal Z. The difference between these two forms can be clarified by determining the underlying argument schemes. In the pragma-dialectial approach by van Eemeren and Grootendorst (1992, p. 96), these argument schemes characterize the way in which the acceptability of the premise that is explicit in the argumentation is transferred to the standpoint. Insight into the type of justification or refutation that is provided for the standpoint is relevant for the evaluation of the argumentation.

A Pragma-Dialectical Reconstruction of Genetic Arguments

An example in everyday language of both forms of the genetic argument may serve to ascertain on which argument schemes the two forms of genetic argument are based. The examples concern an article of the Dutch Road Traffic Act, in which a four-week term is mentioned. The question that has to be answered is whether or not this four-week term should be interpreted as a firm date. If the judge were to make use of the first basic form of the genetic argument in order to justify his interpretation, his argumentation could run as follows:

> The four-week term should be interpreted as a firm date (R') since, from parliamentary documents, it appears that that is what the legislator intended.

In this example, the judge justifies that the four-week term should be interpreted as a firm date (interpretation R') by appealing to an authority: the legislator. In the pragma-dialectical argumentation theory the argument from authority is interpreted as a subtype of symptomatic argumentation. The proposition is regarded as acceptable because an authoritative source says so.[3] In other words, the authority of the source is treated as a sign that the proposition ascribed to this source is acceptable. The scheme of this specific case of symptomatic argumentation could be formulated as follows:

standpoint:	interpretation R'
because:	from parliamentary documents, it appears that the legislator intended R'.
and:	the intention of the legislator is indicative for the acceptability of an interpretation of the law

The following argumentation, as could be brought forward by a judge, may serve to illustrate the second form of the genetic argument as mentioned by Alexy:

> The four-week term should be interpreted as a firm date (R') since a non-firm date (-R') would fail to reduce the number of traffic offences (-Z), whereas a reduction is desirable now that parliamentary documents manifestly indicate that it was the intention of the legislator to reduce the great number of traffic offences (Z).

As was the case in the first example, the judge does refer to the intention of the legislator, but here the standpoint in which the interpretation is expressed is directly justified by a reference to the consequences of the interpretation. Therefore, the argument scheme is not symptomatic, but rather pragmatic. In the pragma-dialectical typology of argument schemes (Van Eemeren, Grootendorst and Snoeck Henkemans, 2002, p. 101) pragmatic argumentation is a subtype of causal argumentation. In this subtype, a certain course of action is recommended in the standpoint and the argumentation consists of summing up the (un)favourable consequences of (not) adopting that course of action. The argument scheme for the second form of the genetic argument could be as follows:

standpoint:	interpretation R'
because:	interpretation – R' leads to -Z
and:	Z is desirable since parliamentary documents indicate that the legislator intended Z

From the analysis of the two basic forms of the genetic argument it becomes clear that a reference to the intention of the legislator may be a justification of the standpoint on its own or that it may be a supplement to pragmatic argumentation.[4] This distinction has consequences for the evaluation of the argumentation. Since both forms of genetic argument are based on different argument schemes, different critical questions should be asked to determine whether the arguments meet the criteria of soundness.[5] If the argument is based on a symptomatic relation it could be relevant to ask whether R' is really intended by the legislator or whether the intention of the legislator should be considered as decisive. On the other hand, if the argumentation is pragmatic, it could be relevant to ask whether the consequences mentioned in the argumentation are indeed unfavourable or whether the consequences actually occur as a result of the proposed course of action.[6]

If, however, we take a closer look at the argumentation in these examples, it becomes apparent that the argumentation is more complex than was first suggested. In both examples, the arguments that underpin the interpretative standpoints are, themselves, supported by arguments. This argumentation on a second or a third level, in pragma-dialectical terms called subordinative argumentation, consists of a reference to parliamentary documents. The relations between the arguments in the first example can be presented in an argumentation structure as follows:

Figure 1. Schematic representation of example 1

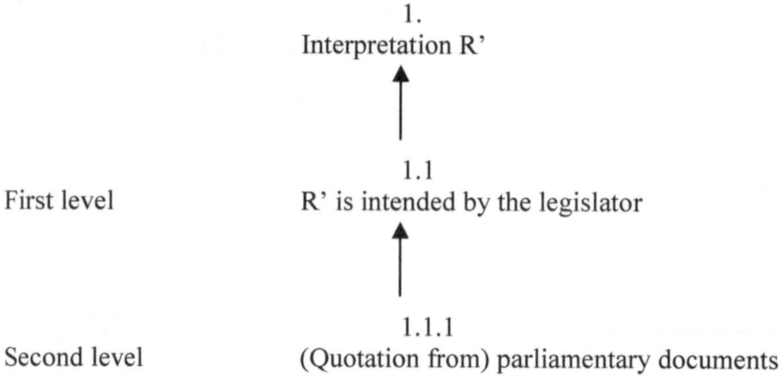

The relations between the arguments in the second example can be schematized as follows:

Figure 2. Schematic representation of example 2

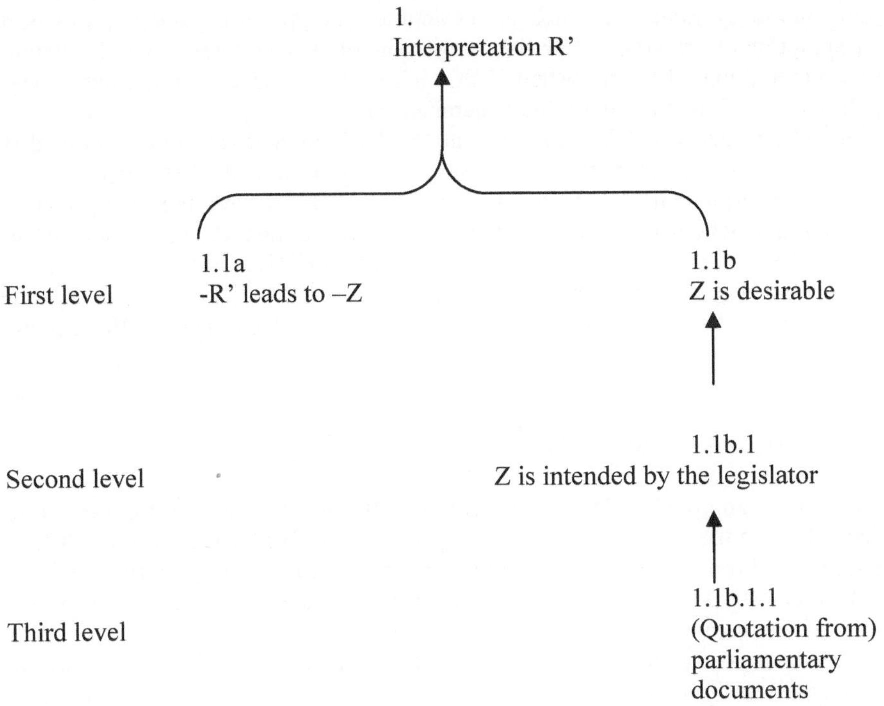

In both examples, arguments on the first level ("the legislator intended a firm date (R')") and ("the reduction of the number of traffic offences is desirable"), are supported by an argument in which a reference is made to parliamentary documents. The argument scheme in these argumentations is based on a specific symptomatic relation: the authority of parliamentary documents is treated as being indicative for the intention of the legislator (directly) as to the interpretation of the rule (example 1) or as to a certain goal (example 2).

In the argumentation in the above cases, the references to parliamentary documents are not specified or made concrete. The judge could, however, anticipate critical questions concerning the authority of the parliamentary documents, by presenting one or more quotations from parliamentary documents, as was done in the Brongersma case that I mentioned in the introduction. According to MacCormick and Summers (1991, p. 522), quotations are in particular relevant where subjective intentions are involved. In a subjective conception of intentions, one ascribes to the legislator some actual subjective motivational state belonging to the legislator (the actual intention), whereas in an objective conception of intention one ascribes an intention to the legislator as a supposedly ideally rational agent (a reasonable meaning). In the former, the quotations may function as evidence of actual denotative or connotative intentions of the legislator. This argumentative use of quotations can be looked upon as argumentation by example, which is yet another subtype of argumentation based on a symptomatic relation.[7] For the evaluation of this argumentation it should, among other things, be established if this quotation is indeed representative and whether it is sufficient to justify the generalization.

The critical questions that are relevant for the argument schemes employed at the different levels in the justification enable us to ascertain whether pragmatic and symptomatic argumentation is an acceptable way to defend the interpretative standpoint and whether the argumentation has been applied correctly. In order to determine whether the argumentation for an interpretative standpoint might be effective, the rhetorical aspects of argumentation should be taken into account as well. In the next section I will concentrate on the effectiveness of the genetic argument.

Limits to Strategic Manoeuvring

In a rhetorical approach to legal argumentation, the acceptability of argumentation is dependent on the effectiveness of the argumentation for the audience to which it is addressed. From this perspective, the justification of an interpretative decision may be considered as a strategic operation. Witteveen (1988, p. 333), for example, states: "If the meaning of a legal rule is unclear or ambiguous, the judge has to operate strategically in order to raise his interpretation above the turmoil beforehand." In his view, it does not suffice for a judge to clarify the meaning of the rule. The judge should also argue why his paraphrase of the rule is the best possible.

In the pragma-dialectical approach to argumentation as developed by van Eemeren and Houtlosser (2002, p. 142), this view on justifying interpretative decisions may be regarded as an attempt both to uphold a reasonable discussion attitude and to further the decision at hand. This means that the arguers' aim for the optimal rhetorical result is not necessarily in conflict with standards for reasonableness. From this perspective, the genetic argument, as well as the other interpretative arguments, may in principle be used to make the strongest case.

Although the genetic argument is often used, the application of the argument in practice is controversial. In order to determine if and how the rhetorical use of the argument may be limited, I will analyse the most important objections against the argument by making use of the insights provided by van Eemeren and Houtlosser (2002) in their study of strategic manoeuvring. These insights offer a framework that enables us to have a closer look at the most problematic aspects of the effectiveness of the genetic argument.

According to van Eemeren and Houtlosser (2002, p. 135) strategic manoeuvring has three aspects; it can take place in:

1. making an expedient choice from the options constituting the "topical potential" associated with a particular discussion stage;
2. selecting a responsive adaptation to "audience demand";
3. exploiting the appropriate "presentational devices".

Making an Expedient Choice from the Options Constituting the "Topical Potential" Associated with a Particular Discussion Stage

In the approach of van Eemeren and Houtlosser (2002, p. 139), the topical potential associated with a particular dialectical stage can be regarded as the set of relevant alternatives available in the stage of the resolution process.[8] If we concentrate on the argumentation stage in deciding on an interpretative issue, the alternatives consist of the various techniques, or methods of interpretation. In a rhetorical approach to legal argumentation, these techniques are considered as *topoi* that can be of help in finding arguments that have convincing argumentative power to justify the preferred interpretation.[9]

When choosing for a genetic argument to justify an interpretative decision, it should be considered that, at least in the Netherlands, in principle there is no ranking order between the various interpretative arguments.[10] However, both in actual practice and in the literature, it is sometimes suggested that there is indeed a hierarchy and that the genetic argument, together with the linguistic argument has preference. This preference is based on the idea that these two arguments express that the judge is bound by the law and in that way guarantee that judicial decisions are not arbitrary. Since it might lend extra argumentative force to the argument, an appeal to this idea might prove effective. This approach could, however, also turn out to be counterproductive, because there is a chance that the judge might be accused of (implicitly) referring to a hierarchy that doesn't exist, if the genetic argument is used as a single argument to justify the interpretation.

In a case where a genetic argument was used in order to decide that certain plants should be considered as drugs within the meaning of the Opium Act, the annotator[11] explicitly made such an accusation.[12] He pointed out that "there is no general hierarchy in a genetic interpretation method, a functional argument and other interpretation methods. A genetic argument does not, as a matter of course, prevail over other arguments". Similar criticism was passed in a case where the Supreme Court had to give an interpretative decision concerning the term "to compete for".[13] The Supreme Court decided that this term had to be interpreted in accordance with how it had been used in earlier legislation and presented a genetic argument. When a genetic argument is put first, this should, according to the annotator, be motivated because "even in criminal law, which is strongly orientated on legislation, altered social circumstances should be taken into account when justifying interpretative decisions". These reactions illustrate that an interpretative decision based on a single genetic argument may encounter serious resistance and is therefore unlikely to be effective if it is not supplemented by other arguments, although the argument may be sufficient in view of formal motivation obligations. In these supplemented arguments it should be demonstrated why a genetic argument is preferable to other interpretative arguments.

Selecting a Responsive Adaptation to Audience Demand

For optimal rhetorical results, in the view of van Eemeren and Houtlosser (2002, p. 140), the moves that are made must, in each stage of the discourse, be adapted to audience demand such that they comply with the listeners' or readership's good sense and preferences. In the argumentation stage, this may be achieved by quoting arguments the readers agree with or referring to argumentative principles they adhere to.

In a legal context an interpretative decision is directed to various addressees. The audience might consist of justiciables, lawyers and the legal community as a whole. For a non-legal audience, such as the justiciables or other parties who might be affected by the rule, the genetic argument is, in comparison to other arguments, more accessible, because the judge refers to statements from politicians that were brought forward in public debates. Often, these statements are comprehensible without specific legal knowledge. The argument may also be appealing to a non-legal audience because, in a democracy, the authority of the legislator is generally accepted and convincing.

The effectiveness of genetic argumentation however is much more problematic for a legal audience. In legal theory many authors point at the fact that one cannot speak of just one legislator, but that there are many participants in the process prior to the enactment.[14] This enables a judge to select those extracts from the legislative process that support his view on the solution of the interpretation and ignore others.[15] In doing so, the legislator is wrongfully made responsible for the interpretation of the judge. The judge interprets the law but presents his interpretation as the intention of the legislator. This suggestion of acting arbitrarily would harm the effectiveness of the argumentation and should therefore be prevented. This could be done by indicating that counter arguments that were brought forward in the legislative process are taken into account as well. These counter arguments could consist of arguments that directly support an alternative interpretative decision as well as arguments that are aimed at the genetic argument and in that way indirectly criticize the interpretative decision that is defended by the judge. The balancing strategy that is used to weigh the pro- and counter arguments should be made explicit.[16]

It should then, however, also be verified whether the quotation of both the counter and pro arguments is complete and correct. The sheer volume of the documents involved in the legislative process may, after all, easily lead to misquotations and thus affect the effectiveness of the argumentation negatively. The Brongersma case, which I mentioned in the introduction, presents us with a telling example of an incomplete quotation by the Supreme Court. The brackets in the aforementioned quotation refer to the original text, the parliamentary record, which reads "as a result of the Brongersma case".[17] By leaving out this reference to the Brongersma case, it is suggested that the issue was discussed in a general sense (whereas in actual fact it was not). It also strays from the fact that the discussions in parliament took place in the year 2000, while the doctor assisted Brongersma to terminate his life in 1998. The doctor could therefore not have foreseen the standpoint of the government on this issue. Examples like these make it easy to understand why legal scholars are rather reticent about the use of the genetic argument.

Anticipating this reticence is therefore crucial for an adequate response to the demand of the (legal) audience. This means that quotations from parliamentary material have to meet certain criteria in order to provide an effective justification of the legislator's intention. Quotations should be correctly reproduced and adaptations such as summaries should not influence the nature and purpose of the cited material. The selected quotations should also be characteristic of the parliamentary material. Furthermore, there should be a plausible relation between the quotation and the intention it substantiates.

In order to procure the effectiveness of the genetic argument as a whole, argumentative quotations should be supplemented by arguments that address relevant criticism brought forward in the lawmaking process. Dealing with counter arguments will increase the argumentation's complexity, as does anticipating criticism on the use of the genetic argument.

Exploiting the Appropriate "Presentational Devices"

According to van Eemeren and Houtlosser (2002, p. 140) the available presentational devices must be put in good strategic use for optimally conveying rhetorical moves. The following example illustrates how possible obstacles to the effectiveness of the genetic argument, which are discussed under (1) and (2), may be increased by the presentation of the argument:

> From the legislative history of the realisation of article 243 and 247 of the Criminal Code (…) it follows that the legislator, by introducing the term "powerlessness", only had in mind a state of physical helplessness originating in the victim's physical inability to act. (Supreme Court 28 February 1989, *NJ* 1989, p. 658)

In this example, taken from Dutch jurisprudence, there is a difference of opinion about how the term "powerlessness" in the Criminal Code should be interpreted. The Supreme Court justifies its interpretation by deploying a genetic argument. In its formulation of the argumentation, the Supreme Court suggests that it is absolutely clear how the term should be interpreted by stating that "From the history … it follows that". This firmness is then reinforced by the word "only" so that other possible interpretations are ruled out beforehand. At a cursory reading, this peremptory formulation might seem effective, but in view of possible objections to the genetic argument that concern "the choice of the topical potential" and "the audience demand", it is not. The ineffectiveness of the presentation also becomes apparent in the critical reaction on this decision from the annotator. He criticizes the formulation as being apodictic and he says: "There are other valid arguments, but by making the formulation absolute, these other arguments did not come to the surface".

Another problem in this presentation is that the argument could not be checked because the reference to the legislative history is too vague. The argument from the legislator is neither a direct quote nor accompanied by any source reference. The Supreme Court should at least have given a reference as to where the argument is mentioned. Argumentation, including arguments that are extracted from parliamentary documents, has to be expressed to be able to determine the discursive effectiveness of the formulation and stylistic framing of it. This illustrates that expression is inextricably bound up with content.

Conclusion

Interpretative decisions are frequently justified by arguments in which the judge refers to the intention of the legislator. By means of these references, arguments from politics may reappear in legal argumentation. In these so-called historical or genetic arguments, the ways in which references to the legislator form part of the justification of the decision may differ. In order to gain more insight in these differences, two types of the genetic argument as distinguished by Alexy were taken as a starting point. In a pragma-dialectic reconstruction of the argumentation of which each of these types is composed, it is shown how the complexity of the argumentation in both types varies. It also became apparent that references to the legislator are situated on different levels.

Furthermore, I have demonstrated that differences between various forms of the genetic argument may be clarified by determining the argument scheme that underlies the argumentation. By making use of the pragma-dialectical typology of argument schemes I have shown that the genetic argument may be based on symptomatic argumentation as well as on pragmatic argumentation. Insight into the argument scheme is particularly important in view of the evaluation of the argument, since for each type of argumentation different criteria of soundness are applicable.

The effectiveness of the genetic argument is discussed by making use of pragma-dialectical insights on strategic manoeuvring. I analysed how problematic aspects of the genetic argument could hinder its effectiveness. From this analysis it seems that the effectiveness of a genetic argument is limited when it is used as a single argument in order to justify an interpretative decision. The effectiveness of the argument may be increased if it is part of a more complex argumentation that anticipates possible objections to the adequacy and the application of the argument.

* Dr. H. José Plug is lecturer in the Department of Speech Communication, Argumentation Theory and Rhetoric in the University of Amsterdam. Her research interests include political and legal argumentation.

Notes

1 Judges in the UK will rarely adduce citations of parliamentary materials and debates for the purpose of genetic arguments aimed to establish the legislature's intention. The objections against the use of legislative history in this way are practical (to read all the materials when preparing a case would be expensive and time-consuming) as well as fundamental (it becomes increasingly impossible to rely on the apparent meaning of a rule). See also MacCormick and Summers (1991, p. 380).

2 Waaldijk (1987) argues that the requirement to justify legislative decisions seems more problematic than the requirement to justify judicial decisions. He nevertheless concludes that it is possible for legislative decisions to conform to the same 'rule of law' as judicial decisions: to be embedded in a system of rational argumentation for reasonable decisions. On differences and similarities between justification requirements that are to be fulfilled by the judge and the legislator, see also Wintgens (this volume).

3 If a person, a written source or an institution is inappropriately presented as an authority, then a fallacy of abuse of authority (*argumentum ad verecundiam*) is committed. See van Eemeren *et al.* (2002).

4 The analysis is in line with the finding of MacCormick and Summers (1991, pp. 522-530) that, since an argument from intention is variable in content, the argument should be considered 'transcategorial'.

5 The set of questions that are relevant for the pragma-dialectical typology of argument schemes are formulated in van Eemeren *et al.* (2002, pp. 95-102).

6 See Feteris (2002, pp. 251-252) for a more extensive discussion on which norms are relevant for the evaluation of pragmatic or teleological argumentation in a legal context and how these norms can be translated to critical questions.

7 See Garssen (2001) who discusses the major theoretical approaches of argument schemes, including argumentation by example.

8 Analytically, four stages can be distinguished: confrontation stage, opening stage, argumentation stage and concluding stage. They correspond with the four different phases an argumentative discourse, in principle, must past through, to be adequate for resolving a difference of opinion (van Eemeren and Grootendorst, 1984).

9 See for example Viehweg (1954) and, in Dutch jurisprudence, 't Hart (Supreme Court 28 February 1989, *NJ* 1989, p. 658).

10 See Plug (2000a, p. 198).

11 An annotator is a legal scholar who comments on an important ruling, by means of an annotation or a note that is published within the final decision.

12 Supreme Court 29 November 1994, *NJ* 1995, p. 292.

13 Supreme Court 19 December 1989, *NJ* 1990, p. 468.

14 The concept 'the legislator' is a complex one. In the Netherlands, for example, 'the legislator' consists of the Government, which is composed of the monarch and the ministers, and the States General, which in its turn is composed of the Upper House and the Lower House.

15 Witteveen (1988, p. 340) demonstrated this point by means of a case in which it had to be decided whether an article in the Betting and Gaming Act permitted the mayor to limit the number of bingo nights in his municipality. The court pointed out that the legislator did not intend a limitation. They referred to a statement that was made during a parliamentary debate by one of the MPs who introduced the bill. On closer examination of the debate, Witteveen concluded that the MP's opinion was much more balanced. Sometimes these inadequacies are brought to light by the annotator of a judgment.

16 Requirements that are to be met when dealing with counter arguments are discussed in Plug (2000b).
17 See also Pans (2003).

References

Alexy, R. (1989), *A Theory on Legal Argumentation. The Theory of Rational Discourse as Theory of Legal Justification*, Clarendon press, Oxford.

Feteris, E.T. (1999), *Fundamentals of Legal Argumentation. A Survey of Theories on the Justification of Judicial Decision*, Kluwer Academic Publishers, Dordrecht.

Feteris E.T. (2002), 'Pragmatic argumentation in a legal context' in F.H. van Eemeren (ed.) *Advances in Pragma-Dialectics*, Sic Sat, Amsterdam/Vale Press, Newport News, Virginia.

Garssen, B. (2001), 'Argument Schemes' in F.H. van Eemeren (ed.) *Crucial Concepts in Argumentation Theory*, Amsterdam University Press, Amsterdam.

MacCormick, D.N. and Summers, R.S. (eds.) (1991), *Interpreting Statutes. A Comparative Study*, Dartmouth, Aldershot.

Snijders, H.J. (1978), *Rechtsvinding door de burgerlijke rechter. Een kwantitatief rechtspraakonderzoek bij de Hoge Raad en de gerechtshoven*, Kluwer, Deventer.

Pans, E. (2003), 'De Hoge Raad en de onzekere arts. Kanttekeningen bij het arrest over hulp bij zelfdoding in de zaak Brongersma', *Nederlands Juristenblad*, Vol. 17, pp. 870-877.

Plug, H.J. (2000a), *In onderlinge samenhang bezien. De pragma-dialectische reconstructie van complexe argumentatie in rechterlijke uitspraken*, Thela Thesis, Amsterdam.

Plug, H.J. (2000b), 'Selecting counter arguments in legal and non legal argumentation' in C.W. Tindale, H.V. Hansen and E. Sveda (eds.). *Argumentation at the Century's Turn*, [on CD-Rom.], St. Catherines, Ontario: OSSA.

van Eemeren, F.H. and Grootendorst, R. (1984), *Speech Acts in Argumentative Discussions. A Theoretical Model for the Analysis of Discussions Towards Solving Conflicts of Opinion*, De Gruyter/Foris, Berlin/ Dordrecht.

van Eemeren, F.H. and Grootendorst, R. (1992), *Argumentation, communication and fallacies. A Pragma-dialectic Perspective*, Erlbaum Associates, Hillsdale, NJ.

van Eemeren, F.H. and Houtlosser, P. (2002), 'Strategic maneuvering: maintaining a delicate balance' in F.H. van Eemeren and P. Houtlosser (eds.) *Dialectic and Rhetoric. The warp and Woof of Argumentation Analysis*, Kluwer Academic Publishers, Dordrecht.

van Eemeren, F.H., Grootendorst R., and Snoeck Henkemans, A.F. (2002), *Argumentation: Analysis, Evaluation, Presentation*, Erlbaum Associates, Mahwah, NJ.

Viehweg, Th. (1954), *Topik und Jurisprudenz*, 5th ed., 1974, Beck, München.

Vranken, J.B.M. (1995), *Mr. C. Asser's handleiding tot de beoefening van het Nederlands burgerlijk recht. Algemeen deel*, Tjeenk Willink, Zwolle.

Waaldijk, K. (1987), 'Can we require legislatures to state the reasons for their legislative decisions?' in F.H. van Eemeren, R. Grootendorst, J. A. Blair and C. Willard (eds.) *Argumentation: Analysis and Practices. Proceedings of the Conference on Argumentation 1986*, Foris Publications, Dordrecht.

Waaldijk, K. (1994), *Motiveringsplichten van de wetgever*, Koninklijke Vermande, Lelystad.

Witteveen, W.J. (1988), *De retoriek in het recht. Over retorica en interpretatie, staatsrecht en democratie,* Tjeenk Willink, Zwolle.

PART V

PRACTICAL ISSUES

Chapter 16

EC-law between Social Message and Record of Agreement. How the Theory of Legislation can Contribute to Understanding Practical Problems of Negotiated Legislation

Tito Gallas*

Legisprudence and the Practice of Legislation

"Legislation is political decision and not a science of legislation" (Sousa Franco, 2003, p. 122). Clearly, this sentence expresses Professor Sousa Franco's thought as a politician, rather than as a scholar. However, even if not formulated in such an apodictic manner, calling into question the very existence of a science of legislation, other authors too tend to limit the role of legistics. Giuliano Amato, also a politician and university professor, is certainly correct in saying that "the legislative techniques ... must respect the choice of values made by the political master" (Amato, 1990, p. 47), but this statement expresses unidirectional view. It considers only the relationship decision-maker → executor and doesn't take into account the input that an expert may provide to the legislator.

This, however, is not the only display of a tendency to lessen the importance of the theoretical reflection on legislation, or of certain forms of this reflexion. Also among the scholars in the science of legislation there are different approaches. Karpen (1996, p. 11) distinguishes six fields of interest. Among these fields we can single out a more abstract level, that Karpen calls "Legis-Prudence" and other forms of research, more practice-linked, among which one finds "the techniques to meet the legislative requirements and to express clearly the legislative will (Legis-Technics, legistics in a narrow sense)". Between the legists interested in one or the other of the different fields, one can often notice incomprehension as to the value of the respective research. It can happen, for instance, that a legist coming from studies in constitutional law looks with distrust at the reflections of a philosopher of law on more communicative legislation, involving several actors in the civil society. The lawyer with a background as a constitutionalist is likely to ask questions about the representative nature of those actors, of the procedures and so forth and to relegate the legisprudence, intended as pure theory of legislation, amongst the reveries of doubtful usefulness or indubitable misleadingness.

This contribution is not intended to contribute to an abstract discussion of these themes. It may nevertheless show, in a limited field, that a theoretical systematisation of a problem may lead to a clearer vision of a given legistic phenomenon – in our case, EC-lawgiving – and consequently to a better comprehension and solution of related practical problems.

Internal Norm (Social Message)

The first part of the title of this contribution says something quite obvious, at least to those used to reasoning on the creation of legislation: the law, the legal rule, is – or can be or should be – a social message.

There are, of course, several other possible definitions of what is law. They are even better known. If one takes a legal dictionary, under "norm, legal " one can find, probably first of all, the characteristics which make the difference between a legal rule and other – social, religious, ethical – norms: the speciality of the obligation or of the sanction or similar distinguishing traits. Then, one may find a description of the different parts of the norm, the descriptive one and the deontic. Often a classification of different types is also given; a rule may be classified as abstract, as concrete etc. And perhaps one can find some explanation about the need for a rule to be socially effective as a condition for its existence as legal norm. More or less information may be given in such a dictionary, but normally one would not find anything about a social message.

The result of the look in our "virtual" dictionary is not by chance. It shows the state of things. In fact, for a lawyer with a traditional viewpoint – one may call him a "normal" lawyer – it must be a discovery, a novelty, that legisprudence defines the legal rule from a rather different perspective and sees it first of all as a kind of social communication (Monrand, 1994, p. 142; Delnoy, 1999, p. 142).

Law has a steering function (*Steuerungsfunktion)* (Noll, 1973, p. 98) for the society addressed. It is intended to lead the citizen to follow the will of the legislator (Delnoy, 1999, p. 141), at least in the current, "instrumental" (Wintgens, 2003, p. 68) conception of legislation. By the law the legislator intends to influence the behaviour of the addressee of the norm: he tells him what he must or cannot do or what behaviour is allowed; or otherwise he instructs him under what conditions he, the citizen, may obtain a certain legal result, for instance, how he can dispose *post mortem* of his property. The aim is that the order or the information on the legal requirements reaches the interested citizen as effectively as possible. From this viewpoint, law is message.

This given is by now obvious among legists. However, for the sake of completeness, it is useful to recall shortly the mechanism of communication. For our purposes, we can take the simplest and plainest scheme that the theory of communication may offer. The communication takes place between a sender and one or more addressees through a common code; in a way, one can think of a wire in a traditional telephone connection. A sender conceives of what he has to communicate, formulates it into an expression corresponding to the chosen code, transmits it via the code to the addressee; the addressee decodes the received impulsion and the communication is successful to the extent that the concept of the addressee corresponds to the concept of the sender. It can be successful only if the code is common to both participants. This means that they must use a language known by all the participants and, further, that the expression used is common to the vocabulary of all of them. It is useless if the sender formulates his thought in a very precise form, but the corresponding word is unknown by the counter-party. Incidentally, one may notice that in the foregoing sentences 'code' and 'language' are used as synonyms. Of course, in general, language is not the only possible code; just imagine a picture and the different means of expression used in it. However, language is the means, per excellence, of communication for the legislator, practically the sole one.

This, extremely simplified but sufficient, model of communication is self-evident in formal legistics. Very slowly, those who also participate in the legislative process become aware of it. This is an important step forward, because this theoretical acknowledgement entails important consequences for the practice of legislative drafting.

International Norm (Record of Agreement)

But now, let us raise the question of whether the scheme just outlined is valid for every legal rule. Is any norm social communication? Are there always a sender and an addressee? This question seems to be completely new.

The means of expression of a legal rule is language. Language does not serve only for communication. One of its functions is to fix what one thinks or says ("*Mnemonik*", von Humboldt, 1994, p. 121). If two parties negotiate a contract, in the negotiation phase the language is the means of communication; it serves to communicate to the other party one's position, a proposal, the acceptance and so on. But the function of the written text of a contract is to record, to fix what has been agreed. Only in the second place may it serve to communicate, for instance to inform the judge or a third party about the content of the contract.

Now, this does not apply only to contractual rules negotiated between individuals; it is valid also for agreements in international law. In this case too, communication is not the main aim. The rules of communication are not necessarely applicable; for example, one does not need to pay attention to the code of the other party. The French *Conseil d'Etat* describes it sharply : "(...) *comme on sait, un traité ne vaut que par les arrière-pensées de ses signataires. Là où les juristes cherchent la précision, les diplomates pratiquent le non-dit et ne fuient pas l'ambiguïté*" (Conseil d'Etat, 1992, p. 48). The translation might run as follows: "(...) as one knows, a treaty counts only having regard to the mental reservations of the signataries. Where lawyers try to be precise, diplomats like to say and not to say and they do not shrink back from ambiguities". The sentence is full of nuances:

arrière-pensée means a mental reservation, maybe known or not by both of the contracting parties, *non-dit* is more than simply silence, it leaves the other party in a situation of uncertainty. Obviously, we are no longer in the realm of communication.

Our first conclusion is now: not every legal rule is social message. Only the norms of internal law, created by a legislator who is clearly distinguished from the addressee of the norm, constitute a social message and have to be drafted as such a message. The rules of international law follow different criteria.

EC-law (between Social Message and Record of Agreement)

Internal law, international law. Where is Community law situated between these two conceptions?

EC-law mainly takes the form of regulations and directives. Regulations are, pursuant to Article 249 of the Treaty, directly applicable. They establish directly rights and obligations for the citizens. *De facto*, this is also true as for directives; formally, directives are addressed to the Member States, but the fact is that they are so detailed that their content doesn't need any more specification for their transposition into national law. Moreover, EC-law can be invoked by any citizen. Thus, in substance, Community law features as internal law. It should be drafted as such, as a social message.

The reality of Community life shows that the actors in the production process of EC-legislation are not conscious or are only dimly – not thoroughly – conscious of their role as legislators. In particular in the Council, they negotiate the regulations and directives as if they were international agreements.

One may, certainly, object that any legislative activity is a balance between different options, each of them being advanced by different actors of the political and social life. This is true: negotiation is the rule in any legislative process. The enlightened vision of the legal norm as a result of logical deduction is belied every day by the sight of the participants in the production of the law, negotiating, sometimes haggling over, the result of the legislative process. The different political parties that form a government, majority and opposition, various organisations and movements, media of opposite tendencies, contribute to the balancing of the interests involved and to a regulation taking all of them into account, in a more or less equitable result.

At first sight, the genesis of EC-law doesn't differ substantially from this picture. In the Community Institutions, Commissioners with different portfolios, Ministers with different competencies, European and national officials coming from the various departments, lobbies representing all kinds of interests, face one another in order to assert one or other standpoint. Ecological requirements may clash with industrial or commercial needs; one has to weigh social considerations against budgetary restrictions; the agricultural interests of a northern region may be opposed to those of a southern country; and so on. It will seem that the same situation occurs at Community level, as is usual in any State, just with one further element of complication, at least as for the Council of Ministers, namely the conflict between national interests represented by the Member States. The other conflicts mentioned above may come into play at the same time, in Brussels, and in this case things are simply more complicated, but not different from what one sees at national level. Alternatively, they may be already settled in advance, in the respective capitals. Anyway, one must recognise that the balancing of interests in the creation of EC-legislation, as described up to now, does not differ substantially from what happens in the Member States.

Thus, the fact that EC-law is the result of negotiations intended to weigh up the various interests against each other does not make it different in nature to internal law in general. The distinguishing characteristic is to be found elsewhere. In this regard, let us think, first of all, of the way in which the legislation of the Community is created. Already in 1983, Ferrari Bravo (1983, p. 135) deplored that the proper original method of legislating was replaced by a "*metodo diplomatico*" consisting of a "meticulous and often laborious negotiation" between the delegates of the Member States. In fact, the work in the Council is led by the diplomats of the Committee of Permanent Representatives (Coreper) and it has already been described how diplomats are used to draft legal norms.

Actually, what counts is not the fact of negotiating, but the mental attitude behind it.

Compromise is not necessarily a synonym for lack of clarity. Suppose two parties, in whatever context, each propose a different figure (for an amount or for a percentage of pollutants and so on) and they reach an agreement on a certain figure between these two. In this case, the compromise will necessarily be expressed in an unambiguous term, a number. A public authority bearing in mind that he is acting as a legislator will take care that the result of a negotiation is such that it can be translated in a message as simple and precise as possible; he avoids having recourse to verbal acrobatics and to covering mental reservations with an obscure drafting. He will do so because it is his duty to address the citizen with clear and simple words. Moreover, he will do it also because he knows that an equivocal proposition is not confined to his interlocutors with whom he sat around the negotiating table, but will be interpreted, with an "*unbescholtener Blick*" (naïve look), as Swiss legists sometimes say, by citizens, officials and judges. An ambiguous formulation may get twisted against the legislator.

Not so as for diplomats. As described in the previous quotation of the *Conseil d'Etat*, they are used to a different kind of drafting, not understood as a message to a third party. It is interesting to notice, that the said quotation of the *Conseil d'Etat* was not intended to describe international lawgiving, but precisely the creation of EC-law. And then, for this law, it coins the terms "*droit diplomatique*" (Conseil d'Etat, 1992, p. 48), as a law created by diplomats, following their mental habits; finally, it characterizes it as essentially "opaque" (Conseil d'Etat, 1992, p. 41).

It is true that since 1992 the Institutions have made some efforts in order to improve the quality of their legislation. If a Council Resolution of 1993[1] was more an example of symbolic law, an Interinstitutional Agreement[2] of 1998 on the drafting quality of EC-law could deserve a better fate. Their guidelines suggest, *inter alia*, that the drafting should be clear, that one has to take into account who are the addressees of the norm, that any draftman must remember the burdens of multilingualism. However, it will take some time, and a long pedagogical process, before such guidelines may prevail on deep-rooted habits.

If we try to answer now the question asked above, namely where is EC-law situated between the two alternatives shown in the title of the present contribution, at the present state of affairs we must say that EC-law has, by its nature, the character of internal law and should thus take the form of a social message, but that it is conceived and drafted as if it were international law and, consequently, as a record of agreement.

Negotiated Law

One could argue that, with the foregoing statement, the subject of the present contribution is exhausted. However, a more detailed study of the Community legislative activity shows certain aspects that hardly fit with the scheme sketched above.

First of all, one may notice that almost from the beginning there existed legislative acts adopted by the Institutions, whose content was already known to the persons to whom they were intended to apply. This is the case of the annexes to the directives for removing technical barriers to trade between Member States; such annexes often reproduce technical regulations drawn up in other – private, public or international – organisations and currently applied, for instance by test laboratories.

Further, one must recall the contribution that the interested parties, addressees of the future legal standards, provide in the drawing up of regulatory proposals of the Commission. This contribution has become increasingly more systematic in the framework of the *ex ante*-assessment strategies applied by the Commission's services. One of the main items of the interinstitutional agreement on "better law-making", that will be signed in the next few months, is just the extension of such pre-legislative consultations.

The most interesting and important recent evolution involving new actors in the regulatory activities of the Community is the phenomenon of negotiated law. This concerns acts not negotiated by diplomats, but by the future addressees of the norm; thus, such acts can be linked not so much to "diplomatic law", but rather to the scheme of international law or to contracts, which, as is well known, constitute law between the contracting parties (see, for instance, Article 1134 of the Belgian civil code).

Among these new regulatory forms, the first that should be mentioned is the system laid down in the field of social policy by Articles 138 and 139 of the EC-Treaty, introduced by the Treaty of Amsterdam. If the Commission intends to submit a legislative proposal in this field, it consults management and labour; these may inform the Commission that they prefer to settle the question by a direct dialogue and if this dialogue leads to "contractual relations, including agreements", the Commission waives the submission of its proposal to the European Parliament and the Council.

The abovementioned Agreement on better Community law-making insists on a greater use of such alternative regulation mechanisms, such as co-regulation and self-regulation. In this case too, in a way creators and addressees of the norm coincide.

This phenomenon is not limited to EC-legislation; the Community simply follows a general trend towards a more and more "negotiated" law, in opposition to the "imposed" one (Supiot, 1996, p. 631).

This trend may give rise to some perplexity. Beside the questions already raised at the beginning of this contribution about the representativeness of the negotiators, the need for clear procedures etc., another question may be asked, concerning drafting: doesn't this new approach, at Community but also at any other level, contain the risk that the negotiators, not conscious of their role as legislators, adopt the same attitude as diplomats, namely neglect the citizen, accept the conclusion of ambiguous compromises, and thus finally create, themselves also, "opaque" law?

This question goes beyond the ambit of the present contribution. We leave it open for further discussion.

* The author, Head of Division at the Council of the European Union, is not presenting the position of the Council, but expressing his personal views.

Notes

1 OJ C 166, 17.6.1993, p. 1.
2 OJ C 73, 17.3.1998, p. 1.

References

Amato, G. (1990), 'Principi di tecnica legislativa' in M. D'Antonio (ed.), *Corso di studi legislativi superiori*, ISLE - Scuola di scienza e tecnica della legislazione, CEDAM, Padova.

Conseil d'Etat (1992), 'Rapport public 1992' in *Etudes et Documents*, nr. 44, pp. 13-66.

Delnoy, P. (1999), 'La communication législative' in C.-A. Morand (ed.), *Légistique formelle et matérielle - Formal and material legistic*, Presses Universitaires d'Aix-Marseille.

Ferrari Bravo, L. (1983), 'Il Consiglio' in E. Pennacchini, R. Monaco, L. Ferrari Bravo and S. Puglisi (eds.), *Manuale di diritto comunitario*, volume primo, UTET, Torino.

Karpen, U. (1996), 'Legislation and Legistics in European Countries - Introduction to the Topic of the Symposium' in U. Karpen (ed.), *Legislation in European Countries*, Nomos Verlagsgesellschaft, Baden-Baden.

Noll, P. (1973), *Gesetzgebungslehre*, Rowohlt Taschenbuch Verlag GmbH, Reinbek bei Hamburg.

Morand, C.-A. (1994), 'Vers une méthodologie de la communication législative', *Gesetzgebung heute*, Vol. 1994, 2, pp. 11-27.

Sousa Franco, A. (2003), 'A economia de hoje ou o peixe de cabeça apodrecida' [Today's economy or the fish with a rotten head], *Visão*, 29.5.2003, p. 122-123.

Supiot, A. (1996), 'La loi dévorée par la convention ?' in Ph. Gérard, F. Ost and M. van de Kerchove (eds.), *Droit négocié, droit imposé?*, Publications des Facultés universitaires Saint-Louis, Brussels.

von Humboldt, W. (1994), *Über die Sprache*, A. Francke Verlag, Tübingen/Basel.

Wintgens, L.J. (2003), 'Het wetsbegrip anders bekeken. Alternatieven voor en in wettelijke regulering. Tevens een inleiding tot de *legisprudentie*, een nieuwe wetgevingstheorie' [The concept of law from another point of view. Alternatives for and in legislation. An introduction to *legisprudence,* a new theory of legislation] in L.J. Wintgens (ed.), *Het Wetsbegrip* [The concept of law], Die Keure, Brugge.

Chapter 17

The Justification and the Optimisation Principle in International Nuclear Law: Theory and Practice

Ludo Veuchelen*

Introduction

This paper consists of a case study on nuclear law giving rise to the following discussion themes.

The Role of the Law and the Courts in Today's "Risk Society"

Although there is an evolution in our law systems to more regulation on prevention and precaution, this is not a new evolution in using General Principles, but the result of our complex technical society. Society and industry expect clarity and security of law where law itself is vague. This point would be a first theme for discussion, i.e. the role of the law and the courts in today's society: Law and Ethics?; Process of law-making: technocrats versus democracy?; Quality of law: why do we accept the law?

Licensing Procedure for High-risk and the use of Broad General Principles of Law such as Precaution and Justification

About the Justification Principle, many questions remain and give rise to further legal challenges. This risk may be reduced by the provision of governmental guidance on practical questions relating to the application of the Justification Principle to new and existing generic practices. This point would be a second theme for discussion, i.e. how is the licensing procedure for high-risk and activities governed to equilibrate the economic and ecological values? Motivation of public decisions; Transparency for the citizen; Proportionality and Precautionary Principle.

Understanding between Technicians, Engineers, Scientists and Lawyers about the Optimisation Principle

The BAT Principle ("Best Available Techniques") compares available techniques of the industrial sector and does not impose an individual or compelling choice on the licensee, which means no direct sanctions are given.

A third theme for discussion is: are we ready for this new evolution? Can we find a common understanding between, technicians, engineers, scientists and lawyers on Optimisation Principles, such as ALARA ("As Low as Reasonably Achievable, taking economic and social factors into account") and BAT?

General Outline

Although nuclear law developed along the lines of a complex, highly technological and international industrial sector, which gave rise to a technical specificity, we cannot speak of nuclear law as a Lex Specialis. On the contrary: nuclear law is often criticised as not being democratic; a clear example of techno-science ruling and set up to promote the nuclear sector (Frydman, 1998a).[1]

It is clear that with the development of the ecological values in society, nuclear law is dependent on the general principles of environmental law (I like to call it "tutorship", where this tutorship belonged to public and administrative law at the beginning of the nuclear era).[2]

Nuclear law is the precursor of internationally established law, or should I say supranational law. To understand the genesis of this law system, we have to go back to both the medical uses of artificial radiation, from which angle the International Commission on Radiation Protection (ICRP) originates (1928), and to the military uses and the "Atoms for Peace" programme from which originates the promotion of civil nuclear uses, which culminated in the EURATOM Treaty (1957).

From the very beginning, the civil nuclear sector was dominated by large international institutions: the IAEA in Vienna and the OECD/NEA in Paris. Both are still very influential besides the Commission of the EU, in regulating the nuclear power sector.

As nuclear law developed earlier than environmental law, a set of general principles and rules of positive law already saw daylight, and there are globally called "nuclear law". Nowadays, some of these principles and rules can be found in environmental law, but new principles and rules emerged and we would like to know how far they coincide. In this part of the book I will try to highlight the principles and rules originating from nuclear law which can be called exemplary for other fields of law.

I will treat two principles of nuclear law, along the life-cycle of a nuclear industrial activity, the justification principle and the ALARA-principle.

For reasons of simplifying the discussion about the definition of General Principles of law, I can state that, to the contrary of a rule of law, such a principle is not applicable to a specific set of facts and gives more flexibility to the law and in particular to the judges. The General Principles are nevertheless an important source of law, not in the least in the field of public and administrative law. These principles are meant to give the rules of law a philosophical and ethical interpretation and are increasingly used to cover the lack of precise rules, or to cover the backlog in defining the rules for new developments.[3]

It goes without saying that we have great difficulty in applying all these general principles in such a way that law is done in a just and coherent way. Besides purely legal general principles, as for the rights of defence, the proportionality principle etc., we have to deal with political principles, which are laid down in sources of law without defining them as for the Precautionary Principle. Especially when the term "reasonable" is used, we know that the appreciation is completely left to the judge.[4] I will come to that point when speaking about ALARA.

In the doctoral research work of Steven Lierman and Chloée Degros, sponsored by SCK•CEN in the frame of PISA (Program of Integration of Social Aspects into Nuclear Research), a lot of attention is devoted to the evolution in our law systems to more regulation on prevention and precaution, as already can be witnessed in some "Risk Informed" and "Performanced Based" regulation. Steven Lierman studied the influence of the Precautionary Principle on the Liability law and Chloée Degros intends to study the legal sanctions in the field of the nuclear law and in particular when Soft Law is applicable.

It is perhaps good to indicate that this is not a new evolution, but that the difficulty of applying such general principles of law, which are the result of an ever more complex and technical society, have grown considerably and that society and industry sometimes expect clarity and security of law from the judges in areas where the law itself is very vague.

In legal doctrine these principles have been treated under different perspectives (Van Gestel, 2000, pp. 56-63):

- "Optimierungsgebote" (Alexy, 1979, pp. 79ff) characterise general principles of law which order, prohibit or allow a safe practice which can be reached entirely or partly (goal-oriented and not a "minimal requirement");
- the difference between "morality of duty" and "morality of aspiration" (Fuller, 1969, pp. 5-6).
  When obligations of result cannot be easily defined, norms with more principal character are more flexible, to give a basis for self-regulation of companies, which is called "morality of aspiration" instead of "morality of duty";
- "Reflexive Regulation" refers to what sociologists call "reflexive modernisation" where the individuals get more influence to define the level of risk they want to incur in society. This often leads to a pessimistic view on how to steer the global result of actions in society (Pieterman, 2000; Beck, 1992; Beck and Giddens, 1994);
- "Procedural Justice" refers to social science research that shows that people are not influenced by the results of the legal process as much as they are influenced by their opinion of whether the system was fairly administered, their

participation in the process, and the dignity and trust of the system. It is comparable to the "informed consent" (Tyler *et al.* 1996; see also the extensive study by Frydman, 1998c).

The protection of man and his environment in nuclear law is founded on the basic safety standards as developed by ICRP[5] and introduced by European Directives, i.e. Council Directive 96/29/EURATOM of May 13, 1996.[6]

It is good to have a close look at the text of the Directive, Title IV Justification, Optimisation and Dose Limitations for Practices:

1. Member States shall ensure that all new classes or types of practice resulting in exposure to ionising radiation are justified, in advance of being first adopted or first approved, by their economic, social or other benefits in relation to the health detriment they may cause.
2. Existing classes or types of practice may be reviewed as to justification whenever new and important evidence about their efficacy or consequences is acquired.
3. In addition, each Member State shall ensure that:
   - in the context of optimisation all exposures shall be kept as low as reasonable achievable, economic and social factors being taken into account;
   - without prejudice to Article 12, the sum of the doses from all relevant practices shall not exceed the dose limits laid down in this Title for exposed workers, apprentices and students and members of the public.

I will try to explain the meaning of these Basic Safety Standards in daily life.

A Legal Case Study on "Justification" and "Optimisation" in the Nuclear Field

Justification

Although the meaning of Justification in legal terms can be very broad, the 1996 Directive already was more explicit than the 1980 Directive, which stipulated in Article 6 (a):

> The limitation of individual and collective doses resulting from controllable exposures shall be based on the following general principles:
> a) the various types of activity resulting in an exposure to ionising radiation shall have been justified in advance by the advantages they produce.

This formula was, to my knowledge, never challenged before Court, except for the case of BNFL Thermal Reprocessing Plant at Sellafield (THORP).

In one of the many cases introduced by Greenpeace, the Judge (Otton J.) stated that "it was relevant to bear in mind that the need for THORP was considered at the planning stage by virtue of a 100 day Public Enquiry ... and during the Parliamentary process, planning approval was given". The Judge concluded that in a broad sense THORP had already been "justified in advance".

From the foregoing one can conclude that justification as a general legal principle leads to court decisions where no specific legal obligation for future activities is applied.

After the 1996 Directive, it was however clear that such legal obligation was imposed on the Member States and clearly directed to the Authority responsible for licensing new practices. One can also read in the 1996 Directive a new legal formula instead of a Cost-Benefit Analysis.

The newly formulated justification principle was again tested before Court, when the Secretaries of State for the Environment and for Health (The "Secretaries of State") in the UK were challenged on their decision (on 03.10.2001) that the practice of manufacturing Mixed Oxide Fuel (MOX) in the UK was "justified" in accordance with EU legislation, namely Council Directive 96/29/ EURATOM. This brought to a conclusion a decision-making process that had commenced almost five years earlier (Leigh, 2003, pp. 43-51). The Sellafield MOX plant is called "SMP".

A key legal point is that the October 2001 decision of the Secretaries of State was based on a view that the 1996 Directive introduced a different legal test to the application of the justification principle than that contained in the 1980 Directive. Article 6 of the 1996 Directive was interpreted as being concerned with a generic approach to a type of activity and not with a site-specific justification.

The case R v. Secretary of State for the Environment, Food and Rural Affairs and the Secretary of State for Health *ex parte* Greenpeace and Friends of the Earth and others led to the Judgment of Mr. Justice Collins of the High Administrative Court in London, which was handed down on November 15, 2001 (Unreported Case N° 4012/2001). Collins J. simply said that "That Submission is in my view correct". Accordingly the claimant's claim failed. However, they quickly lodged an appeal.

The Court of Appeal in London delivered its judgement on December 7, 2001. This decision confirmed the first judgment and favoured the operation license of BNFL for MOX production. For the record, a key passage of the decision by Lord Justice Simon Brown is given here:

> It cannot in my judgment be said that the Secretaries of State were bound to take into account costs which had been incurred in constructing SMP, which plainly cannot be recovered, and which were plainly not going to be incurred anywhere else. Secretaries of State are entitled to decide these cases in the real world. To bring into account sunk costs on a fictional basis that the equivalent costs would be incurred were the approval to be invoked to operate the practice elsewhere in the future would be absurd. It would be to sacrifice reason on the altar of blind theory. I cannot accept that Article 6 on its true construction requires such an economically nonsensical approach.

Because the only main argument used by claimants was that "sunk costs" should not be ignored when applying the justification test in the 1996 Directive, it is of no further help for our discussion to go deeper into the arguments developed in this MOX case.

Perhaps the most remarkable thing about the challenge in the UK Courts is that despite the fact that the October 2001 discussion document, and the several-year decision-making process, covered many complex subjects and issues, environmental discharges, environmental impact, radiological effects, including possible health effects, operational safety, economics, international markets for MOX, transportation, security and so on, in the end the challenge focused on just a single economic issue, the question of the sunk costs.

Many questions remain, e.g. would a new type of reactor system be a new practice? If numbers of particular installations are planned or foreseeable and some costs have been expended prior to a decision on justification having been taken, how should the sunk costs to be taken into account in relation to the generic practice? If existing practices have not been justified (and many existing practices will not have been subjected to a formal justification exercise) is there a legal requirement for them to be justified as new practices? Questions such as these may well give rise to further legal challenges in the future, causing high transaction costs. This risk might be reduced, and greater certainly achieved, by the provision of Governmental (or Community) guidance on practical questions relating to the application of the justification principle to new and existing generic practices.

Although it might seem simple, I have not been able to find an equivalent principle in environmental law. If this point is confirmed it highlights the thorough process of nuclear licensing compared with other industries with high risk for man and his environment.

Justification in Case of Military Uses (Nuclear Warheads)

It might be more appealing to confront this legal mechanism of justification with the military applications and practices.

Indeed, this legal test was also performed in the UK, resulting in a judgment of the Court of Appeal (Civil Division) on January 25, 2002 (Lord Justice Laws). The case concerned certain authorisations that permit the discharge of radioactive waste from two sites for the manufacturing of Trident nuclear warheads, part of the UK Atomic Weapons Establishment (AWE). The proceedings were a vehicle to give effect to the Appellant's objection to nuclear weapons.

The primary case was based on the Justification principle under Article 6 (a) of Council Directive 80/836/EURATOM, whereas the Respondent (the Environment Agency and the Secretary of State for Defence) was called to treat it as a detriment having regard to the "humanitarian" principles of international law.

The Appellant submitted that by regarding the Trident nuclear warheads programme as a given or axiomatic benefit (the Government's commitment to an independent nuclear deterrent, as a principal benefit) the Respondent foreclosed any debate that might be conducted as to whether the justification principle was met or not; the Respondent held itself bound to conclude that the principle was satisfied.

The Court of Appeal dismissed the case saying the law of England will not contemplate what may be called a merits review of any honest decision of government upon matters of national defence policy (the defence policy is within the constitutional framework).

The first and most obvious reason for this is that the court is unequipped to judge such merits or demerits.

> The defence of the realm, which is the Crown's first duty, is the paradigm of so grave a matter. Potentially such a thing touches the security of everyone, and everyone will look to the government they have elected for wise and effective decisions ... There is not, and cannot be, any expectation that the unelected judiciary play any role in such questions, remotely comparable to that of the government...I recognize that the notion of so grave a matter of State lacks sharp edges. But it is now a commonplace that the intensity of judicial review depends upon the context.

(The Lord Justice compared this case with a deportation in the interest of national security, while there was a substantial risk that this person would suffer torture or inhuman or degrading treatment.)

In conclusion, I see many distortions between Theory of Law and its practice. Let's not forget that "law not only has to be done, but also be seen to be done"!

Optimisation

The "As Low as Reasonably Achievable" principle (ALARA) is another basic safety standard developed by ICRP and transposed in EURATOM Directives and in national law. It is common knowledge that the ALARA principle is also used in environmental law, in connection with the principle of "Best Available Techniques, not entailing Excessive Economic Cost" (BATNEEC).

The Integrated Pollution Prevention & Control Directive (96/61/EG, Bd. EG L 257), Article 2, 11 stipulates: "best available techniques shall mean the most effective and advanced stage in the development of activities and their methods of operation which indicate the practical suitability of particular techniques for providing in principle the basis for emission limit values designed to prevent and, where that is not practicable, generally to reduce emissions and the impact on the environment as a whole:

- "Techniques" shall include both the technology used and the way in which the installation is designed, built, maintained, operates and decommissioned;
- "Available techniques" shall mean those developed on a scale which allows implementation in the relevant industrial sector, under economically and technically viable conditions, taking into consideration the costs and advantages, whether or not the techniques are used or produced inside the Member State in question, as long as they are reasonably accessible to the operator;
- "Best" shall mean the most effective in achieving a high general level of protection of the environment as a whole. In determining the best available

techniques, special consideration should be given to the items listed in Annex IV".

Following Annex IV to the IPPC Directive, the Best Available Techniques must take into account, amongst other things, the cost/benefit of environmental measures but also the Prevention and Precaution Principles.

Both principles, ALARA and BATNEEC, seem to create the same troubles for lawyers when they have to be applied:

- is it a principle or a rule of law?
- is it a minimum requirement or an aspiration?
- is it binding for the competent Authority or for the licensee?
- which sanctions of law can be applied, and in particular how to apply these principles in liability cases?

It is not a coincidence that the same questions arose when the precautionary principle was commented by legal doctrine. We can even say that for the very low doses of radiation, the ALARA Principle is a "Precautionary approach *avant la lettre*".

In that sense, nuclear law is a precursor in regulating at the same time with the "command & control" mechanism (prescribing dose limits) and with the goal oriented regulation and self-regulation (ALARA).

Lawyers should ask for more guidance in defining the ALARA Principle. This was already suggested by ICRP in 1988 (see Lefaure, 1996; Govaerts, 1996).

The measures to be taken by the Authorities in order to contribute to the implementation of ALARA by the operators, as listed by ICRP, are:

7.4. General responsibilities of the competent authorities:
(170) Competent authorities may wish to impose general requirements for optimisation of radiological protection to be carried under all circumstances ranging from major designs to individual dose control in the workplace. In order to assist with implementing these general requirements, the competent authority should specify the general criteria needed to implement the optimisation procedures. It must be remembered however that the final responsibility for radiological protection remains with the operating management.

(171) The specific way in, which the competent authorities can assist, are by:
1. encouraging the development of decision-aiding techniques suitable for optimisation assessments and recommending their use,
2. establishing relevant criteria, such as the value of unit collective dose, for performing optimisation assessments,
3. recommending the relevant factors to be taken into account in optimisation studies of different types,
4. guiding designers and managers on how to apply the requirement on a case by case basis,
5. encouraging the provision of information suitable to determine relevant biological protection parameters and models for use in optimisation studies,

6. making or commissioning generic assessments in order to establish optimised design parameters and recommending standards that can be deemed to be optimised,
7. assuring the comprehensiveness and quality of implementation of radiological protection optimisation in design, operation and maintenance BY SUITABLE ENFORCEMENT REGULATIONS AND BY AUDITING THE PERFORMANCE ACTIVITIES.

Every time the word *reasonable* is used in regulation or by judges it seems as if one is trying the impossible: setting rules for a practice we cannot define the boundaries of. In many documents and comments however, "reasonable" is a synonym for "economically feasible" (Van Gestel, 1996, p. 57). In the ALARA acronym, it is added: "taking economic and social factors into account".

That's why the principle is severely criticised by many authors who don't belong to the nuclear sector.[7]

In addition, the ALARA Principle has been tested before the Court in the US, even in the Three Mile Island case.

The many misunderstandings about applying such a general legal principle can be illustrated with a few quotes, taken from: "An overview of the current state of radiation litigation" (Wiedis *et al.* 2001).

- If the vague ALARA language becomes the legal standard of care for a utility, every exposure, no matter how small, can be analysed and criticised with the benefit of hindsight ... ;
- Unfortunately, a lawsuit always places the attention on the plaintiff as if he was the only worker at the plant and the health physics department can devote all of its resources to reducing that one worker's dose as low is reasonably achievable ...;
- An expert can always apply a cost-benefit analysis focused on just one worker and testify that such steps would only cost only a few dollars while greatly reducing his dose.

Needless to say that this is still a minefield for lawyers and, in particular, for judges, who are forced to work with a combination of positive law, soft law and optimisation principles. In case they interpret such optimisation principles as minimum criteria, such judgments can work counter-productively.

Of course this evolution to more rules for prevention and precaution is in line with Soft Law and Quality and Safety Control procedures and standards. These procedures and standards enter the law system via the principles "bonus pater familias" and "duty of care" when activities are brought before the Courts. The new evolution is to leave the "Command and Control" type of regulation for "Risk Informed Regulation" or "Performance Based Regulation", whose evolution is more in line with the common law tradition.

In Europe, the ALARA Principle has not been clarified by the Authorities. Instead it has become a leading principle for the nuclear operators, as part of their licensing permit, which of course is a source of many possible legal sanctions but merely of public and administrative law.

The SCK•CEN is a member of the European ALARA Network, which is not an official network organised by the European Commission but which is strongly supported by it. The ALARA Network organises workshops where a "benchmarking" of ALARA-practices is done and where a "lessons learned" attitude is promoted.

The ALARA Principle has been a prototype for optimisation of a safe plant management and safety culture. The BAT or BATNEEC Principle clearly puts more emphasis on the role of the Authorities which have to deal with licensing dangerous or high-risk operations, not in the least to prevent or minimise pollution.

It seems logical that, in the first place, the BAT Principle aims to compare the available techniques of a given industrial sector and not to impose an individual or compelling choice on the licensee. If this is correct, no direct sanctions can be linked to such a principle.

General Conclusions

In this study, the three "Basic Safety Standards" applicable under nuclear law are shown to be a breakthrough in international law towards better protection of man and the environment.

Maybe "le choc des idées, qui fait jaillir la lumière" has been absent in nuclear law practice and too many are of the opinion that nuclear law is a monolithic bloc of rules, which need no further comparison or re-thinking.

To avoid this isolation the SCK•CEN started with the Programme of Integrating Social Aspects into nuclear research, of which the three PhD projects in law are an integrated part (one project already completed). The programme is called PISA: see http://www.sckcen.be/pisa/.

It is the more remarkable that not only does multi-disciplinary research between the physical sciences and the social sciences seem rare, but also that amongst lawyers it is not common to look over the boundaries of industrial sectors, nor over the walls of the legal specialities or faculties at university level.

* Legal Adviser, Project Leader PISA "Law & Technology", SCK·CEN, The Belgian Nuclear Research Centre.

Notes

1 Under the title "Le développement du pouvoir administratif et technocratique" (Frydman, 1998b, pp. 36-37) the author writes : "Le principe des réformes est décidé au niveau du gouvernement, qui s'en réfère lui-même aux travaux des experts, organisés en autorités indépendantes, en commissions ad-hoc ou en bureaux d'études, ou aux avis des technocrates qui font profession d'administrer. On retrouve, sous une forme positiviste et paternaliste, l'idéal scientiste et techniciste du droit moderne".

2 It cannot be denied that principles such as the Precautionary Principle, Sustainable Development, Biodiversity and the eco-ethics in general, have got an enormous impact on regulation and justification in recent years. See Raes (1995) where he treats Jonas' anti-utopism versus Serres' contractualism and Ferry's antropocentrism. He also cites Kruithof: "Man is the measurer, but therefore not the only measure".

3 "Il y a à la racine de tout système de droit une conception de l'homme et du monde qui implique un certain nombre de postulats; c'est à ce fond éthique que se rattachent les principes généraux; mais la constatation opérée par le juge est en réalité largement créatrice: en affirmant l'existence d'un principe, le juge lui attache la sanction dont il était dépourvu et l'insère par là dans le droit positif" (Rivero, 1985, p. 77ff).

4 "The most common meaning of 'reasonable' is 'governed by reason'. Many interpretations have been, and still are, given to this concept, so central to social and exact sciences. The present author's research in the field of legal theory shows that an appeal to reason in legal discourse plays the essential role of hiding contradictions which this very discourse is incapable of resolving" (Corten, 1997).

5 In Re Ionizing Radiation Protection, ECJ 25.11.1992, Commission versus Belgium, European Court Report, 1992, the European Court of Justice (ECJ) expressly recognised that the standards laid down in Directive 80/836/EURATOM were based on the published recommendations of the ICRP, though in that case the ECJ, when considering the principle of this limitation, decided that the Directive imposed a minimum level of protection thereby allowing Member States to adopt more stringent dose limits than those required by the Directive if they so wished. Meanwhile the possibility of imposing lower dose limits has been incorporated in national legislation as for Article 54 of the new ARBIS in Belgium.

6 OJ L 159, 29.06.1996.

7 Belbéoch, 1998 : "Mais est-ce "raisonnable" de condamner des gens à mourir de cancer en leur imposant certains niveaux de dose parce que la radioprotection coûte cher? Est-il raisonnable de condamner l'industrie nucléaire à dépenser des sommes considérables pour éviter quelques morts alors que ces dépenses pourraient menacer son dévéloppement?"; Lajoirie (2002, pp. 43-57).

References

Alexy, R. (1979), 'Zum Begriff des Rechtsprinzips', *Rechtstheorie*, Beiheft 1, pp. 59-87.

Beck, U. (1992), *Risk Society, towards a New Modernity*, Sage Publications, London, Newbury Park, New Dehli.

Beck, U. and Giddens, A. (1994), *Reflexive Modernization, Politics, Tradition and Aesthetics in the Modern Social Order*, Polity Press, London.

Belbéoch, R. (1998), 'Le redoutable principe ALARA', in I. Rens and J. Jakubec (eds.), *Radioprotection et droit nucléaire, Entre les contraintes économiques et ecologiques, politiques et éthiques*, SEBES.

Corten, O. (1997), *L'utilisation du "raisonnable" par le juge international. Discours juridique, raison et contradictions*, Bruylant, Brussels.

Frydman, B. (1998a), 'Les transformations du droit moderne', *A la rencontre du droit*, E. Story-Scientia, Brussels.

Frydman, B. (1998b), 'Le développement du pouvoir administratif et technocratique', *A la rencontre du droit*, E. Story-Scientia, Brussels.

Frydman, B. (1998c), *Les transformations du droit moderne*, ULB Brussels, Série '*A la rencontre du droit*', E. Story-Scientia, Brussels.

Fuller, L. (1969), *The Morality of Law*, Yale University Press, New Haven and London.

Govaerts, P. (1996), 'Op zoek naar het redelijke, opportuniteiten en beperkingen van de toepassingen van het ALARA-principe', *Refresher Course Document, IRPA – International Congress on Radiation Protection*, Vienna, April 14-19, Centre d'Etude sur l'évaluation de la protection dans le domaine nucléaire (CEPN).

Lajoirie, O. (2002), 'La participation de l'industrie nucléaire à l'élaboration de la norme internationale. Approche du phénomène en droit de la radioprotection', *Bulletin de droit nucléaire*, N° 69, 2002/1, pp. 43-57.

Lefaure, C. (1996), 'How to apply optimisation in radiation protection', *Refresher Course Document, IRPA – International Congress on Radiation Protection*, Vienna, April 14-19, Centre d'Etude sur l'évaluation de la protection dans le domaine nucléaire (CEPN).

Leigh, W.J. (2003), 'The Principle of Justification: the Application of the Principle to the Manufacture of MOX Fuel in the UK', *Nuclear Law Bulletin OECD/NEA*, N° 71, 2003/1, June 2003, pp. 43-51.

Pieterman, R. (2000), 'Risicodenken in het Recht, een cultuurhistorische schets', in R. Foqué en S. Gutwirth (red.), *Vraagstukken van milieurechtelijke begripsvorming*, SI-EUR24, Gouda Quint, Arnhem.

Raes, K. (1995) 'Verantwoording als ethisch imperatief tegenover de ecosfeer', *Recht en kritiek* 21, pp. 355-367.

Rivero, M. (1985), *Droit administratif*, Paris, Dalloz.

Tyler, T., (1996), *Law in a Therapeutic Key*, Carolina Academic Press, Stanford.

Van Gestel, R. (1996), 'ALARA: minimumregel of beginsel met aspiratie', *Refresher Course Document, IRPA – International Congress on Radiation Protection*, Vienna, April 14-19, Centre d'Etude sur l'évaluation de la protection dans le domaine nucléaire (CEPN).

Van Gestel, R. (2000), 'ALARA: minimumregel of beginsel met aspiraties?', *milieu en recht*, Vol. 3, pp. 56-63.

Wiedis, D., Jose, E. and Komer, K. (2001), 'An overview of the current state of radiation litigation', *Health Physics*, Vol. 81, Number 3.